ENID BLYTON

THE UNTOLD STORY

Bloomsfield Publishing
86 – 90 Paul Street
London
EC2A 4NE
England

ENID BLYTON
THE UNTOLD STORY

BRIAN CARTER

RICHLY ILLUSTRATED

Bloomsfield Publishing London England

First published in Great Britain in 2021 by Bloomsfield Publishing

A catalogue recording for this book is available from the British Library.

ISBN 978-1-5272-3723-0

Printed and bound by Ashford Colour Press Ltd
Typeset by 2QT Limited (Publishing)
Dust Jacket Design by 2QT Limited (Publishing)

TO
MY SISTER
JENNIFER THOMSIDE

CONTENTS

Dedication. v

Preface ix

Acknowledgements ix

List of Figures. xii

List of Appendices xv

Epigraph xx

SECTION ONE

CHAPTERS

Introduction 1

I   Enid: The Naturalist 3

II   Enid: The Poet 22

III Enid: The Columnist & Feature Writer . . 39

IV   Enid: The Editor 65

V   Enid: The Universal Teacher 76

VI   Enid: The Prolific Songwriter 85

VII Enid: The Professional Storyteller. . . . 95

VIII Enid: The Playwright 128

IX   Enid: The Artist & Illustrator 144

X   Enid: The Passionate Gardener . . . 155

     Recapitulation & Conclusion 166

SECTION TWO

ARTICLES AND ESSAYS

Why Some of Enid Blyton's Stories Are Not Up To Standard   169

– Rehabilitation & Conclusion   175

Brief History of The Teachers World   .   .   .   177

The Sunny Stories Magazine – A Phenomenal Success   .   180

Brief History of The Enid Blyton's Magazine   .   .   186

A Short History of Darrell Waters Ltd   .   .   .   190

A Short History of Enid Blyton's Literary Estate   .   .   201

The Enid Blyton Trust   207

A Short Treatment of Clairvoyance   209

Physiognomy & Phrenology – The Rise and Fall of Two

Great 'Sciences'   214

Epilogue   223

Endnotes   229

Appendices   243

Bibliography.   339

Index.   361

PREFACE

This new biography of Enid Blyton is an offshoot from studies of precocious and gifted children. It was during these studies I discovered Enid Blyton's artistic and literary gifts, and her amazing photographic memory which became apparent when she was about nine years old. It shows how she developed and used these gifts in her extraordinary work as a universal teacher and professional storyteller.

ACKNOWLEDGEMENTS

My thanks go out to Elizabeth Robins, a retired teacher, who read the first draft of the book and offered valuable advice; to Marsha Rowe of The Literary Consultancy who read the first draft and offered priceless advice; to Tony Summerfield of the Enid Blyton Society whose masterly work in four volumes, *Enid Blyton: An Illustrated Bibliography*, has clarified many details about her books; to Bob Stoney for permission to reproduce extracts from *Enid Blyton: A Biography*, the said book written by his late wife, Barbara Stoney (1924– 2009) and published in 1974 by Hodder & Stoughton; to David Chambers of the Enid Blyton Society who read the typescript in minute detail and whose articles in *The Enid Blyton Society Journal* have opened new lines of research; to Anita Bensoussane from the Enid Blyton Society who has kindly read the first draft of the typescript and made valuable comments and suggestions; to Rosemary Rooke, former P.A. at Ipswich High School, for providing information about Enid Blyton's passage at Ipswich High School; to Elaine Purves, Head of Ipswich High School, for permission to reproduce a group photo showing Enid Blyton during her teacher training at Ipswich High School, carried in Figure 12, page78; to Diana Capatinino of the Haringey Arts Council, who put forward the first draft of the book to the Literary Consultancy for a critical assessment; the staff at the British Library for helping to bring to light her songs carefully preserved in books in the Music Wing of the British Library; to Camden Libraries, for permission to reproduce material from books in the Swiss Cottage Library Reserve Stock. The material reproduced is as follows: two pages from Lavater's *Essays on Physiognomy* showing drawings of nine noses and the characteristics of their owners (Appendix 70); the frontispiece from Dr Spurzheim's book on phrenology showing three views of the surface of the skull and 'Powers and Organs of the Mind' (Appendix 72); a photo of Johann Caspar Lavater in the frontispiece alongside the title page of his book *Essays on Physiognomy* (Figure 30) and in passages drawn from page lxxxi of *Memoir of the Life of J.C. Lavater* carried in this book on page 215 and pages 216/217; to The Herald & Times Group, for permission to reproduce an extract from Anne Johnstone's article in *The Herald* (Glasgow) of July 29, 2006, page 16, carried in this book on page 121; to Imogen Smallwood, for permission to reproduce extracts drawn from pages 59, 102, 120 and 121 from her book *A Childhood at Green Hedges*, published by Methuen in 1989; to Robert Houghton of the Enid Blyton Society, for permission to reproduce an extract from the 'Forum' under the thread: 'Enid's Silver Screen Technique', published Dec 20, 2008, the said extract reproduced on page 120.

The following extracts and poems from Enid Blyton books have been reproduced by permission of Hodder & Stoughton Ltd (Enid Blyton Estate), Carmelite House, 50 Victoria Embankment, London, EC4Y 0DZ:

> Extracts of 1095 words from *The Story of My Life*, carried throughout the book.
> Extract of 13 words from *Five on a Treasure Island*, carried on page 125
> 'A Great Surprise', a poem, from *Real Fairies*, carried on page 27
> 'The Shepherd', a poem, from *The Enid Blyton Poetry Book*, carried on page 31
> 'Speedwell', a poem, from *Enid Blyton's Book of the Year*, carried on page 34

'Magic in the Snow', a poem, from *Silver & Gold*, carried on page 30

'Picking the Apples', a poem, from *My First Reading Book*, carried on page 33

My thanks also go out to the *Daily Mail* for permission to reprint a quotation from Diana Norman's article, 'Noddy Loses his Old Friend' carried in her column in the issue of November 29, 1968, the said quotation reproduced in this book in preliminary page xx.; to Amy Driver, Director, Business Administration, WAMU 88.5 Avenue University Radio, for permission to reproduce and extract from J. K. Rowling's talk on the Diane Rehm Show, first broadcasted Oct 20, 1999, the said extract carried on page 120 of this book; to The Times/ Licensing for permission to reproduce the following:

An extract from Walter Ellis's article, 'Last Stand of the Printed Word', carried in *The Times*, in the edition of Dec 21, 1995, the said extract reproduced in this book on pages 69/70.

Extracts from Nikki Pope and Richard Wood's article 'Enid Blyton Wins Back Her Shelf Space' carried in *The Sunday Times*, in the edition of April 13, 1997, the said extracts reproduced in this book on pages 175/176.

To Tony Buckingham, freelance photographer, for permission to reproduce the photograph of the Trocadero building, first published in the *Evening Standard*, 16 August 2012, and reproduced in this book in Figure 34; to The Beatrix Potter Society for permission to reproduce the photo of Beatrix Potter as a child, carried in Figure 23, bottom row, second, in the group of composers and artists; to the National Portrait Gallery (USA), Smithsonian Institution, for permission to reproduce the photo of Edmonia Lewis by Henry Rocher c 1870, in Figure 23, bottom row, third, in the group of composers, artists and sculptures; to the Library of Congress Prints and Photographic Division, Washington DC, 20540 USA, for supplying a photo of the American composer Amy Beach (1867 – 1944) from the Bain Collection, with no known restriction on publication, the said photo reproduced in this book in Figure 23, second photo, top row (Reproduction number: LC-USZ62-56790).

LIST OF FIGURES

The numbers in italics refer to the page numbers

ENID: THE NATURALIST

1. Graphic illustrations of birds, from Enid's own *The Bird Book, 4*
2. Title page of two books resulting from Enid Blyton's nature study courses in *The Teachers World, 8*
3. Six title pages of some of Enid Blyton's nature books, *9*
4. Old Thatch, Enid Blyton's fairytale-like cottage, on the front cover of *The Teachers World, 10*
5. One of Eileen Soper's 60 'Nature Plates' that illustrated the series *of Enid Blyton's Nature Readers, 18*
6. Front covers of five storybooks resulting from the series of *Enid Blyton's Nature Readers, 19*

ENID: THE POET

7. Front cover of *Child Whispers*, Enid Blyton's first poetry book, and title pages of her other three poetry books, *26*
8. Facsimile reproduction of 'Speedwell', a short poem, from *Enid Blyton's Book of the Year, 34*

POEMS CARRIED IN THE TEXT

'A Great Surprise', from *Real Fairies*, her second book of poems, *27*

'Magic in the Snow', from *Silver & Gold*, her third book of poems, *30*

'The Shepherd', from *The Enid Blyton Poetry Book, 31*

'Picking the Apples', one of a batch of 30 poems, from *My First Reading Book, 33*

'Off To Sea', one of 25 nursery rhymes, from *Noddy's Own Nursery Rhymes, 35*

'Too Hot,' a humorous poem, from an anthology in *The Teachers World, 36*

ENID: THE COLUMNIST & FEATURE WRITER

9. The four books resulting from Enid Blyton's 'Stories from World History', from *The Teachers World, 49*

10. Portraits of 'King Alfred's Mother' & 'Lord Nelson', from *The Teachers World, 59*

ENID: THE EDITOR

11. Title pages of the six publications edited by Enid Blyton, *67*

ENID: THE UNIVERSAL TEACHER

12. Enid Blyton as a trainee teacher at Ipswich High School, *78*

ENID: THE PROLIFIC SONGWRITER

13. Title pages/covers of ten of Enid Blyton's songbooks, *86*

ENID: THE PROFESSIONAL STORYTELLER

14. Title pages, in miniature, of a selection of Enid Blyton's retold story books, *101*

15. Book covers and title pages, in miniature, of a selection of Enid Blyton's religious books, *102*

16. Two fairytale books illustrating Enid Blyton's technique in telling fairytales, *104*

17. Title pages, in miniature, of a selection of Enid Blyton's fairytale books, *106*

18. Photo of Pearl Curran & Frances Browne, two writers who wrote their stories clairvoyantly, *109*

ENID: THE PLAYWRIGHT

19. Title pages, in miniature, of a selection of Enid Blyton's books of plays, *130*

20. Title page, and illustration of costumes, from *The Play's The Thing, 135*

21. Covers of six books of musical plays published individually, from *Blyton - Sharman Musical Plays, 139*

ENID: THE ARTIST & ILLUSTRATOR

22. Photos of a selection of male composers and poets with dimpled chins, *147*

23. Photos of a selection of female composers, musicians and illustrators with dimpled chins, *148*

24. Sketches from Enid Blyton's schoolbook, demonstrating drawing skills, *149*

25. A selection of Enid Blyton's illustrations, from her nature and gardening courses in *The Teachers World, 151*
ENID: THE PASSIONATE GARDENER

26. Elfin Cottage, where Enid Blyton had her first 'real' gardening experience, *158*

27. Illustration of Enid Blyton's gardening & nature study textbooks, *162*

28. Her magnificent garden at Green Hedges, *165*
THE SUNNY STORIES MAGAZINE– A PHENOMENAL SUCCESS

29. Illustration of the front cover of the *Sunny Stories For Little Folks* magazine*,* old series, and of *Sunny Stories,* new series, *182*
PHYSIOGNOMY & PHRENOLOGY

30. Photo of John Caspar Lavater and the title page of his book, *216*

31. Photo of Franz J. Gall and the title page of his book, *218*
ENID BLYTON MAGAZINE

32. Front cover illustrations of two of Enid Blyton's Magazines, *187*
A SHORT HISTORY OF DARRELL WATERS LTD

33. David Haslam's pencil drawing of 'Noddy between two American television evangelists', *196*
A SHORT HISTORY OF ENID BLYTON'S LITERARY ESTATE

34. The Trocadero Building that was managed by Trocadero Plc., *202*

35. Enid Blyton's subconscious mind at work, *124*

LIST OF APPENDICES

The appendices start from page 243

ENID: THE NATURALIST

1. *The Teachers World* announcement of the beginning of Enid Blyton's nature articles in the newspaper
2. The Gorse, Enid Blyton's first nature lesson for children, from *The Teachers World*
3. Enid Blyton's syllabus covering one year's nature lessons for children, from *The Teachers World*
4. 'Big Crabs and Little Crabs' another nature lesson, from *The Teachers World*
5. Sample reading of nature notes, from Enid Blyton's *The Teachers' Treasury*
6. *The Teachers World* announcement of Enid Blyton's 'Hedgerow Tales', in the 'Twenty Teaching Features'
7. Enid Blyton's syllabus for 'Hedgerow Tales', from *The Teachers World*
8. 'Rabbity Ways', first 'Hedgerow Tales' lesson, from *The Teachers World*
9. Sample reading of 'Nature Notes', from *Enid Blyton's Book of the Year*
10. A list of one hundred flowers, compiled by Enid Blyton, from *Enid Blyton's Nature Lover's Book*
11. Sample reading of a page from 'The Swallows in the Barn', one of Enid Blyton's Nature Readers
12. The standard front cover of one of *The Enid Blyton Nature Readers,* with a list of the 36 readers in the series

ENID: THE POET

13. 'March', the first in a series of nature poems, from *The Teachers World*

xv

14. 'An Indian Day', a poem from *The Teachers World*

15. 'Sea Lions', the first in a new series of 'New Animal Poems', from *The Teachers World*

16. 'The Poplar Tree', one of the twelve 'Poems of the Open Air', from *Enid Blyton's Nature Lover's Book*

17. Front cover and first page of *Enid Blyton's Sunny Stories Calendar*

18. 'The Helmsman', a poem to mark the Silver Jubilee celebrations of the then King George V, from *The Teachers World*

19. 'A Lion Once We Had', a poem Enid dedicated to Sir Winston Churchill, from the *Sunday Graphic*

20. 'April Day', Enid Blyton's last known poem, from Barbara Stoney's *Enid Blyton: The Biography*
ENID: THE COLUMNIST & FEATURE WRITER

21. Front cover of an edition of *The Teachers World*

22. Enid Blyton's first article in her column, 'From My Window' from *The Teachers World*

23. 'Green And Blue' Enid Blyton's last article in her column 'From My Window'

24. Enid Blyton's first 'Children's Page' from *The Teachers World*

25. 'A Letter from Bobs', from *The Teachers World*

26. 'Peronel and His Pot of Glue' Enid Blyton's first Friday Afternoon Story, from *The Teachers World*

27. The Board of Education's *Handbook of Suggestions*, with a 'Prefatory Note'

28. 'The Siege of Troy', Enid Blyton's first story in the series of 'Stories of World History', from *The Teachers World*

29. 'Notes for the Teacher', from the series of 'Stories of World History', in *The Teachers World*

30. Enid Blyton's syllabus for her 'Stories of World History', from *The Teachers World*

31. 'King Arthur & The Knights of the Round Table', Enid Blyton's first episode of her 'Tales of Romance', from *The Teachers World*

32. 'A Roland for an Oliver', one of the eighteen episodes of 'King Charlemagne and the Paladins of France', From *The Teachers World*

33. 'The Siege of the Castle of Aiguillon', the first of nine episodes, from Enid Blyton's 'Stories of Chivalry in the Fourteenth Century', from *The Teachers World*

34. 'The Beginning of the Adventures of the Red Cross Knight', one of seven episodes of a story Enid Blyton retold from Spencer's '*Faerie Queene*', from *The Teachers World*

35. Part of a full page in the *Teachers World and Schoolmistress* showing a new 'Programme of Teaching Features'

36. 'King Alfred's Mother', one of the thirty-two stories of historical characters Enid Blyton narrated in the *Teachers World and Schoolmistress*

37. 'A Robin Called Sing-A-Song', the second of a monthly series of stories narrated by Enid Blyton in *The Teachers World*

38. 'The Months', first Feature Article Enid Blyton wrote for *The Teachers World*

39. Enid Blyton's farewell letter to her fans, from *The Teachers World*
ENID: THE UNIVERSAL TEACHER

40. A list of the 30 readers in the 'Enid Blyton Pennant series'

41. Title page of Enid Blyton's *The Teachers' Treasury*

42. A full page advertisement for the *Teachers' Treasury*, from *The Teachers World*

43. Professor T.P. Nunn's introduction to *The Teachers' Treasury*
ENID: THE PROLIFIC SONGWRITER

44. Part of a score for 'The Trees', from *Responsive Singing Games*, Enid Blyton's first songbook

45. Part of the score for 'Little Lambkin' and 'Pop Goes the Weasel!' two songs for infants, from *Two Years in the Infant School*

46. Table I giving details of Enid Blyton's songbooks

47. Part of the score for 'The Singer in the Night', one of Enid Blyton's poems set to music

48. Table II showing Enid Blyton's miscellaneous songs and Noddy songbooks

48A. Tables III and IV giving details of sheet music and songs Enid Blyton wrote specially for her musical plays

49. Part of the score for 'Gardeners Song' in the musical play 'The

Kings Pocket Knife', from *The Play's The Thing*

50. The score for 'The Union Jack', a patriotic song Enid Blyton wrote for the then Empire Day Celebrations

51. One of two pages of the score for 'Shepherd Song', a Christmas carol written by Enid Blyton, from *The Teachers World*

52. Tables V and VI showing Christmas carols and miscellaneous songs written by Enid Blyton

53. 'The Shepherd King', a Christmas carol written by Enid Blyton, on the front cover of the Senior School Edition of *The Teachers World*.

ENID: THE PROFESSIONAL STORYTELLER

54. Inside cover and plan of *The Children's Encyclopaedia*

55. Extract from *The Secret Commonwealth of Elves, Fauns & Fairies* on the nature and characteristics of fairies

56. Title page and preface to *The Mystery of Edwin Drood* written by the spirit pen of Charles Dickens

57. A description of the branches of clairvoyance from various sources

ENID: THE PLAYWRIGHT

58. TABLE I showing a list of Enid Blyton Straight Plays drawn from Enid Blyton books

59. 'King Cole Calling!', one of Enid Blyton's school plays, from *The Teachers World*

60. A review of 'Six Enid Blyton Plays', from *The Teachers World*

61. A full-page advertisement for *The Play's The Thing*, from *Child Education*

62. A synopsis of 'The King's Pocket Knife', one of the 12 musical plays in *The Play's The Thing*

63. TABLE II showing a list of Enid Blyton's musical plays for staging at school concerts etc.

64. A full-page advertisement for Enid Blyton's two stage plays as it appeared in *The Enid Blyton's Magazine*

ENID: THE PASSIONATE GARDENER

65. Enid Blyton's syllabus for her one-year course of Seasonal Nature Study, from *The Teachers World*

66. A lesson on germination, from *Round the Year with Enid Blyton*,

from *The Teachers World*
THE SUNNY STORIES MAGAZINE

67. Enid Blyton's 'Letter to Boys and Girls', from the *Sunny Stories* magazine
68. Photo of Marion Crawford who took over writing stories for the *Sunny Stories* magazine, when Enid Blyton retired
BRIEF HISTORY OF THE ENID BLYTON MAGAZINE

69. Information about Enid Blyton's fan clubs, in six pages in miniature, from *Enid Blyton Diary*
PHYSIOGNOMY & PHRENOLOGY

70. Two page showing nine noses, from J.C. Lavater's *Essays on Physiognomy*
71. Dr. Gall's map of the surface of the skull showing his system of organology
72. Dr. Spurzheim's map of the surface of the skull showing his refined system of Gall's organology that he renamed phrenology
A SHORT HISTORY OF DARRELL WATERS LTD

73. First page of the Memorandum of Association, showing the main objectives of Darrell Waters Ltd, Enid Blyton's company
A SHORT TREATMENT OF CLAIRVOYANCE

74. A copy of The Fraudulent Mediums Act that repeals the Witchcraft Act 1735

Opening an Enid Blyton book was
like getting into a warm bath or
starting a box of chocolates.
It might not be good for you,
but by gosh, it was luxury.

A quotation from Diana Norman of the *Daily Mail*, in her column of November 29, 1968, announcing the passing of Enid Blyton on November 28, 1968, in a Nursing Home. Enid Mary Waters née Blyton (1897 – 1968)

INTRODUCTION

Enid Mary Waters née Blyton, born August 11, 1897 at 354 Lordship Lane, East Dulwich, London, has been described as a prolific and successful writer of children's books, with over 700 books and innumerable contributions to national and regional newspapers and magazines to her credit.

Since the publication of her first book, *Child Whispers* in 1922, some 500 million copies of her books have been sold worldwide. Some of them were made into films and stage plays, serialised in certain newspapers as cartoon strips, recorded on audio cassettes and adapted for radio and TV programmes for children. Moreover, by having her books translated into more than 90 languages, she had brought them to non-English speaking children in countries all over the world.

Now if these facts come as news to some of us, they would come as even bigger news when we learn that she was not just a prolific and successful writer of children's books, but also a naturalist, poet, editor, columnist and feature writer, universal teacher, prolific songwriter, professional storyteller, playwright, artist and illustrator and a passionate gardener and that she was just as successful in each of these fields as she was in writing storybooks for children. Bringing these facts to the attention of the public is the main reason this book has been written.

The material is presented in two sections. That in Section One is divided into ten chapters, each dealing with a particular aspect of her work. It begins with *Enid: The Naturalist* and ends with *Enid: The Passionate Gardener*. They all revolve around two main chapters: *Enid: The Universal Teacher* and *Enid: The Professional Storyteller.* This is because I put her work into two distinct categories: teaching

1

and storytelling. A short recapitulation is given at the end of the ten chapters before the section is brought to a close.

Section Two reveals why some of her stories are not up to standard followed by short histories of *The Teachers World*, a newspaper that provided an early outlet for her literary and artistic productions; the *Sunny Stories* magazine in which some of her popular books, such as, *The Naughtiest Girl in the School*, started out as serials and of *The Enid Blyton's Magazine*, through which she interacted with hundreds of thousands of fans. It also carries a *Short History of Darrell Waters Ltd*, Enid Blyton's own company, and in another article, A *Short History of Enid Blyton's Literary Estate* after her passing in 1968.

Moreover, it gives a short history of phrenology and physiognomy so that readers may find background information when they meet with references to these two subjects in the book. Extras provided to close the section are the *Epilogue, Bibliography* and the *Index*.

Finally, notwithstanding the order in which the chapters are presented, feel free to begin from any chapter you may fancy. If you are interested in her poetry, then start with that chapter, and so on. The slight inconvenience of cross-references will soon be overcome when you tackle the other chapters. You should also bear in mind that the main chapters around which the others revolve are *Enid: The Universal Teacher* and *Enid: The Professional Storyteller*. Reading the book from the beginning will eventually lead you to these two chapters.

With the conviction that the material in this book is necessary to clear up misunderstandings about her work, I now hope that the book will give you as much pleasure to read as it has given me to write.

CHAPTER I
ENID THE NATURALIST

OVERVIEW

In this first chapter we see Enid Blyton in a field we've never seen her in before. From her instructive expeditions in the countryside with her father to explore the wonders and beauty of nature to her qualifications in zoology and botany, we follow her as she receives one commission after another to write nature articles, books and readers. Then we take a look into the nature sections of books she wrote for teachers and learn about the nature books she wrote for children. The chapter ends with a brief reflection of how many children she must have inspired or encouraged to go into fields such as botany, zoology and ornithology through her nature study courses, nature books and readers.

If there's one person to whom Enid should be grateful for setting her on course to become a naturalist, that person would be her father. A self-taught naturalist himself, he made sure he imparted his knowledge of animals and plants to the young Enid by taking her with him whenever he went on expeditions in the countryside.

'*Look – there goes a coal tit,*' he said to her during one of their nature walks together. '*Watch for the white streak on the nape of his neck and you'll always be able to pick him out from the other tits.*

'*Listen,*' he continued, '*do you hear that call? It's a yellowhammer, and he's crying for "A little bit of bread and no cheese!" Listen again – now you'll know it.* (See Figure 1).

Yellowhammer.   House-sparrow.
Spotted Flycatcher.
Bullfinch.   Linnet.
Pied Wagtail.
Tree-Sparrow.   Whitethroat.

FIGURE 1: Graphic illustration of birds from Enid Blyton's own The Bird Book showing the yellowhammer (top left) and other birds she first learnt about from her father, Thomas Blyton, during their regular excursions in the countryside (see Enid: The Passionate Gardener, Chapter X, for more information about this book). © British Library Board (SM 7286.d.17 p073).

'See this hazel twig? It has two flowers on it. Find them both. Yes, the yellow catkin is one – but where's the other? Good girl, you're right, it's the little bud-like thing with the red spikes hanging out...'

Enid remembered this conversation so well she was able to reproduce it faithfully on page 56 of her autobiography *The Story of My Life,* first published by Pitkin in 1952.[1]

'We explored everywhere and everything,' she recalled further on in another passage on page 57 of the same book, *'watching the lizards play on the sunny banks, listening to the willow-warblers (small woodland birds) singing, poking down a hole that my father said badgers had been in and looking for the white violets we knew always blossom in a certain dell.'*

Many years later, after she had fully taken in these early nature lessons, she went on to gain first-class passes in geography, botany, handwork (including drawing) and a distinction in zoology during her first year of training at Ipswich High School to become a teacher.

Then, after her final year, she gained first class passes in the practice of education, child hygiene and the history of education and class teaching of children for her National Froebel Union Higher Certificate.[2] With this qualification, she became a teacher and soon found herself following in her father's footsteps by taking her pupils out on nature walks in the countryside to explore the wonders and beauty of nature.

In 1924, when she gave up classroom teaching altogether, apparently, to keep up with her growing writing commitments, the emphasis was no longer on teaching Nature Study in the classroom and taking her pupils out on nature walks, but on writing about nature.

The opportunity to do this came in 1925 when she received a commission from *The Teachers World*, an independent educational weekly newspaper for teachers, to write a series of nature articles (later to be termed 'nature lessons') for children eleven years and younger in the then public elementary schools. The announcement to this effect was made in the edition of April 1, 1925 (see Appendix 1).

From examining the wording of this announcement we find that Enid was no stranger to *The Teachers World*. She was already contributing poems and stories that earned her the title of Children's Poet and Storyteller, and teachers were delighted that she had been commissioned to write the series of nature articles. (The subject of her contributions of poems and stories to *The Teachers World* is discussed in full under *Enid: The Poet*, Chapter II and *Enid: The Columnist & Feature Writer*, Chapter III.)

This need to write nature articles came about when it was recognised that the fortnightly Nature Lessons for seniors (eleven years and older) contributed by one Richard Morse, F.L.S were not suitable for juniors and teachers began calling for simple lessons they could teach to small children.

But how, some of us may ask, did *The Teachers World*, an influential newspaper for teachers, come to be running nature lessons in the newspaper in the first place? Well, in those days lessons in English, nature study, mathematics, geography and so on were carried in newspapers aimed at teachers and teachers were free to incorporate them in their syllabuses or teaching programmes.

Included in these newspapers was *The Teachers World,* whose editorial team would often commission graduates and teaching professionals to contribute lessons on various subjects to guide teachers in drawing up their syllabuses. This can be seen from the following extract from an announcement made on page 940 in the edition of August 25, 1926 under the caption: "Indispensable":

The Teachers World is already the weekly guide and helper of more than 50,000 teachers in the planning and preparation of lesson series in all the main subjects of the curriculum...

It was therefore this favourable situation that gave Enid a 'window of opportunity' in the newspaper to write fortnightly nature lessons for juniors.

Her first article in the newspaper of April 15, 1925 appeared under the heading: ENID BLYTON'S NATURE LESSONS with the title 'Gorse' (see illustration, Appendix 2).

Then, after presenting lessons with titles such as 'The Bunny', 'The Bluebell', 'The Dragonfly', 'The Wild Rose', 'The Fly', 'The Kingfisher' and 'The Snake' she published a syllabus outlining all the lessons she intended to present for the coming year: September 2, 1925 – to August 18, 1926 (see Appendix 3). With this syllabus in hand, teachers could then plan ahead for an entire year of Nature Study for their pupils.

If we go back to the syllabus we've just seen (Appendix 3) we'll see that the nature lessons were scheduled to end August 18, 1926 with a lesson on 'Crabs and Lobsters', but in fact it did not end there. For the next week after the last lesson in the syllabus was published, *The Teachers World* slipped the following announcement on page 940, in the edition of August 25, 1926:

NATURE STUDY

For the Juniors Enid Blyton is preparing a new series of illustrated Nature Lessons. Her delightful manner of presenting this subject to the younger children has been so successful that the new series is being prepared on the same lines.

Thus the series was to continue faithfully, fortnight after fortnight, for almost another year, with a new lesson with the title 'Big Crabs and Little Crabs' appearing September 1, 1926 (Appendix 4). The series eventually came to an end on August 17, 1927 with a lesson with the title 'Starfish'.

If we take another look at the illustrations of her lessons given in Appendices 2 and 4, we'll see that they took up a full page in the newspaper. A rough count will put the words at between 1,500 and 2,000. The fine print is a feature throughout the newspaper to preserve its small, magazine-like format.

In all she wrote sixty-two nature lessons for the course and in August 1929 Evans Brothers Ltd republished some of them in book form with the title: *Enid Blyton's Nature Lessons* (see title pages illustration, Figure 2). The twenty-six nature lessons in this book are those we have seen in the syllabus in Appendix 3. The remaining thirty-six are those she wrote before and after the publication of the syllabus. It's not known why the publisher did not bring them all out in book form.

From these nature lessons, we now turn our attention to another set of nature lessons she was working on at the same time. These she termed 'Nature Notes' and was for her three-volume *Teachers' Treasury* that she wrote for teachers (see title page illustration, Appendix 41).

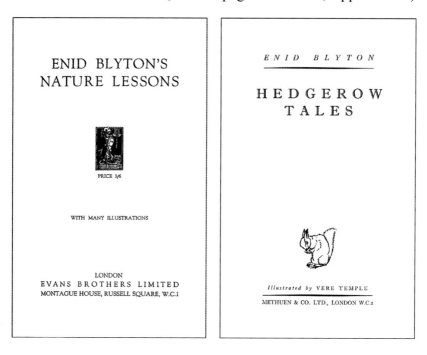

FIGURE 2: Title pages of two books resulting from Enid Blyton's nature study courses in The Teachers World. In all she wrote 62 Nature Lessons, serialised in The Teachers World from April 15, 1925 to August 17, 1927, and 24 Hedgerow Tales seven years later, from Sept 5, 1934 to July 24, 1935. Only 26 of the 62 Nature Lessons were published in the book shown above. The rest remain in the newspaper to this day. © British Library Board (SM: left, 7003.r.11 title page; right, 20055.c.4 title page).

More information about these volumes is given in Chapter V, under *Enid: The Universal Teacher*. In the meantime, let us take a look inside to get an idea of what these 'Nature Notes' are all about.

All the information we need is contained in her long foreword or introduction appearing in Volume I. Here we learn that there are twenty-six different lessons covering a year's course in nature and that they had been written with a view to helping teachers to prepare lessons for their pupils.

Supported by drawings where necessary, these lessons cover

subjects with titles such as 'winter buds', 'the primrose', 'frog', 'gnat', 'squirrel', 'wild rose', 'seed dispersal', 'migration of birds' and so on. Essential information and curious facts about each of these subjects are presented in an orderly manner, as can be seen in the illustration in Appendix 5.

Soon after this book went into circulation, she brought out *The Bird Book* (see title page illustration, Figure 3). However, since this book has a lot to do with her gardening experience it's treated fully in Chapter X, under *Enid: The Passionate Gardener*.

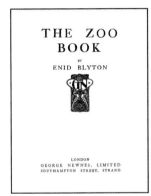  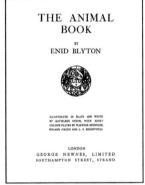

 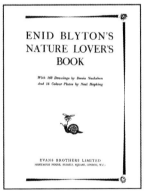 

FIGURE 3: A selection of title pages of nature books Enid Blyton wrote for children and teachers. Details of publishers and publication dates can be found in the Bibliography in this book. © British Library Board (SM: top row, The Zoo Book (12805.m.46 title page); The Bird Book (7286.d.17. title page); The Animal Book (7208.g.38. title page). Bottom row: Rambles with Uncle Nat (12831.g.6. title page); Enid Blyton's Nature Lover's Book (7008. bb.3.title page); Enid Blyton's Animal Lover's Book (12833.d.41.title page).

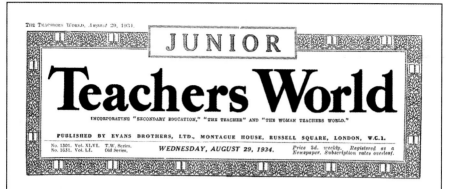

THE TEACHERS WORLD, *August 29, 1934.*

JUNIOR
Teachers World

INCORPORATING "SECONDARY EDUCATION," "THE TEACHER" AND "THE WOMAN TEACHERS WORLD."

PUBLISHED BY EVANS BROTHERS, LTD., MONTAGUE HOUSE, RUSSELL SQUARE, LONDON, W.C.1.

No. 1301. Vol. XLVI. T.W. Series.
No. 1631. Vol. LI. Old Series.

WEDNESDAY, AUGUST 29, 1934.

Price 3d. *weekly. Registered as a Newspaper. Subscription rates overleaf.*

OLD THATCH.—The old English cottage at its best. The thousands of children to whom Wednesday morning means Enid Blyton's page in T.W. will scrutinise this picture carefully in search of the well, the tit bells, the seed hoppers, etc., and they will find at least two of the pets. They will be glad to hear that, in addition to her children's page, Enid Blyton (here seen at work with her portable typewriter) will contribute a year's Nature Study Course, "Hedgerow Tales". See page 771.

FIGURE 4: Old Thatch, Enid Blyton's fairytale-like cottage that made it on the front cover of the Junior Teachers World in the edition of August 29, 1934. Here she's seen sitting outside with her typewriter on her lap. Image restoration credit: 2graphic Photo Restoration. Website: www.photo-restoration.co.uk

10

Then, in 1927, when *The Bird Book* and her *Teachers' Treasury* were helping to make a name for her in educational circles, she turned her attention to writing a book exclusively on the subject of animals. With the title *The Animal Book* (see title page illustration, Figure 3), this richly illustrated book of 124 pages gives children curious facts about the different types of animals and their characteristics, and describes places where they are most likely to be seen or found.

It was not, however, her first book on the subject of animals. For even before she got the commission to write the series of nature lessons for *The Teachers World* in April 1925 she had already written *The Zoo Book* that George Newnes Ltd published in 1924 (see Figure 3 for title page illustration). In this beautifully illustrated book of 96 pages children learned things such as how the zoo came into existence, how animals are caught and taken to the zoo and about the secrets of the keepers along with vivid descriptions of monkeys, bears, snakes, birds, horned or hoofed animals and so on.

By that time, Enid was in her early thirties and had just moved to her new home in Bourne End, Buckinghamshire – a fairytale-like cottage that, surprisingly, did make it on the front cover of the *Junior Teachers World* (Figure 4). This place was to give her the comfort and security she needed to plan and execute all her writing projects. Moreover, with her first husband, Hugh Pollock, whom she married in 1924, her two young daughters Gillian and Imogen, a housekeeper, cook and a chauffeur, she had everything a woman could have hoped for at that time. Some of her best work was produced during this period of peacefulness and apparent happiness.

It was also the time when the nation was plunged into mourning the death of King George V in January 1936 and Neville Chamberlain became Prime Minister (1937). On the cultural side, English people were getting used to listening to radio broadcasts – or wireless as it was known at that time – in their own homes, thanks to the BBC (British Broadcasting Corporation) that was incorporated in 1922.

Five years after her last commission to write nature lessons for *The Teachers World*, we find her working assiduously on another commission to write a comprehensive nature and gardening course for juniors with the title 'Round the Year with Enid Blyton'. However, since this extensive course deals principally with gardening themes, it's treated in full under *Enid: The Passionate Gardener,* in Chapter X.

The successful fulfilment of this second commission in August 1933 was to leave her with all the time she needed to concentrate on a host of ongoing projects that were engaging her attention. These included holding down a children's page – 'Enid Blyton's Children's Page' – as well as writing a series of biographical sketches of historical characters; writing new poetry books, storybooks and musical plays; editing educational and teaching books and working with composers to set her songs to music. We'll soon be learning about these activities in other chapters of this book.

While all this was going on, *The Teachers World*'s editorial team was busy drawing up a plan for a new series of teaching features for 1934 – 1935. Contributors were given the task of coming up with a year's course of lessons in their respective fields and that the courses themselves should have some aspect of novelty. Thanks therefore to the new teaching features, Enid landed a commission for the third time to write a brand new series of nature lessons.

When all the contributions were received, *The Teachers World* published a provisional syllabus on page 751 in the edition of August 29, 1934, outlining all the teaching features – twenty in all – as they would appear fortnight after fortnight (Appendix 6). A close look at the contents reveals the announcement of Enid's forthcoming contribution – Hedgerow Tales: A Novel Nature Study Course (first column, No. 12). As we go along, we'll find out why the nature study course was termed 'Hedgerow Tales' and why the editor described it as a 'Novel Nature Study Course'.

On page 771 in the same edition, Enid published her syllabus or timetable of all the lessons she intended to present for the coming year September 5, 1934 to July 24, 1935 (Appendix 7). Notice the headline in bold letters: Hedgerow Tales – A Year's Course in Nature Study by Enid Blyton. As we'll see in other illustrations, Enid's work in the newspaper was always prominently displayed.

The editorial team must have anticipated the reception the series would be met with by publishing the following announcement that precedes the timetable in Appendix 7:

The many friends and correspondents of Enid Blyton – and they number, literally, thousands of teachers and children – will be glad to hear that she is to write the Nature Study lessons for the school year 1934 – 35. The scope of the series is described in characteristic terms by the author herself in column 3.

In this column (third on the page in Appendix 7) headed: 'From the Author to the Reader', Enid gave a bird's eye view of what the new course was all about. It's centred on a particular hedgerow with its overshadowing tree, sunny bank, moist ditch and a little pond nearby and depicts the lives and 'personalities' of all the creatures living therein.

Her first lesson in the fortnightly series, 'Rabbity Ways', appeared on page 792 in the edition of September 5, 1934 (Appendix 8). Here, in the first three paragraphs, Enid set the stage for what was to follow in all the lessons by giving teachers a description of the hedgerow itself along with the atmosphere at daybreak before the creatures begin to stir. Then she plunged into the lesson by presenting facts about rabbits in a roundabout way, that is, in the form of a tale or story, with the creatures acting as if they had human thoughts and feelings. This can be seen from the following extract:

In venturing out of her burrow, a rabbit was startled to see a hare.

Suddenly she stopped and stood so still that it seemed as if she had frozen stiff…

As soon as the rabbit saw that it was a harmless creature she ran on again and came up to the hare.

"You scared me, cousin hare," she said, "Is your burrow round here?"

"Burrow!" said the hare, looking in surprise at the rabbit, her soft eyes gleaming in the grey light. "I have no burrow. I live above ground."

"But how dangerous!" said the rabbit in alarm. "Stoats and weasels could easily find you! Do you make a nest like the

birds?..."

Let us consider another example to see her presentation of facts in a roundabout way. In one of the nature lessons presented by Richard Morse F.L.S. (Fellow of the Linnean Society), who began writing general nature lessons for *The Teachers World* and ended up writing exclusively for seniors (children eleven years and over), we find the following in a lesson on the hare and rabbit he gave on page 893, in the edition of January 30, 1924:

The newborn rabbit is blind, helpless and devoid of fur. Hares are born covered with fur, and are active and able to see and to care for themselves almost immediately.

Now compare this with the long-winded version in the following passage from her first lesson Rabbity Ways:

The rabbit went to the hare's form which was simply a dent in the earth. Near it were other small holes, and in each lay a young hare, a leveret, its eyes wide open, its body warmly covered with fur.

'They have made forms of their own,' said the hare, proudly. 'Even when they are young they like to live alone.'

'My young ones were not like this,' said the rabbit in surprise, looking at the leverets. My children were born blind and deaf and had no fur on them at all...I should not think of leaving them out in the open like this. It is a good thing your children are born able to see and hear or they would certainly be eaten by an enemy!'

Facts conveyed in other lessons in this roundabout way include:

- Moulting: the process whereby snakes shed their skin and new skin is formed (Creepy Creatures, April 17, 1935)
- Metamorphosis: the process whereby the grub of the water beetle emerges from the water to become a dragonfly (The Fish That Built A Nest, July 24, 1935).
- The water spider that makes a marvellous web of silvery water bubbles, neatly tied by silken ropes to the stem of water weeds, to trap insects in the pond (The Fish That Built A Nest, July 24,

1935).

- Deer whose antlers drop off in the spring and grow again in a few weeks (The Little Fawn, July 10, 1935).
- The cuckoo that lays its eggs in other birds' nest to 'to give other birds the trouble of bringing up her young' (The Strange Egg, May 15, 1935).

At the end of each lesson were Things to Do in the form of Oral Composition or Role Playing, Written Composition and Drawing.

Accompanying the series was a large four-page picture of the hedgerow in autumn for the children to cut out and mount on cardboard for displaying on the classroom wall. The children were then encouraged to cut out the drawings of animals, birds, fish and insects featured in the 'tales' and put them in the appropriate place in the picture. As the series progressed, new pictures for winter, spring and summer were published. To crown it all, Enid provided a drawing or 'key' to guide children on where to put the animals etc., in the pictures for each season. The remaining twenty-three lessons in the series were all presented along the same lines.

This is an excellent example of Enid carrying out one of the suggestions in the *Primary School report* of 1931, wherein it is stated, among other things, '*that lessons should be thought of in terms of activity and experience rather than knowledge to be acquired and facts to be stored*' [3]

Now we know how the word 'Tales' came to be used to describe the Nature Study course and why *The Teachers World* termed it a 'Novel Nature Study course' (see reference to the entry, Appendix 6, column 1, No 12).

The series eventually came to an end on July 24, 1935 with a lesson with the title 'The Fish that Built a Nest'. This title differed from the original in the timetable, A Friend and an Enemy, for by that time Enid had steered the lesson in another direction (see the last entry in the timetable, Appendix 7).

In November 1935, Methuen & Co published the twenty-four novel nature lessons in book form with the same title: *Hedgerow Tales* (see title page illustration, Figure 2). The teaching features, such as

Things to Do and the large drawings to cut out and put on the wall in the classroom were not reproduced.

Finally *Hedgerow Tales* can be put on a par with 'Enid Blyton's Nature Lessons' in that they have been well thought out, carefully written, easy to read and designed to capture a child's imagination. The roundabout way Enid presented facts is interesting and the way she made the creatures express themselves with human thoughts and feelings is entertaining.

The nature books that followed this elaborate course are *Animals at Home* (1935), *Birds at Home* (1935), *Birds of Our Gardens* (1940), *The Enid Blyton's Book of the Year* (1941) *The Enid Blyton's Nature Lover's Book* (1944) and *Rambles with Uncle Nat* (1947) – see a selection of title page illustrations, Figure 3).

Of special mention is *The Enid Blyton's Book of the Year* that she wrote for teachers. Among the many sections in this book of 352 pages is one devoted entirely to nature study, covering topics such as the weather situation each month of the year and its consequences for plant and animal life; flowers in and out of bloom; flowering plants in and out of season and so on (see Appendix 9 for a sample reading).

Then there's *The Enid Blyton's Nature Lover's Book* in which we find a list of exactly one hundred flowers, with brief information given on each of them at various pages in the book (see Appendix 10 for illustration).

In 1945 when the Second World War had just come to a close, we find her branching out into another field – writing nature readers for five to seven-year-old children. For her, it was just a change from a previous commission Macmillan & Co gave her to write general readers for schoolchildren.

What set these nature readers apart from the previous set of reading books is her skill in presenting basic facts of nature, such as germination, pollination, the migration of birds, seed dispersal etc., wrapped up in interesting stories (see Appendix 11 for sample reading from one of the Nature Readers).

Children reading this story for reading practice would have understood that it is about a group of swallows, whose home is in a barn, leaving suddenly on a long journey to some unknown destination. But it's really about the migration of birds, a nature lesson Enid neatly wrapped up in the story. It was then up to the teachers to bring out the nature lesson after the reading exercise.

In drawing up the syllabus for the nature themes to be covered in the series, Enid sought the help of Professor L.J.F. Brimble, B.Sc. F.L.S (1904 – 1965) who, at that time, was holding several posts, including that of a lecturer in botany at the University of Manchester. Together they decided on thirty Nature Readers, each containing two stories to be released in batches of ten. The first batch was released in July 1945 and by October, a second batch was released. In July of the following year, the third batch was released to complete the target of thirty.

It was at this point that the books changed from being simple Nature Readers for the children's own use to being special teaching books designed for teachers to bring out the nature facts wrapped up in the stories. To do this Enid collected all the stories and published them in a single volume with the title: *Stories and Notes to Enid Blyton Nature Plates* that Macmillan & Co. published in 1949. This is how she presented the features of the new publication in the following extract from the foreword:

FOREWORD

This book is for the teacher's use, and can be used to great effect with the big wall pictures that illustrate the stories. It contains all the sixty Nature stories that are given in the thirty readers which have been prepared for the children's own use. There are two stories, well and accurately illustrated, in each of the thirty readers. Here the stories are printed all together, and I have written teaching notes for each one…

The big wall pictures she referred to in the foreword were done by Eileen Soper (see her photo, Figure 23) and this was the third feature in the elaborate project. These were intended to be placed on the wall in classrooms so that children might see them as they read the stories. The drawings, with the title: 'Enid Blyton Nature Plates' complemented the stories, in which the main points were beautifully

FIGURE 5: One of Eileen Soper's 60 'Nature Plates' that illustrated the series of Enid Blyton's Nature Readers. It refers to germination, the main nature fact she presented in 'The Wonderful Conker', the first of two stories in Nature Reader No. 27. The drawings were originally done in colour. © British Library Board (SM: Cup.1250.d.3 plate 27).

illustrated in colour (see illustration, Figure 5).

Finally, Professor Brimble, who had worked with her to draw up the syllabus, wrote a reference book to be used in conjunction with the Nature Readers. It contained exclusively background information of the nature facts in each story. Enid welcomed this initiative and wrote a short foreword to the book which Macmillan & Co. published subsequently in 1949 with the title: *A Reference Book to Enid Blyton Nature Readers*.

Ten years after the Nature Readers had ran their course in schools, Enid added six more to the series, bringing it to thirty-six in all, encompassing a total of seventy-eight stories (see Appendix 12 for a list of all the Nature Readers and stories in the series).

In November, 1952, even before the six Nature Readers were added to the list, Macmillan & Co. republished the thirty Nature Readers

FIGURE 6: Front covers of five storybooks encompassing the series of Enid Blyton Nature Readers. The 36 Nature Readers in the series were so popular in schools in the mid-1940s that Macmillan & Co republished them in 1952 and 1953 as storybooks, as shown above. (See also Appendix 12 for the list of all the Nature Readers and stories in the series.) Image restoration credit: 2graphic Photo Restoration. Website: www.photo-restoration.co.uk

as special storybooks under the heading: *My First Nature Book (The Brownie's Magic*) and *My Second Nature Book (The Spell That Went Wrong*). Then, in July, 1953, they published three more books, under the heading: *My Third Nature Book (The Wonderful Carpet), My Fourth, (The Rabbit's Party*) *and My Fifth Nature Book (Susan and the Birds)* – (see front covers illustration, Figure 6).

Finally, if the thirty-six nature readers were to be reintroduced to primary schools today to teach children to read, or to fight against illiteracy, they would, undoubtedly, measure up to any that is in use for that purpose. The subject of the readers would fascinate schoolchildren and they would want to know more. However, since the elaborate system described in the preceding paragraphs is no more, the books would be regarded as nothing more than reading exercises, unless teachers take the trouble to research the nature lessons wrapped up in the stories and bring them out after the reading exercise. On the other hand, those republished as storybooks (see again illustration, Figure 6) would go down well with parents who want storybooks with a difference to read to their children.

Her last known Nature Book, *The Enid Blyton's Animal Lover's Book*, was published by Macmillan & Co in 1952, when she was about fifty-six years old (see title page illustration, Figure 3). In this book, Enid resorted to her old technique of wrapping up nature lessons in interesting stories. The story is about two children, Richard and Suzanne, who befriended one Zacky Boswell, a Gypsy farmer, while they were sojourning in the country with their mother. This person was to share with them his knowledge of nature by taking them on regular nature walks.

Notwithstanding her extolling Zacky Boswell's knowledge of wildlife in the countryside and casting him as a good mentor to the two children, she allowed a character in the book to voice disparaging remarks about Gypsies, remarks that were to land her in trouble many years later when critics began to question the contents of some of her storybooks.[4] To find out how she could have avoided such a situation, see Why Some of Enid Blyton's Stories Are Not up to Standard in Section Two of this book.

On the whole, Enid presented nature facts and the descriptions of animals, birds and plants so clearly that children in any age group could easily read and understand them all by themselves. Moreover, when we take into account the beautiful true to life illustrations of boys and girls wearing recognisable clothes – doing things and going places readers themselves could not go without parental approval or permission – along with beautiful black and white (and sometimes colour) illustrations of birds (see again Figure 1), animals, trees and plants in vivid countryside settings, the pleasure children must have derived from reading these books is incalculable.

Finally, with her knowledge of birds, animals and plants, no one would ever know how many children she had encouraged or inspired to move into fields such as botany, zoology and ornithology through her nature study courses in *The Teachers World,* nature books and readers, and in the poems and songs she infused with nature themes.

Let us now turn to something else she was interested in – poetry – where we have another opportunity to see how her knowledge of birds, animals, plants and flowers shone even more brightly in this field.

NOTE: The thirty-six Nature Readers as well as Eileen Soper's sixty beautiful colour plates that accompanied them are carefully preserved by the British Library, 96 Euston Road, NW1 2DB, London, England and can be read in the Reading Room of the Rare Books and Music Wing by applying for a temporary readers pass. *Enid Blyton's Nature Lessons* and *Hedgerow Tales* in book form, as well as all the other books described in this section are also preserved and can be read along the same lines.

CHAPTER II
ENID THE POET

OVERVIEW

By the time we get to the end of this chapter, we'll see how Enid Blyton became aware of her gift of poetry, her struggle to develop it and the opportunities that came her way to see her poems in print. We'll also see how she rose from obscurity to become *The Teachers World* adorable poet. We then move on to review her poetry books and take a look at her poems published in periodicals and anthologies, and at those she wrote for people in high places. The chapter ends with a call for her achievement in this field to be recognised.

Just as Enid's father is credited with setting her on course to become a naturalist, so he may also be credited with setting her on course to become a poet.

'*My father was fond of poetry*,' she recalled on page 50 of *The Story of My Life*, '*and he used to quote it so often that it became part of my life*.' This repetition stimulated or aroused her interest in the subject and was to lead directly to the discovery that she too had a gift of poetry.

This gift began to show itself at an early age in the frivolous rhymes she used to make up at home to amuse her two brothers, Hanly and Carey, when they were growing up:

'*I remember quite well the first rhyme I ever made up*,' she recalled in a passage on page 66 of *The Story of My Life*. This was it:

My kitten cat is white and fat,
His eyes are green and round-o,
Along he goes on tippy-toes
And never makes a sound-o.

'*From these first beginnings*', she continued in another passage, '*and from the pleasure I took in the sound and meaning of words, came all my other poems. Anything that aroused my love or admiration seemed to need special words and special lilts, and gradually I left the little 'nursery rhymes' and began to experiment with the making of poetry.*'

Scarcely had she become fourteen years old when she put her experiment to the test by sending in a poem to a children's magazine edited by Arthur Mee. Incidentally, this was the same person whose eight-volume *Children Encyclopedia* she had read from cover to cover and then read it all over again (see Chapter VII, *Enid: The Professional Storyteller* for more information). It was therefore a bold step for a fourteen-year-old to take, but it did pay off:

'*To my utter amazement and delight, I had a letter back from the great man himself. He liked my poem. He would print it. But more than that, he told me that he liked the letter I had sent with it ... when [eventually] my little poem was printed on the children's page in the magazine I could have cried for joy!*' [5]

Encouraged by this small success she went a step further and sent in a humorous poem to *Punch*, one of the leading magazines of the day, only to find that the response was not as encouraging as that from Arthur Mee. When the self-addressed envelope came back, her excitement soon turned to dismay:

'*I opened it. There was my poem – but written at the side was a sentence or two in a small, neat handwriting:* "Idea good. Spoilt by wrong accent in line 10 and bad rhyme in line 12. Try again sometime". *It was signed O.S., the initials of Owen Seaman, the then famous editor of Punch. I stared at the magic initials as if I had been struck by lightning.*' [6]

However, this criticism did not discourage her. For it was not long before she set to work in earnest to find out why her poetry was not up to standard.

'I bought books on the technique of poetry – 'prosody' as it is called. I was ashamed to find that I didn't know how to write poetry properly at all, according to these books.' [7]

So it was that by the time she was in her early twenties she had so mastered the art of writing poetry that she was confident enough to start sending out poems again to various periodicals of the day, all of which were accepted and published without question. According to her biographer, Barbara Stoney, in various passages in *Enid Blyton: A Biography*, *Nash's Magazine* published three of her poems entitled: 'Have You?' 'My Summer Prayer' and 'Do You?' in various editions between 1917 and 1918; *The Poetry Review* published another, 'The Poet', in 1919, and a small Presbyterian church magazine, published yet another: 'The Messenger', sometime in 1920. [8]

By this time, she had already completed her teacher-training course at the Froebel Wing of Ipswich High School where, as stated in the previous chapter, she obtained her National Froebel Union Higher Certificate. Here we are in 1918 – the year that witnessed the end of the First World War (1914 – 1918) – and it was during this year she began working for the first time as a teacher at Bickley Park School for Boys in Kent. While she was holding this position, a fortuitous event occurred and this event was to give her the unique opportunity of seeing many more of her poems published regularly in a single medium: the sudden availability of a slot for poetry in *The Teachers World*.

In this slot, one H. M. Crawford used to feature every month a verse on some nature theme along with an illustration and a few Nature Notes. It is not known how the slot became available. Neither is it known what arrangements had been made for Enid to take it over. Nevertheless, from June 1922, Enid quickly filled the vacuum with a long poem on a nature theme and her best friend from school days, Phyllis Chase, provided an illustration to go with the poem. For every other month that followed Enid was to thrill readers of *The Teachers World* with a poem about some happenings in nature until the series came to an end in June 1923 (see Appendix 13 for illustration of one of the poems in the series).

Now while she was busy writing these long poems for her monthly poetry page in *The Teachers World*, she was also accumulating a stock of her own poems. It would appear that the purpose of the exercise was to have enough poems on hand for the children in her class to read or recite to her. However, as time went by the children appeared to like her poems so much that she decided to have them published so that schoolchildren everywhere might enjoy them as much as her pupils did. The publisher she eventually found was J. Saville & Co. who published them in June 1922 with the title: *Child Whispers,* which, incidentally, was her first book ever to be published! (See Figure 7 for front cover illustration.)

With titles such as 'Fairy Sight', 'A Fairy Necklace', 'Poppies', 'Goblins', 'Lovely Frocks', 'Fairy Music' and 'A Happy Ending', the twenty-eight poems in this first book of poems soon became as popular as ever with children who were easily captivated by references to fairies, elves, goblins and other folks. Moreover, we can imagine how pleased she must have been to see not only so many of her poems in print all at once, but also the many interesting reviews her book of poems received from newspapers and magazines to which her publisher had sent in a copy. Prominent among them is one that appeared in *The Supplement to The Schoolmistress*, a weekly educational newspaper for teachers, in its edition of August 10, 1922. Here is an extract from this review:

CHILD WHISPERS

(Publishers: Saville and Co. 2s. 6d. net.)

A NICE little booklet of verses for children. Witches, fairies, goblins, flowers, little folk, butterflies, and other delights all live between its pages. Teachers who like easy simple verse for their children will find what they want here...

Children whose imaginations were fired by her poems and who enjoyed reciting them at school, or reading them at home for pleasure, were in for a bigger treat when Enid wrote thirty-three more poems which were published subsequently by the same firm, J. Saville & Co. in 1923 under the title: *Real Fairies* (see title page illustration, Figure 7).

 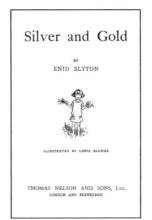 

FIGURE 7: The front cover of Child Whispers, and title pages of her other three poetry books. Child Whispers, published in 1922 by J. Saville & Co is her first book ever to be published. © British Library Board, (SM: Child Whispers, (12802.aa.65 cover); Real Fairies (011645.de.68 title page); Silver and Gold (11643.m.11 title page); The Enid Blyton Poetry Book (11654.a.39 title page).

A remarkable feature of these new poems whose titles include 'Real Fairies' – the title of the book – 'Wall-Flowers', 'The Mermaid's Ribbon', 'The Open Window', 'The Workmen' and so on, is that they are all suitable for recitation. At least this is the opinion of *The Teachers World's* reviewers, when they were reviewing the book in the edition of July 18, 1923. Here is an extract from this long review:

MISS BLYTON'S NEW BOOK.

REAL FAIRIES

By Enid Blyton (J. Saville, 3s.6d.)

"REAL Fairies" will need no recommendation to readers of The Teachers World, for Miss Blyton's name alone will be sufficient to ensure a welcome for her latest volume of poems ... Unlike so many collections of "child poetry" they are particularly suitable for recitation by children, for the language and thought are simple and attractive, and in most cases each poem introduces an original and dramatic story...

Here is a poem selected from page 43 of this book that reflects these qualities and confirms the reviewer's opinion about its suitability for recitation:

A GREAT SURPRISE

This morning when the sun was hot,
I took my watering-can,
I filled it full of water cool
And down the path I ran.
I watered all my candytuft,
And all my poppies red,
And then I emptied all the rest
Upon my pansy bed.
But oh! I dropped my watering-can,
And stared in great surprise,
For up a little fairy flew
Before my very eyes!
She shook her little dripping wings,
As cross as she could be,
"I'm not a thirsty flower," she said,
"How dare you water me!"

The image of fairies so vividly presented in this poem must have been enough to make children believe that fairies really existed. Whatever the case, Enid's depiction of fairies in verse in some of the poems in this book, as well as in *Child Whispers*, was nothing more than the depiction of fairies in children's literature – such as the fairy godmother in *Cinderella* – that was prevalent at that time.

No sooner had this second book of poems seen the light of day than Enid turned her attention to writing a new series of poems for *The Teachers World*, this time on the subject of each day of the week.

Her first poem in the series 'Monday' was published on July 6, 1923 in *The Teachers World Extra Number* – a special edition issued separately to focus attention on some particular subject. The next poem in the series 'Tuesday' appears in the *Extra Number* for August, and 'Wednesday', in the edition for September and so on until the series came to an end in December 1923.

This new series of poems, as well as the one that preceded it, was so well received that when the editor of *The Teachers World* was putting together material for *The Extra Numbers* or special editions to mark Empire Day celebrations, they turned to Enid, once again, to write a new series of poems. The new poems were to go with articles about each country in the then British Empire – now the Commonwealth.

Enid began writing the new series in March 1924 with a long poem about the far away country of India. With the title: 'An Indian Day', this poem tells the story of a day in the life of the Indian people where the sweltering or hot climate makes life so unbearable that human activity grinds to a halt, forcing everyone to seek the shade, until the sun goes down later in the day, and the resulting cool makes life worth living again (see Appendix 14 for a facsimile reproduction). By the time the series came to a close one year later Enid had written one such poem every month about Burma, South Africa, New Zealand, Australia, Canada, Ceylon, The British Isles, and so on.

Scarcely had she written the last poem in the series when her talent was required, once again, to write another series of poems the editor was planning to feature in the newspaper. On this occasion, the subject was to be about animals, a subject Enid was quite capable of handling.

So it was that as early as February, 1925 Enid's first poem in the new series with the title: 'The Fox' appeared on a full page in *The Teachers World* to the delight of teachers and their pupils who were seeing, perhaps for the first time, peculiarities of familiar animals portrayed in poetical form (see Appendix 15 for a reproduction of 'Sea Lions', one of the poems in the series). As the series unfolded readers were treated to a poem on 'Squirrels', 'Dogs', 'Cats', 'Monkeys', 'Pigs', 'Cows', 'Horses' and so on until it came to an end one year later.

In the meantime, readers of *The Teachers World* who were enjoying her poems in the series but knew nothing about her had the opportunity to learn a great deal when an interviewer wanting to be known only as H.A.[9] interviewed her for a special article in a series with the title: *The Children's Poets*. This article, which was published in the edition of October 1, 1926, carried a small picture of Enid sitting by a round pond in her garden and took readers on an imaginary tour of the inside and outside of her home before touching on the subject of her poetry:

> *Her first poem was published in her teens, long before she left the school-room or thought of becoming a teacher,* the article informed readers*, and since then she has written for many of the best known mediums of the day, including Punch, The Morning Post, Nash's Magazine, and others. ... Strange to say, as the quantity increases, the quality improves. Year by year Enid Blyton's poems for children grow richer in understanding [and] become more tender in their appeal...*

Even before this article was published, Enid had already released *Silver & Gold*, another book of thirty poems that Thomas Nelson published in 1925 (see Figure 7 for title page illustration). So the reference made in the article to her poems growing year by year 'richer in understanding' and 'more tender in their appeal' could apply, not only to the series of poems she wrote for *The Teachers World* (see again examples given in Appendix 13 to 15), but also to the thirty poems in *Silver & Gold*.

Moreover, anyone who has read her earlier poems in *Child Whispers* and *Real Fairies* and compared them with the poems in *Silver And Gold* would have noticed the clear break from simple verses about fairies, elves and so on to verses about things which children can relate to. In other words they are, for the most part, poems about everyday things in a child's world.

Here's a review of *Silver & Gold* carried in *The Teachers World* in the edition of April 22, 1925 under the caption: Last Week's Books:

SILVER & GOLD

By Enid Blyton (Nelson, 3s 6p 5" X 6 ½" 71 pp)

It is quite unnecessary to describe for T W readers the contents of this dainty little volume. In each a real child speaks as a real child really would, and the verses, both by their sound and sense, will be loved by all children who see the little book. An ideal illustration for these jolly verses has been chosen in Mr Lewis Baumer.

Let us now look at a poem selected from this book so that we may appreciate the change in subject and style. This poem, 'Magic in the Snow' – the thirteenth poem in the book – gives a vivid picture of a landscape transformed by snow falling through the night. By putting herself in the picture, Enid gave the impression she had just got out of bed and was taking in the scene from her bedroom window:

MAGIC IN THE SNOW

I LOOKED from my window this morning
And saw such a wonderful sight,
For all of the trees and the houses
Were covered in blankets of white.
The sky was as blue as a harebell,
With wee misty clouds all around;
And purple and blue were the shadows
That lay here and there on the ground.
And when I went out in the garden
There wasn't a sound to be heard –
Not even the wind in the bushes,
Not even the song of a bird.
And I knew that the garden was waiting,

And keeping as still as could be,
Watching for something to happen –
Something perhaps I could see.

Children living in cold climates have seen this phenomenon year after year, especially during Christmas, and reading this poem would have helped them to relive the experience in their imaginations.

This writing of poems about familiar things in a child's world was to reach its peak in her fourth book of poems: *The Enid Blyton Poetry Book* that Methuen & Co. published in 1934 (Figure 7). In this book we find ninety-six poems, written in batches of eight for each of the twelve months of the year. We also find a leading or introductory poem for the name of the month followed by a short nature poem about flowers, birds, insects, animals, the seasons, weather and so on. Children who enjoyed her nature poems in *The Teachers World* and were asking for more had more than their fair share in this book. Here is one of these poems, 'The Shepherd', which appeared in the first batch of eight poems for the month of January:

THE SHEPHERD

I know a man who's old and wise,
He reads the wind, he reads the skies,
He knows when storms will blow his way,
He knows what rain will fall each day.
He'll take you where the primrose shines,
He knows the early celandines,
He names each bird that by him flies,
His eyes are very blue and wise.
All day and night he tends the sheep,
He hears them bleating in his sleep,
There's not a lamb upon the farm,
He hasn't carried in his arm.
I wish I knew the things he knows
The night-time skies, the wind that blows,
The singing birds, the bleating cries –
I wish I were a shepherd wise.

Poems such as this would not fail to delight schoolchildren by the vivid pictures they would conjure up in their imaginations. Moreover, if there's one of Enid Blyton's books of poems that deserve to be brought back into circulation – especially in schools – it would be *The Enid Blyton Poetry Book* (see title page illustration Figure 7).

Incidentally, the poems in this book were to become a source of inspiration for Enid when she was writing songs for schools. Among the poems she successfully turned into songs are 'A Frosty Morning', 'The First Crocus', 'The Singer In The Night' and 'The Wild Rose' (see *Enid: The Prolific Songwriter*, Chapter VI, for development of this theme).

Besides these two new books of poems, Enid also published many other poems for children in some of her nature and storybooks. Among these books is *Enid Blyton's Book of the Year* to which we have already been introduced in the previous chapter, *Enid: The Naturalist*. In one of the sections of this book we find fifty-two short poems – reduced to forty-five in subsequent reprints – about birds, animals, flowers, trees and some other aspects of nature (see Figure 8 for a sample reading of one of these poems).

Then there's *Enid Blyton's Nature Lover's Book* mentioned in the previous chapter. Under the heading: 'Poems of the Open Air' she presents twelve poems, mostly about trees and birds, in the usual style (see Appendix 16 for illustration).

Even when we turn our attention to her storybooks for children we find batches of poems appearing either alone or as an additional treat to each of the stories in the book. For example, in her *Enid Blyton Book of Fairies,* published by George Newnes Ltd in 1924, there are thirteen poems about fairies, elves, goblins and so on scattered among the many stories in the book. Another batch of her poems can be found in *The Marigold Storybook* (eight poems), and in *The Foxglove Storybook* (another eight poems), two books which John Gifford published 1954 and 1955 respectively.

Other batches of her poems can be found in some of the 200 reading books she wrote for schools. This is especially the case in *My First Reading Book*, first published by Birn Brothers in 1933. In this book of 160 pages, we find thirty poems, presented as an alternative method to teach children to read. Here's one of the poems selected from this book:

PICKING THE APPLES

Let's pick the apples off the tree,
They're very ripe and red,
And if we do not pick them soon,
They'll tumble on our head.
Where's the ladder? Here it is,
Lean it on the tree.
I will climb it to the top,
Hold it straight for me.
Oh! What lots of apples here!
Juicy, ripe and sweet,
Scores and scores are tumbling down,
Round about our feet.
Put them in the basket, please,
Fill it to the top,
Look at all the fruit there is,
What a splendid crop.

Other books for children in primary schools containing her poems are *Read To Us* (14 poems), *How To Count* (12 poems) and *How To Multiply* (12 poems) – all published by Birn Brothers in 1929.

Another outlet for her poems is *Enid Blyton's Sunny Stories Calendar* for 1942 that George Newnes Ltd published in September 1941 (see illustration Appendix 17). Here we can see three poems: one on the cover with the title: 'Good Luck!' – which takes the place of the introduction – and two others, 'The Quiet Snow' and 'The Little Tree-House' on the page with the calendar for January 1942. For every other month of the year Enid presented two poems, bringing it to twenty-five by the time the year was out. On the other side of the calendar is Nature Notes – not shown in the illustration in Appendix 17 – for every month of the year describing things such as flowers and trees in season, with activities for children to do such as looking out for particular types of flowers.

The title was changed to *Sunny Stories Calendar* in subsequent issues after 1942 and it was published every year after until 1951 when it made its last appearance.

With the twenty-five poems in the first issue and twelve in every other issue – thirteen in the issue for 1943 – we get 134 poems in all.

Even Noddy, the little wooden boy created by Enid Blyton in 1949, whose series of books was popular with children, had his own book of nursery rhymes. With the title: *Noddy's Own Nursery Rhymes: A Nursery Colour Picture Book*, published by Samson Low in 1958, it contains twenty-five verses that children could recite in the nursery.

SPEEDWELL

LIKE A LITTLE pool of blue
    On the bank we shine,
    With brilliant eyes we gaze at you
When the day is fine.
The blue of summer skies we hold
    In our blossoms frail,
Like little jewels we unfold,
    Fit for fairy-tale.
Germander is the name we bear,
    You call us " Speedwell," too,
See, we're shining everywhere,
    Dressed in vivid blue.

130

FIGURE 8 The 'Speedwell', one of a batch of fifty-two poems (reduced to forty-five in subsequent editions) with nature themes. Enid Blyton included these poems in the nature section of her Enid Blyton Book of the Year, first published by Evans Bros in 1941. © Hodder & Stoughton Ltd. Reproduced by permission of Hodder & Stoughton Ltd.

Here's one of the nursery rhymes from this book:

I'M OFF TO SEA

I'm off on a trip
In a big, big ship,
Yo-ho for a life at sea!
The waves go splash
And I make a dash
To take the captain his tea!
The wind goes by,
And the sea is high,
And everything's wet as can be,
I'm kept on the run,
But really it's fun
For Bruiny, Bumpy and me!

This piece was carried in the book below a picture of a big ship with Noddy and all the toys on deck. He is seen performing a balancing act with the captain's breakfast on a tray.

Enid was also lucky to have some of her poems published in anthologies or collections of poems from time to time. The first anthology in which her poems appear is believed to be one that was carried in *The Teachers World* in its edition of January 1, 1923. Here, two new poems with the title: 'A Lively Horse' and 'The Railway' were featured among twenty other poems from famous poets of the day such as John Drinkwater, John Marefield, G K Chesterton, and so on.

Eighteen months later the editor of *The Teachers World* published a second anthology in the supplement or *Extra Number* to the regular edition of July 4, 1924. Here we find thirty-two poems classified under different headings such as Adventure & Travel, Ships & The Sea, Armistice Day, and so on. Enid contributed a single poem with the title: 'Too Hot' to this anthology and this poem appears under the heading: Humorous Poems For Juniors. Here is this poem in full:

TOO HOT

I'm hot to-day, simply dreadfully hot
You just touch my hand – no you'd p'raps better not,
I'm 'fraid it would burn you, it's hot as can be,
Oh! I wonder if *anyone's* hotter than me!
My clothes are all stuck to me tighter than glue,
And I just can't unstick them, whatever I do,
I've wriggled and pulled till my breath is all gone,
Oh why can't I have just a bathing-dress on?
I wish I could sit in a nice little pool,
And get just a bit of me lovely and cool
I wish I could water myself with a can,
But I know I'd be scolded if once I began.
I believe I am melting, I'm feeling so queer,
It'll serve people right, if I do melt out here!
They'll feel sorry then when they come out and see
There's nothing but bundles of clothes left on me!

Then, when she brought out her three-volume *Teachers' Treasury* in 1926, (see title page illustration, Appendix 41), she presented in Volume II, in the poetry section, a collection of thirty poems from poets such as Walter de la Mare, Robert Louis Stevenson, and Oliver Herford and included ten poems of her own.

Moreover, in another anthology published by Collins Educational in 1942, in a book entitled: *A Book Of One Thousand Poems – The Classical Collection For Children*, four of Enid's poems with the title: 'What Piggy Wig Found' (page 104), 'Fairy Music' (page 150), 'Winter' (page 206), and 'The Field Mouse' (page 329), were included in the collection.

There's another collection worthy of mention at this time: *Enid Blyton's Treasury of Verse* which Purnell Books published in 1979 for Darrell Waters Ltd, a company Enid formed in 1950 to help manage her business affairs. For information about this company, see *A Short History of Darrell Waters Ltd* in Section Two.

This collection features 110 of Enid's best poems collected from some of her books and periodicals. Here we find poems about flowers, animals, fairies, nature, the weather, seaside, and so on. It is beautifully illustrated throughout with an introduction by her elder daughter Gillian Baverstock

As time went by Enid tried her hand at writing poems for adults, but these were not as numerous as those she had written for children. Among them can be found 'The Helmsman' which she wrote to mark the Silver Jubilee (25 years) of the reign of the then King George V. On that occasion, the editor *of The Teachers World* did her the honour of publishing this poem on the cover of the Junior Edition of May 1, 1935 when the celebrations to mark the occasion were at their peak (see Appendix 18 for illustration). Then there's 'A Lion Once We Had': a poem Enid dedicated to Sir Winston Churchill who had led the nation to victory in the Second World War (1939 – 1945). This poem was carried in the *Sunday Graphic* in the edition of March 16, 1947 (see Appendix 19 for illustration).

'To Hang Or Not To Hang', another poem for adults, was written in 1950 on the occasion of the government discussion on the Abolition of Capital Punishment, and is carried in full by her biographer, Barbara Stoney, on pages 199 and 200 of *Enid Blyton: A Biography*.

Her last known poem with the title: 'April Day', which she wrote when she was advancing in age, is featured prominently by her daughter, Imogen Smallwood, on page 153 in her book, *A Childhood At Green Hedges*, and by her biographer, in Appendix I, page 185 of *Enid Blyton: A Biography*. A transcript of this poem can now be seen in Appendix 20.

Finally, when we take into account the large number of poems referred to in this chapter as well as the uncollected poems Tony Summerfield listed in his four-volume *Enid Blyton: An Illustrated Bibliography,*[10] we can see that they're enough to give her a place in any standard reference book on the subject of poets and poetry.

Yet if we go through any of these books today, we find no mention of her name, much less her achievement in the field of poetry. Whatever be the reason for this omission, it is hoped that the documentary of her poems in this chapter would bring her name and achievement to the attention of future editors of such publications so that she may be placed, posthumously, among the finest children's poets of the 20th century.

CHAPTER III

ENID THE COLUMNIST & FEATURE WRITER

OVERVIEW

In 1919, when Enid Blyton began teaching at Bickley Park School for Boys in Kent for the first time, she was attracted to a newspaper that was circulating in schools throughout the country. Entitled: *The Teachers World*, this newspaper was packed with news, views and interviews of interest to teachers. A brief history of *The Teachers World* is given in Section Two and a reproduction of the front cover of one of the editions can be seen in Appendix 21.

One reason for this attraction could be that since it carried from time to time stories and poems for children, she could try to see whether the editor would also publish her own stories and poems. Little did she know that some seven years later she was going, not only to be the biggest contributor of stories and poems to the newspaper, but would hold down a column, 'From My Window', faithfully for over four years.

Neither did she ever dream that as time went by, she was going to have a whole children's page, write feature articles, and run Nature, World History and Gardening courses in the same newspaper. In this chapter we take a look at the origin, development and termination of her column and its transformation, first into 'Enid Blyton's Letter to Children' and subsequently, into 'Enid Blyton's Children's Page'. Then we move on to consider other pages she held in the same newspaper and in other periodicals from time to time.

When Enid received the invitation to write a weekly column in *The Teachers World*, it took her completely by surprise.

'Will you write a weekly column for The Teachers World?'

'I would love to,' I answered, 'but what about? Salaries, conferences, lockouts? Impossible. I couldn't.'

'No, other things you're interested in, and that might interest other teachers – books and theatres, education, children, Nature…

'Thus it was settled and I visioned a new and delightful task before me every week.'

These are the opening lines of her first article in 'From My Window', the title of her column, which appeared in the edition of July 4, 1923. This article, which was about children in general, could have easily been termed 'On Genius in Children'. Here she is comparing the workings of a child's mind to that of a genius whose characteristic attitude, she points out, is a questioning one:

'…The questioning, wondering mind that analyses and puts together, that observes and records for itself, and that finally bursts out into an expression of the many impressions – there is a description equally applicable to mature genius, or to immature childhood', she tells teachers in the article as her thoughts on the subject unfold. *'What is the explanation of the curious similarity? Why does it in all but a few cases cease as the child grows? Is it some fault of our education that has not recognised the real trend of a child's mind, which is, surely, genius-ward, in its simplicity and need for expression? … If only we could train our children in the way that geniuses perforce [unavoidably] have to train themselves, we should get a wonderful type of ordinary men and women.'*

(See Appendix 22 for the full text of this first thought-provoking article in her column.)

With such an impressive beginning, she knew she was on course to fulfil the charge given to her.

All the articles she eventually wrote during the four years she held the column may be put into the following categories:

- Human Interest, often with practical precepts & moral over-tones
- Miscellaneous
- Personal

Let us begin with the first: Human Interest

HUMAN INTEREST

Here are three brief extracts from some of her articles in this category, written between 1925 and 1926:

The Best People In The World (January 28, 1925 page 887)

... The naturally happy spirit is a rare and beautiful gift. People who have it are the luckiest folk on earth ... If only it were a duty to be happy! We are thought that we must be good, that we must have common sense and that we must love one another; but we are not told that we must be happy. It would need a happy person to teach that properly ...

A Sense of Humour (March 4, 1925, page 1129)

...Certainly life is a serious business – so serious sometimes that it is not to be greatly wondered at if bitterness and prejudice creep into our character. And then only a sense of humour can save us. I think if people realised the real power of this underestimated sense, they would not readily either part with it or leave it undeveloped...

Kindness (March 31, 1926, page 1347)

...Kindness consists of smaller acts, and is more apparent between strangers than between friends where it gets swamped by the bigger virtues of love and unselfishness ... There is a tremendous lot of kindness in the world. It pops up unexpectedly everywhere, and gives you a delicious warm feeling round your heart...

Other articles in this category with practical precepts or moral overtones include: On Being Surprised (July 25, 1923), Romance (Aug 29, 1923), On Little Things (Sept 5, 1923) Faces (Oct 17, 1923), Other People's Shoes (Nov 7, 1923), On Asking Questions (Jan 30, 1924),

Friendly Things (Feb 18, 1925), Surprising People (Sept 8, 1926) and An Exciting Life (Aug 17, 1927).

MISCELLANEOUS

From time to time Enid wrote articles on current affairs of a cultural character. These included visits she had made to exhibitions and shows, such as The Ideal Home Exhibition (March 26, 1924,); The Royal Tournament (June 11, 1924); The Rodeo – a show of cowboys and horses – (July 2, 1924) and the new aquarium at the Zoo (July 9, 1924). In these articles, she would give brief descriptions of what was taking place, along with her comments and observations.

She also reviewed books in her column, among which were: *Riceyman Steps* by Arnold Bennett (December 5, 1923); *Man and the Attainment of Immortality* by Prof. James Young Simpson (August 15, 1923); *Exploring England* by Charles Bayne (June 2, 1926) and *The London Child* by Evelyn Sharp (August 10, 1927). Here is a brief extract from the review of *Man and the Attainment of Immortality:*

> *... Here is just the book for the teacher for it contains a clear, scholarly, up-to-date account of the world and its inhabitants and also an inspired and beautiful attempt to point out the future of mankind...*

The book reviews appeared to be for new books she had read and was keen to share with teachers, rather than for those submitted to her by publishers for reviewing.

PERSONAL

Had it not been for her growing popularity, it's unlikely the numerous articles in this category would have flourished in the newspaper. This popularity stemmed from the success of her earlier articles and from her poems, plays, stories and nature lessons in other sections of the newspaper. No sooner had she written a piece or published a poem than her newly-found fans flooded her with letters of appreciation, as can be seen from the account she gave in the following extract:
'Happiness' (February 18, 1925, page 1037)

> *WHEN, a few weeks ago, I wrote about "Happy People," I didn't*

foresee the increase it would bring me in my correspondence. Now, as I write, I have before me letters from grown-ups and letters from children – wistful letters, sincere letters, and quaint letters. Everybody does so badly want to be happy…

Her column therefore became the medium of interaction with teachers and fans and this was the beginning of all the articles of a personal nature she wrote for the newspaper. Hence, when she moved house, started up a garden, visited the theatre or went on holiday, an entire article was devoted to the event and this in turn brought an even bigger increase in her correspondence.

As time went by she was including in the column material that was more suitable for children than for teachers and this must have given rise to a longing to write articles especially for them. Whether there had been negotiations with the editor to have this wish fulfilled is not known, but from August 24, 1927, teachers who were reading her column 'Green and Blue', in which she contrasted the blue of the sky with the green of the countryside, suddenly found at the bottom the following message:

In place of this feature Miss Blyton will write – directly to the children – a Weekly Letter, commencing next week.

So it was that 'From My Window', the title of the column she held for over four years, had abruptly come to an end on August 24, 1927 (see Appendix 23 for the last article in her column). In its place was 'Enid Blyton's Letter to Children' the first one of which appeared in the edition of August 31, 1927. Here are the opening lines of this letter:

Dear Boys And Girls,

A lovely thing has happened. It has been decided that I can write you a letter every week for your own, instead of writing a talk for the grown-ups, which you sometimes shared … I can tell you about all sort of things, especially those you would see if you lived here in Elfin Cottage with me – jolly things, lovely things, funny things … I think I know the things you like to hear about – animals and gardens, adventure, the Zoo, exciting books, birds and hundreds of other jolly things…

This was the beginning of her interaction with children, which eventually led to a fan base with hundreds of letters to reply to every week. It also gave her another opportunity to interact with teachers. From then onwards, they would be reading her 'Enid Blyton's Letter to Children' in classrooms and sending her their comments, along with letters from children, just as they had been doing with her poems, stories and nature lessons.

Then in 1929, nearly two years after she had started writing the 'Enid Blyton Letter to Children', an event took place that was to give her the opportunity to have a whole page to interact with children.

It all happened when the editor decided sometime in 1929 to divide the newspaper into two distinct editions: a Junior Edition for teachers of children younger than eleven years, and a Senior Edition, for those of children eleven years and over. Therefore, in recognition of her increased contributions for children, both in her regular column and in separate parts of the newspaper, the editor terminated her column and created a children's page for her to run in the Junior Edition.

Her pleasure in having this Children's Page can be seen from the opening lines of her first 'Letter to Boys And Girls' that appeared in the edition of September 4, 1929 (see Appendix 24).

Here we can see that this 'Letter' was retained from the previous arrangement as the main feature, along with a story and a poem. We can also see a picture of Enid sitting in the grass with her pets whose strange behaviour was to be the subject of many of the 'Letters'.

It was also in this Children's Page that Enid started to write a weekly letter purporting to come from 'Bobs', the name of her fox terrier (shown on her lap in Appendix 24). This colourful addition never ceased to fascinate children (see Appendix 25, third column, for illustration). Here we can see immediately what it was about them that captivated children's imaginations. Indeed, so popular had these letters become that Enid had them published privately in 1933, under the title: *Letters From Bobs.*[11]

Finally, to come back to the termination of her column, 'From My Window', we find that the event was not handled in a proper way. In the first place, the editor trivialised the event in a few words at the bottom of her last article 'Green And Blue' instead of making a proper announcement in the newspaper. Secondly, Enid too did not make an announcement to let teachers and her fans know she had terminated her column. With 211 articles to her credit over four years, that certainly was not the right thing to do.

In the end it turned out that it was Enid herself who terminated her column. Barbara Stoney gave a summary of this situation in a passage on page 141 of *Enid Blyton: A Biography*:

> '... She decided to wind up her column on the retirement of Mr. E. H. Allen, who had taken her first contribution to the magazine and had continued to follow her career with friendly interest throughout his editorship. Enid disliked changes not of her own making, and did not feel inclined to fall in with any fresh ideas that a new editor might bring ...'

This statement therefore unravels the mystery of the failure of Enid, or her editor, to make a formal announcement in the newspaper of the termination of her column.

However, notwithstanding this situation, Enid was lucky to have been given a replacement, in the form of another column, to present a 'Letter to Boys And Girls', as discussed in a paragraph earlier in this section. Some two years later, she got an even bigger opportunity to interact with children when, as stated earlier, the newspaper was divided into two separate editions and she was given a whole page for that purpose. So her decision to wind up her column, 'From My Window' did pay off in the end, after all!

Let's now take a look at the other pages she held in the newspaper from time to time to see what they're all about. For convenience, I put them into three categories:

- Weekly Pages
- Fortnightly Pages
- Monthly Pages

WEEKLY PAGES

Her first Weekly Page was the 'Friday Afternoon Stories' page she shared with other contributors. The editor provided this page for teachers and others to narrate a story that, in turn, teachers would tell to children in classrooms. Her first story in this page was 'Peronel and His Pot of Glue' that was carried in the edition of February 15, 1922 (see illustration, Appendix 26). Beautifully illustrated by Phyllis Chase, it's a wonderful story about a little dancing fairy called Peronel who restored the king's broken dish with glue made from a mixture of fairy ingredients.

This was her first story ever to be published in *The Teachers World*. Had the editor rejected it, along with a batch of other stories, the door to *The Teachers World* would have been closed and all the contributions described in these pages would not have been! [12]

From then onwards she contributed many more stories to the page, whenever she had the opportunity to do so for, as stated earlier in this section, she had to share the page with other contributors. Sometimes the page was withdrawn without notice, and then suddenly reappeared. In the end, it was discontinued and when that happened, Enid collected some of the stories and carried them in her fairytale book, *Enid Blyton Book of Fairies,* which George Newnes Ltd published in 1924. [13]

The second Weekly Page Enid was holding started out fortnightly and was given to her for teaching purposes. Here she had the opportunity to run an elaborate course in world history, all wrapped up in stories. These stories fell into two distinctive groups as follows:

- Stories of World History
- Tales of Romance

STORIES OF WORLD HISTORY

The series of stories Enid presented under this heading stems from suggestions the Board of Education – now the Ministry of Education – put forward in a new edition of *Handbook of Suggestions* for the consideration of teachers (see title page illustration, Appendix 27).

One of the suggestions, carried on page 118, states that '*In junior classes ... simple, attractive stories should form the substance of the instruction ... They should be so arranged as to introduce the child to a gallery of striking pictures drawn from the whole range of history.*'

No sooner had the handbook came out than *The Teachers World* organised in the newspaper a World History course for children eleven years and younger to help teachers to carry out the specific suggestion just quoted from the 'Handbook of Suggestions'.

Moreover, since Enid had already run teaching courses in the newspaper, she was given the commission to write stories for the World History course with the caption: 'Stories of World History'.

A brief announcement to this effect was made in *The Teachers World*, edition of August 24, 1927, and the following week Enid's first story: 'The Siege of Troy – 1. How the Trojan War Began' appeared in the newspaper under the caption: 'Stories of World History', in the edition of August 31, 1927 (see Appendix 28 for illustration).

In this first story in what was to become a series, Enid gave an account, in her own words, of the beginning of the Trojan War and described the events that eventually led to the fall of Troy. This was followed by Notes For The Teacher, to provide teachers with background information and prepare them for questions the children might ask after listening to the story in classrooms (see Appendix 29, column 3, for illustration).

Then in October 1927, when the episodes were appearing with nothing to guide teachers about what was to follow, she published her syllabus outlining all the 'Stories of World History' she intended to cover in the course (see Appendix 30 for illustration). At the bottom of the syllabus is the mention that the course was to run for one year and that the episodes would appear weekly instead of fortnightly. So with this syllabus, teachers could then look forward to a series of World History stories to read to children in classrooms.

As the weeks progressed, the stories were unfolding smoothly according to the plan outlined in the syllabus. By the end of May 1928, she had already presented six episodes of the 'Siege and Fall of Troy', six episodes of 'The Adventures of Odysseus' and twelve episodes of

'The Ancient Greeks and Persians'. She then moved on to 'Stories of The Arabian Nights', told in two episodes, before ending these groups of stories.

Then in June, 1928 she moved on to another group of stories in the syllabus about the Romans and their conquest. Here are the opening lines to introduce this group of stories:

I. Tales of the Romans – Romulus and Remus

I have told you of many great cities and of many great peoples. Now I want to tell you of the beginning of a city which was to become the most famous in the world – the city of Rome. Find it on your maps and see where it stands in Italy on the banks of the River Tiber…

In telling the stories in this group, Enid placed emphasis only on significant events in early Roman history. These events included the rise of the twins Romulus and Remus and the part they played in giving Rome its name and status; the bravery of Horatius who kept the bridge from the invading Etruscans and the squawking of Juno's geese that saved the Capital from the deceitful Gauls.

However, the event that featured strongly in the stories is the bitter enmity between Rome and Carthage. In four episodes, each of between 1500 and 2000 words, she described the rise of Carthage, its troubles with Rome and the battles that were fought between them. She went on to narrate the circumstances of Hannibal's birth, his rise to commander of the Carthagian armies and described how he crossed the Alps to invade Rome. Eventually Rome succeeded in destroying Carthage. Here are the final words of the story Enid used to dramatise this historic event:

Rome had commanded that Carthage should be utterly destroyed and that not one stone should be left upon another. So day after day the destruction went on and smoke rose day and night into the sky … The city was soon a sight of terrible desolation and ruin and no one looking on it could imagine it to have been a great and beautiful place.

When it was burnt to the ground still one other thing remained

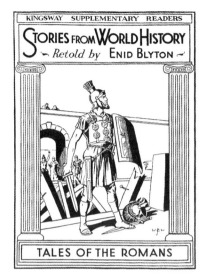

FIGURE 9: The four books resulting from Enid Blyton's 'Stories of World History' serialised in 36 episodes in her Weekly Page in The Teachers World from August 31, 1927 to August 15, 1928. The books became part of a series of The Kingsway Supplementary Readers for schools, published by Evans Brothers in 1934. Notice that the main title has been changed from 'Stories of World History' to 'Stories from World History'. © British Library Board, (SM: Tales of the Romans (W10/2428 cover); The Adventures of Odysseus (W10/2430 cover); The Story of the Siege of Troy (W10/2431 cover); Tales of the Ancient Greeks and Persians (W10/2429 cover).

to be done. The ground was to be ploughed up. Scipio saw this done and then indeed Carthage was destroyed. No longer had Rome any cause to fear her enemy. Carthage was no more.

In carefully prepared Notes For The Teacher at the end of this final episode, Enid explained that the wars between Rome and Carthage came to be known as the Punic Wars. There were three in number, but she dealt with only the last of the three wars. She even recommended books children and teachers should read to learn more about the events described in the stories. Included in these books are *The Tale of Ancient Peoples*, *Book I*, published by Cassell & Co. for class reading and *Stories from Ancient Rome* by Professor Church, also published by Cassell & Co. for teachers' use.

In 1934, five years after the 'Stories of World History' came to an end, Evans Brothers Ltd who, incidentally, were the owners of *The Teachers World*, published some of them in book form (see illustration of front covers, Figure 9).

If we go back to the syllabus in Appendix 30, we find that it was supposed to be fulfilled in one year. However, by the time the year ended Enid had covered only those stories relating to Ancient History. In such cases the editorial team would place a small announcement somewhere in the newspapers to let teachers know that the stories would continue until the syllabus came to an end. In this case, they decided to incorporate the rest of the syllabus into a new series of teaching features they prepared for the coming year August 1928 – August 1929. In doing so, they changed the name from 'Stories of World History' to 'Tales of Romance' to reflect the character of the stories remaining to be told.

Let us now turn our attention to the group of stories, under the new heading 'Tales of Romance' (Medieval or Middle Ages stories of bravery, heroes and chivalry) to see, once again, Enid's storytelling ability in action.

TALES OF ROMANCE

Under this heading, we find the following stories:
1. King Arthur and the Knights of the Round Table
2. King Charlemagne and the Paladins of France
3. Stories of Chivalry in the Fourteenth Century
4. Tales from Spenser's *Faerie Queene*

Let us start with the first, not only to see how Enid presented it in her Weekly Page, but also to learn something about the story.

KING ARTHUR AND THE KNIGHTS OF THE ROUND TABLE

The first episode of this legend appeared in the edition of August 29, 1928 (see illustration, Appendix 31). Notice the announcement in the box near the top of the second column. It tells teachers that the stories of Ancient History had drawn to a close and that Enid will start the new series from the period of early Romance, that is, of adventure and chivalry in the Middle Ages. In this way teachers of children eleven years and younger could make provision in their timetables to continue the oral teaching of the lessons.

As we can see from reading this first episode, it shows the curious circumstances of Arthur's birth, the death of his father, King Uther Pendragon, his being brought up by a nobleman called Sir Hector and a number of significant events leading up to his being crowned King of England.

As the story progressed, children learned that a magician called Merlin led Arthur to a lake where a hand suddenly emerged from the water holding the sword Excalibur that was to be forever associated with him (The Finding of the Sword Excalibur, Episode II); witness the treachery of his half sister Queen Morgan Le Fay (The Treachery of Queen Morgan Le Fay, Episode III); marvel at how a youth called Gareth sacrificed his noble birth, became a kitchen-boy in the King's kitchen, suffered humiliation and finally got a chance to go out on adventures. His brave deeds eventually earned him respect and a knighthood (Gareth, the Knight of the Kitchen, Episodes V and VI);

listen to adventures of other brave knights and so on until the story reaches to a point where the knights all go out in search of the Holy Grail, the cup from which Jesus is said to have drunk before his death.

The story ends with King Arthur being wounded in a battle and, realising the end was near, directed a faithful knight to throw his sword Excalibur back into the lake before sailing away in a barge, with three mysterious women in black, to go to the Valley of Avalon to die (The Passing of Arthur and the End of The Round Table, Episode XV). Here are the final lines of this fascinating legend:

No more is known of the great and noble king, but some say that he did not die but lives still in the happy valley of Avalon.

Now in case teachers were wondering who King Arthur was, Enid had already taken care of the question in Notes For The Teacher at the end of the first episode:

History tells us little of King Arthur. He is supposed to have lived in the sixth century just after the Romans had left Britain, and it was probably about this time that he and his knights performed the deeds of chivalry which for centuries afterwards were told of in story and song...

She also believed that the representation of the Knights of the Round Table in plate armour and trappings of the era of the Crusades is historically inaccurate, as we can see in the following extract from the said Notes For The Teacher:

It would strike the thoughtful reader as curious that these heroes are dressed in the plate armour and trappings of the time of the Crusades, engage in tournaments and live in moated castles, whereas the warriors of the sixth century probably wore mail shirts and lived in wooden houses. She then went on to give the following explanation:

The stories were written down in the time of the second and third Crusades, during the reigns of Henry II and Richard I. Those who listened to these stories of deeds of chivalry preferred to picture the heroes in trappings they knew ... thus did all the picturesqueness of the Crusade period creep into the centuries-

old stories making them historically inaccurate but nonetheless thrilling and absorbing.[14]

Two years after the series came to an end, the stories were collected and given a new lease of life when George Newnes Ltd brought them out in book form in April 1930 under the title: *The Knights of the Round Table.* The book contained 14 stories spread over 126 pages, with four colour plates (see title page illustration, Figure 14). Latimer House reprinted it in 1950 with 96 instead of 126 pages. The book is still in print and can be purchased through booksellers advertising on the web.

As was her custom, Enid always announced the next story to follow when the first one came to an end: NEXT WEEK: 'King Charlemagne and the Paladins of France'.

KING CHARLEMAGNE AND THE PALADINS OF FRANCE

This story is even more fascinating than 'King Arthur and the Knights of the Round Table'. It's centered, not on the battles of the French King Charlemagne and the adventures of the Paladins,[15] but on two colourful characters: Roland and Oliver. In the first episode that appeared in the edition of December 12, 1928, Enid tells the story of Roland, dressed in rags and living in a cave in the hillside with his mother, and of Oliver, the son of a Governor, living in luxury in the city. The two boys soon came to blows when they first met in the countryside, tested each other strength, found that they liked each other and became friends for life.

In time, children learned that Oliver was really the nephew of King Charlemagne and that his mother, living in poverty, was really King Charlemagne's sister. The story of how his mother came to be living in poverty was told and through a strange set of circumstances, they both managed to get back into the high life again. Meanwhile Roland had lost touch of his friend Oliver when he was taken into the service of a wealthy nobleman. Then one day a curious circumstance brought the two friends together again. In a joust[16] arranged after a draw of lots to settle an important issue for their masters, they fought each other without knowing it, but neither could defeat the other. Let's now turn to Enid to find out what happened next:

> *'They rode full upon one another and when their lances encountered each other's shields they broke into pieces. Neither was unhorsed, but each jumped to the ground and drew his sword to fight on foot. They rushed upon one another and the watchers on the banks held their breath to see the fury of the combat ...'*

After one hour, they ended up with broken swords and then began the hand to hand fight:

> *'...They rushed together striving to pull one another to the ground, but they could not. Then they tried to tear the helmets from each other's head and both did so at the same time. They both stood there bareheaded, about to renew the fight when they suddenly recognised one another. Oliver saw Roland, his boyhood companion and Roland saw Oliver his long-ago friend and companion! For a moment they gazed in amazement and then they rushed upon one another with joy. They embraced and all the onlookers gasped in surprise.*
>
> *'I surrender!' cried Oliver.*
>
> *'I yield me!' cried Roland.'*

(See Appendix 32 for the sixth episode describing in full the fight between the two friends.)

As the episodes unfolded, Enid introduced characters, such as Ogier the Dane, the son of the King of Denmark; Malagis the Enchanter; Genelon the betrayer, and others, and their clashes with Roland, Oliver and King Charlemagne became the subject of the rest of the story. In some of the eighteen episodes, Enid touched upon King Charlemagne's campaigns against the Heathens[17] and his quarrels and battles with noblemen who refused to pay him homage in money. However, she gave him little prominence in the story, preferring to focus on the heroes Roland and Oliver, as pointed out in a previous paragraph.

The story ends with the death of both Roland and Oliver in a battle at a place called Roncesvalles in which they were outnumbered while fighting for a cause (The End of the Battle of Roncesvalles, episode 18).

STORIES OF CHAVALRY IN THE FOURTEENTH CENTURY

These stories that Enid drew from Froissart's *Chronicles*, differ fundamentally from those we've just considered in that they deal with clashes between the English and the French during the so-called Hundred Years' War between the two nations. Here we are in the fourteenth century where the French embarked upon a ruthless campaign to drive from the soil of France English noblemen who had settled in castles in various regions of France.

In the first episode, under the caption: 'The Siege of the Castle of Aiguillon' she told children how the French had taken one castle after another and finally laid siege to the Castle of Aiguillon (see illustration, Appendix 33). She then went on to describe how the King of England, upon hearing the news, went over to France to rescue his compatriots: 'The King of England Does Battle In The Fair Land Of France', (Episode II), and the battle that ensued: 'What Happened At The Battle Of Crecy', Episode III). In this episode Enid provided a map showing the march of Edward III to Crecy and Calais, enabling children to follow the events described in the story.

This was followed by a description of how the town of Calais was taken (Episode IV), how Sir Aymery, in an act of treachery, sold the town of Calais after it had been taken (Episode V), The Battle of Calais and how it went (Episode VI), how The Prince of Wales makes ready for battle (Episode VII), what Happened at the battle of Poitiers (Episode VIII) and ended with King John made a prisoner and the return to England (Episode IX).

For those of us versed in English History, we see at once that these accounts cover only a fraction of the battles and happenings of the so-called Hundred Years' war between England and France, as described by John Froissart in his *Chronicles*.[18] Nevertheless, in telling the stories Enid had to be selective. She told only those events she thought children eleven years and younger would be interested in, hoping that what they had learned from the stories would form the basis for studies in English History at an advanced level.

TALES FROM SPENSER'S *FAERIE QUEENE*

This is the last story in the group of 'Tales of Romance' to appear in Enid's Weekly Page, the first episode of which appeared in the edition of July 10, 1929 (see illustration, Appendix 34). It's based on allegorical events described in Book I of Spenser's *Faerie Queene*.[19] The principal characters Enid portrayed in the story are George, later to become the patron saint of England, and Una the daughter of a great King. They were brought together for the first time when, at an annual feast given by Queen Gloriana, George appeared on the scene dressed in rough clothes to ask the Queen for an adventure and Una, to ask for help to destroy a dragon causing havoc in her hometown. The Queen then assigned George the adventure to accompany Una back home to destroy the dragon, knighted him, and from then onwards he was known as Sir George.

However, before they could reach Una's hometown, Sir George had to fight a dragon on the way; fall under the spell of Archimago – a wicked magician – deserted Una and, after a fight with the giant Orgoglio, got thrown into prison. Meanwhile Una set out on a quest to find Sir George and found herself in a series of dangerous situations, but was rescued by a lion that became her protector. Then Prince Arthur made his entry into the story, defeated the giant Orgoglio and freed Sir George from prison. After a series of adventures, Sir George was reunited with Una who was overjoyed to find him alive. With all obstacles out of the way, they finally returned to Una's hometown where Sir George destroyed the dragon after a long and fierce fight. The story ends with Sir George getting married to Una. Here are the final lines of this wonderful story:

Many more adventures did Sir George have and so good and noble a knight was he that he was made a saint. We know him now as Saint George of Merry England and his red cross shines bravely on our Union Jack.

This then is a summary of the last story in the series of 'Tales of Romance' that came to an end August 28, 1929.

Overall, the stories under this heading, as well as those under the heading 'Stories of World History', were well organised, beautifully written and admirably presented in Enid Blyton's Weekly Page. If teachers had to retell them from original sources, where the text was still in Middle English with all its anachronistic or outdated expressions, children would have been bored to death. However, thanks to Enid's remarkable storytelling ability and her mastery of the English language, she not only made them intelligible to children, but also brought them to life on the pages of *The Teachers World*.

In this respect, we have to agree with the editor's assessment of her storytelling ability, carried in the second paragraph, in the box that appeared at the top of the second column of the first episode of 'The Siege of Troy – 1. How the Trojan War Began' (see again Appendix 28, for illustration). For not only did she stand in the front rank among the tellers of tales to children, but she had proved her storytelling ability, with the narrations of the 'Stories of World History' and 'Tales of Romance' we have just considered in this section.

For some of us who have read translations from the Greek of the twenty-four books of Homer's *Iliad*, another twenty-four, of *The Odyssey*, Sir Thomas Malory's translation from the French of *La Morte d'Arthur* (The Death of Arthur), the works of Froissart's *Chronicles*, the six books of Spenser's *Faerie Queene*, and other sources of Ancient and Medieval History Enid consulted to expound the stories, it would be a miracle if we could recall all that we had read, much less to retell them in the form of elaborate stories for children. But that was exactly what Enid did – thanks to her amazing photographic memory and strong powers of retention, subjects which are discussed in full under *Enid: The Professional Storyteller* in Chapter VII.

WINNERS AND LOSERS IN THE SYLLABUS

The syllabus Enid published in *The Teachers World,* edition of October 5, 1927, (see again Appendix 30) was so comprehensive that it would have surprised teachers if she had managed to fulfil it in one year. However, even with the extension of another year – from August 1928 to August 1929 – she still did not manage to complete it. By the time the second year was up, she had covered only stories relating to

Ancient and Medieval History. Those she was not able to tell are as follows:

- Julius Caesar and his Visit to Britain.
- The Story of Jesus and his Place in History. The Beginning of Christianity.
- Roman Rule in Britain. Caractacus. Boadicea.
- Christianity comes to Britain through the Romans. St Augustine.
- The Coming of the Northmen. Story of St. Edmund.
- Tales from The Eddas and the Sagas of the Northmen.

It's not known why Enid did not tell these stories she outlined in the syllabus we have seen in Appendix 30. However, since the groups of stories carry no dates, we can surmise she placed them there provisionally, to be developed and presented in due course. Nevertheless, time was not on her side so some of the stories had to go to end the History Lessons within the time allocated to her. In all she had written sixty-one episodes within the two years, each containing between 1,500 to 2,000 words, taking up a full page and sometimes overflowing to other pages – a remarkable achievement that cannot be matched by any other contributor of stories to *The Teachers World*!

PORTRAITS OF HISTORICAL CHARACTERS

With the syllabus out of the way, Enid took a break from teaching through the medium of her pen, but not a break from *The Teachers World*. Up and still running was her weekly 'Enid Blyton's Children's Page' in which she continued to fascinate children with her stories, poems, competitions and her 'Letter to Boys And Girls'.

Then in 1932, we find her working assiduously on another comprehensive teaching project. Entitled: 'Round The Year with Enid Blyton', it was centered on another group of suggestions the then Board of Education made with regards to the teaching of Nature Study to children eleven years and younger in public elementary schools. However, since this project has a lot to do with her gardening experience, it's treated fully under *Enid: The Passionate Gardener* in Chapter X.

With the completion of this comprehensive course, in August, 1933,

FIGURE 10: Top half of a full page showing a drawing of 'King Alfred's Mother', left, and of 'Lord Nelson', right, in the middle pages of The Teachers World Supplement in the editions of September 4, 1935 and December 16, 1936 respectively. The Teachers World commissioned artists to draw these pictures and then commissioned, in turn, Enid Blyton to write biographical sketches, in the form of stories, to go with the pictures. Image restoration credit: 2graphic Photo Restoration. Website: www.photo-restoration.co.uk

Enid took a break again until 1935 when *The Teachers World* offered her another commission, this time to write a series of biographical sketches of historical characters.

It all began in September 1935, when the editorial team came up with another 'Programme of Teaching Features' to help teachers prepare interesting lessons for children in public elementary schools. In this programme, they included a plan to present twenty portraits of historical characters whose names can be seen in Appendix 35). Then they commissioned Enid to write biographical sketches in the form of stories to go with each portrait. A summary of this plan can be seen in the following announcement:

The beautiful seven-colour plates of great figures of history will dominate your classroom. Your class will want the story of each of these famous characters, and we have chosen Enid Blyton to be the narrator – for reasons which need no elaborating either for teacher or child.

This announcement was made in Enid's first story in the series: 'King Alfred's Mother, The Story of a Great Queen', which appeared in the edition of September 4, 1935 (see illustration, Appendix 36).

From this story, children learned about his mother and father, his four brothers and especially about the teachings his mother gave him during his formative years, teachings that were to prepare him for great things in life. In the middle page of the edition was a beautiful, full-length picture of his mother. This was to be placed on the blackboard so that children could see it as they listened to the stories (see illustration, Figure 10). When the session was over, the picture was placed on the wall to decorate the classroom and children could then look forward to listening to the next story of another historical character.

In telling the stories of the historical characters Enid often began by describing briefly, in simple language, the circumstances of their birth, their struggles to overcome limitations or infirmities, their education or lack of it, the opportunities that came their way for advancement, the people who helped them along the way and their ascension to power or fame. Some attention was paid to their achievements, but she always emphasised characteristics of their early childhood to show children that it was during this time they began to show what sort of men or women they were going to be.

For example, to emphasise the trait of fearlessness that was characteristic of Horatio Nelson (1758 – 1805) otherwise known as Lord Nelson, she told the following story:

Once when he was lost, and had been found late at night all alone in the countryside, his grandmother said to him:
'I wonder you did not feel fear Horatio.'
'What is fear?' said the small boy. 'I never saw fear.'
'It really seemed as if all his life long he did not know what fear was.'

In time, children were learning about famous characters, such as, William the Conqueror, Joan of Arc, Caxton, Cabot, Sir Thomas More, The Empress Matilda, Robert Bruce and the others in the list.

Soon Enid had successfully covered all the twenty historical characters, but instead of the series ending there, twelve more names were added in with no announcement to let teachers know about the change. (A list of the twelve names added in can be seen in Appendix 35.) Nevertheless, the stories continued as usual, week after week, until December 16, 1936 when she successfully completed the stories of the additional twelve characters and ended the assignment. The last story was about Lord Nelson whose illustrated picture, as it appeared in the series, is shown in Figure 10.

Finally, although chronicles, biographical dictionaries and encyclopedias were available in the then public elementary schools, teachers would never have thought of consulting them to find interesting stories of the lives of the great and famous to tell to children in classrooms. So schoolchildren at that time ought to have been grateful to *The Teachers World* for coming up with the idea in the first place, and to Enid Blyton, whose unique storytelling ability brought the historical characters alive in the classroom.

FORTNIGHTLY PAGES

The fortnightly pages Enid held were entirely for teaching purposes. These were for her 'Enid Blyton's Nature Lessons' and 'Hedgerow Tales', subjects we have already considered under *Enid: The Naturalist* in Chapter I.

MONTHLY PAGES

The earliest monthly page she held was for her nature poems. She held this page from June 1922 to June 1923. This was followed by a page for her 'Days of the Week Poems' that she held from July to December 1923. A discussion of these poems, and others she presented subsequently, is presented under *Enid: The Poet* in Chapter II.

Then, in 1926, we find her holding another monthly page, this time for storytelling. This page appears to be the reappearance of the weekly 'Friday Afternoon Stories' page that was discontinued. However, instead of sharing it with other contributors, she held it exclusively for one year. Her first story, The Golden Promise, appeared in the page in the edition of January 8, 1926. For every other month teachers could look forward to another story to tell children in classrooms. A sample reading of one of the stories, 'Lost – A Robin Called Sing-A-Song', along with a list of all the stories in the series is provided in Appendix 37. The series came to an end on December 3, 1926 with a Christmas story called 'The Astonishing Christmas Tree'.

FEATURE ARTICLES

Three years later, Enid began writing a series of feature articles about each of the twelve calendar months of the year. Entitled 'The Months', the series began in January 11, 1929 with an article on January. In this article, she traced the history and folklore behind the name January and gave general information about happenings during this first month of the year (see Appendix 38 for illustration). Teachers and pupils alike were treated to a similar article for every other month of the year until the series came to an end in December 1929.

ENID'S WITHDRAWAL FROM *THE TEACHERS WORLD*

After twenty-three years of writing for teachers and children in *The Teachers World*, Enid withdrew, but not before making an announcement in her 'Letter to Boys And Girls' which appeared in her 'Enid Blyton's Children's Page' – later changed to 'Enid Blyton's Children's Corner' – in the edition of November 14, 1945 (see Appendix 39, under Green Hedges, second column, second paragraph for illustration).

However, since she had already stopped writing for teachers when her column had been terminated and replaced with 'Enid Blyton's Children's Page'; her teaching courses came to an end when her syllabuses were completed and her feature articles were completed in the time allocated to her, the only activity she held on to in the newspaper was writing for children in her 'Enid Blyton's Children's Page'. Therefore, the withdrawal stated in the previous paragraph is from this last activity. However, the real reason for this withdrawal could be that since her popular *Sunny Stories* magazine – presented in Section Two under the *Sunny Stories Magazine – A Phenomenal Success* – was up and running at the same time she was holding that 'Enid Blyton's Children's Page' in *The Teachers World*, and that the material she was preparing for both publications – a 'Letter To Boys

And Girls', poems, stories, competitions, puzzles and so on – differ only in content, she could gain time to work on her *Sunny Stories* magazine by cutting out the duplication, and, simultaneously, to continue with her other writing projects outlined in this book.

Let us now turn out attention to her contributions to periodicals and the columns or pages she held therein from time to time.

CONTRIBUTIONS TO PERIODICALS

In 1934, a curious magazine made its appearance in England. Entitled *The Nature Lover: The Magazine of the Countryside*, it was a magazine with a difference. Enid soon got to know about it and before long, she was contributing articles, in the form of a monthly 'Country Letter'.

Under the title: 'A Country Letter from Enid Blyton', readers could find there news about her fairytale-like cottage for which we have seen a picture in Figure 4, her pets, and especially about developments in her garden. As we'll see when we get to *Enid: The Passionate Gardener*, Chapter X, her garden was well furnished with every kind of flowering plant we can think about, vegetables of all kinds, an orchard with fruitful pear, apple and nut trees, a bird table and a pond with aquatic life. This richness of flowering plants, fruit trees and birds that regularly visited her bird table furnished material for her 'Country Letters'. As the months progressed, she introduced material such as weather conditions in each month of the year and birds that are most likely to be seen in certain months of the year. Enid contributed 21 'Country Letters' and one poem to the magazine before it ended sometime in 1950.[20] Other magazines in which Enid held a full page include *My Magazine, Woman's Life, Wife And Home: The Married Woman's Magazine, The Lady, The Bystander, Punch, Child Education* and *Home Weekly* in which she narrated a story or presented poems on a variety of subjects.

Of special mention is *The Busy Bees News* that was a publication of the Busy Bees Society, the youth section of the P.D.S.A. – People's Dispensary for Sick Animals. According to her biographer, Barbara Stoney, in a passage on page 143 of *Enid Blyton: A Biography*, '*Enid had been interested in the society since 1933 and began writing articles and short stories for its publications …'*

She eventually became head of the society and through her *Letters to Boys & Girls* in *The Teachers World* and in the *Sunny Stories* magazine she would give news of its activities and encourage children to become members. Then when she carried information about the society in her *Enid Blyton's Magazine*, the membership jumped to some three hundred thousand children. Enid then organised them into a club – The Busy Bees Club for Animal Lovers – and regularly contributed a monthly letter to give news, results of competitions and to let children know what the members were doing to help birds and animals.[21] According to David Chambers, a researcher and contributor to *The Enid Blyton Society Journal*, '*Enid was to lend her name to the magazine right up until her death in 1968.*'[22]

Enid also contributed to national and regional newspapers, the chief among which was the *Sunday Graphic*. According to David Chambers, her contributions to this newspaper included 68 stories about a pixie called Pip, published between May 6, 1945 and August 18, 1946. The stories were later brought out in book form (see front cover illustration, Figure 16). It was also during his research that he made the startling discovery that Noddy had first made his appearance in this newspaper before he became the children's favourite character in the 24 books Enid eventually wrote about him.[23] Other newspapers with her contributions are the *Evening Standard*, the *Sunday Dispatch*, the *Sunday Mail*, *The Sunday Times* and *The Outline*.[24]

So ends this presentation of Enid Blyton's extraordinary contributions to newspapers and magazines. If this had been her only job, she would have undoubtedly made a comfortable living. However, as we have already seen in the preceding chapters, and will be seeing in chapters to follow, her wide field of interests did not allow her to focus her attention in a single direction – hence the variety of activities we are learning about in this book.

CHAPTER IV
ENID THE EDITOR

OVERVIEW

In this chapter, we take a look at another type of work Enid Blyton was doing when she was holding down a column in *The Teachers World* and writing nature, poetry and storybooks for children. Here she is presented as Editor – General and Associate – of educational and other related publications. Let us begin with the first, Editor of Educational Publications.

The known educational publications with which she had been associated, and her editorial roles, are as follows:
- 1928 – Modern Teaching: Practical Suggestions for Junior & Senior Schools (General Editor)
- 1930 – Newnes' Pictorial Knowledge (Associate Editor)
- 1932 – Modern Teaching in the Infant School (General Editor)
- 1938 – Two Years in the Infant School (Supervisor)

Let's now consider each of them in turn, beginning with *Modern Teaching*, to find out, not only what her editorial responsibilities were, but also what the books are all about.

———————————

MODERN TEACHING – PRACTICAL SUGGESTIONS FOR JUNIOR & SENIOR SCHOOLS

In 1918 when Enid obtained first-class passes in the practice of education, child hygiene, history of education and class teaching of children for her National Froebel Union Higher Certificate, and was awarded a distinction for her paper on the principles of education,[25] she had no idea that that qualification was going to prepare her for an important job as General Editor of Educational Books at the publishing firm George Newnes Ltd.

At that time, her first husband, H.A. Pollock, was editor of the book department at the same company. So, in the absence of information to tell us whether the job was proffered or she had to apply for it, we can assume that it was he who recommended her for the job.

For management, appointing her as General Editor was probably the best decision they ever made in relation to editing educational books for schools. For, apart from her qualifications outlined in the first paragraph, they were to benefit from the wealth of facts stored away intact in her photographic memory. (The subject of her photographic memory is treated in Chapter VII, under *Enid: The Professional Storyteller.*) They were also to benefit from her knowledge of History – Ancient, British & European – evidence of which we have already seen in Chapter III, under *Enid: The Columnist & Feature Writer*, in the form of the elaborate 'Stories of World History' course she ran in *The Teachers World*. In any case, the company had already seen a demonstration of her ability to undertake important jobs when they published her three-volume *The Teachers' Treasury*, a book she wrote for primary school teachers (see Appendix 41 for title page illustration).

The material to be edited was to be contained in a book of six volumes entitled: *Modern Teaching: Practical Suggestions for Junior & Senior Schools.* It consisted of manuscripts for a number of courses in History, Geography, English, Nature Study & Science, Art, Handwork, Housecraft and Needlework written by graduates and teaching professionals. It also included: specimen lessons, models of syllabuses, maps, charts and a bibliography. Her role as General Editor therefore was to prepare the six volumes for publication.

BRIEF ACCOUNT OF THE CIRCUMSTANCES GIVING RISE TO THE PUBLICATIONS

Improving the way subjects of the curriculum were taught in public elementary schools in the early 1900s and updating teaching methods were matters high on the agenda of the then Board of Education – now the Ministry of Education. Coupled with this was the need to bring teaching methods in line with the rapid technological, political, educational, social and cultural changes taking place in England and

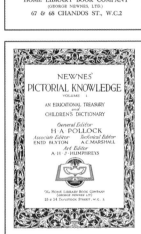

FIGURE 11: Title pages of the six publications with which Enid had been associated in various editorial capacities. © British Library Board: Modern Teaching (SM: 8311.f.10, title page); Modern Teaching in the Infant School (SM: 8305.g.25, title page); Two Years in the Infant School: (SM (X24/1058, title page); Newnes' Pictorial Knowledge: (SM: 12217.d.9, title page); Birds of the Wayside And Woodland (SM: W39/2925, title page); Daily Mail Annual: (SM: PP.6754. BBK, title page).

the world at large. To this end the Board published a *Handbook of Suggestions* to bring the curriculum in line with these changes, to modernise teaching methods and to guide teachers in drawing up meaningful time tables or programmes (see illustration, Appendix 27).

Therefore, *Modern Teaching* was meant to be an embodiment of the suggestions in the handbook, as pointed out in the following extract from the foreword to *Modern Teaching*:

Teachers in every part of the country have welcomed these Suggestions and many of them have wished that somewhere was to be found a volume, or a series of volumes, in which the Suggestions were faithfully followed, extended and developed. With the publication of Modern Teaching this wish was fulfilled...

The course of study in each of the six volumes starts with a treatment, in brief, of the salient points of each subject that teachers were expected to expand by supplementary reading. Then there are outlines of model lessons and a suggested syllabus.

If we take just one subject treated in the Handbook – history – we find the following features of the suggestions put forward by the Board:

- Syllabuses should vary with the circumstances of the school.
- The History Course should always be continued to modern times.
- Regular revision throughout the course is essential.
- The inter-relationship of *history and geography* must be borne in mind.[26]

These then were the peculiar set of circumstances surrounding the works that had been passed to Enid for editing. Her efforts were rewarded when the Home Library Book Company, a division of George Newnes Ltd, published the six volumes of *Modern Teaching* in September 1928 to the acclaim of head teachers and teachers everywhere (see Figure 11 for title page illustration). Moreover, the fact that it was republished three years in a row after the first edition shows how popular the volumes were with teachers in primary schools up and down the country.

NEWNES' PICTORIAL KNOWLEDGE

Sometime after *Modern Teaching* had seen the light of day, we find her working, once again, for the same company on an even bigger educational project. This time she was working directly with her first husband, H.A.Pollock, to bring into being a *Children's Encyclopaedia and Dictionary* whose richly illustrated material was to leave a strong impression on the minds of children everywhere. In this case the editorial roles were changed. Whereas she was General Editor of *Modern Teaching* and her husband, apparently, playing no role in its production, he was the General Editor of the new project and she was designated Associate Editor. The project was so big that other specialist editors, such as A. C. Marshall (Technical Editor), and A. J. Humphreys (Art Editor) had to be recruited.

Entitled: *Newnes' Pictorial Knowledge*, this *Children's Encyclopaedia and Dictionary* combined involved culling from various sources documentaries, pictures, drawings, illustrations, maps, charts, etc., and co-ordinating contributions from experts in various fields. In helping her husband to put together the material, Enid was to draw on knowledge gained from reading Arthur Mee's ten-volume *Children's Encyclopaedia* from end to end and then reading them all over again, when she was a child. (See *Enid: The Professional Storyteller,* Chapter VII, for more about this.) Moreover, with her photographic memory she was in a good position to assist with verifying facts researchers presented for the Encyclopaedia.

The material took a long time to put together, but when all the hard work was completed, The Home Library Book Company published it in 1930 in eight volumes, under the title: *Newnes' Pictorial Knowledge – An Educational Treasury and Children's Dictionary* (see Figure 11 for title page illustration).

This popular Encyclopaedia for children quickly ran through several editions, with the volumes increasing from eight to ten over the years to provide updates in various branches of knowledge. Moreover, for some unknown reason, each new set of volumes came out with a different editor, but Enid's place as Associate Editor remained constant.

One of the people who had benefited from reading an updated edition of *Newnes' Pictorial Knowledge* as a child was Walter Ellis. In an article he wrote for *The Times* in December 1995, he had nothing but praise for the volumes:

FOR MANY of my boyhood years, I had a source of information on which I felt I could always depend. Newnes Pictorial Knowledge, a **ten-volume** *set that had Enid Blyton, no less,* *as associate editor, gave me a basic understanding of nature, history and my favourite fable, myth and legend, as well as providing a guide to such arcana as How Television Works, The Art of Walt Disney and Good Manners for Boys and Girls. When I outgrew Newnes, I felt genuinely sad and never really found an adequate substitute...* [27]

The basic understanding he got of his favourite fable, myth and legend came from a section in Volume IV entitled Fables, Myth & Legends that Enid compiled and edited. The contents of the section, which included stories such as 'Brer Rabbit and the Tar Baby', 'The King with the Golden Touch,' 'Aladdin and the Wonderful Lamp', 'Roland Sounds his Horn', 'Una and the Faithful Lion' and so on, is reminiscent of the stories she retold in the *Sunny Stories For Little Folks* magazine, treated in this book under the *Sunny Stories Magazine – A Phenomenal Success* in Section Two. It is also reminiscent of those in 'Tales of Romance' under *Enid: The Columnist & Feature Writer* in Chapter III.

The idea of putting fables, myths and legends in an Encyclopaedia for children must have come from her recollection of Arthur Mee's *Children's Encyclopaedia* where hundreds of fables, myths and other stories were carried alongside subjects such as the story of the earth, the great wonder of human life, rise of nations and races and so on (see Appendix 54 for illustration of *The Children's Encyclopaedia*).

The successful completion of this project in 1930 was to free up time for her to concentrate on keeping alive her 'Enid Blyton's Children's Page' in *The Teachers World*; continue with writing stories for the *Sunny Stories for Little Folks* magazine; help her publishers promote her poetry books, songbooks, books of plays, nature and storybooks; catch up with business correspondence and reply to hundreds of letters from devoted fans. Notwithstanding this heavy workload, she was still able to find time to work on another editorial project George Newnes Ltd had in store for her – to edit another teaching book: *Modern Teaching in the Infant School*.

MODERN TEACHING IN THE INFANT SCHOOL

Modern Teaching in the Infant School is a book that should have been written soon after *Modern Teaching: Practical Suggestions for Junior & Senior School* was published in 1928. As the former put forward suggestions for senior and junior schools, it was expected that a similar project would follow for infant schools. Whatever the reason for the delay, plans to produce the work were finalised sometime in 1930-31 and the task of editing fell, once again, to Enid Blyton. The four volumes into which it falls are as follows:

Volume I – Reading & Writing
Volume II – Approach to History, Geography and Psychology
Volume III – Handwork, Games and Music
Volume IV – The Story Hour, Nature Talks and Hygiene

In preparing the volumes for publication, Enid was entirely in her element. For she was dealing with material that resembled that in her own *The Teachers' Treasury*, a book in three volumes she wrote for infant and primary school teachers. However, what must have given her pleasure to edit was the material in Volume IV, especially 'The Story Hour' and 'Nature Talks'.

It's easy to imagine that telling stories to children is a simple matter, but when we read the material in 'The Story Hour' in Volume IV we realise that this is not the case. For in this section we find in Chapter I under How to Tell Stories, topics such as the Purposes of Storytelling, Knowing the Story, Memorising the Story, Adapting a Story, Presentation of the Story and the Re-expression of the Story by the Children. In other chapters we find: The Choice of Stories (II), Sources of Stories (III), Examples of Stories to Tell (IV and V) and Stories for Special Occasions (VI). Finally, there's a Bibliography of Fairytales and a List of Storybooks of literary quality. In short it was like an abridgement from a dissertation on storytelling. Teachers of children in infant schools were expected to develop the themes by studying the books recommended in other chapters.

The other source of pleasure in carrying out her editorial duties was in the second item in Volume IV – Nature Talks. At the time of preparing the four volumes for publication, she was also putting together material for her own comprehensive Round the Year with Enid Blyton Gardening and Nature Study course to be serialised in *The Teachers World* (see *Enid: the Passionate Gardener, Chapter X,* for more information about this course). Included in the material to be edited were topics such as Nature Study Activities (II), Making Friends with the Birds (IV), The School Aquarium (VI), The School Garden (XI) and Germinating Seeds in the Classroom (XII), topics with which Enid was entirely familiar.

The four volumes finally saw the light of day when The Home Library Book Company published them in May, 1931(see title page illustration of one of the volumes, Figure 11). Like *Modern Teaching*, it soon became popular with teachers and ran through several editions, notably in June 1933, August 1934 and July 1936.

TWO YEARS IN THE INFANT SCHOOL

This publication in four volumes is exceptional in that it has been prepared for publication, not by an editor, but by a team of teaching professionals, all working together under Enid Blyton's supervision. It is also unique in the sense that it covers a complete course of lessons for two years, just the time a child entering school for the first time will spend in the classroom before moving on to primary school. Hence the title: *Two Years in the Infant School* (see title page illustration, Figure 11). Here we are dealing with children who are starting school for the first time. What should be taught to these children? What material should be used to help teachers teach these inquisitive, sometimes fearful children in a classroom setting that is fundamentally different from their homes? *Two Years in the Infant School* provided answers to these questions.

In the four volumes we find a total of eighty-four topics or subjects, one for each week of two school years. In each topic there is material for a Talk, Oral Composition, Preparation for Reading, Writing & Number; Drawing & Handwork; Games, Dramatisation, Musical Activity, Poems and Stories – in short, a complete scheme of work that experienced or inexperienced teachers could use immediately in the classroom, as can be gathered from the following brief extract from the preface:

> ...*By means of the eighty-four Topics, which are in effect, weekly programmes of work centred round a new idea each week, the whole of the curriculum of the Infant School is covered ... The Topics, or weekly programmes of work, follow on smoothly and consecutively, and unfold a progressive scheme of work in every subject, so that the teacher, by beginning at Topic No. 1 and working through to the last Topic, will find that every week is excellently planned for her in an original and delightful way...*

Unlike the other publications she had been commissioned to edit, this one contains many of her own contributions. These take the form of an astonishing forty-five songs and two Christmas carols for infants, set to music by Cecil Sharman; over 200 stories and a number of poems.

The four volumes were accompanied by a box containing supplementary teaching material, such as colour pictures, diagrams, picture sentence cards, sentence sheets, drawings and eight-four colour plates for decorating the wall after their use in the classroom to illustrate the topics. The works also exist in five boxes – four, containing the teaching material on pages for file binders, with the fifth containing the supplementary teaching material just described.

The British Library[28] has preserved copies of the works and teachers and others who are interested can consult them at the Rare Books & Music Wing by applying for a temporary readers pass. Members of the library can use their readers pass for admission. The two *Modern Teaching* books and *Newnes' Pictorial Knowledge* are also preserved and can be consulted along the same lines.

This project marks the end of a chapter in Enid's life where her teaching qualifications and experience had been used to contribute to the successful publications of teaching books. Teachers who are consulting these books today to find out what teaching was like in the 1920s and 30s would possibly marvel that the works had all been edited or prepared for publication by Enid Blyton, whom they know only as a famous but controversial writer of storybooks for children!

RELATED PUBLICATIONS EDITED BY ENID BLYTON

The related works Enid Blyton edited are as follows:

- *Birds of the Wayside & Woodland,* 1936 (Editor)
- *Daily Mail Annual for Boys & Girls*, 1944 (Editor)

BIRDS OF THE WAYSIDE AND WOODLAND

This book stems from T.A. Coward's marvellous three-volume *The Birds of the British Isles and Their Eggs*, published in 1920 by Fredrick Warne. It's not known exactly how she got the job, but it may well have resulted from her successful editing of the teaching books. In the following brief extract from the preface, we have the opportunity to witness how Enid herself summed up her editorial responsibilities:

BIRDS OF THE WAYSIDE & WOODLAND
By T.A.COWARD
PREFACE

I have counted it an honour, as well as a great pleasure, to be asked to edit and to add to the late Mr. T.A. Coward's work on the Birds of the British Isles. This book, as it stands, is mainly his, and I have tried to make all the necessary alterations, cuts and additions in the same spirit and, I hope, in more or less the same way that Mr Coward himself would have done. It is a short and condensed version of his three finely written volumes on British Birds, with various general chapters added by myself on aspects of bird-life not directly dealt with by Mr. Coward. My knowledge of birds must be small compared with his lifetime study but in our love for them we are perhaps on an equal footing...

ENID BLYTON

Tony Summerfield of The Enid Blyton Society, in his masterly publication in four volumes: *Enid Blyton – An Illustrated Bibliography*, describes the first edition of the book on page 32 of Volume I, as being '6 ½ X 4 ¾ (352 pages). Red cloth boards embossed in black with a dustwrapper (300 coloured illustrations and 8 black & white photographs)'. Frederick Warne & Co. published it in 1936. The book ran through several editions in succession before going out of print sometime in 1952 (see title page illustration, Figure 11).

THE DAILY MAIL ANNUAL

In 1944 we find her once again deeply engrossed in fulfilling another editorial commission, this time to edit the first edition of the *Daily Mail Annual for Boys and Girls,* published by the *Daily Mail* (see title page illustration, Figure 11). Providing children with short stories, puzzles, games, cartoons, poems and short articles of general interest they had missed during the Second World War (1939 – 1945) was the chief aim of the new publication. Enid's role was to put together contributions in these fields and to write a preface.

She also contributed eight stories – all from her *Sunny Stories for Little Folks* magazine. The *Daily Mail* went on to produce more *Annuals for Boys and Girls* – from 1944 to 1954 – but this was the only one she edited. These then are the known related publications with which Enid Blyton had been associated as editor.

Now as she went through life, wearing all the 'hats' previously described, and those yet to be described in other chapters, she was slowly becoming aware of her mission in life. What is this mission? This is what we'll be finding out in the next chapter.

CHAPTER V

ENID THE UNIVERSAL TEACHER

In 1905 when Enid was about eight years old a strange thing happened to her. She was at home one day when a gentleman, whom her father had invited, sat her in a chair and pressed his hands over the entire surface of her head. He was looking for signs, in the form of bumps, that would tell him whether Enid had any gift, talent or special ability.

In those days, such a person was known as a phrenologist and this strange art of revealing gifts, talents or special abilities from examining the surface of the head is called Phrenology. Notwithstanding the controversy surrounding the subject in the early 1900s, many people still went to consult a phrenologist for career guidance and character reading and those who had the means, like Enid's father, would often invite a phrenologist to their homes so that their children might receive special attention. More information about this subject can be found in Section Two, under the heading: *Physiognomy & Phrenology – The Rise and Fall of Two Great 'Sciences.'*

To come back to our subject, when the phrenological examination was over, it was expected that the phrenologist would reveal his findings on the spot, so that those present might know what discovery he had made, but her father quickly stopped him from doing so. Let's turn to Enid's own recollection for the rest of the story:

'Don't say anything in front of the child,' my father said to the man, who was quite bald and had about the bumpiest head I had ever seen in my life. 'You can give me a written report,' Enid recalled in a passage on page 77 of a 'Momentous Day', the title

of Chapter 13 of *The Story of My Life*.

'I didn't see the report until years later,' she continued in the same passage. *'Then one day my mother showed it to me. She had unearthed it with a lot of old papers. I read it with interest: "This child will turn to teaching as she develops,' the report said. 'It is and will be her great gift.'"*

It was only after she had read the report that she learned from her mother what her father's reaction was when he received it:

'Your father was disappointed in it. He was so sure that you were a musical genius that he was certain your bumps would prove it, young as you were. But they didn't!' [29]

This disappointment however did not put an end to the music lessons he had been giving her on the piano at home, lessons that started sometime before he asked the phrenologist to visit his home. These lessons were to continue even after he had left the family home following a series of rows with his wife Theresa over another woman,[30] for he had made an arrangement with her to see that Enid put in the hours required by her music teacher. So pleased was he with the progress she was making that when she reached eighteen years of age he arranged for her to sit the LRAM (London Royal Academy of Music) examination. If successful she could then take up a place at the Guildhall School of Music to gain a professional qualification.

By that time her education at the St Christopher's School for Girls in Beckenham, Kent had come to an end. By all appearances, she enjoyed her stay there and left with an excellent school record and a good character reference. According to a passage on page three of a booklet the school published in 1993 to mark its centenary, she became a pupil at the school in 1907. She stayed there for nine years and was Head Girl for her last two years. She enjoyed life at the school, was top of her class, excelled in music and used to organise the end of term senior girls concert parties. She was also tennis champion, captain of lacrosse and a keen member of the debating society, the minutes of which are still to be seen in a book at the school.[31]

This termination of her college education was to give her all the time she needed to prepare for the LRAM examination, a preparation that

FIGURE 12: An outside photograph of Enid Blyton (centre, back) taken during the summer term 1916, when she was a trainee teacher at Ipswich High School. The staff, seated from left to right: Miss Fryer, Miss Flear and Miss Gale (headmistresses). The children are believed to be those in her charge. Reproduced with permission of the Head of Ipswich High School.

started sometime during her last year at the St Christopher's School for Girls. Therefore, with her academic schooling out of the way, she was kept busy with piano practice, study of harmony and singing.[32] This was a private arrangement her father had set in place and he was looking forward to seeing her take up a place at the Guildhall School of Music sometime in 1916.

We can now imagine how astonished he must have been when Enid announced one day she was giving up music to start training immediately to take up teaching. The announcement was made, not face to face in the family home, but by telephone. This was because, as stated in a preceding paragraph, he had left the family home and was living somewhere else. Having made the announcement, Enid had two objectives in mind: to get him to cancel the music examination and to sign the enrolment forms to give consent for her to start the Teacher

Training course. She knew that getting him to change his mind was no easy task. However, after pleading with him from the telephone box where she put through the call, she managed to break down his resistance to her plans. Consequently, he agreed to cancel the music examination and asked her to send the forms by post for him to sign. It was a victory she never imagined she would have achieved, as she expressed many years later in a passage on page 77 of *The Story of My Life*:

> '*I couldn't believe it. I had got my way – my father did not sound too angry, or too upset. I was filled with gratitude and love. Ah – now I would write to him – a letter he would like to get!*' [33]

Relieved that the music examination was out of the way, she turned her back on a career in music and began to make plans to enter an exciting new world: the world of teaching.

Therefore, when Enid finally became a teacher in 1919, after some three years of strict training at the Froebel Teacher Training Wing of Ipswich High School (see Figure 12 for group photo), the phrenologist's prediction came true, or so it seemed, for after five years of teaching – one year at Bickley Park School for Boys in Kent, and four years as a governess or tutor to four boys in their own home, later to become a small private nursery school with many more children [34] – she gave up teaching altogether to take up writing. When her poor father eventually heard about this, he must have been as astonished as ever.

Now the question that arises here is this: considering that Enid did turn to teaching as the phrenologist predicted and she had the ability to become a successful classroom teacher, why did she suddenly give up teaching for writing? The answer is that Enid never *really* gave up teaching. For her, writing was just another form of teaching, one that would enable her to reach and to teach many more children than the dozen or so she had been teaching in the classroom. To do this she was going to write, not just books to entertain, but educational books to teach children to do many things, and to instil in them sound morals, without her having to be physically present in the classroom to plan and organise her lessons, mark papers, put up end of term reports and so on. Through writing therefore, she was going to become a universal teacher, as the following examples demonstrate:

The 200 reading books she wrote under titles such as *Easy Reader*, *My First Reading Book*, *Let's Read*, *Enid Blyton Readers*, *Treasure Trove Readers* and *The Enid Blyton Pennant Series*, whose series alone contains thirty reading books, were all written to teach schoolchildren in England and in some of the English speaking countries abroad to read (see Appendix 40 for illustration of a list of the 30 reading books in the Pennant Series and a book cover from another series).

Likewise, the 36 Nature Readers we learned about under *Enid: The Naturalist,* Chapter I, teach schoolchildren many facts about birds, animals, insects and reptiles that they assimilate effortlessly during the exercise of learning to read (see again Appendix 12 for illustration of one of the book covers and a list of the thirty-six readers in the series).

Her Nature Study courses under the headings: 'Enid Blyton's Nature Lessons', 'Hedgerow Tales' and 'Round The Year With Enid Blyton', which were serialised in *The Teachers World*, teach school-children many facts about flowering plants, trees, birds, the weather, pollination, hibernation, and so on. Teachers everywhere used to incorporate these lessons in their teaching programmes, and thousands of schoolchildren used to follow them in public elementary schools up and down the country (see again Appendices 3, 7 and 65 for her syllabuses for these courses).

Her gardening book referred to under *Enid: The Passionate Gard-ener,* Chapter X, was written to teach children secrets of growing flowering plants and vegetables successfully in a garden. Here they learned how to use gardening tools, choose seeds to grow, prepare beds, sow seeds, care for seedlings and so on.

Her History Lessons, in the form of 'Stories of World History' and, subsequently, her 'Tales of Romance' (Medieval or Middle Ages stories of bravery, heroes and chivalry) which were elaborated under *Enid: The Columnist & Feature Writer,* Chapter III, teach schoolchildren about the ancient Greeks and Persians, the Romans and their conquests, the state of Europe in the Middle Ages, the Hundred Years' War between England and France and introduced them to the English version of Homer's *Iliad* and the *Odyssey* and to translations from the French of

Froissart's *Chronicles* (see again Appendix 30 for her syllabus for the World History course).

Her songbooks contain songs used by music teachers to teach schoolchildren to sing and by creating roles in the numerous plays she wrote for schools, she was teaching them to act (see the chapters *Enid: The Prolific Songwriter,* Chapter VI and *Enid: the Playwright,* Chapter VIII for details).

Her early poems were written specifically for recitation in her own classroom. By publishing them in book form, she brought them to a wider audience of schoolchildren everywhere. Moreover, by slipping them in various parts of her storybooks, she was teaching children to appreciate poetry at an elementary level.

Then there are religious books she wrote to teach children stories from the bible, just as she had been doing when she was a Sunday school teacher at the Elm Road Baptist Church many years earlier.[35]

Included in this wide range of books are: *The Children's Life Of Christ* (59 titles), *The Enid Blyton Bible Stories* (14 titles from the Old Testament), *The Enid Blyton Bible Stories* (another 14 titles from the New Testament), *The Boy With The Loaves And Fishes* and *The Little Girl At Capernaum* (see Figure 15 for front covers and title pages illustration). She even wrote a book to teach children about the bible itself. Entitled: *The Greatest Book in the World*, it tells children about the history, authors, translations and versions of the bible along with curious stories of bibles that had been miraculously preserved after authorities stamped out their reading in some countries.[36]

Moreover, since bible stories and prayers often go together she also wrote a book to teach children to pray. Entitled: *Before I Go To Sleep,* it was translated into many languages and quickly ran through several editions. Another prayer book she prepared for children is *The Children's Book of Prayers* containing twenty prayers selected from *The Book of Common Prayer.* [37] (See again Figure 15, the tenth and third items, for title page and front cover illustration.)

Even when we turn to her *St. Clare's* and *Malory Towers* series of school stories, we find there some form of teaching. In these books, there're so many moral lessons 'between the lines' that teenagers reading them had the opportunity to witness the consequences of gossip, criticism, pride, arrogance, playing practical jokes, and so on. In this way, she was teaching them to cultivate good qualities and repudiate unfavourable ones. (See Bibliography at the end of this book for a list of books in the school series.)

Now this is not all for while she was busy writing educational and religious books for children, she was also writing educational books for teachers. Principally among them is her three-volume *The Teachers' Treasury* which The Home Library Book Company, a division of George Newnes Ltd, published in 1926 (see Appendix 41 for title page illustration and Appendix 42 for information about these volumes).

From examining the wording of this title page we cannot fail to notice the mention: Edited by Enid Blyton. Don't be mislead by this, for apart from two sections dealing with poetry and handwork which she did edit, everything else in the book had been written by her, as can be verified from the introduction to the works by Mr. Percy Nunn who was holding at that time the prestigious position of Professor of Education at the University of London. This introduction can be read in full in Appendix 43.

This new role as a universal teacher also shows itself in her association with the educational publications discussed under *Enid: The Editor* in Chapter IV.

Finally, if we go through the hundreds of stories she wrote to entertain we find there's invariably a moral lesson or two neatly woven into them. It was this tendency to teach children how to behave, with over-emphasis on punishment for wrong deeds that caused critics to brand her a moralist.

She was however no more a moralist than all the historical writers of fables, allegories, parables and other fictional creations, who wove moral lessons into their stories. Furthermore, if we examine some of the traditional stories such as *Cinderella, The Three Little Pigs, The Sleeping Beauty* on the one hand, and fables such as 'The Fox and The Crow', 'The Dog and His Shadow', 'The Lion and The Mouse' on the other, we'll be surprised to find how many moral lessons are skilfully woven into them. These are stories successive generations of children read and enjoyed yet no one has ever accused the authors of being moralists!

Therefore, by turning to writing, Enid demonstrated her teaching ability more effectively than if she had still been teaching in a classroom. Moreover, she was to receive a remuneration or reward, sometimes in the form of royalties[38] higher than that which she would have received as a classroom teacher and a job satisfaction that's better than that she would have got from classroom teaching.

Now to come back to the subject of phrenology, when Enid saw the word *teaching* in the phrenologist's report it took her completely by surprise, for that was the last word she expected to see in the report she never thought she would get to read. At that time she was determined to become a writer and would have been delighted if the report stated she was cut out to be a writer. That would have given her the encouragement she needed to get her writing off the ground. So when she took up teaching, she saw it, not as a career, but as a stepping stone to achieve her goal in becoming a writer.

"*I was going to train as a teacher because I wanted to know exactly how and what to write for children later on,*" she thought, after her father had told her that by taking up teaching it would put the idea of being a writer out of her head.[39] However, it was an unexpressed thought, for when she was pleading with him to sign the forms to start the Teacher Training course, she could not bring herself to tell him that was what she was thinking.

So she refused to believe the phrenologist's prediction that she would turn to teaching as she developed and that teaching would be her great gift. Neither did she believe she had a bump for teaching. For her, he had made a mistake, as she so lively expressed in the following passage on page 78 of *The Story of My Life:*

'*...He was wrong, of course – writing is my career, with a love of teaching to help it, so why he thought I had such a wonderful bump for teaching I don't know. Maybe I had bumped against a door or table and raised a lump somewhere on my head!*'

It was not until she had settled down in life and had taken stock of her achievements that she realised she had fulfilled his prediction.

For she did turn to teaching as she developed, even though, as stated in a preceding paragraph, she saw it as a stepping stone to further a career in writing. Moreover, she was so good at teaching through the medium of her pen, as demonstrated in previous paragraphs, that she had fulfilled the second part of the prediction – teaching would be her great gift.

Nevertheless, she did manage to come round to accept the statement in the report that teaching was her great gift and recognised from the particular form of teaching she had been doing that her mission in life was to teach, as can be seen from the following brief extract from the foreword to *A Complete List of [Her] Books*, published by Menzies in 1951:

> *'...I must just add one other note here. I do not write merely to entertain, as most writers for adults can legitimately do ... I am also a teacher and a guide...'*

Therefore, in making such a statement she had fully acknowledged the phrenologist's prediction, even though she did not realise it. So that when all these factor are taken into account, it has to be admitted the phrenologist was right, after all. For not only did she turn to teaching as she developed, but teaching was, indeed, her great gift!

CHAPTER VI

ENID THE PROLIFIC SONGWRITER

As stated in the previous chapter, teaching, through the medium of her pen, was Enid's great gift. By turning to teaching, she sacrificed years of music training that would have resulted in her becoming a professional pianist, with unlimited possibilities for giving concerts to packed halls and revelling in the applause and publicity.

Music, however, did not go out of her life entirely. Waiting silently in the background, it was to find full expression in a field she never knew she would venture into. That field is songwriting. With her Frobel teacher training that places emphasis on all round development of the child and her musical background, she set out to write songs, not for the songwriting market, but for use in her own classroom. The songs proved to be so successful that she had them set to music and brought them out in songbooks for other teachers to use in their classrooms. One thing led to another and before long she was writing songs for schools, patriotic songs for *The Teachers World* and songs for her musical plays. In time, she arranged with composers to set some of her poems to music and tried her hand at writing Christmas carols. Without her realising it, she had become a songwriter!

To crown it all, she developed working relationships with some of the leading composers of the day, such as Alec Rowley, Cecil Sharman, Sydney Twinn, R. C. Noel Johnson, Percy Judd, Philip Green and her own nephew Carey Blyton. These working relationships were to take her songs to a higher level, spreading them far and wide in schools,

FIGURE 13: Title pages/front covers of 10 of Enid Blyton known songbooks. Centre: Responsive Singing Games, her first songbook. Other songbooks not shown here can be seen in Tables I & II, Appendix 46 and 48. ©British Library Board: Round the year Songs (SM: MUSIC W87/9406 cover); Enid Blyton's "Happy Year Song Book" (SM: Music Collections G.1276.q.(6.) cover); Songs of Gladness (SM: Music Collections F.637.xx.9. cover); Snowy Days (SM: Music Collections F.280.d. cover); Responsive Singing Games (SM: Music Collections VOC/1923/Blyton cover); ten songs from child whispers (SM: Music Collections VOC/1934/Twinn, cover); Autumn Days (SM: Music Collections F.280.d. cover); Enid Blyton's New Noddy Song Book (SM: Music Collections VOC/1958/Johnson cover); Enid Blyton's Noddy Song Book 1. (SM: Music Collections VOC/1952/Johnson cover); Mixed Bag (SM: Music Collections H.1984.k.(1.) cover).

music shops and in some theatres throughout the land.

With these facts in mind, let us now take a close look at her songwriting activities. For convenience, I put them in the following categories:

- Singing Games or Action Songs
- Songs Specially Written for Infant Schools
- Songs for Unison Singing
- Songs based on her Poems
- Sheet Music
- Songs for her Musical Plays
- Patriotic Songs
- Christmas Carols
- Miscellaneous Songs

SINGING GAMES

This is the first type of song Enid became interested in writing. The intention was to use them in her own classroom to enliven the games she devised for the little ones to play. First she would teach the children to sing the songs until they learned them by heart. Then she gave them roles to play in the games. The children would then play the games afterwards in a large room while singing the songs to the accompaniment of piano music.

It's this type of song or singing games – sometimes called action songs – we find in her first songbook, *Responsive Singing Games* that J. Saville & Co. published in 1923 (see title page illustration, Figure 13). Here we can see on the front cover a beautifully illustrated scene from one of the games, *The Railway Train*. The girl at the back is pretending to be a guard, with a flag in her hand, ready to give the signal for the train to move off while the children move around in a circle, as if they were parts of a train, singing as they go along.

Written specially for teachers, the songbook contains eight songs that may be sung with or without musical accompaniment (see Appendix 44 for an illustration of one of the scores in this songbook). It's believed Enid herself composed the music for the songs. This is because there's no mention of the name of a composer in the songbook.

Three years later, she wrote songs for ten more singing games and instead of publishing them in a songbook she chose to put them in Volume II, Section V of her three-volume *The Teachers' Treasury,* a book we have met with under *Enid: The Universal Teacher* in Chapter V. The titles of the Singing Games include 'The Railway Train' – a repeat from *Responsive Singing Games* – 'Rowing Boats', 'A Bus Ride' and 'Soldiers' March'. Percy Judd, one of the little known composers of the day, set the songs to music.

From Singing Games for infants we now turn our attention to songs she wrote specially for infant schools.

SONGS SPECIALLY WRITTEN FOR INFANT SCHOOLS

If we go back to *Enid: The Editor* in Chapter IV, we find there a review of a book that was prepared under Enid Blyton's supervision. Entitled *Two Years in the Infant School,* this book in four volumes contains eighty-four topics, one for each week of two school years. If we have already read the chapter we would remember much more about this book. However, what is reserved for this section is the large number of songs Enid contributed to the project.

Drawing on experience gained from writing songs for her songbook *Responsive Singing Games* and for her *The Teachers' Treasury* and knowing the project required eighty-four new songs, each of which should relate to the weekly, changeable topic, she set to work to write new songs for the assignment. In time, she wrote forty-five songs and two Christmas carols and then made arrangements with Cecil Sharman, a composer she had worked with before, to set the songs to music. The titles of the forty-five songs she wrote include: 'The Rain Song' (Volume I, pp 72 – 73; 'The First Swallow', Vol. I, pp 131 – 133; 'Acorn Girls', Vol. II, pp 456 – 457; 'The Apple-Tree Song', Vol. II, pp 488 – 489; 'His First Friends' (a Christmas carol) , Vol. II, pp 626; 'The Wind Song', Vol. III, pp 775 – 776 and 'Night Lights', Vol. IV, pp 1204 – 1205.

However, as the forty-five songs were not enough to cover all the topics, the organisers had to resort to folk songs and nursery rhymes to achieve the target of eighty-four songs. In all, they secured ninety-six songs from all sources, twelve more than the project required!

Finally, those of us who can remember singing songs such as 'Pop Goes The Weasel', 'Bye, Baby Bunting' and 'Twinkle Twinkle Little Star' in our early years of schooling will get some idea of the nature of the songs Enid wrote for five to seven-year-old children in infant schools. If not, have a look at the score for one of her songs, 'Little Lambkin', carried alongside that for 'Pop Goes The Weasel!' in Appendix 45.

SONGS FOR UNISON SINGING

Many of us who have successfully passed through the school system would recall the pleasure we got from either singing in a group or watching others sing in groups. Whether it was singing the national anthem or folk songs, it was always a joyful event to look forward to. Songs of this type are known as unison songs, where members of the group sing in harmony with the music.

It's this type of song we find in Enid's second songbook, *Songs of Gladness*. These are nine songs she wrote for children of all ages to sing in schools for singing practice (see front cover illustration, Figure 13). Here we can see the mention of Alec Rowley (1892 – 1958), the distinguished English composer, pianist and teacher who composed the music and went on to compose the music for many more of her songs. Other songs for unison singing soon followed and these I have listed in Table I, which can be seen in Appendix 46. The last entry in the list, 'Mixed Bag', published by Boosey & Hawkes in 1965, is believed to be her last known songbook containing songs for unison singing. Her nephew, Carey Blyton (1932 – 2002) composed the music for the six songs in this songbook.

Thirty-two more songs for unison singing can be seen in Table II, Appendix 48. Twelve of these were published in *The Enid Blyton's Book of the Year* and twenty, in Volume II, Section VI of her *The Teachers' Treasury*. Of the twenty, eleven were drawn from *The Morning Post*, and three from *Teacher's Times*.

As time went by it must have dawned on Enid that writing songs for schools was not as profitable as writing storybooks. It was probably for this reason she took a clear break from writing songs outright to using some of her own poems as the basis for songs.

SONGS BASED ON HER POEMS

The first set of poems Enid successfully turned into songs was drawn from *Child Whispers*, her first book of poems. Here she selected ten of the best poems from the twenty-eight in the book, had them set to music by Sydney Twinn and brought them out in a songbook entitled: *Ten Songs From Child Whispers*, published in 1924 by J. Saville & Co. (see front cover illustration, Figure 13).

Between 1924 and 1955, she successfully turned 57 more poems into songs and the songbooks, composers, publishers and source of the poems are presented in Table I, (II) which can be seen in Appendix 46. Title page illustrations for some of the songbooks in this Table can be seen in Figure 13.

SHEET MUSIC

Besides publishing her songs in batches, Enid also published some of them individually, as sheet music. These were pieces any music teacher could buy in those days for a few pence and take to school to give their pupils for piano practice. Music students also had the option to buy one of them from a music bookshop and take it home for practice.

The first song in this category, 'The Singer In The Night', is based on one of her poems published in *Punch*. Cecil Sharman composed the music and Novello & Co published it in *The School Music Review* in its edition of November 15, 1925 (see illustration, Appendix 47).

Between 1925 and 1958 Enid wrote ten more songs and these are listed in Table III, in Appendix 48A. Included in the list are two *two-part songs* and a *four-part song* also written by Enid Blyton. In *part-songs*, the singers are given different voice parts.

SONGS FOR HER MUSICAL PLAYS

It's in this category, more than in any other, that we find evidence of Enid's ability to write songs by the scores at one go. These she wrote, not for publications in songbooks, but for her own musical plays. The subject of her plays is fully discussed under *Enid: The Playwright* in Chapter VIII, so we'll be considering in this section only the songs that appeared in some of those plays.

The first set of songs for musical plays she wrote was for the twelve plays in *The Play's The Thing,* her first book of musical plays for schools. Here we find a staggering 66 songs all set to music by Alec Rowley (see Appendix 49 for illustration of a part of the score for 'Gardeners' Song' in 'The King's Pocket- Knife*'*, one of the musical plays in the book).

Twelve years later she repeated the same feat, this time for six musical plays in *The Blyton-Sharman Musical Plays*, for which she wrote another batch of 40 songs (see Table IV, Appendix 48A for more information about these songs).

Cecil Sharman composed the music which was published in the same book under the subtitle: *How The Flowers Grow & Other Musical Plays.*

This knack for writing songs in batches was to continue when she wrote her first musical play for the theatre, *Noddy in Toyland*, that was first staged in 1954 at the Stoll Theatre in London. According to her biographer, Barbara Stoney, in a passage on page 162 of *Enid Blyton: A Biography*, '*she wrote some thirty-three lyrics in all – far more than were eventually needed...*' More information about this musical play is given under *Enid: The Playwright* in Chapter VIII.

So if we've been taking stock, we'll have arrived at 139 songs in this category alone, and this without taking into account the others we have previously considered earlier in this chapter (see Table IV for a recap of the songs in this category).

PATRIOTIC SONGS

In the early 1900s, schoolchildren in public elementary schools used to look forward to the annual celebrations to mark Empire Day – a special day set aside in May for them to reflect on the peoples and cultures that were a part of the then vast British Empire. They had the chance to dress up in fancy costumes worn by children of different lands, eat exotic foods, take part in marches and sing patriotic songs.

Up to that time the leading patriotic songs were 'Rule Britannia' and 'Land of Hope and Glory'. However, by the time the celebrations came round in May 1925 they had a new patriotic song to sing: 'The Union Jack'. This patriotic song was Enid's contribution to the celebrations and her aim was for it to be sung in schools where the celebrations were observed. The medium she chose to do this was *The Teachers World*, as usual, where it was well received and given prominence in the Music Supplement of April 29, 1925 (see illustration, Appendix 50).

Here we can see lyrics that measure up to those in 'Rule Britannia' in so far as they express ideas of the might and glory of Britain that were prevalent at that time. The song survived for some time until 1958 when the celebrations gave way to another type, Commonwealth Day – the result of the disbanding of the Empire when Britain granted independence to the majority of its colonies.

From 'The Union Jack' we move on to another patriotic song, 'The League Of Nations', which she wrote for the annual celebrations to mark the anniversary of that august body. The song, which was set to music by Alec Rowley, was published in the Music Supplement of *The Teachers World* in the edition of February 3, 1926. Like 'The Union Jack', it circulated in schools for some time until 1945 when the League of Nations was dissolved and the United Nations took its place soon after the end of the Second World War (1939 – 1945). More information of these two patriotic songs can be seen in Table VI, Appendix 52.

In spite of this, Enid never lost interest in writing songs associated with celebrations and was quick to spot another occasion for her talent to come to the fore: Christmas.

CHRISTMAS CAROLS

Her first Christmas carol with the title: 'Shepherd Song: A New Carol', appeared in *The Teachers World* in the edition of November 7, 1924 (see illustration, Appendix 51). Between 1924 and 1955 she wrote five more Christmas carols and these I have presented in Table V, Appendix 52. They have been drawn from various parts of her books, including her songbooks. One of them, 'The Shepherd King', even made it on the front cover of *The Teachers World*, in the Senior School Edition of December 18, 1929, and this can be seen in Appendix 53.

Finally, like the patriotic songs we encountered in the previous section, her Christmas carols soon fell into oblivion. Had she striven to have them published in some medium other than *The Teachers World*, where they would have received a wider coverage, they might have survived to this day and become as popular as 'Mary's Boy Child' or 'God Rest Ye Merry Gentlemen'.

MISCELLANEOUS SONGS

In this category we find songs written specially for fans of the popular Noddy series of books. This is the impression we get when we read the letter Enid included in the opening page of *The Enid Blyton's Noddy Songbook* that came out in 1952 at the height of the popularity of the Noddy books. Here is a brief extract from that letter:

> *Most of you know the little Noddy books – and you know the funny songs that Noddy sings in them ... Well, here are twelve little Noddy songs and Mr Noel-Johnson has set them to the kind of music all children like. The tunes are as easy to learn as the words and you will love to sing them ...*

(Another song was added to the list when a new edition came out in 1959, making the contents 13 songs in all.)

Then, in 1954, another Noddy songbook made its way in the world. Entitled: *Enid Blyton's Noddy in Toyland: Selection for Piano*, it was a spin-off from songs in the popular 'Noddy in Toyland' musical play (see *Enid: The Playwright*, Chapter VIII for details about this play). Phil Green and R.C. Noel-Johnson set the songs to music and the songbook was published by G. Ricordi, a music publisher, who also published the first songbook referred to in the preceding paragraph.

Five years later, she brought out *Enid Blyton's New Noddy Songbook* with eight more songs for children to sing, once they had the chance to learn the tunes. R. C. Noel-Johnson, once again, set the songs to music and the book was published in 1959 by Ascherberg, Hopwood & Crew Ltd. (See Figure 13 for front cover illustrations of two of the three Noddy songbooks treated in this category and Table II, Appendix 48 for a recap of information about the songbooks.)

Besides the miscellaneous songs in these Noddy songbooks, there're more of them scattered in her work.[40] The reason for this could be that she had lost track of them or she knew where they were but had no time to collect them.

CONCLUSION

From this presentation of her songwriting activities, we can see that she was truly a prolific songwriter. To have found time to write so many songs despite her heavy workload described in previous chapters, and in chapters to come, is truly remarkable.

However, what is surprising is that we've never heard from her about her songs and how she wrote them. In her semi-autobiographical book *The Story of My Life,* there's hardly a mention. Neither is there a mention in the opportunities that were available to her to talk about her work as a storyteller. The reason for this would always remain a mystery.

Finally, given that the facts now presented in this chapter are not generally known, it is hoped that they may get the attention of publishers of biographies or biographical sketches of famous writers so that they might amend the entries in future publications to include her songwriting activities and give her due credit for her songs.

CHAPTER VII

ENID THE PROFESSIONAL STORYTELLER

OVERVIEW

The whole of Enid Blyton's work may be said to fall into two distinct categories: teaching and storytelling. As we have seen in previous chapters, teaching was her great gift, but it was through storytelling, and not through classroom teaching, that the gift was to find full expression. For if we examine the 200 or so reading books she wrote to teach children to read, her Nature Readers, History Lessons and her poems, songs and plays, we find that there's a story in all of them, although many of us might never have looked at it in this way.

This chapter is divided into two sections. In Section One, we endeavour to find out how it all began. How did she become interested in storytelling? What were her qualifications for the art? Did she possess some talent that other storytellers lack? If so, what was that talent? Then we inquire into her strong belief in fairies, look at her technique in telling fairytales and examine some theories about the nature and characteristics of these curious folks.

In Section Two we find an analysis of her curious writing method followed by a presentation of three theories to account for the way she wrote her stories. Did she invent them? Were they the work of some supernatural agent, given to her ready-made through a process known as Automatic Writing? Did they come from her subconscious mind, through a process called the Association of Ideas? Or can they be put down to clairvoyance and other unknown psychic phenomena? The section concludes with the theory that, in my opinion, is the most satisfactory.

SECTION ONE

QUALIFICATION FOR THE ART OF STORYTELLING

VAST READINGS

In the famous book *The Story of My Life* that Enid wrote as a form of collective answers to questions from her fans, we find on page 106 of the first edition a reference to her Irish grandmother, Mary Ann, telling her 'a great many queer old Irish tales'. We would never know how many tales she learned from her. Neither would we ever know how many tales or stories her father or mother used to tell her, nor of those she learned from her teacher at Tresco,[41] the private preparatory school to which she was sent when she was about six years old.

Her first big opportunity to read stories on her own came when she discovered *The Children's Encyclopaedia* edited by Arthur Mee (see Appendix 54 for an illustration of one of the inside covers next to the Plan of the Encyclopaedia). This extraordinary book in eight volumes that was first published in 1908 by the Educational Book Company, London, was packed with hundreds of stories of every description from the British Isles and all around the world. The way the stories were presented: short, often illustrated and in the simplest language imaginable, would fire any child's imagination and Enid soon lost herself in reading the stories.

So that when she stated in a passage on page 48 of *The Story of My Life* that she had read every single old myth and legend she could get hold of – the old Norse myths, the old Greek myths … and every old folk tale she could find from countries all over the world, it was in this *Children's Encyclopaedia* that she first had the opportunity to do so. She also had the opportunity to read for the first time the fables of

Aesop[42] – some seventy-five were carried therein – and a variety of illustrated bible stories drawn from both the Old and New Testaments.

Apart from the abundance of stories scattered throughout the eight volumes, there are also sections in the encyclopaedia where background information is given of the writers of the stories and their works, where necessary. In this way Enid was introduced to Homer's *Iliad* and *The Odyssey*, the works of Shakespeare, Chaucer's *Canterbury Tales*, the works of Charles Dickens, Thomas Carlyle, Charles Kingsley and others and many writers of fairytales, such as the German Brothers Grimm, the Danish Hans Christian Andersen, the Irish Thomas Crofton Croker, Frances Browne and the French Perrault and Madame D'Aulnoy. Enid was so fascinated by the way the stories and other material were presented in the eight volumes of the encyclopaedia – designed to be read like a book – that she read it from end to end and then read it all over again. [43]

'It gave me my thirst for knowledge of all kinds and taught me as much as ever I learnt at school', she stated in a passage on page 49 of *The Story of My Life*. *'It sent me questing through my father's vast array of bookcases for other books – books on astronomy, nature, poetry, history, old legends. There were many volumes above my head that I found and read because I had to know more about the things I read in The Children's Encyclopaedia.'*

In searching her father's bookcases, she wasted no time in reading many of his other books, the discovery of which horrified him:

'I will not have you borrowing adult books like this. I shall lock up the book-cases in future.' [44]

It was not long before he did carry out his threat, with no harm to the young Enid. For, as she was to recall, *'By that time there wasn't a book I hadn't read.'*[45]

This locking up of the bookcases however did not put an end to her love of reading. To fill the gap she quickly turned her attention to other books that were not under lock and key:

'When I hadn't a book to read I took down one of his enormous

encyclopaedias and dipped into that. I learnt some very peculiar facts, which pop up now and again in the books I write ... [Facts about] Stalagmites, stalactites, copper mines, great auks, sea-tunnels, whirlpools – and many, many more.' [46]

From this we can see that this vast reading of stories in *The Children's Encyclopaedia* and of everything else in her father's encyclopaedias was to prepare and qualify her for the art of storytelling, even though she might not have realised it at that time.

In this respect she ought to have been grateful to her father for having in his bookcases books of every description and for buying *The Children's Encyclopaedia* for his three children, Enid, Hanly and Carey. For had the books not been there in the first place to provide her with hundreds of models of stories, it is probable she might not have developed such a strong interest in storytelling.

Apart from this vast reading in her childhood, she also had something else that was to ensure she did not forget one iota of what she had read: a photographic memory.

PHOTOGRAPHIC MEMORY – A PRICELESS GIFT FAR ABOVE THE AVERAGE

According to Leonard Guthrie, M.A. M.D. (1858–1918) in his book *Contributions to the Study of Precocity in Children,* [47] memory is the foundation of scholarships and the secret of brilliancy in school examinations. This we all know. We also know that some people can remember certain things only by learning them by heart. Not so with Enid Blyton. She had a photographic memory, that is, the faculty or ability to 'scan' the contents of a page then close her eyes and recall what she had read word for word, as can be seen in the following account she gave on page 47 of *The Story of My Life:*

'When I was eight or nine I could read down a page once, then shut my eyes and repeat it word for word. I never forgot what I had read. I can still shut my eyes and see a page of my geography book – "Manufacturers: Macclesfield for silk. Luton for hats. Leeds for woollen goods. Sheffield for steel goods."'

In this respect, Enid was among a minority of adults and children who had this faculty or ability well developed. Such was the case of the Rev. Thomas Threlkeld. According to an account given in an article on page 143 of *The Spectator*, in the issue of Feb. 1st 1879:

> *...He could at once recite any text in the English Bible when the book, chapter and verse were named to him and who had a profound and critical knowledge of nine or ten distinct languages and a fair knowledge of no less than seventeen, without counting distinct dialects.*

Moreover, on page 37 of *Contributions to the Study of Precocity in Children* just mentioned, the author cites many interesting cases of people who, when they were children, had shown early signs of a photographic memory. Among them is Thomas Edison (1847 – 1931), one of America's most prolific inventors who, when he was ten to twelve years old, could '*refer usually to the very book and page, to fact, incident, and words used by certain authors who impressed him*' and of Thomas Macaulay (1800 – 1859) the English historian, essayist and statesman who at the age of four was taken to the Oxford Collection and remembered the catalogue ever afterwards.

Finally, Sir Francis Galton (1822 – 1911) the English scientist and cousin of Charles Darwin gave in two papers, one published in *The Fortnightly Review* and the other in *Mind*, many cases of English men, women, children and foreigners with well-developed photographic memories.[48] Readers who are interested in this subject will find therein many interesting cases to convince them that the possession of a photographic memory is no frivolous matter.

These are all cases of people born with that hitherto inexplicable power to retain a vivid picture of what they had read or seen, in every detail, and to recall it at a later date or time. Moreover, judging from Enid's own account in the quotation just cited, she is definitely in this small class of people. Furthermore, since she stated that she never forgot what she had read, we now have the key to unravel the mystery of her ability to retell so many stories.

We find evidence of this in all the traditional stories she retold in the *Sunny Stories for Little Folks* magazine (see the Sunny Stories magazine – A Phenomenal Success in Section Two for details), in the fables of Aesop, the Brer Rabbit tales, the tales from 'Arabian Nights', *The Pilgrim's Progress* under the title: 'The Land of the Far Beyond' and all the Old English stories and legends she retold, including *Tales of Robin Hood* and *The Knights of the Round Table* (see Figure 14 for illustration of title pages of some of the books containing stories she retold).

Evidence of her power of retention of all that she had read can also be found in the large number of Bible stories she retold from both the Old and New Testaments (see Figure 15 for illustration of front covers and title pages of some of her books of bible stories). In order for her to do so with such vividness and clarity, she had to read the Bible from cover to cover, just as she had done with *The Children's Encyclopaedia*, and retain all that she had read.

Moreover, it was in the 'Stories of World History' and in the 'Tales of Romance' she wrote for *The Teachers World* that we find an extraordinary demonstration of her photographic memory. (See again her syllabus, Appendix 30). In order to write these elaborate stories, she had to read translations from the Greek of Homer's *Iliad* [24 books] and *The Odyssey*[49] [another 24 books]; Sir Thomas Malory's translation from the French of *Le Morte d'Arthur* (The Death of Arthur); translation from the French of Froissart's *Chronicles*; Spencer's *Faerie Queene* [6 books] and other Ancient and Medieval History books from which she was able to draw material to retell the stories (see again Appendices 28, 31, 32, 33 and 34 for illustrations of episodes from her ' Stories of World History' and from the 'Tales of Romance').This then unravels the mystery of how she was able to retell so many stories while doing all the things described in this book. It's all down to her photographic memory!

From this extraordinary faculty Enid possessed and used to her advantage, we now move on to consider another factor that was to enhance her storytelling ability: her strong belief in fairies.

STRONG BELIEF IN FAIRIES

A strong belief in anything is often planted in the mind when we were children. If therefore we wish to learn how Enid developed such a

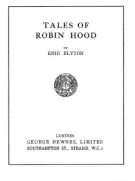

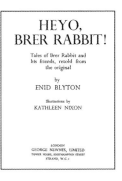

FIGURE 14: Title pages, in miniature, of a selection of books containing stories retold by Enid Blyton. 'Tales from the Arabian Nights' and 'The Knights of the Round Table' are book forms of stories Enid Blyton narrated in the 'Stories of World History' course she ran in The Teachers World. © British Library Board: Old English Stories, classed under Reading Practice No 5, (SM: 20031.a.8, cover); Tales of Robin Hood, (SM: W.P.4815/4 title page); Heyo, Brer Rabbit! (SM: 12819.i.9 title page); Tales of Babar (SM: W.P.8307/17 title page); The Land of Far-Beyond (SM: 12815.aa.58 title page); The Knights of the Round Table (SM: 12831.c.41 title page); Tales of Brave Adventure (SM: 12845.l.7 title page); Tales from the Arabian Nights (SM: W.P.4815/2 title page).

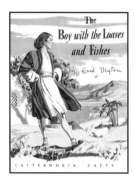
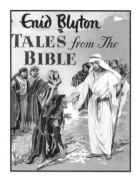
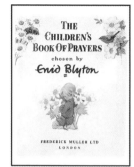
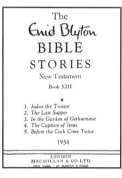

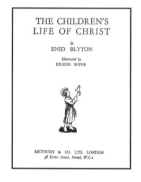

FIGURE 15: A selection of front covers and title pages, in miniature, of Enid Blyton's religious books for children. ©British Library Board: The Boy with the Loaves and Fishes (SM: 4809.aa.6, cover); Tales from the Bible (SM: 3130.r.16, cover); The Children's Book of Prayers (SM: 3458.b.58, title page); The Enid Blyton Bible Stories, New Testament (SM: 03128.f.103, title page); The Enid Blyton Bible Stories. Old Testament (SM: 3130.h.35, title page); The Children's Life of Christ (SM: 4225.h.117, title page); Before I go to sleep (SM: X.200/9278, title page); The Greatest Book in the World (SM: 3130.p.8, title page); The Little Girl at Capernaum (SM: 3228.c.8, title page).

strong belief in fairies and their kind, it's to her early childhood that we'll have to look.

When we begin to look in this direction, we find that it was, once again, 'the queer old Irish tales'[50] her Irish grandmother, Mary Ann, used to tell her that must have sparked her interest in these strange folks:

'...I sometimes find her long-ago voice whispering in my mind still, when I think of leprechauns or banshees!' [51]

Then there's the influence of her father, who was bound to know many Irish and other fairytales, judging from his Irish background. Later on, when she learned to read and discovered Arthur Mee's *Children's Encyclopaedia*, she found so many stories of fairies that it was enough to fix in her mind the idea that these folks probably had some existence in fact.

Moreover, since *The Children's Encyclopaedia* introduced her to Thomas Crofton Croker and his *Fairy Legends and Traditions of the South of Ireland* – a volume packed with a collection of fascinating stories of fairies, banshees, leprechauns, gnomes and so on, in their encounters with humans in a variety of situations – we can speculate she must have eventually found this book and read it to her heart's delight.

Furthermore, in the old Norse myths she told us she had read, there's a treatment of elves – referred to as the Dark Elves and Light Elves – in two of the nine worlds of the Yggdrasil or World Tree. So that by the time she began writing stories, her belief in fairies had already been established.

Another hint she gave of how strong her belief in these folks can be seen in a passage from an article she wrote for *The Teachers World*, in the edition of March 3, 1926, to introduce her new home, Elfin Cottage, to her fans:

'...Flowers "belong" to Elfin Cottage. They look at home there – and that confirms me in my secret belief that fairies and elves, brownies and gnomes, have visited the house and left some of their flower-loving, sunshiny personalities behind.'

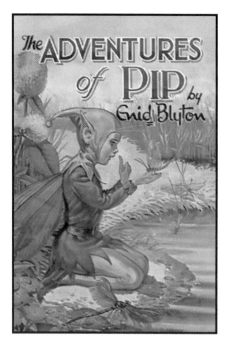 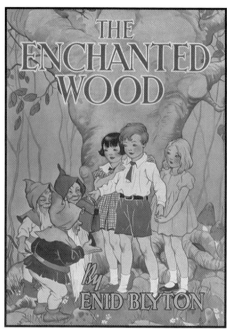

FIGURE 16: Two fairytale books that may be regarded as models to study the techniques Enid Blyton used for her fairytales. Left: Pip, a pixie, visits and explores the natural world. Right: boys and girls visit the world of fairies, elves and so on. Information about these two books is given in the Bibliography. © British Library Board: The Adventures of Pip (SM: 12830.f.19, cover); The Enchanted Wood (SM: 12824.c.7, cover). Photos restoration credit: 2graphic Photo Restoration. Website: www.photo-restoration.co.uk

Yet another hint can be can be seen in the following passage from page 102 of *The Story of My Life*:

> *'I saw pantomimes, of course, as you do, and the children's plays – Peter Pan I saw some time ago with my own two girls, and, you can imagine, we all shouted out that we believed in fairies!'*

Indeed, so strong was her belief in fairies that bits and pieces slipped out unexpectedly in unusual places, as shown in the following extracts from her 'Enid Blyton's Nature Lessons' in *The Teachers World*:

> *...There are ten stamens hidden away, and each has at its tip a bag of pollen – fine golden dust fit for a fairy's baking powder...*

'Gorse', column 2, page 138, April 15, 1925

Now for a little talk about Buttercups in general. Have you noticed their glossy petals? They look as if they have been freshly polished by small fairies with pots of polish and dusters…

'The Buttercup', column 2, page 119, April 14th 1926

One of the prettiest sights to see is a wild rose bush by a river, dropping its petals on to the ripples, where they float like fairy boats…

'The Wild Rose', column 1, page 556, June 10, 1925.

This demonstration of her strong belief in fairies gives us the impression that fairies really exist, something that is still open to doubt. So where can we look to find certainty to clear up the matter? The main sources that are still open to us today to investigate the matter are *The Secret Commonwealth of Elves, Fauns and Fairies,* written by the Scottish clergyman Robert Kirk;[52] J.A. MacCulloch's article on fairies in *The Encyclopaedia of Religion & Ethics*[53] and *The Science of Fairytales* by Edwin Sidney Hartland.[54] A brief extract from *The Secret Commonwealth of Elves, Fauns and Fairies* can be found in Appendix 55. Other sources are listed in *the Bibliography* under the subject of fairies at the end of this book. In this way we have the opportunity to study the subject at length and draw our own conclusions.

Having thus found out how Enid's strong belief in fairies came about, let us take a look at its reflection in her work. In some of the fairytales she recounted, we find cases in which fairy folks leave fairyland – the home of the fairies – and visit the natural world, where they learn many interesting facts about insects, reptiles, birds, flowers and animals. They marvelled at the sea anemone that looks like a plant growing underwater, the chrysalis in which the butterfly develops, the hermit crab that changes its shell, the ladybird with its colourful spots, the caterpillar, centipede and so on. The more unusual or strange the characteristics of these creatures are, the more they charmed the fairies that were looking on in awe and wonder. This is especially the case in *The Adventures of Pip,* that was first published in the *Sunday Graphic*[55] and later brought out in book form (see front cover illustration, Figure 16).

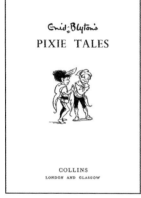
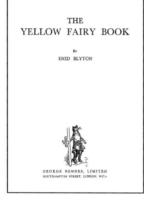

FIGURE 17: A selection of title pages, in miniature, of Enid Blyton's fairytale books (See Bibliography for information about these books and other fairytale books not listed here).
© *British Library Board: The Enid Blyton Book of Fairies (SM: 12829.cc.45, title page); The Enid Blyton Book of Brownies (SM: 012803.k.21, title page); The Red Pixie Book (SM: 20053.i.23, title page); Enid Blyton's Pixie Tales (SM: X.998/611, title page); The Yellow Fairy Book (SM: 12812.aa.95, title page); The Green Goblin Book (SM: 20053.d.40, title page).*

Then there's the reverse, in which boys and girls visit the world of fairies and their like and have adventures with them. An example of this can be found in *The Enchanted Wood, The Magic Faraway Tree* and *The Folk of the Faraway Tree,* published by George Newnes in 1939, 1943 and 1946 respectively. In these books, three children: Jo, Bessie and Fanny, climbed the 'Faraway Tree' and met all the fairy folks who lived there before being taken to different 'lands' at the top of the tree. (See front cover illustration of *The Enchanted Wood,*

Figure 16.)

Furthermore, if we study the other fairytales she has written, we'll find that they're a reflection of the characteristics, clothing and habitat of fairies described in *The Secret Commonwealth of Elves, Fauns and Fairies* and other books referred to earlier in this section.

From this we gain the impression that her knowledge of these folks went far beyond the mere reading of fairytales in *The Children's Encyclopaedia* and other fairytale books that fell into her hands. She was bound to read serious books on the subject, books which might have been in her father's vast collection of books. What these works were we'll never know (see Figure 17 for illustration of title pages of some of her fairytale books).

When we add this last factor of her strong belief in fairies to those we have previously considered, namely, her vast readings and her photographic memory, we have the ingredients for a professional storyteller of the first order, although some of us, when we take into account the criticism of her stories, would not agree with this assertion. In order to redress the balance, I've included in Section Two an article: Why Some of Enid Blyton's Stories Are Not Up To Standard.

Finally, what better way to close this section than with the following assessment of her storytelling ability from Iona Opie, co-author of *The Oxford Dictionary of Nursery Rhymes:*

> *'She was a first-class story-teller. She used a very simple vocabulary and the words came around regularly. Children knew what to expect ... She had an excellent system, well-disguised, to get children reading and to keep them reading...'*[56]

This assessment, short and to the point, will most likely find favour with many professionals in the field of children's literature, especially those who were avid readers of her storybooks before they took up studies in this field.

Let us now move on to Section Two of this chapter to have a look at her writing method, or the way the stories came to her, and consider three theories I put forward to account for the fascinating phenomenon.

SECTION TWO

ANALYSIS OF ENID BLYTON'S WRITING METHOD

The first account Enid gave the world of how she wrote her stories can be found on page 3 of the foreword to *A Complete List of [Her] Books*, published by John Menzies in 1951. At that time, she was fifty-four years old.

One year later, she wrote *The Story of My Life*, published by Pitkin in September, 1952. Here she gave a fuller account of her writing method in Chapter 14 in such a way that the children, for whom the book was intended, could understand it without having to ask an adult to explain what they were reading.

Then in 1953, Peter McKellar (1921 – 2003), a Professor of Psychology, took the liberty to write to her asking for information about her writing method. At that time he was writing a book – later published as *Imagination & Thinking* by Cohen & West in 1957 – and he felt that her contribution would help him to understand the role of the imagination in the writing process. In her reply she gave a professional account, such as would be given from one expert to another, drawing on her knowledge of psychology she had to study while training to become a teacher.[57]

From studying the account she gave in each case, we find a common thread running through them all – the stories came to her ready-made. She had no control over the process. Before starting a new story she would ask herself what type of story should be written. Having decided that it should be, say a fairytale, she would close her eyes for a minute or two and wait, with her fingers on the typewriter keys ready to go into action. Then the story would flow into her imagination, complete with characters, setting, adventure and all. She saw her characters in every detail – hair, eyes, expression, clothing, etc., as clearly as if they were right before her as she wrote, and saw the setting with equal vividness. It was – she emphasised in each case – like looking out of a window, or having a private cinema screen in her head, and what she saw and heard she wrote down.

When the story came to an end, the characters would fade away. Then all she had to do, whenever she sat at her typewriter again, was to wait and see what new story would be *presented* to her to write. Finally she maintained that the stories that came to her were better than anything she could ever invent herself and that she could take no credit

PEARL CURRAN   **FRANCES BROWNE**

*FIGURE 18: Left: **Pearl Lenore Curran** (1883 – 1937), The Illinois (American) woman of English parentage, who saw her characters and scenes clairvoyantly. From the frontispiece of The Case of Patience Worth, by Walter Franklin Prince, first published in 1927 by the Boston Society of Psychic Research, USA. Photo credit: Alamy Stock Photo. Website: www.alamy.com.*
*Right: **Frances Browne** (1816 – 1879), Irish poet and novelist, was known as the Blind Genius of Stranorlar. Although she was blind from infancy, she was nevertheless able to give vivid descriptions in her storybooks of people, places and scenes through exercising the faculty of clairvoyance or inner vision. (See Enid: The Professional Storyteller, Section II for details). Photos restoration credit: 2graphic Photo Restoration. Website:www.photo-restoration.co.uk*

for the phenomenon. This then is a summary of her writing method drawn from the three sources stated in the preceding paragraphs.

Now as astonishing as this account may be, it is in no way unique. In 1929, a psychic researcher, Hannen Swaffer (1879 – 1962) set out to investigate how some famous writers and playwrights came up with plots for their stories and plays. The answers they gave surprised him.

These he put together in a book *Adventures with Inspiration*, published by Morley & M. Kennerley, London, in 1929.

Among the numerous cases cited in the book is that of Edgar Wallace (1875 – 1932), the famous British novelist, playwright and journalist who was considered at that time the king of the modern thriller. Like Enid Blyton, he was a prolific writer with 175 novels, 24 plays and countless articles to his credit. He was said to be the second biggest seller after the Bible. In a conversation with Hannen, he confessed that '*he never thought of his plots but they came into his head ready-made.*'[58]

Then there's the case of George Bernard Shaw (1856 – 1950), the distinguished Irish novelist and playwright who has given the world, among many others, *Arms and the Man*, *The Man of Destiny* and *The Doctor's Dilemma* and whose complete works appeared in thirty-six volumes. Like Enid Blyton, when he had chosen his subject the play wrote itself. He could even begin without a subject, with the same result, he confessed to Hennen: '*The characters come and talk and define themselves and explain their business and there is your play for you.*'[59]

A third case that can be cited is that of Henry Arthur Jones (1851 – 1929), the English playwright whose plays were widely acclaimed. A year before he died he told Hannen: '*God seems to give me plots ready-made.*'[60]

But the case that towers above them all is that of Pearl Lenore Curran (1883 – 1937). (See her photo, Figure 18.) Much has been written about this American woman of British parentage who produced a prodigious output of stories, poems and other articles for which, she claimed, she could take no credit. At the time of the events now being described, she was living in St. Louis, Missouri, USA.

Like Enid Blyton, she would sit at her desk, with a notebook or typewriter, in full consciousness of herself and surroundings, and wait for a story to flow into her imagination. Before long the pen would start to write or her fingers would become active on the typewriter keys and the story would unfold from start to finish. As she wrote the narrative, she would see in her imagination, not only the characters and the setting in the story, but also the entire surrounding area, as she so lively expressed in the following extract from an account she gave to Dr Walter Franklin Prince (1863 – 1934), a psychic researcher who was studying her case:

> *'When the stories come the scenes become panoramic, with the characters moving and acting their parts, even speaking in converse [talking among themselves]. The picture is not confined to the point narrated but takes in everything else within the circle of vision at the time. For instance, if two people are seen talking on the corner of the street, I see, not only them, but the neighbouring part of the street, with the buildings, stones, dogs, people and all, just as they would be in a real scene. If the people talk a foreign language … I hear the talk, but over and above is the voice of Patience either interpreting, [or] giving me the part she wishes to use as story.'* [61]

'Patience' referred to in the extract is Patience Worth, a 'dead' woman from earlier times who identified herself as the author of the stories and poems that Pearl Curran wrote out automatically. In the part dealing with Supernatural Agent soon to be presented, we'll find out who this Patience Worth could be.

After considering these accounts from novelists and playwrights and comparing them with that given by Enid Blyton, we begin to wonder whether the attributes described earlier in this chapter – her vast readings, her photographic memory and her strong belief in fairies – were of any use in the writing of her stories, the more so because the stories appear to come to her ready-made. Nevertheless, when we come to consider one of the theories about her writing method, we'll see how indispensable these attributes were in the writing of her stories.

Moreover, since she claimed she could take no credit for the stories, to whom should credit be attributed? This is what we'll now find out. The theories to be considered are presented in the following order:

1. The stories were the work of some supernatural agent, given to her through a process known as Automatic Writing.
2. They stem from her Subconscious Mind, through the Association

of Ideas.

3. Clairvoyance and other psychic phenomena might have been at work in producing the stories.

Let us now consider each in turn and afterwards draw our conclusion.

THE WORK OF SOME SUPERNATURAL AGENT THROUGH AUTOMATIC WRITING

The more we read the accounts Enid and the others gave of how they received plots ready-made for their stories and plays, the more we are inclined to think that the plots could be the work of some supernatural agent, such as the soul of someone who lived on the earth before. However, before we come to consider this possibility, let us pause to examine the word *soul*, an examination that will give us an understanding of the nature of supernatural agents and how they operate.

The word *soul* refers to the invisible part of our being. Some people use the word *spirit* to refer to the same thing. It is found in the vocabulary of Spiritualism, a religion whose adherents hold that when people die only the physical body is buried or cremated. Their souls survive and pass into an invisible realm. They may return invisibly, under certain conditions, through someone known as a 'Medium', to communicate with the living.[62] One of the ways these departed souls can do this is through a process known as Automatic Writing.

In this way the medium, who may be a man or woman, either goes into a trance or may be fully aware of the surroundings. He may be in a group of strangers who have come to witness the phenomenon or sitting at his desk at home. In the case now being described, he's in a group of strangers at a spiritualist meeting called a séance. With a pencil in his hand and sheets of writing paper ready, he stays still for a few minutes, waiting for the communication. Like Enid Blyton, he has no idea beforehand what's going to happen.

As the people in the group look on in wonder, the pencil in his hand begins to write. In reality, it is not the medium who is writing but the disembodied soul who has taken hold of his hand to write the message in his own handwriting.

In the end what he has written turns out to be a message for someone in the group. From the highlights given such as a brief description of the illness the sender suffered from before passing or a reference to something no one else is supposed to know about, someone in the group recognises that the message is from a relative or friend who passed away some time ago and claims it from the medium. This then is the way disembodied souls – souls without bodies – often return to communicate with the living through automatic writing.

To give a more concrete illustration of this phenomenon, let us take the case of Charles Dickens (1812 – 1870) and the controversial book he's written sometime after he passed away. This famous English novelist, who has given the world *David Copperfield*, *Oliver Twist*, *Great Expectations*, and *Hard Times*, among many others, was working on a novel *The Mystery of Edwin Drood* when he died suddenly, leaving the novel unfinished. Nevertheless, a reputable publisher, Chapman & Hall, published the unfinished novel in 1870, and that, apparently, was the end of the matter.

Three years later Charles Dickens 'came back from the dead' to complete the novel through T. P. James, a well-known Medium of the day. With some eight months of dictation from the departed Charles Dickens, the Medium took the novel from where he left off and brought it to the final page. When it was completed, he published extracts in the press to generate interest in the book and, eventually, published it himself (see title page illustration, Appendix 56). What was even more astonishing, the departed Charles Dickens dictated to him the preface to the novel in which he expressed his concerns about the controversy that might inevitably arise when the Second Part of his novel was published (see again Appendix 56 for illustration).

Needless to state that when the book was published it did stir up a great deal of controversy. Critics went through it with a fine-tooth comb, scrutinising the style and vocabulary to see whether they were those of Charles Dickens. Some even put forward the theory that Charles Dickens completed the Second Part before he died but nobody knew about it. When it was discovered, a relative sent it off to the

Medium, as one would send a manuscript to a literary agent, to have it published. He therefore could not have written it after his death.[63]

Like Enid Blyton, who suffered the same fate when she described her writing method to the world, the brave medium weathered the storm, and fans of Charles Dickens who, after reading the First Part, had been left wondering how the story would end, soon had their wish fulfilled, thanks to the return of the soul of Charles Dickens to complete the novel in a most spectacular way.

To this fascinating account of how the novel was completed could be added the case of Patience Worth, a 'dead' woman of earlier times whom we have met earlier in this chapter. She claimed to be the author of the stories, poems, and other articles dictated to Pearl Curran through the process of automatic writing. Somewhere in the process of dictation, she described herself as a 17th century Quaker woman who had lived on a Dorsetshire farm in England, in 1649, before emigrating to America where she met her death at the hands of hostile Indians.[64] Pearl Curran, who saw her clairvoyantly, described her *'as a young woman of about thirty years as she was leaving England for America. Dressed in a coarse cloth cape, brown-gray, with a hood like a cowl, peaked. She is small and her feet are small---with coarse squared-toed shoes and gray woolen stockings. Her hair was dark red, mahogany in big glossy, soft waves, her eyes brown and deep, her mouth firm and set.'*[65]

Some of her stories written through Pearl Curran were in 17th century English and dialects that Pearl Curran knew nothing about. Therefore, Patience Worth could really be the soul of the17th century Quaker woman who was using Pearl Curran as a medium to get out her stories and poems. A short list of some of Patience Worth's storybooks and books of poems written automatically by Pearl Curran is presented in the *Bibliography* at the end of this book.

Finally if we visit any New Age bookshop in London, England or surf the Internet, we'll find there English books written by famous 'dead' authors, such as Sir Arthur Conan Doyle, H. G. Wells, T. S. Eliot and Nikola Tesla, through mediums who knew nothing about them or their work. A short list of these books is given in the *Bibliography* at the end of this book.

This then is evidence to substantiate the theory that the stories written by Enid Blyton could have been the work of some supernatural agent, such as the soul of someone who lived on this earth before. A hypothetical case could be that of a storyteller whose ambition to have her novels, poems and so on published was thwarted when some untoward event cut short her life. Could her soul have come back, like the souls of Charles Dickens and Patience Worth, to get Enid Blyton to fulfil her ambition? Before coming to such a conclusion, let us turn our attention to the second theory to be considered, namely, that the stories could have been culled from the vast storehouse of material locked away in her subconscious mind and put together spontaneously through the process of the Association of Ideas.

THE SUBCONSCIOUS MIND, THROUGH THE PROCESS OF THE ASSOCIATION OF IDEAS

(Or Unconscious Mental Activity)

There are in the mind of Man many faculties which are outside of the realm of consciousness. *

The subconscious mind is said to be the most mysterious part of our being. It's supposed to be operating in the background, below our conscious mind, hence the prefix 'sub' meaning 'below'. It's that place where *everything* that comes to us through the senses is unconsciously stored or put away while we are busy getting on with our lives. For example, when we read a book, watch television, listen to a story or gather facts about some subject, we do not consciously say to ourselves we're going to put away this or that fact or information. It automatically goes into storage.

Then one day when we're called upon to say or write something impromptu, that is, without preparation, on a subject, we find that the subconscious mind springs to our aid in a most astonishing way. It searches for the information we need and presents it to us, as if on a platter, for our talk or writing. What surprises us after the talk or writing is over is the way everything seemingly falls into place spontaneously, with no apparent effort on our part to organise the material.

We see the same process at work when we learn to do things such as drive, type or speak a foreign language. After doing the same things over and over again we find that the process becomes automatic. We drive or type with such ease or speak the foreign language with such fluency that we marvelled at *how* we're able to do it. Imagine our astonishment if we had been told that it was all done subconsciously, through a mysterious process known as the Association of Ideas or the spontaneous or unconscious putting together of ideas of a similar of contrasting nature.

In the case of Enid Blyton we see this process at work in a variety of ways. It appears to have begun in her childhood, when she used to immerse herself in reading the hundreds of stories she found in Arthur Mee's *Children's Encyclopaedia*. Then when she went to bed, before she fell asleep, she became aware that something was at work putting together bits and pieces of all that she had read or experienced to form new stories in her head. To these stories she gave the name 'Night Stories' or 'Night Thoughts':

'Every night they went on and on in my head until I fell asleep. They were about children I knew and children I didn't know. They were adventures, some with animals in them, and soon I found that they appeared to be made up of many of the things that had happened to me, or that I had read about or heard of in the months that had passed.' [66]

As time went by she noticed that a pattern was emerging. Instead of the stories being all mixed up or confused, as in dreams, they became structured:

'It was almost as if, instead of some part of my mind mixing up everything into a senseless muddle, as dreams are mixed up, that part of my mind had gone carefully and miraculously to work, and had sorted out all the odd bits and pieces of my life and thoughts and reading, and had produced an interesting pattern

of them – a kind of design. And the pattern or design it produced was a story ...' [67]

This was done without her conscious mind taking any part in the phenomenon. So much so that she was astonished when she realised what was happening:

> *'To take a jumble and make of it, not a silly dream, but a sensible story without even trying to is most strange. Who does the sorting out and piecing together? How is it done? How does it come back into my mind all finished and perfect, unwinding itself from beginning to end? Do I do the sorting out; do I arrange the pattern of the story?'* [68]

With experience and practice, the whole process had become so spontaneous that her subconscious mind could furnish her with whole stories on any subject she chose to write about, be it fairies, nature, adventure or even some subject that came to her out of the blue, as can be seen in the following extract drawn from her letter of February 26, 1953 to Professor Peter McKellar:

> *'...For instance, I have been asked to write a book, which will deal with a scout or scouts, with kindness to animals and with a definite religious thread going through it. No more instructions than that ... and when, on Monday, I sit down to begin the book, it will already be complete in my imagination – characters (a scout or scouts will be there) – setting, animals, everything. No thought or planning would have gone to the book ...'* [69]

That she had had ample practice in writing stories to bring about the spontaneous effect, even before she had anything published, can be seen from the following account:

> *'All through my teens I wrote and wrote and wrote – everything I could think of! Poems, stories, articles, even a novel ...'* [70]

In another passage, we find the following statement to substantiate this account:

> *'I had no success at all at the beginning. I had at least **five hundred things** sent back to me and on only one of them was there even a personal note ...'* [71]

Many years later, when she began writing stories that publishers accepted for publication, she realised that that early writing was *'all good practice for me.'* [72]

Moreover, in as much as she did not know how the stories come back into her mind 'all finished and perfect, unwinding itself from beginning to end', as quoted in an earlier passage, she was nevertheless able to recognise the process, and even master it, as can be seen in the following extract from another letter to Professor Peter McKellar of February 26, 1953:

'I did not know that I was 'training' my under-mind (or sub-conscious) in its ability to create and imagine, but I was, of course, and have been all these years. I knew how to get in touch with it, I knew how to be at one with it, I knew how to pull out the imaginings or put them into words – and now, with so much practice, a whole book is formed in a few days, characters alive and complete, incidents, jokes, everything – and my conscious mind has nothing whatever to do with it except record what it sees ...' [73]

This then is evidence to support the theory that the hundreds of stories Enid wrote had been furnished spontaneously to her by her subconscious mind. The expertise she had built up, first from listening to, then reading, and finally writing hundreds of stories had produced patterns which the subconscious mind presented to her ready-made whenever she thought of writing some new story.

Let's now turn our attention to the last theory to be considered: Clairvoyance & Other Psychic Phenomena.

CLAIRVOYANCE & OTHER PSYCHIC PHENOMENA

As stated in the description of Enid's writing method given earlier in this chapter, the first thing she would do, when she sat down to write a new story, was to close her eyes for a minute or two, make her mind blank and wait.

The following account of how the first 'Faraway Tree' story came to her gives us an example of what happens next:

'... Then, as I sit still and look into my mind's eye, my characters

appear. What do I see? Yes – three children, and I know their names – Jo, Bessie and Fanny! They stand there in my mind's eye and I can see them as clearly as I see you when I look at you. I can see if they are tall or short, dark or fair, fat or thin … They stand there complete before me, exactly as they would in real life and I can see every single detail of them … As I look at my new characters … they seem to come alive. They move and laugh and talk – they are real to me now.' [74]

What Enid has given us in this passage is a demonstration of clairvoyance, that mysterious ability to see in the mind's eye people, objects and scenes independent of the eyesight. It has many branches, a description of which is given in Appendix 57.

Enid was, however, not the only fiction writer to see her characters and scenes clairvoyantly. Among those who had this faculty well developed is Frances Browne (1816 – 1879), a successful writer of stories for children (see her photo, Figure 18). This Irish woman who wrote *Granny's Wonderful Chair* in 1856, a fairy story about a girl called Snowflower moving through the air in a chair, has given descriptions of the places the chair took the girl, the people whom she met, the costumes they were wearing and the splendour in the palaces she visited, as well as intense descriptions of characters and scenes in the stories themselves.

However, what is spectacular about her is that she had never seen people in real life and knew nothing about the world around her. She was blind from infancy and could only have written the stories through an inner vision, or clairvoyance, which enabled her to see in her imagination all that she could not see in the real world.

Then there's the case of Robert Houghton, a Scotsman who joined the Enid Blyton Society in 2005. He is well known for his reviews of a cross section of Enid Blyton's books in *The Enid Blyton Society Journal* and for his contributions to its forum. In a post he made to the forum on December 15, 2008 on the 'thread' or subject of 'Enid's Silver Screen Technique', he asserted that when he was writing fiction he could usually 'see' his characters clearly in his head and followed this statement with details in another post dated December 20, 2008:

'...When I imagine characters they do come alive for me in 'glorious technicolor' and I DO see them in my mind's eye: I see how they move, how they talk, what they are wearing, the colour and style of their clothes and hair ... likewise I see the sun and the shadow, the village or churchyard they are standing in, the house they are living in or visiting and it is just as if I could go there myself ...'

Finally, there's the case of J. K. Rowling, the author of the successful Harry Potter stories. During her North American tour in 1999 to promote the Harry Potter books, she appeared on the Diane Rehm show aired on WAMU Radio in Washington D.C., October 20, 1999. Here she told Diane Rehm, and listeners throughout the USA, how Harry first came to her in her imagination:

'It all began when I was travelling by train from Manchester to London ... I saw Harry very, very clearly, very vividly and I knew he didn't know he was a wizard. So I see this skinny little boy with black hair, and green eyes and glasses ... patched up glasses, you know, that got scotch tape around them, holding them together.' [75]

These are all possible explanations of clairvoyance that could fit into the first category in the 'Branches of Clairvoyance' outlined in Appendix 57, namely, Simple (Full or Partial) Clairvoyance (see also Section Two for 'A Short Treatment of Clairvoyance').

So it could be said it was the gift of clairvoyance that brought to life in Enid's imagination all the characters and settings in her stories. For without the animation the stories would have existed in her mind in the form of narratives. Other gifts she's said to possess were clair-audience (clear hearing), clairsentience (clear feeling), clairalience (clear smelling) and clairgustance (clear tasting). A reference she made to these gifts can be found in a passage in another letter to Peter McKellar of February 26, 1953:

'My night 'images' were always more than merely 'images' – they were a coherent line of events in the form of a narrative ... complete with sound, smell, and taste – and feeling!...This is

why I can describe things so realistically in my stories...' [76]

These are all astral counterparts of our physical senses of seeing, hearing, feeling, smelling and tasting and some people with the gift of clairvoyance possess them in varying degrees. However, space does not allow a full treatment of these subjects in this book about Enid Blyton. Readers who are interested and want to know more are advised to read the books listed in the *Bibliography* under Clairvoyance and Spiritualism.

Now it would appear that the gift of clairvoyance had been with her from an early age and not acquired as she developed. This fact was brought to light by a chance remark her elder daughter, Gillian Baverstock, made to a reporter one month before the celebration of the 60th anniversary of Enid Blyton's 'Malory Towers' series of school stories. Here is an extract from the conversation during their encounter:

Gillian: *'By the time she was a teenager, her two brothers were at boarding school. I think she was terribly lonely and withdrew into herself.'*

Anne: *'Was this the origin of her vivid and fecund imagination?'*

Gillian: *'Oh no. She had that right from before she could read and write. She told me once: 'When I was a girl, people I had met or places I had been would come into my head in bed. Then when I grew up I would lie down at night and wait for the stories to come. The characters would walk in fully formed - dress, character, even voice - then the setting ...'* [77]

Had Enid been moving in spiritualist circles, her clairvoyance and other gifts might have been made known to her. And with the possibility of having them fully developed, she could have gone on to become a medium, psychic or seer, giving readings, finding missing persons or making predictions. In this way her life would have taken a different course and all the activities described in this book might not have been!

Nevertheless, she was still able to use the gifts for the benefit of children, whose imaginations were fired by the vivid pictures she reproduced from her imagination, in the countless numbers of stories she had written for them.

So the theory that is now being put forward is that it was clairvoyance and other gifts that provided the animation and dialogues in her stories. It may be regarded as going hand in hand with the previous theory we have just considered, namely, that her subconscious mind was the force behind the automatic production of her stories. This subconscious mind supplied the material and Enid saw the fictitious characters and setting in her mind's eye in every detail and listened to the dialogues.

Now that we have reached the end of the three theories about Enid's writing method or how the stories came to her, it's time to sum up in the conclusion that follows.

CONCLUSION

In summing up the evidence presented to support the three theories, let me remind readers that Enid insisted she could take no credit for her stories. She knew that she did not invent them, but at the same time, she did not know *how* the stories came to her. Therefore the three theories are put forward to find a reasonable explanation for the phenomenon.

Concerning the first theory, that her stories had been written by a supernatural agent through the process of automatic writing, the first thing to take into account is that Enid was writing much more than just fictional stories for children.

Her writing can be put into two categories, namely, imaginative or fictional and thinking or factual. In the first category we find all her stories, poems, plays and songs, and in the second, her Nature Lessons and Nature books; her Nature Readers and Reading Books; her World History courses in *The Teachers World*; her newspapers and magazines articles on a variety of topics and the articles in her column 'From My Window' in *The Teachers World*.

However, in the nine letters she wrote to Professor Peter McKellar, the psychologist who was investigating her writing method, she referred only to the work described in the first category and made no reference at all to how she did the work in the second.

In reality the work in the second category is work for which she could take credit and must have been proud to do so, because it stemmed from her schooling, her vast readings and from her teacher training course, all of which was neatly filed away in her photographic memory to recall and use at will.

However, in as much as she claimed she could take no credit for her stories while silently taking credit for her thinking work, if she somehow knew that a disembodied soul – a soul without a body – used her as a medium to get out the stories, and gave the world the impression she knew nothing, then it would have been one of the most carefully guarded secrets she took with her to the grave.

There's however no reason to believe that was the case, for everything points to the second theory, which is, that her subconscious mind was the force behind the automatic production of her stories. That she herself had been aware of this can be seen in the following extract from an account she gave to Professor Peter McKellar in her letter to him of Feb 26, 1953:

> *'I think my imagination contains all the things I have ever seen or heard, things my conscious mind has long forgotten – and they have all been jumbled about till a light penetrates into the mass, and a happening here or an object there is taken out, transmuted, or formed into something that takes a natural and rightful place in the story – or I may recognise it – or I may not – I don't think that I use anything I have not seen or experienced – I don't think I could…'* [78]

This statement alone sums up the evidence for this second theory. For when we examine a cross section of her stories, we find traces of all that she mentions. For example, the title of Robert Louis Stevenson's adventure book, *Treasure Island*, resurfaced in the title of her first Famous Five book, *Five on a Treasure Island*.

In Stevenson's plot we find a wreck, seaweed, boat, map, bars of gold, island inlet, along with words such as torch, rope, axe and spade, all of which featured prominently in the plot for *Five on a Treasure Island*.

(It should be pointed out that Enid stated on page 52 of *The Story of My Life* that she used to read her brother's books. So that's possibly where the key elements might have come from.)

FIGURE 35: Left: Snowflower, sitting in 'Granny's Wonderful Chair', as it moves through the air, taking her wherever she wanted to go. From the cover of Granny's Wonderful Chair by Frances Brown, published in 1857 by unknown publisher. Right: Peter and Mollie, sitting in a chair in Enid Blyton's Adventures of the Wishing Chair, as they too move through the air in a series of adventures. From an illustration by Hilda McGavin on page 11 of the first edition of The Adventures of the Wishing Chair, published by George Newnes in 1937. Images restoration credit: 2graphic Photo Restoration. Website: www.photo-restoration.co.uk

In her story *The Adventures of the Wishing Chair*, we can clearly see the association with *Granny's Wonderful Chair* by the blind Irish author, Frances Browne. The idea of Frances's chair responding to the wishes of Snowflower, the heroine in the story, by taking her wherever she wanted to go, was retained in *The Adventures of the Wishing Chair*, with the exception that there are two children, Peter and Mollie commanding the chair rather than just one child, in a series of new adventures, far removed from those in *Granny's Wonderful Chair* (see illustration, Figure 35).

The description of the activities in the Yggdrasil or World Tree that she had retained from reading the Norse Myths in the *Children's Encyclopaedia* was to create the setting for *The Magic Faraway Tree*. The nine worlds under this tree were transposed into seven lands at the top of *The Faraway Tree*. Even the squirrel that runs up and down the

Yggdrasil tree to carry messages has been retained to coordinate the children's movements in *The Magic Faraway Tree.*

In Lewis Carroll's *Through the Looking Glass*, Tweedledum, wearing a saucepan for a helmet, resurfaced in the Faraway Tree trilogy as the Saucepan Man, with many more saucepans.[79]

In *Little Women* by Louisa Alcott, a book Enid said she had read 'again and again', Josephine, one of four sisters, was disappointed at not being a boy: '*... I can't get over my disappointment at not being a boy.*'[80]

In *Five on a Treasure Island*, Enid made Georgina, the cousin of Julian, Dick and Anne, express the same sentiment, but with different words: '*I hate being a girl ... I like doing the things that boys do..*'[81] Henceforth, she refused to respond to the name Georgina and insisted on being called George.

Furthermore, her eagle eyes and photographic memory had retained all that she had seen and heard during her cruise to Madeira and the Canary Islands aboard the Stella Polaris in October 1930. These were to provide the setting for the eight books in her Adventure Series.

These examples are only a fraction of the material in her subconscious mind that flowed spontaneously and unintentionally into her stories as she wrote them, through the process known as the Association of Ideas. They also help to substantiate the theory that it was her subconscious mind that was the force behind the seamless production of her stories.

In the light of this situation we can now clearly see the role her attributes such as her vast readings and photographic memory played in the production of her stories. For it was the stories that were told to her as a child, the patterns or models of the hundreds of stories she read in *The Children's Encyclopaedia*, the practice she got from writing hundreds of stories before she even got one of them published, and the fixation of all this in her photographic memory that was to set the stage for the automatic production of her stories.

For just as how, in the examples stated earlier in this section, the subconscious mind would furnish us with the material for out talk or writing spontaneously, once the topic is known, with no effort on our part to organise it, so her subconscious mind *presented* whole stories to her every time she sat to write a story. The only condition was for her to decide beforehand what story to write and the subconscious mind did the rest. So here in a nutshell the mystery of how she was able to get 'ready-made' stories every time she sat down to write a story is unraveled.

However, what she was not aware of was that she possessed clairvoyance and other gifts, which is the third theory put forward for consideration. It was this faculty that brought to life in her imagination images of all the new stories that were spontaneously concocted by her subconscious mind. Having thus seen the whole story in her mind's eye, it was easy for her to write it out exactly as she had seen it, as opposed to struggling to write out a plot that she had consciously invented. So the two theories to be retained as the most plausible are the workings of her subconscious mind and clairvoyance and other psychic gifts. The theory of a disembodied soul, that is, the soul or spirit of someone who has lived on this earth before, using her as a medium to get out his/her stories through the process of automatic writing, is rejected.

Notwithstanding this result, it could be said that the initiator in the entire process is her strong will without which the stories would not have come into being at all. An example of this can be seen in an account she gave to Professor Peter Mc Kellar in her letter of February 26, 1953. In this account, she stated that she had been asked to write a story about scouts, with kindness to animals and a religious thread running through it. No other instructions had been given:

> '...All I have done is to say **firmly** to myself – there must be a scout or scouts – animals – and ethics – and I leave it at that and don't think another word about it. But those conscious directions penetrate down into the imagination and when, on Monday, I sit down to begin the book, it will already be completed in my imagination – characters, (a scout or scouts will be there) setting, animals, everything. No thought or planning will have gone to the book ...' [82]

From this we may infer that if there was no will or desire to write a story, then it would not have come into being at all. For it was her strong will that sent her subconscious mind searching for material for her stories and the exercise of her clairvoyant and other faculties enabled her to see the entire stories presented to her in response to the demand of her will.[83] This then is my conclusion after summing up the evidence presented to support the three theories.

What conclusion would you arrive at?

---

*The epigraph, *There are in the mind of Man many faculties which are outside of the realm of consciousness,* cited earlier in the section of the Subconscious Mind in this chapter, is drawn from Chapter IX, page 51 of *The Law of the New Thought* by William Walker Atkinson (1862 – 1932), published by Psychic Research Co. Chicago, 1902.

CHAPTER VIII
ENID THE PLAYWRIGHT

OVERVIEW

That Enid branched out into playwriting at a time when she had so many things going on will surprise many of us. With no formal training in this field she was, apparently, ill-equipped to practice the art. Yet by the time she was twenty-five years old she was writing plays for schools at first, and then for the theatre many years later, plays that captivated audiences of children everywhere and earn her warm praise and admiration from all quarters.

In this chapter we find out how it all began, learn something about her plays published in books and other media and marvel at how she was able to harness or adapt her writing method, as described in the previous chapter, to the new medium. Then we take a look at the two stage plays she wrote for performance in the theatre and at the only one she wrote for adults. Finally, we try to find out why her plays did not survive and consider what can be done to bring them back into circulation. The headings under which these matters are presented are as follows:

1. In the Beginning
2. Musical Plays for Schools
3. Adapting her Writing Method to Stage Plays for the Theatre
4. Plays for Staging in the Theatre
5. 'The Summer Storm' – A Stage Play for Adults
6. Why her Plays did not Survive

IN THE BEGINNING

Enid's ability to write plays for schools really began to show itself in January 1920, when the Thompson Family[84] engaged her as Nursery Governess to teach their four children in their own home. At that time, she had just left Bickley Park School for Boys, where she taught for about a year, and was delighted when her close friend, Mabel Attenborough, recommended her for the job. In time, the class expanded when neighbours asked for their children to be taught along with the boys.[85] In this new setting, she was free to use her plays, poems, stories and songs for the children in her charge.

According to Barbara Stoney, her official biographer, on page 42 of *Enid Blyton: A Biography,* '*she would write small plays for the children to act, poems for them to recite and songs for them to sing and twice a year these would be incorporated into a concert for parents and friends.*' Then, when she gave up classroom teaching altogether to concentrate on teaching through the medium of her pen, several outlets for her newly found talent soon presented themselves. The first was her *The Teachers' Treasury* that Georges Newnes Ltd published in 1926. In this book she created a whole section for six plays, in addition to sections she created for her songs, poems and stories (see Appendix 58, Table I for a list of the plays in this book).

Another outlet for her plays was *The Teachers World.* This newspaper that gave her such a wonderful opportunity to showcase her poems, songs, Christmas carols, 'Stories of World History' and numerous articles for her column, soon began accepting her plays for publications (see illustration, Appendix 59 for *King Cole Calling!,* one of her plays carried in this medium). Other plays she wrote for this medium include *A Regular Muddle* (edition of October 31, 1923), *The Union Jack* (April 29, 1925), *The League of Nations* (February 5, 1926), *The Princess and the Enchanter* (July 24, 1935).

A third outlet for her plays was her *Enid Blyton's Book of the Year,* published by Evans Brothers Ltd in 1941. In this book, which she wrote for teachers, we find a whole section packed with twelve of her plays, complete with detailed instructions about how they were to be staged in schools (see Appendix 58 for a list of the plays in this book).

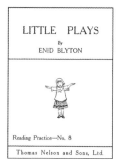

FIGURE 19: A selection of book covers of plays Enid Blyton wrote for performance in schools between 1927 and 1955. A Book of Little Plays at the bottom was also used in schools to give children reading practice. © British Library Board: Six Enid Blyton Plays (SM: 011779.e.163, title page.); The Wishing Bean, and Other Plays (SM: 11782.c.20, title page.); Mr. Sly-One and the Cats (SM: 11785.a.22, cover); Finding the Tickets (SM: 11785.a.23, cover); Who will hold the Giant (SM: 11785.a.24, cover); The Mothers' Meeting (SM: 11785.a.25, cover); Little Plays, classed under Reading Practice No 8, (SM: 20031.a.8, cover.).

In 1955, the publisher selected four of these plays and brought them out individually under the following headings: *Mr. Sly-One and the Cats, Finding the Tickets, Who Will Hold the Giant* and *The Mothers' Meeting*. The front covers illustration for these four plays can be seen in Figure 19.

Apart from her plays being published in the two books for teachers, she also released batches of her plays in standard books. The first in this category is *Six Enid Blyton Plays* which Methuen & Co published in 1935. Here we find six plays in one, two and three acts whose titles can be seen in Appendix 58, Table I. An interesting review of these plays was carried by *The Teachers World and the Schoolmistress* in the edition of October 23, 1935, a facsimile of which is presented in Appendix 60.

This was followed by two plays she published in *Cameo Plays*, Book III and eight, in Book IV, edited by G. Holroyd and published by E. J. Arnold in 1939. One of the plays in Book III, *The Spick-And-Span Stone* is recycled from her *The Teachers' Treasury* and the other, *Brer Rabbit Tricks Mister Lion*, is specially written. These plays, along with those in Book IV, are listed in Appendix 58, Table I.

Then in 1939, another batch of six plays saw the light of day in *The Wishing Bean and Other Plays*, published by Blackwell. The titles of the six plays are presented in Appendix 58, Table I.

Here's a passage from a review of The *Wishing Bean* that was carried in the 'Book Review' section of *Hull Daily Mail,* in the edition of Friday, October 20, 1939:

Plays for Children

'If you had three wishes ...' is a proposition of interest not merely to those young enough to profess without shame a belief in fairies. But magic appeals for its own sake ... and for that reason Enid Blyton's book of little plays should delight hosts of young readers – and actors. "The Wishing Bean and Other Plays" (Basil Blackwell, 2s 6d) should be a useful book to have about the place when the children are home for Christmas – or in 'foster' homes for evacuees. Altogether, there are six plays, each of them enormous fun to act...

Here are some more reviews of her straight plays, this time culled from the regional press:

The Dover Express & East Kent News

Friday, December 18, 1931

ADISHAM

A well attended concert was held in the school on Wednesday evening, given by the school children of Adisham school and organised by Miss Golding (Headmistress) Miss Marsh and Mr. Smith (teachers) ... The chief item was the play 'The Wishing Glove' by Enid Blyton, well acted by the following children ...

(A list of the names of the children was given and the writer went on to give news of other performances by senior children at the concert before bringing the review to a close).

The Tamworth Herald

April 10, 1943

BROWNIES BRIGHT ENTERTAINMENT

At the Assembly Rooms, Tamworth on Wednesday evening (April 7, 1943) members of the Tamworth Brownies Pack gave a capital entertainment to a crowded audience...

'The main feature of the entertainment was "The King's Jester," a play in three acts by Enid Blyton, produced by Miss J. Laidler. The performance was greatly enhanced by brightly coloured costumes and effective scenery and was a highly credible show for such young children ... The company was composed of girls from Tamworth, Wales, Coventry, Birmingham, London, Liverpool, Broadstairs and Margate...

The Western Times, Devon

Friday June 23, 1950

GOOD SHOW BY JUVENILES

Scholars of Okehampton County Primary School distinguished themselves on Wednesday evening when they were responsible for one of the best juvenile performances seen in the town for many years. Seven-year-olds were seen to advantage in "The Toys That Came Alive," a play by Enid Blyton. The cast consisted of fourteen boys and girls (whose names were given in the article) *and the play was produced by Miss M.C. Rowe.*

Another Enid Blyton story, "Crying for the Moon," was presented by the eight-year-old children who provided first-class entertainment. The cast consisted of fifteen boys and girls (whose names were given in the article) *and the show was produced by Mrs. F.G. Yeo.*

Enid also wrote a curious little book of plays, not for staging in schools, but to give children reading practice. Entitled: *Little Plays* (the title was changed to *A Book of Little Plays* in another edition), it contains five small plays with simple dialogues that read as if they were part of a story (see title page illustration, Figure 19). After each reading exercise, children were tested for comprehension and were given oral and written exercises. The titles of these special plays are presented in Appendix 58, Table I.

MUSICAL PLAYS FOR SCHOOLS

In Chapter VI, *Enid: The Prolific Songwriter*, we learned about the staggering amount of songs Enid wrote for her musical plays. Here we now have the opportunity to have a close look at these plays. There are two books of plays in this category: *The Play's The Thing!* and *The Blyton – Sharman Musical Plays for Juniors*. Let us start with the first: *The Play's The Thing!*

THE PLAY'S THE THING!

Her first book of musical plays, *The Play's The Thing!* That was first published in 1927 by The Home Library Book Company Ltd contains twelve musical plays in one, two, three and four acts (see title page illustration, Figure 20).

To give an idea of the structure of one of the plays, I have included a synopsis of *The King's Pocket Knife* in Appendix 62. The surprising ending in this play is a strong feature of most of the plays in the book.

To generate interest in the book, the publisher ran brilliant display advertisements in the school press. Beautifully written by copywriters and advertising professionals, the advertisements highlight all the features that make the plays unique. A facsimile reproduction of one of these advertisements, carried in *Child Education*, in the edition of January, 1928, can be seen in Appendix 61.

Moreover, her publisher commissioned Alfred Bestall, a talented illustrator of the day, to design the costumes for the characters to wear in the plays (see Figure 20 for a facsimile of costumes he designed for one of the plays, *The King's Pocket Knife*).

Thirteen years later, George Newnes republished the twelve plays in two separate volumes: *Plays for Older Children* and *Plays for Younger Children.*

My assessment of these musical plays in several acts is that they have been carefully written, with well-constructed plots. In fact, everything about them – from the preface that gives guidelines for staging the plays to the description of the scenes and props to be used – gives an impression of professionalism. It's these musical plays, more than any other she has written, that mark her out as a talented playwright. A list of the twelve plays can be seen in Appendix 63, Table II.

THE BLYTON-SHARMAN MUSICAL PLAYS FOR JUNIORS

This is the second and last set of musical plays Enid wrote for performance in schools under the title: *The Blyton-Sharman Musical Plays for Juniors,* published by A. Wheaton in 1939. Those of us who have the opportunity to examine this book today will notice that there's another title inside the book: *How The Flowers Grow and Other Musical Plays.* It is these two different titles that led researchers to believe they are two separate books but, in reality, they both refer to the same book.

A further examination of the book will show that it contains only the scores for the music in the plays. The plays were published separately. An illustration of the front covers of these plays can be seen in Figure 21, along with an illustration of the two titles relating to the same book.

THE PLAY'S THE THING!

The
MUSICAL PLAYS
FOR CHILDREN
BY
ENID BLYTON

WITH MUSIC BY
ALEC ROWLEY

AND TWENTY-FOUR FULL PAGE DRAWINGS BY
ALFRED E. BESTALL

THE
HOME LIBRARY BOOK COMPANY
(GEORGE NEWNES LTD)
67 & 68 CHANDOS STREET W.C. 2.

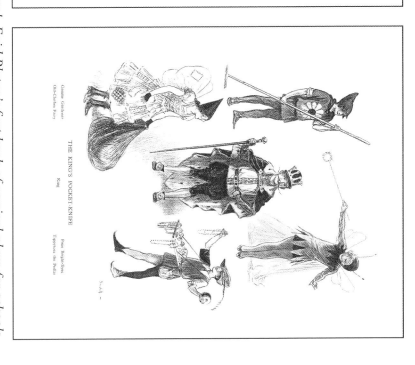

Gnome Gardener
Old-Clothes Fairy

THE KING'S POCKET KNIFE

King

Pixie Bright-Eyes
Tippytoes the Pedlar

FIGURE 20: Left, title page of The Play's The Thing!, Enid Blyton's first book of musical plays for schools. Right, Alfred E. Bestall's illustration of costumes for actors to wear in 'The King's Pocket Knife', one of the twelve musical plays in the book. © British Library Board (SM: L.R.261.a.8 title page and plate 4).

135

In one of the preliminary pages of the book the publisher slipped in the following note for the attention of head teachers browsing the pages before buying the book for their schools:

Six Musical Plays for Juniors

The name of Miss Blyton as author of plays for young children and of Mr. C. Sharman as a composer of music carry full conviction. We have much pleasure in announcing the publication of the following plays by Miss Blyton with incidental songs set to music by C. Sharman:

How the Flowers Grow

The Fairy in the Box

The Magic Ball

The Toys at Night-Time

Who Stole the Crown?

Santa Claus Gets Busy

Elsewhere it is stated that the six plays referred to can be purchased separately.

This then is a chronicle of her plays, both straight and musical, that many of us reading this chapter are seeing for the first time. Starting in 1926, they reached their peak in 1939 and would have continued to shine in schools, had it not been for the turbulent events of the Second World War (1939 – 1945) that disrupted normal school activities and put an end to her creativity in this field.

Nevertheless, her ability to write plays did not go away entirely, but came back in full swing many years later when she discovered another medium for staging plays, and, eventually, adapted her new writing method to write them. Let us now turn our attention to this new medium to witness, once again, her extraordinary writing method in action.

ADAPTING HER WRITING METHOD TO STAGE PLAYS FOR THE THEATRE

If we go back to the description of Enid's writing method given in Chapter VII, Section Two, *Enid: The Professional Storyteller*, we find that when the story came to an end the characters would fade away. Where they went to no one knows. Then one day a host of them suddenly reappeared from their own stories and congregated in her imagination. They all came back to feature in her first stage play for the theatre – *Noddy in Toyland!*

Although Enid herself appeared to be surprised when this happened, their reunion was something she herself had brought about in her imagination many years ago, but soon forgot in the hustle and bustle in getting her other projects going. This we can clearly see in the following extract from an account she gave on page 102 of *The Story of My Life*:

> *'...I sometimes think I would like to write a stage-play for you children – perhaps a kind of mixture of a pantomime [Christmas play] and a play, because then I could bring in the Saucepan Man and Moonface, Little Noddy, Josie, Click and Bun, Mr. Pink-Whistle, the Three Golliwogs and all the rest. What do you think?'*

These lines were penned in 1952, when *The Story of My Life* was published, and since that time the idea of writing such a play was brewing in her mind so that when the opportunity presented itself in 1954, she sat down and used her powerful writing method to bring the play into being.

At first it was not easy, for her writing method was adapted for writing stories, not stage plays. But after two to three days of trying, she succeeded in getting the 'cinema screen' in her imagination to function once again. The rest is like magic, as can be seen from the following extract from an account she gave to Professor Peter McKellar in another letter of January 28, 1955.[86]

> *'...For the first two days I endeavoured to use the same process of writing as I use for my books – finding characters and settings and then using the 'cinema screen' in my mind ... This method was a complete failure for the writing of the play ... I stumbled over the writing. I laboured, I could not draw on my imagin-ation at all. Then like a flash I seemed to discard the old way of writing, and instead of needing to see characters in their story*

setting ... into my mind came the stage itself, all set with scenery. And then in came the characters of this stage, singing, talking, dancing – and once again something went 'click' and the whole writing of the play went out of my hands and was taken over by my imagination again...'

Now if we reflect on what she wrote in the passage drawn from page 102 of *The Story of My Life* cited earlier, we see that it was her strong will to reunite a host of characters from her books that led to the creation of the new stage play, *Noddy in Toyland*. The instructions were sent to her subconscious mind and when she found time to write the new stage play, it furnished her with all the characters and scenery she wanted to see reunited on the stage.

Moreover, with the faculty of clairvoyance, which we have seen at work in the previous section, the whole play was brought to life from start to finish, complete with the characters in their favourite clothes and with bits and pieces from her books, such as Noddy's car, Big Ears bicycle and so on. It took her sometime to get started, for the method was new, but when it was over she had already become familiar with it and was able to use it, once again, to write what was to be her second and last stage play for the theatre: *The Famous Five*.

Now that we've seen how some of the characters from her storybooks came back to feature in *Noddy in Toyland,* and how the stage play came into being, let us now take a close look at the play itself, and at another*, The Famous Five* to see what we may learn about them.

PLAYS FOR STAGING IN THE THEATRE – NODDY IN TOYLAND

Noddy in Toyland is a musical play in three acts, produced by Bertie Meyer and directed by Andre Van Gyseghem. The musical director was Philip Green. Act 1 is set in Toyland Village and The Enchanted Wood. Act II, in Moonface's room in the Faraway Tree and a market in Goblin-Town. Act III, in Toyland Village.

It was first performed at the Stoll Theatre, London, on December 23, 1954. Promotion for the show was done in Enid's own *Enid Blyton's Magazine* whose fortnightly circulation was about 60,000 copies (see Appendix 64 for a full-page advertisement for the play). It was

FIGURE 21: *Front covers of the six musical plays for juniors Enid Blyton wrote for performance in schools. These books were published in: The Blyton-Sharman Musical Plays, the seventh item listed here, and appear here individually. The songs for the six plays in: How the Flowers Grow, and other Musical Plays, the eight item on this list, were also bound in this book. © British Library Board: The Blyton-Sharman Musical Plays for Juniors (SM: 11782.b.46, cover.); How the Flowers grow, and other Musical Plays (SM: Music Collections H.3830, cover.) Image restoration credit: 2graphic Photo Restoration: Website: www.photo-restoration.co.uk.*

139

therefore a fitting medium to carry advertisements to promote the show.

The tickets were quickly snapped up by her fans that came to the show in droves, displaying their badges for the various fan clubs into which Enid had organised them. These clubs were: The Busy Bee Club, The Famous Five Club, The Enid Blyton's Magazine Club and The Sunbeam Society whose meeting place was in the magazine itself (see A Brief History of *The Enid Blyton's Magazine* in Section Two for more information about these fan clubs). Enid herself was there to greet them at the opening performance.

Soon the children were carried away by brilliant performances from child stars such as Bunny May who played Noddy and Susan Hatch who played Silky the Pixie.

'*As each character made his appearance at the opening matinee*', states *Plays & Players* in reviewing the play, '*the youngsters let out shouts of recognition that would scare the lives out of the toughest commandos ... The story evolves with the utmost simplicity, the settings by Richard Lake are enchanting in their bold colours and Philip Green's music is often captivating.*' [87] The play also received publicity in the *Tatler & Bystander*, in the issue of December 15, 1954, and a favourable review in *The Daily Telegraph*, in the issue of December 24, 1956, soon after its third annual performance.

Finally, according to an account given by Barbara Stoney on page 163 of *Enid Blyton: A Biography, 'Noddy in Toyland continued to play to packed houses in London, the provinces and overseas during the nine years that followed its first performance.'*

Two years after its first staging in 1954, Sampson Low, one of Enid Blyton's numerous publishers, published the play in book form under the title: *Enid Blyton's Book of Her Famous Play Noddy in Toyland* (see Appendix 64 for the cover page illustration).

THE FAMOUS FIVE STAGE PLAY

Very little was known about this play other than that which was carried in an advertisement in *The Enid Blyton's Magazine* in the issue of December 7, 1955 (see Appendix 64 for illustration). Here we see that it had its premier at the Princes Theatre in London December 23, 1955 and was staged nightly, while *Noddy in Toyland* was staged earlier in the day. It's a straight play of adventure and mystery for older children, hence being staged at night. Based on her Famous Five series of books, it features Julian, Dick, Anne, George and Timmy the Dog, characters whose names rang a bell for her many fans all around the world.

The mystery surrounding the play is deepened because it was not even published in book form. Curious to know why that was so, Norman Wright of the Enid Blyton Society began investigations that led him to discover a carbon copy of the play in the archives of Darrell Waters Ltd, Enid Blyton's own company. Typed by Enid Blyton herself with her hand-written corrections, this carbon copy of some 35,000 words gave him only some of the information he was seeking.

Nevertheless, after studying it carefully, he was able to glean it was a new story in the form of a full-length play in three acts. The first act is set in Kirrin Cottage, the second at a fairground and the third, on Kirrin Island. After successful negotiations with the officials of the company he brought the book out in a limited edition of 350 copies. [88] This then is all the information available for this remarkable stage play for older children.

THE SUMMER STORM – A STAGE PLAY FOR ADULTS

This full-length play of 90,000 words was written by Enid Blyton, under the nom-de-plume of Justin Geste, for the adult theatre, but its production never got off the ground. Let's turn to the following account her biographer, Barbary Story, gave in passages drawn from pages 169 and 170 of *Enid Blyton: A Biography* to find out the reason:

> *'The play – The Summer Storm – was duly sent to several theatrical managers for consideration but it was apparent ... that as it stood it was totally unsuitable for staging. The over-dramatised theme was one of marital intrigue and mistaken parentage, set in an upper-middle-class background. It had ten characters, required five different stage settings ... and would have involved drastic rewriting, great ingenuity over the changing of the sets and weighty production costs which, it*

would appear, no one was prepared to risk ...'

It was probably these considerations on the one hand, and the fact that it did not find favour with her literary agent, George Greenfield, on the other, that caused her to put the play aside and never look at it again. A fuller account of this situation can be found in *Enid Blyton* by her literary agent, George Greenfield, published by Sutton Publishing Ltd in 1998.[89]

SOME REASONS ENID BLYTON'S PLAYS DID NOT SURVIVE

If there was one factor that signalled the end of the staging of her plays in schools, it would be the Second World War (1939 – 1945). The disruption to the school system during the conflict is incalculable. Apart from schools being closed permanently as the conflict escalated, thousands of schoolchildren were evacuated from cities to the counties and even overseas for their own safety.

When the war was over in 1945, the entire teacher training system was eventually overhauled, new curricula were devised and new teaching methods brought in to respond to the rapid political, cultural and economic changes taking place in the country.

So it was that teaching methods that relied on productions from educators, professional textbooks writers and from former teachers such as Enid Blyton, were either sidelined or cast aside to make way for the new. Because of this, the material Enid produced for schools such as *The Teachers' Treasury, The Enid Blyton's Book of the Year,* reading books, nature readers, poetry and songbooks and her books of plays, soon fell into oblivion.

In the light of this situation, the question that now presents itself here is this: Can the plays chronicled in this chapter be brought back into circulation in schools? The answer is yes, possibly, but to do this, they would all need to be reviewed and only those plays deemed relevant to modern living would then be selected and modified where necessary.

With regards to her two stage plays, *Noddy in Toyland* and *The Famous Five* they too can be brought back into circulation and given a new lease of life. After all, her Famous Five books and films as well

142

as the Noddy series of books are now enjoying a revival. Why not her stage plays? [90]

CHAPTER IX
ENID THE ARTIST & ILLUSTRATOR

OVERVIEW

In previous chapters, we've seen Enid as a poet, songwriter and playwright and learned about her poems, songs and plays. In this chapter, we look at the last and least known of all her artistic endowments – that of an artist and illustrator.

In doing so, we are taken first of all into the field of physiognomy – the science of reading character and revealing gifts, talents and special abilities from studying the features of the face. A brief history of physiognomy is given in Section Two, under the heading: Physiognomy & Phrenology – The Rise and Fall of Two Great 'Sciences'.

Is it true that they're signs in the face for gifts, talents and special abilities? If so, did Enid's face show any such sign(s)? The answers to these questions can be found in this chapter. We then move on to consider evidence to support the assertion that she was an artist and illustrator. After considering the debt she owed to her numerous illustrators, we take a quick look at theories about where artistic gifts come from.

If we study any photograph of Enid Blyton in circulation, we'd be struck by a particular feature – a round dimple in her chin, (see example in her photo, below). We marvel when we see it and wonder if it has a meaning, the more so because it is not present in the chin of every face we see. Well, it does have a meaning, which is this: it indicates a tendency towards some form of art such as music, drawing and painting, or poetry. This meaning forms part of a theory John Spon, a theoretical and practical physiognomist, put forward in his book: *The Science of Physiognomy: Theoretical and Practical*, which Herbert Jenkins published in 1947 in London, England.

Photo credit: Evening Standard

This is how he summed up the theory in a passage on page 178 of the book:

'A round dimple in the chin denotes art-loving tastes. It is caused by a blending of round muscles and round bones, and this combination is best adapted to assist every species of art except sculpture ... Nearly all great poets, painters, actors, writers, athletes, etc., have either a round or cleft dimple ... it is a direct indication of their talent ... in all faces in which the muscular or artistic chin is observed, when not dimpled, it is nevertheless well rounded and is soft and mobile, and should be classed with the dimpled chin.'

Here he's referring to three types of formation in the chin: a round dimple, a cleft dimple and a well-rounded or 'ball-shaped' formation, soft and mobile, that should be classed with the dimpled chin. We'll soon see examples of each type as we go along.

Evidence to substantiate the assertion can be seen in the chins of musical masters such as Beethoven, Bellini, Schumann, Bach, Handel,

Liszt, and Schubert and in those of poets such as W.B. Yeats and Lord Byron (See Figure 22 for particular examples of a dimple in the chin of a selection of male composers, poets and painters). It's also seen in the chins of actors such as Sir Laurence Olivier, Kirk Douglas, George Montgomery, Christopher Dean and Cary Grant and in those of illustrators such as Matthew Pritchett MBE, *The Daily Telegraph's* cartoonist, and Peter Wienk, illustrator of the Noddy books.[91]

Furthermore, it can be seen in the chins of female painters, composers and illustrators such as Marianne von Martinez (1744 – 1812) Austrian, singer, pianist and composer; Margaret Isabel Dicksee (1858 – 1903) British painter; Sofonisba Anguissola (1532 – 1625) Italian Renaissance painter; Eileen Soper, British illustrator (1905 – 1990); Edmonia Lewis (1844 – 1907), African-American sculptor and artist; Amy Beach (1867 – 1944) American composer and pianist; Beatrix Potter (1866 – 1943) English writer and illustrator, and Enid Blyton (1897 – 1968) who was, as we've seen in other chapters, a pianist turned songwriter, playwright, poet, author and, as we'll soon see, an artist and illustrator (See Figure 23 for particular examples of a dimple in the chin of a selection of female composers, painters and illustrators).

Having understood that the round dimple in Enid's chin is indicative of, among other things, her talent for painting and drawing, let us look for supporting evidence. The first reference we find is in a passage on page 75 of *The Story of My Life*. Here she stated that she had once spent a part of her holiday on a farm and that every Sunday she used to go off to teach in the Sunday school:

'I told stories – Bible stories – to a class of wide-eyed, listening children ... I drew and painted big pictures for the Sunday-school wall. I helped in the handiwork the children often did in that well-run and interesting Sunday school.'

Since this is just about all we can find on the subject in that book, let us turn to a passage on page 33 of Barbara Stoney's *Enid Blyton: A Biography,* to fill the gap. Here she's telling us something about what Enid used to do during her teacher training at Ipswich High School:

VINCENZO BELLINI   **WILLIAM YEATS**   **ROBERT SCHUMANN**

LORD BYRON   **JOHANN SEBASTIAN BACH**   **S. COLERIDGE-TAYLOR**

FIGURE 22: A selection from male composers and poets whose chins show one of the three formations, namely, a round dimple, cleft dimple, well-rounded or ball-shaped.
Top, from left to right: Vincenzo Bellini (1801 – 1835) Italian composer (round dimple); William Yeats (1865 – 1939) Irish poet (well-rounded or ball-shaped); Robert Schumann (1810 – 1856) German composer (round dimple); Lord Byron (1788 – 1824) English poet (cleft dimple); Johann Sebastian Bach (1685 – 1750 German composer (round dimple) and Samuel Coleridge-Taylor (1875 – 1912) English composer (cleft dimple). Photos restoration credit: 2graphic Photo Restoration: Website: www.photo-restoration.co.uk.

'...She was no mean artist and carried a small blue book with her everywhere, in which she sketched her charges at play or drew birds and animals seen on the 'nature walks'. She kept a similar book during her last year at school and these two volumes of pencilled drawings provide an interesting insight into how Enid viewed her world at that time ...'

ENID BLYTON   AMY BEACH   MARGARET DICKSEE

EILEEN SOPER   BEATRIX POTTER   EDMONIA LEWIS

FIGURE 23: A selection from female composers, poets, sculptures and artists whose chins show one of the three formations, namely, a round dimple, cleft dimple, well-rounded or ball-shaped.

Top row: Enid Blyton (1897- 1968) whose talents include writing children's books and illustrating her own articles in The Teachers World (round dimple); Amy Marcy Beach (1867 – 1944) American composer and pianist (round dimple); Margaret Isabel Dicksee (1858 – 1903) British painter (well-rounded or ball-shaped).

Bottom row: Eileen Soper (1905 – 1990) illustrator of children's and wildlife books, including Enid Blyton's Famous Five series of books (well-rounded or ball-shaped.); Beatrix Potter as a child (1866 – 1943) English children's writer, illustrator and painter (well-rounded or ball shaped); Edmonia Lewis (1844 – 1907) Black American sculptor and artist (well-rounded or ball-shaped formation).

Photo credits: Enid Blyton, Evening Standard. (The photo was restored by 2graphic Photo Restoration.) Amy Beach: Library of Congress/Bain Collection; Margaret Dicksee: Alamy.com; Beatrix Potter as a child: The Beatrix Potter Society; Edmonia Lewis: National Portrait Gallery (USA), Smithsonian Institution. The photo of Eileen Soper is drawn from the back page of Wildings: The Secret Garden of Eileen Soper by Duff Hart-Davis. The source of the photo was stated nowhere in the book.

(See figure 24, for a reproduction of a selection of these sketches Barbara Stoney presented between pages 48 and 49 in the same book.) Barbara Stoney also tells us on page 17 of the biography that Miss Read, the teacher at a small nursery class she attended at a house called 'Tresco', found, among other things, that Enid '*was one of the best pupils at art and nature study*'… From this statement, we can see that the aptitude for drawing was present from early childhood but gave way to her other interests as she developed.

This aptitude for drawing, somewhat neglected after her spell of classroom teaching, was to come to life again when *The Teachers World* commissioned her to write a series of nature lessons for schoolchildren (see *Enid: The Naturalist*, Chapter I, where this theme is fully developed). Instead of commissioning in turn an artist to illustrate her lessons, she did all the illustrations herself. Take another look at the illustration in Appendix 2. This fine pen and ink drawing of 'Gorse' is Enid's first public demonstration of her aptitude for drawing. A closer examination of this illustration reveals her initials, E.B. at the bottom left-hand corner of the drawing. She went on to illustrate every other

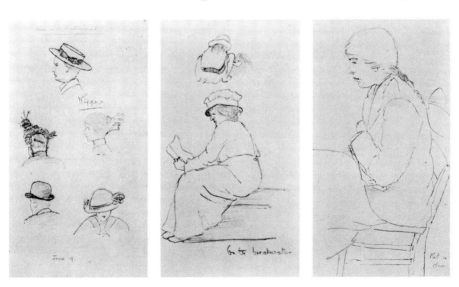

FIGURE 24: Sketches from Enid Blyton's drawing book, during her last year at school. Reproduced from a copy carried between pages 48 and 49 of Barbara Stoney's Enid Blyton: A Biography, published in 1974 by Hodder & Stoughton Ltd. Courtesy Bob Stoney.

lesson in the series until it came to an end August 17, 1927 (see Figure 25 for examples of some of these illustrations, drawn from a cross-section of her 'Nature Lessons' and from her 'Round The Year With Enid Blyton', another nature study course she had been commissioned to write). As this latter course borders on her gardening experience it is treated fully in the next chapter, *Enid: The Passionate Gardener.*

With such fine drawing skills, Enid was in a very good position to illustrate her stories in the numerous storybooks she wrote for children. Yet she and her publishers found it convenient to engage outside illustrators and artists to do the job. The decision to involve outsiders is commendable, for taking on the additional task of illustrating her stories would have robbed her of valuable time to get out her poems, songs, plays, stories and nature lessons, and to keep abreast with her numerous writing and editorial commitments.

Therefore, by commissioning others to do work she herself was quite capable of doing, she was acting wisely. For what would her book covers have been like without the inspired illustrations or drawings of her friend from school days, Phyllis Chase who illustrated, among many others, the cover of her first book, *Child Whispers* and, subsequently, *Responsive Singing Games* (see again Figures 7 and 13 for illustrations of the book covers). Among the other illustrators are Ronald Green, Hilda McGavin, Kathleen Nixon and Grace Lodge.

But the illustrator that towers above them all, in my opinion, is Eileen Soper (1905 – 1990) to whom she owed the biggest debt of gratitude (see her photo, Figure 23). This gifted artist and illustrator was responsible for the beautiful drawings of Julian, Dick, Anne, George and Timmy the Dog, in The Famous Five adventure series of books. It was these true to life drawings that made the series of books so lively and attractive to children.

She's also the illustrator of the sixty beautiful drawings to accompany *Enid Blyton Nature Readers* (see again Figure 5 for one of the drawings) and countless front covers, and scenes in a variety of Enid Blyton's storybooks. The story of the life of this exceptionally gifted woman can be read in *Wildings, The Secret Garden of Eileen Soper*, by Duff Hart-Davis, first published in 1991 by H. F. & G. Witherby.

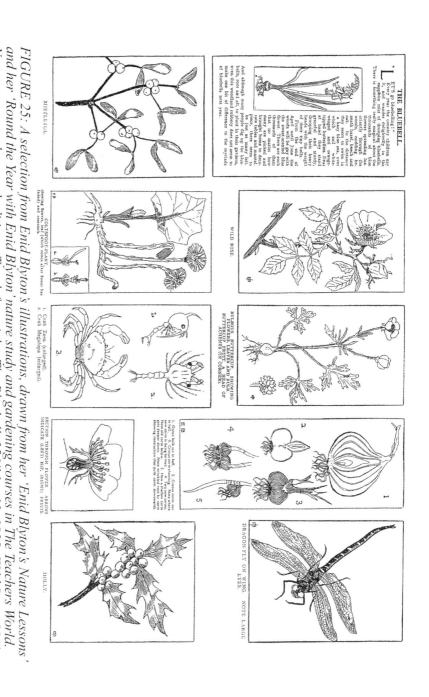

FIGURE 25: A selection from Enid Blyton's illustrations, drawn from her 'Enid Blyton's Nature Lessons' and her 'Round the Year with Enid Blyton' nature study and gardening courses in The Teachers World. Name, page numbers and editions: Top, left to right: The Bluebell, 356/May 13, 1925; Wild Rose, 556/June 10, 1925; Bulbous Buttercup, 119/April 14, 1926; Onion, 666/Feb 8, 1933; Dragon Fly, 444/May 27, 1925. Bottom: Left to Right: Mistletoe, 552/December 9, 1925; Coltsfoot Plant, 1029/February 17, 1926; Crab, 929/August 18, 1926; Section of Flower, 556/June 10, 1925; Holly, 552/Dec 9, 1925. Image restoration credit: 2graphic Photo Restoration. Website: www.photo-restoration.co.uk.

To return to Enid Blyton's illustrations in *The Teachers World*, when she finished the work of illustrating her own articles, she never took up the pen and ink again to do any more illustrations, at least that is as far as I have been able to ascertain.

Neither did she take up the paintbrush to paint, something that she was equally capable of doing. It was not until she was advancing in age that she did exercise the talent, but only after her daughter, Imogen Smallwood, encouraged her to do so. This is how Imogen put it over in a passage on page 59 of her book *A Childhood at Green Hedges*, published by Methuen & Co. in 1989:

'Once a good artist, she never drew or painted at Green Hedges until, when her mind began to let her down, I bought her some water colours and she began, hesitantly at first, to paint her beloved garden.'

Imogen featured prominently a reproduction of this painting on the dust jacket of her book and this gesture, in my opinion, is the highest tribute she could have paid to her mother in recognition of her artistic endowments. With this evidence, we have no doubt now that Enid was indeed a fine artist and illustrator, even a painter.

To come back to the subject of physiognomy, although it has demonstrated that a round dimple in the chin is a direct indication of artistic gifts – and not the cause of them – it has given us no clue about where artistic gifts and talents come from. So let's now see whether folk wisdom can provide us with some explanations.

Among the common sayings is that artistic gifts or talents are innate, that is, they existed from birth. This may have something to do with the theory of reincarnation, the essence of which is that we have all lived on this earth before and that when we come into the world again, we bring with us any gift or talent we might have had in a previous life. This is the explanation some people come up with for genius. A case in point is that of Wolfgang Mozart (1756 – 1791) the Austrian composer who, by the time he was six years old, was already composing music. He might have been an accomplished musician in a previous life and reborn with his previous musical accomplishments intact!

Another explanation is that an artistic gift is hereditary, that is, that children inherit it from their fathers or mothers through some mysterious 'code' scientists have not yet been able to decipher. Good example of this are Pablo Picasso (1881 –1973), the exceptionally gifted Spanish-born French painter whose father was a painter and art teacher; Eileen Soper (1905 – 1990), one of Enid Blyton's illustrators, whose father, George Soper and sister Eva Soper were both painters and Amy Beach (1867 – 1944) American composer and pianist, whose mother was a talented pianist and singer.

However, the most popular explanation of them all is that it runs in families, sometimes absent from one generation only to show up in another. An excellent example of this can be seen in the Bach family. Many of us are familiar with the music of Johann Sebastian Bach (1685 – 1750) the German composer (see his photo, Figure 22). However, we marvel when we learn that his great-great grandfather played the lute, his great-grandfather played in bands, his grandfather played the organ, his two granduncles were musicians, his father was a professional musician, his sons all turned out to be musicians, his grandsons were all musicians and so were his cousins and their sons.

In the case of Enid Blyton, her Aunt May Crossland was a professional musician, her nephew, Carey Blyton ((1932 – 2002) was a composer and her father, multitalented. He wrote poetry, painted in watercolours, sang with a fine baritone voice and played both the piano and banjo.[92] It was no wonder he believed that Enid, his only daughter, would turn out to be a professional musician.

Nevertheless, notwithstanding the failure of physiognomy to explain where artistic gifts and talents come from, it has given us an infallible means of 'spotting' people with artistic gifts: the presence of a round or cleft dimple, or 'ball' in the chin! Teachers, educators, talent scouts and all those who have something to do with the arts, would do well to take note of this physiognomical fact as a guide to selecting pupils who would do justice to scholarships or other means provided for their training.

After reading this, the most thoughtful among us would raise an objection by saying that they know many people who are accomplished artists, actors, musicians and so on, and in whose chins there is no round or cleft dimple. How can this be accounted for?

The physiognomic response would be as follows: some musicians, painters, artists, dancers and so on with no round or cleft dimple in the chin often acquired their art through long periods of training. In the process, some of them found it so difficult they never finished the training. The few who persevered never felt they were in the right field but continued because they saw it as their livelihood. On the contrary, dimpled-chinned children and adults can practice the art with no training at all. Even when training is given, they progress so rapidly that teachers had better be highly qualified, else their pupils would surpass them. In short, the difference between the two is that for one, practising the art is acquired and for the other, natural.

Finally, it's a pity that Enid did not start to paint in the prime of her youth, with the intention of mounting small exhibitions of her work from time to time. For if her young fans had been taken on a trip to any art gallery, they would have undoubtedly been both surprised and pleased to see paintings and pencil drawings by their favourite storyteller adorning the walls. This however was not meant to be, so we have to accept that she used the talent as best as she could while doing all the other things described in this book.

CHAPTER X

ENID THE PASSIONATE GARDENER

OVERVIEW

In this last chapter we're going to learn about Enid Blyton's gardening experience and its impact on her work as a universal teacher and professional storyteller. We'll also learn about some of the houses she lived in and the reasons for her moving from time to time. As the chapter develops, we'll see how this extensive gardening experience eventually led to her writing a book about birds, *The Bird Book*, and her elaboration of 'Round the Year with Enid Blyton', an extensive Nature Study & Gardening course for schools. We'll then move on to consider in turn *The Bird Book*, the four books resulting from the Nature Study course and *The Children's Garden*, the only textbook on gardening she ever wrote for children. The chapter ends with the description of a magnificent gardening project that was the pinnacle of her gardening experience.

Writing in her column 'From My Window' on May 19, 1926, Enid surprised her fans with the following revelation: '*THREE months ago, if I had had to sign one of the forms that ask you what you are, I should have put down "Writer." But now I'm not sure that I shouldn't put down something else instead – and that is "Gardener."'*

At that time she was in her second year of marriage to Hugh Pollock, her first husband, approaching her twenty-ninth birthday and enjoying the modest success of her books and contributions to *The Teachers World*.

'*I can't stop gardening,*' she continued in another paragraph immediately after revealing her secret, '*It's got into my bones, so that I find myself pulling up weeds in the garden when I ought to be making beds, and scribbling the names of plants on labels when I ought to be doing accounts.'*

This love of gardening really began when she was about ten years old and living with her parents and two brothers, Hanly and Carey, at Clockhouse Road, Beckenham, on the outskirts of London. At that time her father, who had taught her so many things, gave her a patch from his own big garden to do whatever she wanted.

'*… I can remember my little patch perfectly,*' she recalled in a passage on page 25 of *The Story of My Life*. '*It was square, and ran from the path to the wall. I knew what to do because I had often watched my father in the big garden, and had helped him. I dug it over well, as deeply as I could. I then got a trowel and broke up the earth as finely as possible, and made it smooth and level. It looked very nice, I thought.*'

It was not long before she had, in her own words carried on page 26 of the same book, '*a gay border of virginia stock … patches of gay candytuft, spires of graceful, brilliant clarkia, dancing poppies of all colours, sweet smelling mignonettes, and many hardy nasturtiums that climbed high over the wall, thick with orange flowers.*'

This pleasure she derived from preparing the soil, watering and watching her plants grow and flower, soon came to an end when the family moved out unexpectedly; and the disturbing changes that were to follow rapidly in succession banished from her mind all thoughts of taking up gardening again.

These changes included her father moving out following disagreements with his wife Theresa over her discovery that there was another woman; her estrangement from her mother and her decision to leave home to avoid her mother's constant naggings.[93] However, although gardening was no longer uppermost in her thoughts, it was her secret wish to have another garden someday to recreate the experience that had given her so much pleasure.

Twenty long, turbulent years were to pass before this wish was fulfilled, and when the day finally came, she was just as excited as she had been when she got her first patch. It all happened when, looking for a home to settle down after her marriage to Hugh Pollock on August 28, 1924, she spotted a house which, in her own words, *'was peeping at her from behind a large chestnut tree'*. As the house was for sale, she fetched the keys from the neighbours and went inside to look around.

That this new house situated at 83 Shortlands Road, Bromley was charming, there is no doubt (see Figure 26 for illustration). But what captivated her attention and kept her spellbound throughout the inspection was the large stretch of uncultivated land at the back of the house with its field of wild buttercup plants. She could not contain her excitement:

'All my life I have said "One day I will have a garden that is every bit my own... And now my dream has come true,"' she told readers in her column in *The Teachers World of Jan 20, 1926*, *'...Imagine a garden which is just an enclosed piece of meadow-land – a garden for which you can make your own plans, mark your own paths, plant your own flowers. Never in my life has there been such an exhilarating moment, not even when my first book came out!'*

When the deal was finalised and she and her husband moved in, she set to work to transform the enclosed piece of 'meadow-land', as she termed it, into the garden of her dreams. Indeed, its cultivation had given her so much pleasure that she did not hesitate to share it with her fans:

'Every day I walked round the garden,' she told them in another article in *The Teachers World of August 4, 1926, 'and saw how much everything had grown since the day before. It takes me half-an-hour to go round properly – not because the garden is*

big, but because I am so slow about it. I count how many poppy buds have opened since yesterday. I measure myself by the tallest hollyhock. I always look to see if any new fuchsias are out. I marvel at the way the sweet alyssum spreads and I wonder if the flower stems of carnations ever stop growing. I smell everything I can, especially the roses which I love best of all...'

FIGURE 26: Elfin Cottage at 83 Shortlands Road, Bromley where Enid's dream to have a garden 'every bit my own' came true. In 1992 Bromley Council placed a blue plaque on the building, top, left, in memory of her having lived there. Photo credit: PippaStef of the World of Blyton. Website: https://worldofblyton.com

It was from this garden that she was able to get fresh ideas and first hand material for her ongoing course of nature lessons in *The Teachers World*. Details of this course are given in Chapter I, *Enid: The Naturalist*. It was also in this garden she began to document the habits, ways and peculiarities of the different types of birds frequenting her bird table.

The result of this detailed observation and note taking was *The*

Bird Book which George Newnes Ltd published in October 1926 (see Fig. 3 for title page illustration). It supplied children with information such as the wonders of migration, with detailed descriptions and illustrations of beaks and claws; colourful descriptions of birds of the garden, shrubbery, field and hedgerow, and of those whose habitats include the woods, commons, hills, the sea and seashore. There are also chapters covering subjects such as birds' eggs – their size, shape and colour – how birds build their nests and how the children can make friends with the birds (see again Figure 1 for illustration of birds from a page in this book).

Now just when Enid and her husband were getting accustomed to their new home and garden, news came from out of the blue about a project to construct an arterial or main road near their home. After considering the threat it would pose to their newly found happiness, Enid and her husband decided to look for a new home straightaway.

'I'm going to look for another little cottage, far away from anywhere busy, with a bigger garden than this one ... I shall choose somewhere tucked away cosily, with lovely views of hills and fields, and the garden must be very quiet, full of wild birds, butterflies and bees,' she told her fans in her 'Letter to Boys & Girls', in *The Teachers World*, in the edition of July 10, 1929, soon after telling them how worried she had been when she first heard about the project.

One week after penning these lines she was able to report in another letter, in the edition of July 17, 1929, that she came across a house whose owners were going to India and who were only too happy to sell it to her.

It was not long before the deal was sealed and she and her husband moved into the house that became known as 'Old Thatch', situated in Bourne End, Buckinghamshire on August 2, 1929 (see Figure 4 for illustration).

The speed with which she made up her mind to buy this house was surprising. What could have been the reason for this? The answer could be that apart from its beauty, its spaciousness and its location far away from the flow of noisy traffic, it had, as part of the bargain, a well-stocked, ready-made garden that more than compensated for the one she reluctantly left behind at Elfin Cottage!

For, according to an account she gave in *The Teachers World* of July 24, 1929, shortly before moving in, this new garden she inherited contained '*a lot of grass and big beds full of flowers, roses blossom everywhere ... climbing over poles and trellises ... a long rose walk ... old yew hedges thick and cool in which hosts of little birds had built their nest ... [and] a fine kitchen garden with everything growing there that you could possibly want ...*'

She followed up this description with more details, especially about the orchard, in another article of August 28, 1929: '*I have a large number of apple and pear trees in my garden and they are so full of fruit that the branches are bowed right down ... My nut trees are full of nuts, too – they look so exciting, hanging down in pretty green bunches. I think the garden must have known I was coming to it this year, and that is why all the trees have done their best to be fruitful!*'

In the meantime, the task of maintaining this new garden, which in her own words, '*was nine times bigger than the one she left behind at Elfin Cottage,*' was so demanding that she found it necessary to hire a full-time gardener. In this way she could concentrate on fulfilling a number of commissions that were pouring in from all quarters. Among them was a new one from *The Teachers World* to do another course on Nature Study and Gardening for children, one that was to draw not only on her gardening experience but also on her knowledge of zoology and botany, gained from her teacher training course at Ipswich High School.

Entitled: 'Round the Year with Enid Blyton – A Weekly Course of Seasonal Nature Study', it was by far the most comprehensive course on Nature Study for children ever published in the newspaper. In working out the course, Enid took into consideration the 'Primary School Report' that was published around that time.[94] This report suggested that Nature Study should include the following:

1. Weather observations, charts and calendars
2. Common animals and insects found in gardens
3. Common birds, their habits and appearance
4. Common plants and trees, bulbs, etc.

'*Taking Nature under these four headings,*' Enid wrote in the introduction to the course, published in the edition of August 24, 1932, '*I have allotted one of the above subjects to every month, making 48 lessons in all, so that, whilst each lesson is topical, the teacher will be able to follow out four different courses covering all the activities suggested in the Report...*'

Indeed, so meticulously did she plan the course that one week before the first lesson appeared in print she published her syllabus in the newspaper for teachers to work out in advance how they were going to teach the lessons in their classrooms (see Appendix 65 for a reproduction of this syllabus).

Moreover, if we examine this syllabus carefully we find that for each of the twelve months there is a lesson on some aspect of gardening – to find this, run a finger down the first column where the words 'Weather Lessons' appear and stop at the heading 'Plant and Tree Lessons'. The gardening lessons are presented here vertically, under each month.

Of special interest is the one appearing under March entitled: *Our School Garden*: (*How to make it a success.*) This is how she began this lesson which appears in *The Teachers World* on March 8, 1933:

'*I WANT you this summer to have a lovely, flowery garden, a place where bees and butterflies come, a place of delicious scents and gay colours. We have made wormeries* [a place or container where worms are kept] *aquaria* [artificial ponds or tanks for fish] *and bird-tables successfully, and now we will do an even bigger thing, and have even more fun in doing it...*'

That even bigger thing to which she referred was to make a school garden. The rest of the lesson was packed with instructions and suggestions about how to draw up a garden plan, prepare the soil, choose seeds, care for seedlings and so on (see Appendix 66 for a full-page illustration of a lesson on Germination). Soon teachers everywhere were preparing patches of soil in school grounds to give the children practical gardening experience.

When eventually the course came to an end in August 1933 all the lessons were collected and published in four separate volumes under the title: *Round The Year With Enid Blyton – Spring, Summer, Autumn and Winter.* In 1950 Evans Brothers Ltd, the publisher, combined all the lessons and republished them in a single volume (see Figure 27 for front cover illustration).

*FIGURE 27: Left, a display advertisement for The Children's Garden, published in The Teachers World edition of June 12, 1933 to promote Enid Blyton's first and only textbook on gardening for children. The name was changed to Let's Garden when Latimer House republished it in 1948. Image restoration credit: 2graphic Photo Restoration. Website: www.photo-restoration.co.uk_*
Right: One of the front covers of Round the Year with Enid Blyton, a nature study textbook that resulted from her one-year course of 'Seasonal Nature Study' in The Teachers World. (See her syllabus for this course, Appendix 65.) © British Library Board: (SM: W10/4348, cover).

The success of these four volumes and the growing number of letters Enid was still receiving from children who wanted more information about how to get started with a small garden at home, encouraged her to write *The Children's Garden* that George Newnes Ltd published subsequently in 1935 (see Figure 27 for a display advertisement that was published in *The Teachers World* to promote this book).

Thirteen years later, after the book ran through several editions, Latimer House, one of her many publishers, republished the book under the title *Let's Garden*. This was a wise move, for with the wonderful changes such as a more attractive typeface, new illustrations by William McLaren and a better presentation of the subject matter, the book became even more attractive to the next generation of children who were to read it.

In the meantime, Enid wasted no time in keeping her fans abreast of the progress of her own garden through her 'Enid Blyton's Children's Page' in *The Teachers World*. In doing so she would often give news about her home, Old Thatch, that looked like a house taken straight from a fairytale book (see again Figure 4 for illustration). Here we can see some of the beautiful scenery of her wonderful garden that is hidden on the other side of the house. Since its appearance on the front cover, as shown in the illustration, her fans liked this house so much that when she announced one day that she was moving out, they were taken completely by surprise. Why did she want to leave this house whose countryside location and quiet surroundings were ideal for her writing projects? The answer she gave was convincing:

'Old Thatch became much too small for us, and although we built on to it once, we couldn't do so again, for if we did we would be making a really old cottage into something that was neither old nor new just a hotch-potch. So we decided that we must look for another house, bigger than Old Thatch, with just as nice a garden ...' she stated in her 'Letter To Girls And Boys' of July 27, 1938.

Having made her point, she updated them on what she had been doing to find a new place: *'I hunted and hunted and hunted. I rushed around the countryside in our car and looked at about five hundred houses all over the place. And at last I found one I really like.'*

She then went on to tell them that the house she found had a bigger garden than the one at Old Thatch, with a great many little lawns surrounded by green yew hedges, an orchard with all kinds of fruit trees and a big vegetable garden that seemed to grow prize vegetables.

So after all the arrangements for moving had been finalised, Enid said goodbye to Old Thatch and moved to Green Hedges, the name readers helped her to find for the new place, situated in a tree lined road in Beaconsfield, Buckinghamshire. The move took place in August 1938.

Moreover, as Enid hinted in her column of July 27, 1938, the place she found had a garden that was bigger than the one at Old Thatch. What she did not state was that both the garden and the house were situated on over two and a half acres of land! With all this space at her disposal, Enid decided to go into gardening on a large scale. To do this, she quickly found a new full-time gardener to help her put her plans into operation.

It was not long before she had hundreds of crocuses – in gold, white, mauve and purple – an abundance of daffodils and a rose garden filled with roses of all scents and colours. *'There are deep red velvety ones, pure white ones, golden-yellow roses and brilliant pink. There are orange ones and bluish pink ones, and every one is lovely'*, Enid recalled in various passages on page 16 of *The Story of My Life*. Moreover, with the help of her new gardener, she was also able to grow, once again, vegetables for her enlarged household which by then included her two daughters, Gillian and Imogen, their nanny, a housekeeper and a cook.

This lovely garden which was brought into being purely for the pleasure it brought her and her family, and for the pleasure it gave to many children who had taken up her invitation to visit her home and garden from time to time, was the pinnacle of her gardening experience. For all that she had not been able to do both at Elfin Cottage and Old Thatch, was comfortably achieved here at Green Hedges. After seven years of maintaining this garden, she and her second husband, Kenneth Darrell Waters, whom she married in 1943, decided one day to replan the garden. According to her daughter, Imogen Smallwood, in a passage on page 102 of her book, *A Childhood At Green Hedges*, first published in 1989 by Methuen & Co., this replanning began sometime in 1947:

'On her own, my mother probably would not have bothered. She liked her garden as it was; but she was happy to see my

stepfather make plans and to give her own ideas, so that it was to an extent a joint venture, and one that continued for the next ten years at least.'

Without going into details about the replanning, she recalled that Sid Hearne, a local contractor, had been engaged to carry out the first stage, which was the construction of a small round pond, surrounded by paving stones.

'*The following year the plans became more ambitious,*' she continued in another passage on the same page. '*Landscape gardeners were called in from Windsor to make a rose garden out of the croquet lawn. This was less pleasing for all the beds were rectangular or L-shaped; too many straight lines, and the rose bushes within them were planted in straight rows as well ...*' (see Figure 28 for illustration).

On page 104 in the same chapter, she stated that '*the orchard at the bottom of the garden was levelled and a hard tennis court was built with a little wooden summer house beside it.*' Furthermore, in another passage on page 41 of the chapter entitled: The Garden, she stated that '*there was a big cold greenhouse with a warm, pungent smell for tomatoes; cold frames for the cucumbers and glass cloches to cover the strawberries.*'

FIGURE 28: A part of Enid Blyton's magnificent garden at Green Hedges, after it had been replanned. Reproduced from a copy Imogen Smallwood carried on page 103 of her book: A Childhood at Green Hedges, published by Methuen Children's Books in 1989. The owner of the original photograph cannot be traced. Image restoration credit: 2graphic Photo Restoration. Website: www.photo-restoration.co.uk

Moreover, although her writing from her new home had increased beyond measure, she was to produce no new book on gardening. It was, however, from here that she wrote another bird book, *Birds Of Our Gardens*, published by George Newnes Ltd in 1940; another book about nature, *The Enid Blyton's Nature Lover's Book*, published by Evans Brothers Ltd in 1944, and began to write the series of thirty-six Nature Readers for juniors, that Macmillan & Co. began publishing from 1945, just after the end of the Second World War (see again Figure 3 for illustration of covers of her Nature Books – and Appendix 12 for illustration of the standard book cover and list of Nature Readers).

Finally, when Enid wrote in 'From My Window', her column in *The Teachers World* of May 19, 1926, that given a form on which she had to state her occupation, she was not sure whether to put down Gardener instead of Writer, she was in some way making a self-fulfilling prophecy. For she possibly never envisaged that some twelve years later she was going to have a garden bigger and lovelier than the one she had when she penned those famous lines from Elfin Cottage.

Moreover, although it must have been her dream to write a book on gardening, she never envisaged, not only writing a textbook on gardening for children, but also running two separate courses of Nature Study and Gardening in *The Teachers World*, both of which helped to cultivate the gardening spirit in two generations of children who, in turn, passed their knowledge on to the next generation. So that whenever we hear the saying, England is a land of small gardeners, let us spare a thought for Enid Blyton and the part she had played in helping to keep the saying alive!

RECAPITULATION & CONCLUSION

Now that we have come to the end of this section we have been able to see that Enid Blyton was much more than a prolific and successful writer of storybooks for children. From her dominant interest in zoology and botany in Chapter I to her passion for gardening in Chapter X, we have seen how the bulk of her work fell into two distinct categories: teaching and storytelling. We have also seen how she progressed from classroom teaching to becoming a universal teacher through the medium of her pen.

As we moved through the chapters, we saw how she became interested in poetry and playwriting, and how her musical ability, thought to be lost, was to find full expression in songwriting. We discovered that she could draw and paint and learned – perhaps for the first time, how she wrote her stories. Finally, we saw how physiognomy, a little known 'science', threw light on her artistic endowments.

That someone from a broken home could have risen to such a position in life is truly remarkable. In this respect she was lucky to have benefited from her father's wide knowledge of nature, poetry and music before he left the family home for good. She was also lucky to have had the opportunity to indulge in reading books from his vast collection before she too left home because of disagreements with her mother.[95]

With regards to the other activities described in this book, many of them came about as a result of fortuitous happenings, such as her spell of classroom teaching that gave her the opportunity to try out her talents on the children in her charge; her marriage to Huge Pollock, editor of the book department at the publishing firm George Newnes Ltd, who had put an end to rejections by helping to get some of her earlier books published, and her discovery of *The Teachers World* newspaper that was to give her, not only an outlet for her early poems, stories and plays, but also the opportunity to continue teaching through the medium of her pen.

Finally, if we reflect on the following extract from her very first article in 'From My Window', her column in *The Teachers World*, on the implied subject of Genius, we shall find in it a summary of her intellectual life:

> '...I do not think genius is a mysterious something with which one must be born. I think it is the natural result of using one's mind to the fullest extent, of loving beauty in any form, and of directly expressing the powerful spiritual effects which clamour for release...' (See Appendix 22 for the full text of this article.)

When we take into account the hundreds of stories, songs and poems she published in book form; the plays she wrote for schools and the theatre; the 200 or so reading books and the thirty-six Nature Readers she wrote for schools; the nature and gardening books she wrote for children; the teaching books she wrote for teachers; the Bible stories and classics she retold; the elaborate World History, Nature and Gardening courses she ran in *The Teachers World;* the 250 stories she wrote for the *Sunny Stories for Little Folks* magazine and, subsequently, the 553, for the *Sunny Stories* magazine; the running of her own *Enid Blyton's Magazine* which ran into 162 issues; the 1271 contributions she made to *The Teachers World* from 1922 to 1945, including the 211 articles she wrote in her column 'From My Window'; the running of a children's page in *The Teachers World*; the educational books she edited; the innumerable articles she wrote for national and regional newspapers and magazines, and all the other activities described in this book, we have to admit she did use her mind to the fullest extent. Therefore, on the basis of the point of view she expressed in her article and its reflection in her professional life, we have to concede she was indeed a genius!

SECTION TWO

WHY SOME OF ENID BLYTON'S STORIES ARE NOT UP TO STANDARD

As pointed out in the Overview to *Enid: The Professional Storyteller*, Chapter VII, there's a story in every poem, song and play and in every Reading Book and Nature Reader Enid had ever written. Because these stories were little known they somehow escaped criticism of her stories in other categories, such as in her adventure, mystery, suspense, fairytale, Noddy and other storybooks.

Included in this criticism are unrealistic plots (Famous Five books); limited vocabulary, flatness of style, racism and providing children with a poor role model (Noddy books); sexism (Adventure books); thin characterisations (Fairytale books) and others, such as irresponsibility, inconsistencies, incredibility, inaccurate facts, repetitions and irrelevancies. As a result, critics branded her a mediocre writer of children's storybooks. How did such a situation come about? What was it about her work or her way of working that exposed her to such criticism? This is what we'll now find out. The material to be considered in this section is presented in the following order:

1. Absence of private editorial and secretarial assistance
2. Problems arising from distractions
3. Problems arising from writing books in series

Her rehabilitation and the conclusion to this section are presented afterwards.

ABSENCE OF PRIVATE EDITORIAL AND SECRETARIAL ASSISTANCE

In a letter Enid Blyton wrote to Professor Peter McKellar, the psychologist who was investigating the source of inspiration for her stories, she explained that she was in the happy position of being able to write a story and read it for the first time.[96] Here she is writing the story according to the method described in Section Two of Chapter VII: *Enid: The Professional Storyteller.* To recap, she would sit before the typewriter with fingers on the keys, make her mind blank and wait for a story to come. The story would then flow into her imagination and her fingers would spring into action, often with the opening lines: Once upon a time...

Now in the process of typing the story, if there was something that didn't sound right, or appeared to be out of place, that something was automatically corrected, as can be seen from the following extract from an account she gave in her first letter of February 15, 1953 to Peter McKellar:

> '...*Another odd thing is that sometimes something crops up in the story which I am sure is wrong, or somehow out of place. Not a bit of it! It rights itself, falls into place – and now I dare not alter a thing I think is wrong...*'.[97]

From this we can see that she was a silent witness, looking on in amazement at the way everything was falling into place as the story developed.

Hence all she had to do was to relax, keep up the pace and change the typewriting paper and ribbon as necessary. It was only when the story came to an end and she was reading it over to correct typographical, syntactical and spelling errors that she had the opportunity to question or criticise what she had written. After all, it was a story that came to her ready-made. So it's reasonable to expect that she would read it as if it were given to her to review or edit to prepare it for publication.

However, as every writer knows, it's no easy task to criticise his or her own work. There's a tendency to be carefree or light-hearted when reviewing the stories, and the critical eye that comes into play when

170

reading someone else's work appears to be closed. There's therefore always a need for a second pair of eyes to provide a critical analysis.

This is exactly what was lacking in the reviewing and editing of her stories. For what she needed was a private, dedicated reader or editor to read or edit the stories that came to her automatically, to point out flaws in the plots, inaccurate facts, irrelevancies, inconsistencies, incredibility, repetitions and so on that she might have overlooked in the process of checking or reviewing the stories.

The more so because, as she became proficient in the use of the typewriter, she was typing more than 4,000 words a day and was said to be capable of typing a book of some 40,000 words and deliver it to her publisher in less than a week. Furthermore, with her heavy workload as described in these pages she could not afford to work full-time to give the typescript for a new book the attention it deserved.

There was however, a chance to do some of this work, and that was when her publishers sent her the proofs. But here again, this should have been sent, in turn, to a proofreader before sending them back to her publishers.

The only person known to have provided such assistance was George Greenfield who became her literary agent in 1954. But Enid began writing stories long before she engaged him and there is no evidence she had a private reader or editor before that time.[98]

Therefore, with no such arrangement in place for her stories, when she finished writing a story that came to her ready-made, she would do the editing herself, which was her duty, with hand-written notation on each page before sending it off to a publisher. In this way she was more concerned with the correction of typographical and other errors rather than with flaws in the content. The books eventually reached her impatient fans in the nick of time with all their imperfections, and this situation was to be the cause of a controversy that saw her books banned from libraries and some public schools throughout the country.[99]

Coupled with this situation is that of her working from home, alone, with no secretarial support or filing system in place. Instead, she relied on her powerful photographic memory to keep track of her books and to manage her business affairs.[100] This is how her literary agent, George Greenfield, summed up this situation in a passage on pages fifty to fifty-one in *Enid Blyton* published in 1998 by Sutton Publishing Ltd:

> *Until her last few years, she had the most extraordinary memory ... she replied to all correspondents, whether it be a six year old or the chairman of a large publishing house, by handwritten cards and letters. She took no copies and, as far as could be seen, had no filing system at Green Hedges...*

Therefore, if she had a filing system in place and a secretary working from her home, along with a dedicated reader or editor to whom she could send typescripts for a critical analysis before sending them off to her publishers, she could have had her stories so refined as to leave no room for critics to have a 'field day' in criticising her work.

PROBLEMS ARISING FROM DISTRACTIONS

In writing stories using her clairvoyant and other faculties, Enid needed a quiet place to work so that she might hold in her imagination the entire sequence of pictures of characters in a story and listen carefully to their dialogues. In this way she could type as quickly as possible what she was seeing and hearing until the story reached a point where she could take a break, as for lunch. If all went well the process unfolded smoothly and the result was a wonderful story.

If however she had been disturbed or distracted in the process, the thread of the story could be broken in her imagination, and the story would be lost. The same thing could result if, while working on a story, she had missed a full day's work, for one reason or the other, as can be seen from the following extract from an account she gave to Professor Peter McKellar in another letter to him of January 28, 1955:

> *'...I have just finished a book for Macmillans ... I began it on Monday and finished it this afternoon (Friday). It is 60,000 words long and flowed like its title (River of Adventure). All the same I know quite well that if I had had to miss even a day in the writing of it I might have had to give it up. Once the river is dammed anywhere, it won't flow again in that particular direction ...'*

In such situations the course of action opened to her would have been either to try to save the story by inventing the missing parts that would have come to her automatically or abandon the story altogether.

The nearest we can get to understanding this strange phenomenon is to think about what happens when we hold a chain of thoughts in our minds and something suddenly disturbed us, chasing away those thoughts and causing us to think instead about how to deal with the disturbance. When it's all over and we regain our composure, we try to recall what we had been thinking about only to find that our minds had gone blank. For some of us the thoughts come back unexpectedly, but for others they are lost forever.

From this we can infer that whenever there were inconsistencies in some of her stories they might have resulted from her having lost the thread somewhere along the line and making up parts to save the story, parts that would have come to her automatically, had the process not been interrupted.

PROBLEMS ARISING FROM WRITING BOOKS IN SERIES

Authors who write children's books in series are said to have a one-track mind. The series of books they write is on a particular theme or subject such as fairytales, fantasy, science fiction, animals, and so on. By focusing their attention in a single direction they are able to do a good job at seeing that the plots are realistic, the events credible and in some cases, the character(s) grow up and mature. They may bring the series to a close whenever they deem it fit to do so, or reopen it whenever their fans protest.

This was definitely not the case with Enid Blyton whose wide field of interests and heavy workload made it difficult for her to proceed in this manner. Yet she was able to write, not a single series, as in the case of J.K.Rowling and many other children's writers, but series of series of books. These series included The Famous Five, The Secret Seven, Adventure, Mystery and Noddy.

In addition to this, her method of working and the unpredictable nature of the stories should be taken into account. For example, when she sat down to write a new book in a series, she had no idea what the story in the new book would be. It might be a sequel to the last book or a brand new story. Moreover, since the stories came to her ready-made, she would have to wait until the story began to unfold in her imagination to understand what it was all about. In any case it was only when the story came to an end and she was reading it for the first time she could come to grips with the story.

Therefore, it's no wonder the books that came under 'heavy fire' from critics were those she wrote in series. Among the anomalies critics found in such books are unrealistic plots, incredulity, irresponsibility, inconsistencies, inaccurate facts and so on.

Now if her wide field of interests, heavy workload and commitments didn't allow her the necessary time to devote to each book in a series, why did she continue to write them? Two answers immediately spring to mind. The first is pressure from her publishers. Seeing that the early books in a series were making money for them, they naturally encouraged her to bring out more.

An insight into this situation can be gained from the following extract from David Lister's article in *The Independent*:

Enid Blyton grew tired of writing her Famous Five books, and only continued because her publishers insisted, the author's daughter Gillian Baverstock told the Edinburg Book Festival yesterday. Miss Baverstock said her mother had only wanted to write six of the Famous Five series but churned out 21 between 1942 and 1963...[101]

The other answer is that she could find no suitable way to say no to her fans. As we have seen in Chapter III, *Enid: the Columnist & Feature Writer*, she had built up a huge fan base that had its origin in her 'Enid Blyton's Children's Page' in *The Teachers World,* the *Sunny Stories* magazine and, subsequently, in her *Enid Blyton's Magazine*. In time her fans began writing to her by the hundreds demanding more of her books they had enjoyed reading. This is how she assessed the situation in the following short passage drawn from page 97 of *The Story of My Life*:

'If I happened to write two books about the same characters, in

came floods of letters, saying that it must be a series, when was the third one coming out?'

Another example of overpowering demands from her fans can be seen from the additional account she gave on page 98 of *The Story of My Life*. Here she is at one of her autographing afternoons in some unspecified hall in London where she had the opportunity to interact with her fans. With pen and paper in hand, she listened as they told her what they wanted:

'Another Farm book, please!'

'A Nature book – about birds, please, but you can put in animals too, if you like.'

'A new Secret Seven – no, two new Secret Sevens, Miss Blyton!'

'A book about Robin Hood. I love Robin Hood! Can you write a whole book about him, please?'

'No, I want Brer Rabbit, write a Brer Rabbit book first, Enid Blyton.'

Then comes a chant. 'Another Five book, another Five book, another Five book.'

'I look up from writing down your list and I say: Nonsense! You've got eleven of those already. Surely you don't want another one. But still you chant, smiling broadly: 'Another Five Book!'

Enid's response was to write down everything the children asked for. Then she looked down the long list and told them, *'I may not be able to write all these for you this year – but I do promise you this one – and that one – and that one. Now, surely you don't want me to work day and night for you, without any sleep at all?'* [102] Nevertheless, presence of mind or quick thinking might have provided an appropriate response to stop her books going into long series for which she lacked the necessary time and dedication to see them through to completion.

REHABILITATION & CONCLUSION

Enid Blyton, despite her flaws, is a jolly good read! This was the verdict of a team of experts in children's literature who met in 1997 at a conference to mark the centenary of her birth. At that conference, run by the Centre for Research into Children's Literature, one expert after another told the conference why they thought Enid Blyton should be rehabilitated:

'Enid Blyton should be saluted for her contribution to children's literacy by hooking millions of us on reading,' said Anne Fine, a distinguished author of children's books.

'The unrealistic plots are heroic daydreams that children find flattering,' said Nicholas Tucker, a child psychology lecturer at Sussex University.

'The thin characterisations do not matter because children create their own,' said Michael Wood, a psychologist.[103]

So it was that after years of enduring criticism, Enid Blyton had finally been rehabilitated. Passages in some of her books deemed offensive were swiftly rewritten to reflect changing times and her elder daughter, Gillian Baverstock, who was a strong defender of her mother's reputation and works, breathed a huge sigh of relief.

Meanwhile, The Enid Blyton Society that came into being in 1995 to provide a focal point for collectors and enthusiasts is flourishing and its quarterly *The Enid Blyton Society Journal*, circulated privately, is as popular as ever. In 2002, the society launched its own website www. enidblytonsociety.co.uk

Finally, notwithstanding the passage of time, her books still enjoy an enormous popularity, selling in excess of seven million copies a year. Some of her most popular series of books, such as Noddy, The Famous Five, The Secret Seven, and the adventure, school and fantasy storybooks are all enjoying revivals. Libraries are stocking her books, once again, and the children of today who know nothing about Enid Blyton other than she is the author of storybooks for children, still find her books fascinating.

Enid Blyton passed away peacefully in her sleep in a nursing home November 28, 1968 following a period of disorientation and loss of memory, symptoms associated with Alzheimer's disease. She was cremated at the Golders Green Crematorium, London.

BRIEF HISTORY
OF
THE TEACHERS WORLD

When *The Teachers World* was launched by two Irish brothers, Robert and Edward Evans, in 1911 from a small office in Fleet Street, London, it was greeted with a barrage of criticism.

According to an article in the issue of March 6, 1929, written principally to honour one of the brothers, Robert Evans, who had just received a knighthood, "competent observers' foretold that the venture was doomed to failure. Well-established competitors were in the field', states the writer of the article, 'and in any case there was neither room nor demand for another educational weekly for teachers'. Even the approximate date of the decease of the paper was mentioned.

These 'competent observers' referred to in the article were to be silenced forever. For not only did *The Teachers World* succeed in becoming one of the leaders in educational journalism, with a circulation estimated at around 100,000, but as time went by it incorporated several other educational journals, including *The Teacher, Secondary Education, The Woman Teachers World* and *The Schoolmistress*.

So popular did this newspaper become with teachers that in 1929 the editor divided it into two editions: a Junior Edition, for teachers of children younger than eleven years, and a Senior Edition, for those of children eleven years and over. In this way the editors had more space in each edition to present new material stemming from 'Suggestions' from the then Board of Education about what should be taught in junior and senior classes.

As time went by the editor introduced an Extra Number or a Special Edition, which was published separately, and this edition was devoted to a particular subject, such as literature, science, mathematics, art, music and so on.

A typical edition before the division would have contained, inter alia: the Editorial; News and Views of the Week; Weekly Suggestions for Infant Teachers; reviews or analysis of new teaching methods; specials on the NUT (National Union of Teachers) conferences; Enid Blyton's column 'From My Window'; stories and poems for children by Enid Blyton and other contributors, and weekly lessons in English, mathematics, nature study, handicraft and so on by graduates and teaching professionals – lessons that teachers could use straightaway in the classroom.

After the division, the main features, such as the Editorial and News & Views of the Week, were retained in both editions, with the exception of Enid Blyton's column, 'From My Window', which was discontinued and replaced with 'Enid Blyton's Children's Page' in the Junior Edition.

The newspaper went on to celebrate over sixty-five years until December 1976, when it was replaced with a new journal *Junior Education.* The last issues announcing this change appeared on Friday, December 31, 1976. Here is an extract from this last issue:

Teachers World

No. 3501 Friday, 31 December, 1976

A Continuing Tradition

Mr L. J. Browning, Chairman and son-in-law of Sir Robert Evans, the founder of the firm.

It is of course, with great sadness that we reach the 3,501[st] and final issue of *Teachers World*, a journal which, as our contributor describes on another page, has an honourable place in the history of education in the twentieth century. At Evans we feel the loss particularly keenly because it was Sir Robert Evans' creation of *Teachers World* in 1911 that laid the foundations of the publishing house which now has a world-wide reputation both for its school-books and its range of educational periodicals...

Through war and peace, through the years of the consensus curriculum and the age of innovation, through periods of teacher shortage and teacher unemployment, it has kept teachers informed week by week and guided them through the maze with which education has been faced. Now we ourselves, as publishers are having to take account of that change – but we are doing so constructively, as we have always urged teachers to do; in our case by replacing *Teachers World* with a new journal, *Junior Education*, which will continue our tradition of practical service to the teaching profession ...

The British Library Newspaper Division has carefully preserved every edition of *The Teachers World*. Applying to the appropriate section for a temporary readers pass would enable anyone today to have access to these volumes. The bulk of Enid's tremendous contributions can be found in the standard editions before 1929 and in the Junior Editions and The Extra Numbers thereafter.

THE SUNNY STORIES
MAGAZINE – A PHENOMENAL
SUCCESS

OVERVIEW

In Chapter VII under *Enid: The Professional Storyteller*, we learned about Enid's amazing photographic memory and saw how she used it to retell hundreds of stories. In this article, we now have another opportunity to see her photographic memory in action, this time to retell the traditional stories in the *Sunny Stories For Little Folks* magazine and, eventually, the *Sunny Stories* magazine. Here we'll also learn about the origin, development and demise of these two singular publications.

Children growing up in England today can visit a bookshop or library and choose any books they would like to read. By contrast, children growing up in the early 1900s were not so fortunate. Any storybook they happened to read would have been purchased for them by a parent or relative, either through mail order or from a pedlar or roving salesman, who was often acting independently. Moreover, while children of well-to-do parents had many such books to read, those of parents of average means had none, and had to be contented with reading the stories at school for reading practice, or else, to listen to the stories told by a teacher, parent or grandparent.

So it must have been a godsend when George Newnes Ltd brought into being a magazine called *Sunny Stories for Little Folks* that would carry exclusively the traditional stories for mass circulation. They then gave Enid Blyton the job to come up with the stories. The nature of the contract between her and the publisher is not known today, but it is believed the two books they published for her before, namely, *The Enid Blyton Book of Fairies* and *The Enid Blyton Book of Bunnies* in 1924 and 1925 respectively, as well as her stories published in *The Teachers World*, qualified her for the job.

This magazine, which was to appear fortnightly, cost 2d (two pence) a copy and parents could buy a copy from a newsagent, bookstall or by post to read to their children at home or the children themselves could buy a copy with their pocket money.

When the arrangements were finalised Enid set to work to write the stories. Beginning with 'Golden Hair and the Three Bears', 'Cinderella', 'Aladdin and the Wonderful Lamp', 'The Sleeping Beauty' and 'Dick Whittington and His Cat' in the first issue of the magazine that came out in July 1926, she went on to retell the 'Adventures of Sinbad the Sailor', 'Gulliver in the Land of Lilliput', 'Robin Hood and His Merry Men', 'King Midas and the Golden Touch', 'The Fables of Aesop', 'Puss in Boots', 'Beauty and the Beast', 'Jason and the Golden Fleece', and many more, including Joel Chandler Harris's Brer Rabbit tales that eventually became some of the most popular stories in the magazine. [104] Written in simple language in a lively entertaining style, the stories soon became popular with children who were looking out every week for the next issue to see what new stories the magazine would carry.

Moreover, if there was one feature of the magazine that enticed parents and children to buy a copy, that feature was the attractive picture on the front covers (see illustration, Figure 29). Internal illustrations were gradually introduced as the sale of the magazine progressed. When Enid reached the limit of the traditional stories to retell, she quickly filled the vacuum with her own stories.

Then in 1937 after the magazine had reached a staggering 250 issues, a strange thing happened. The editor, for a reason that's not clear, changed the title from *Sunny Stories for Little Folks* to *Enid Blyton's Sunny Stories*, changed the frequency, and included new features, such as Enid Blyton's 'Letter to Boys and Girls', poetry and a variety of competitions. After the 278th issue, the name was changed again to *Sunny Stories* (see Figure 29 for illustration of one of the front covers in the new series).

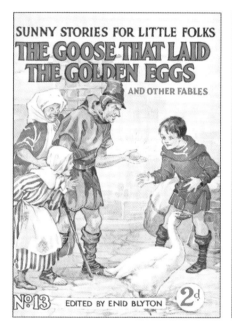 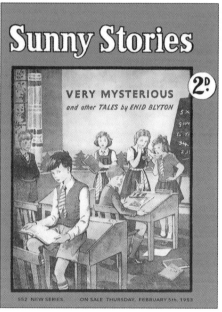

FIGURE 29: Left: a cover of one of the Sunny Stories For Little Folks magazine in the first series Enid Blyton began retelling in 1926 (Vol. 13, January, 1927). Right: One of the covers of the new series, when the name was changed to Sunny Stories in 1937 (Vol. 552, Feb 5, 1953). The mention 'Edited by Enid Blyton' that appeared on every cover of the first series is misleading, for all Enid Blyton did was to write the stories and submit them for publication. © British Library Board (SM: left, 12814.i No 13, cover; right, 12814.d Vol 552, cover).

During the war years (1939 – 1945), children everywhere who couldn't wait for the next issue to appear, suddenly found in issue No. 272 of March 27, 1942 an announcement that left many of them wondering if they would ever see the magazine again. The announcement appeared at the bottom of Enid's 'Letter to Children' [105] as follows:

P.S. – I can't tell you how sorry I am to let you have Sunny Stories only once a fortnight now, but we haven't enough paper owing to the War. You shall have it once a week again as soon as possible!

Therefore, because of restrictions on paper during the Second World War, the publisher reverted to issuing the magazine fortnightly. But whether it was issued weekly or fortnightly, it was more than welcomed by countless numbers of children who were displaced during those turbulent years. With no school to go to and nothing to do, the only happiness they could look forward to was reading the next issue of Enid Blyton's *Sunny Stories* magazine and other publications for childrren that were in circulation at that time.

Now like everything to which Enid had turned her hand to up to that time, her *Sunny Stories for Little Folks* and eventually, her *Sunny Stories*, were a resounding success both in England and abroad. So much so that in 1952, some twenty-six years after the publication of the first issue in July 1926, she was still receiving hundreds of letters from children overseas telling her how much they had enjoyed the stories (see Appendix 67 for one of her 'Letters to Boys and Girls' describing this situation).

Then all of a sudden, without notifying the thousands of devoted fans whose support contributed to that resounding success, she suddenly withdrew or retired from contributing stories to the magazine. Her last 'Letter to Boys and Girls' in the issue of February 5, 1953, Volume 552, gave absolutely no hint that a withdrawal was forthcoming. The following issue of February 19, 1953, Volume 553, contained her contribution of new stories, with a full-page announcement that the magazine would henceforth be published weekly and that it would contain a number of wonderful new features such as a free picture-circus, a painting competition and exciting new serials. Such an announcement would have been made by Enid herself in the 'Letter to Boys and Girls', but there was no letter. Her devoted fans, therefore, must have been as astonished as ever. The following week, the editor wrote the usual 'Letter to Boys and Girls', but with no reference to Enid's withdrawal. It was only in the issue of Tuesday March 24, 1953, Volume 558, that her fans really got to know what was going on.

For in that issue the editor, who had been keeping the magazine going in Enid's absence, introduced Marion Crawford, the person who had been writing the stories in the issues following Enid's withdrawal (see Appendix 68).

As it turned out, the reason for the withdrawal was to start up her own magazine: the *Enid Blyton's Magazine.* According to Barbara Stoney, her official biographer, in a passage on page 142 of the first edition of *Enid Blyton: A Biography,* '*She had already circulated teachers, librarians and educationalists and advertised widely in newspapers and other periodicals that she would soon be starting up her own fortnightly magazine ...*' However, it still does not explain why she made no announcement in her last 'Letter to Boys and Girls', in the issue of February 5, 1953, that she would be leaving and that someone else was going to take her place.

Nevertheless, her disappointed fans soon had reason to be cheerful again when the first issue of her new *Enid Blyton's Magazine* came out in March, 1953. For all their favourite features, such as the famous 'Letter to Boys and Girls', poems, stories, picture-painting competitions, puzzles and so on suddenly sprang to life in the new medium. More information about this magazine is given in *A Brief History of* the *Enid Blyton's Magazine* in this section.

In all she had contributed stories exclusively to the 250 issues of the *Sunny Stories for Little Folks* magazine and, subsequently, another set, to the 553 issues of the *Enid Blyton's Sunny Stories* magazine that was renamed *Sunny Stories* magazine, for thirty-seven years – a remarkable feat for someone who already had a heavy workload to carry, as shown in the other chapters of this book!

Finally, for her grown up fans who had read the early issues of the *Sunny Stories For Little Folks* magazine when they were small, nothing could take the place of the pleasure they derived, perhaps for the first time, from reading the traditional stories that up to that time, no one had taken the trouble to write in a way small children could read and enjoy. In fact, the presentation was in no way close to what it is today. The advanced production techniques, improvements in the quality of printing paper and the revolution in colour printing along with excellent reproduction of illustrations are things children at that time could only have dreamt of. Nevertheless, both Enid and her publishers should be complimented for bringing out the traditional stories for mass circulation at a time when they were most needed![106]

BRIEF HISTORY
OF
THE ENID BLYTON'S MAGAZINE

One of the smartest moves Enid Blyton ever made during her lifetime was to produce her own magazine – *Enid Blyton's Magazine* (see front covers illustration, Figure 32). Coming hot on the heels of the *Sunny Stories* magazine from which she withdrew in 1953, it was to take the children's world by storm, for it gave her the opportunity to recover the huge fan base that was left in abeyance when she withdrew from *The Teachers World* and the *Sunny Stories* magazine.

The news that she was starting up a new fortnightly magazine probably filled her fans with delight, especially when they discovered that it contained all the features they had missed from the *Sunny Stories* magazine – features such as her 'Letter to Boys and Girls', stories, poems, competitions, puzzles, hunts for flowers and so on.

The first issue, published by Evans Brothers Ltd, came out on March 18, 1953 and was an instant success. So much so that some four months later, Enid was still receiving hundreds of letters from children in England and all around the world thanking her for starting up the magazine and telling her what they would like to see in it. Here is an extract from one of her 'Letters to Boys and Girls' in the edition of July 8, 1953 describing the situation:

Here we are with number nine of our magazine already – it seems only a few weeks ago since we first saw Number 1 on March 18th! I am so very glad you all like our new magazine and read every word of it ... I think you would like to have a look at my post every morning. Ideas pour in from you, news comes in from all parts of the world, photographs arrive, thank you letters (what nice manners most of you have!), and all sorts of suggestions for this and that. Dear me, if ever Readers help to run the magazine, it is you…

FIGURE 32: Front covers of two of Enid Blyton's Magazine that she started up in 1953 after withdrawing from the Sunny Stories magazine. It enjoyed a fortnightly circulation of around 60,000 copies and ran through 162 issues before coming to a close in 1959.© British Library Board (SM: left, pp.5992. hc Vol 2, No 7; right, pp.5992.hc Vol 7, No 6). Images restoration credit: 2graphic Photo Restoration. Website: www.photo-restoration.

Sometime afterwards, many of these children were writing to her again, this time to order badges to become members of one of her three fan clubs and a society whose meeting place was in the magazine itself. The names of the fan clubs and society were: *The Famous Five Club*, *The Busy Bees Club*, *The Enid Blyton's Magazine Club*, and *The Sunbeam Society* which was the youth section of the National Institute for the Blind (see Appendix 69 for brief information about each of these fan clubs and the society, drawn from the 1957 issue, in pocket format, of *Enid Blyton Diary*, published by W. M. Collins Sons & Co Ltd, London & Glasgow).

Indeed so great was this organisation of children that by 1957 the membership of one club alone, *The Enid Blyton's Magazine Club*, had reached a staggering 100,000. To mark the occasion, Evans Brothers invited Enid and some of the children who had worked for the clubs to a celebration party at Montague House in London. There was a special cake and Enid was presented with an initialled and dated gold replica of the magazine's club badge. [107]

Apart from entertaining children everywhere with her stories, poems and giving them things to do in the form of hunting for flowers, working out puzzles and so on, Enid also used the magazine to advertise her new and existing books. It was also the perfect medium to announce the wide range of commercial products that were coming on the market as spin-offs from her famous Noddy books – products such as jigsaw puzzles, Noddy car games and ornaments.

After running the magazine single-handedly for some six years, pressure of work, new projects and failing health constrained her to bring it to a close, as can be seen in the following extract from her farewell letter that appeared in the last issue of September 9, 1959:

Green Hedges
September 9, 1959
Dear Boys And Girls,

I have some very sad news for you today. This is the last issue of our much loved magazine ... I will tell you now why I so suddenly decided that I could no longer write our magazine. It is because of two things. The first is that all kinds of interesting work keeps coming along which unfortunately no one but myself could do – making films for you – T.V. programs – the making of new records – overseas radio programs – the Noddy In Toyland pantomime, which is now to be put on in other big towns as well as in London – and new books of course! And going all the time is my magazine, of which, as you know, I write practically every word (except the advertisements!) ...

ENID BLYTON

In this way, the fans she restored from the *Sunny Stories* magazine and mobilised subsequently into fan clubs soon disintegrated. To find out what happened to the clubs themselves, let's leave the last word to Barbara Stoney:

> *'... With the exception of The Famous Five Club, which was then handled by the books' publisher, all were kept alive through the organisation they had helped – and by the Enid Blyton diaries (first published by Collins in 1950) which continued to give news of all four and the charities they supported.'* [108]

A SHORT HISTORY OF DARRELL WATERS LTD

ENID BLYTON'S COMPANY

If you ever wanted to find out why Enid formed this company, what its objectives were and what has become of it after her passing in 1968, then this article is for you.

EVENTS LEADING TO THE FORMATION OF DARRELL WATERS LIMITED.

From reading through the ten chapters in this book, we've seen Enid Blyton coping with a heavy workload that expanded in all directions. Moreover, in Section Two under *Why Some of Enid Blyton Stories Are Not Up To Standard,* we learn she was doing all that work with neither secretarial nor editorial assistance and that she relied on her powerful photographic memory to keep track of her business affairs.

However, as the years went by she must have found doing everything herself burdensome. By 1950, she was contracted to more than twenty publishers, apart from those overseas, with over 300 of her books in circulation both in England and around the world.

She also had to manage her domestic affairs such as paying her household staff, planning the day's meal with the cook, paying utility bills, ordering stationery and so on.

On the other hand, she had no system in place to protect her books, plays, songs and poems against copyright infringements, especially in overseas countries, and never fully recognised the potential for profits by granting licences to third parties, such as TV, film and audio companies, to adapt her books for this media.

Neither did she know at that time about merchandising, that is, arranging with companies to use images of her favourite characters such as the Famous Five, Secret Seven and Noddy to sell their products. It was these situations that must have given rise to the formation of a company.

Exactly where the idea to form a company came from we are entirely in the dark. It could have come from her dealings with her publishers, from her attorney or from a suggestion from her husband. But the person whom she eventually found to help her to form a company was Eric Rogers. The little we know about him is gleaned from her daughter, Imogen Smallwood, who states in a passage on pages 119 to 120 in *A Childhood at Green Hedges* that he was the senior partner in a firm of City stockbrokers. She also tells us in the same passage that he was an ambitious and gregarious man, and that his lifelong dealings in the stock and money markets made him, in his own eyes, the ideal person to set up and direct the running of a company that was to conserve and use the prodigious income her mother's writing produced.

Therefore, it was most likely this person, in his capacity as financial and business advisor, who set the stage for the formation of her company.

Accordingly, after they had identified the key persons to run the company and the legal requirements were met, an inaugural meeting was held on Friday, March 31, 1950 at the solicitors' office of Langton & Passmore, situated at 8 Bolton Street, London. At this meeting, Enid Blyton was appointed chairman and her husband, a director. Eric Rogers was appointed Company Secretary and eventually, Managing Director. Arnold Thirlby, was appointed solicitor, and John Basden, from the firm Holden Howard & Co, accountant. Both of them were also appointed directors. When the Memorandum and Articles of Association were read and approved, Darrell Waters Ltd – named after her second husband, [Kenneth] Darrell Waters – was incorporated.

SHARE CAPITAL

The first thing we find when we try to understand the nature of this new company is that it was a company established with a share capital of £10,000, divided into 10,000 Ordinary Shares of £1.00 each. The directors alone had the power to issue shares and everything to do with the transfer of shares, the increase of the share capital, the payment of dividends, general meetings and so on were set out in the company's Articles of Association, the provisions of which are too long to include in this short history.

MEMORANDUM OF ASSOCIATION

This is a legal document setting out the objectives of the company. In this carefully worded document, we find that its objectives went far beyond the mere management of Enid Blyton's intricate business affairs. Among the objectives set out in the document were:

- To purchase or acquire real and personal property
- To purchase rights of copyright in literary, dramatic, musical or pictorial works
- To carry on the business of printers, publishers and distributors of newspapers, magazines and periodicals
- To carry on the business of literary & dramatic agents
- To carry on the business of an investment and holding company

(See Appendix 73 for the first page of the Memorandum of Association giving details of some of the objectives just listed in brief.)

However, many of the twenty-five elaborate objectives in the document were to remain dormant for a number of years while the directors concentrated on the main task ahead – to sort out her business affairs. In time Enid Blyton's two daughters, Imogen and Gillian, joined the board as directors.

DARRELL WATERS TAKES OFF

No sooner had the company been incorporated than the managing director, along with the appointed staff members, set about the task of sorting out Enid's intricate business affairs. The first thing they did was to take stock of all her publishers, both at home and abroad, and reviewed their contractual arrangements.

Then they drew up an inventory of all her books, in print and out of print. It is believed that *A Complete List of [Her] Books* that John Menzies published in 1951, some one year after the company was incorporated, was commissioned by Darrell Waters Ltd. This book contained a list of some 300 books she had written up to that time and classified in such a way that readers could easily find the titles, names of publishers, the price, the categories – Nature, Adventure, Circus etc – and the age groups, along with a complete alphabetical listing.

The next thing they did was to register Enid Blyton's signature, and that of the word *Noddy*, as trademarks.

Now it would appear that the company was set up at the right time to deal with a sensation that was caused by Enid Blyton's new creation – Noddy. His books, and play *Noddy in Toyland* that was staged in theatres up and down the country, were to take the children's world by storm.

Soon the company was caught up in publishing, or commissioning the publication of, new Noddy books that were not already contracted to publishers since his creation in 1949, one year before the formation of the company. It was also caught up in the tasks of merchandising – doing deals with manufacturers and companies to carry the likeness of Noddy on children's clothes, stationery, toiletries and in the manufacture of inanimate and animated toys, games and puzzles. The company also profited from granting overseas publishers translation rights to have the Noddy books appear in foreign languages all over the world.

From 1950 to 1954, Darrell Waters Ltd went from strength to strength and with competent staff, managed to achieve its immediate objective to put Enid Blyton's business and financial affairs in order.

Then all of a sudden they had to deal with a crisis – Enid Blyton, for whom the company was set up, suddenly resigned, in December, 1954, from the post of chairman and director of Darrell Waters Limited!

ENID BLYTON RESIGNED AS CHAIRMAN & DIRECTOR

It is not known why Enid Blyton resigned, but we can identify at least two factors that might have contributed to her resignation. The first could be pressure of work. Her many writing projects did not allow her to carry out the duties of chairman effectively. Secondly, her insistence that she should be allowed to negotiate contracts with her publishers while the company already had a provision in the Memorandum of Association to do so on her behalf must have set her at odds with the board of directors.

Her younger daughter, Imogen Smallwood, appeared to have known the reason for her mother's determination to have her own way:

'My mother could not have tolerated the other directors interfering in such matters, and neither would the publishers, who dealt with her so confidently, have been pleased at the change,' she states in a passage on page 120 of her book: *A Childhood at Green Hedges.*

Nevertheless, the real reason could have been that the role of chairman and director did not suit her. She had an artistic cast of mind and must have found it strange to be sitting at board meetings among the other directors who were experts in the field of business and finance. She was in her element when she was using her imagination to create songs, plays, stories and poems. Hence she would have shone brilliantly if she had been chairman of some literary society where the topics of discussions centered on such subjects. Whatever the case the directors had to accept that she was no longer on the board and move on.

MAKING PROGRESS

Having come to terms with Enid's resignation, the company turned its attention to the fulfilment of the objectives outlined in the Memorandum of Association. Chief among them was the systematic copywriting of her new books using the formula: © Enid Blyton: Darrell Waters Ltd. They also did something that Enid herself could never have done alone – police her copyrights and trademarks and guard against infringements and fraud of all kinds.

The first case that came to their attention was that of the German author and journalist, Brigitte Blobel, who claimed to have translated two Famous Five books written by Enid Blyton. The books in question are: *The Famous Five on the Forbidden Island* – German Translation: *Fünf Freunde auf der verbotenen Insel* and *The Famous Five and the Blue Diamond* – German translation: *Fünf Freunde und der blaue Diamant* both of which were published by the German publisher Bertelsmann, in 1977 and 1979 respectively.

As it turned out the two Famous Five books never existed in English at all. They were in fact her own original books in German. Strong objections from Darrell Waters Ltd caused the publisher to withdraw the two books from circulation. It's not known what action Darrell Waters eventually took against the impostor and her publisher.

Then there was the case of David Haslam, aged 35, from Newlyn, Cornwall, England whom the company accused of Noddy trademark infringement. The alleged infringement occurred when he did a pencil drawing entitled: 'Noddy vs the Real World' which showed the character on a podium between two American TV evangelists looking down on a mob in a picture that was taken from a 19th century German book (see illustration, Figure 33).

The company subsequently tried to force Mr. Haslam to remove the drawing from an exhibition at Kettering, Northamptonshire, but before he could do so Kettering Council officials confiscated the drawing and posters reproduced from it after they had received a letter from the company's solicitors threatening action.

The company said it would sue Mr. Haslam unless he gave an undertaking not to display the drawing or posters in public again, an undertaking which Mr. Haslam refused to give; whereupon the company took him to court. Before going to court his solicitor, Stuart Lockyear, counter-threatened Darrell Waters Ltd with the European Declaration of Human Rights Article 19 (Freedom of Expression) and the company backed down. They returned his drawing under the threat that if he tried to sell the picture or the posters he would be sued.[109] These two cases might have been the tip of the iceberg, with others the company resolved privately, without their reaching the attention of the public.

Coming back to the subject of the company turning its attention to the fulfilment of its objectives, another objective they managed to fulfil, with varying degrees of success, was the granting of licences to third parties to exploit Enid Blyton's creations. In the forefront was BBC Enterprises – later to become BBC Worldwide – to whom a licence had been granted to do a series of television programmes and cartoon series about Noddy, Big Ears and his Toyland pals. According to an article in *The Guardian*, in the edition of May 7, 1996, during 1995 alone, the BBC had released seven Noddy videos (selling 500,000 of them), launched a Noddy comic and sold two million copies of the thirty-seven Noddy books (some with tapes attached) and four *Learn-with-Noddy* board books.

FIGURE 33: David Haslam's pencil drawing: 'Noddy vs. the Real World' showing Noddy between two American TV evangelists. Darrell Waters Ltd, Enid Blyton's company, accused him of Noddy trademark infringement. Source: David Haslam's website: www.agraphic.co.uk/nod.htm which is no longer accessible on the Internet.

Come to think of it, it was this same company, whose executives deliberately kept Enid Blyton off the airwaves in the mid-1930s and branded the work submitted to them for approval as 'second rate' and of 'no literary merit', that's now taking the liberty to promote her stories in the form of cartoons, films and television programmes. How times have changed!

Then there was a production company called Family Feature Films based in Germany to whom a licence had been granted to make Blyton films for both cinema and TV. Others to whom licenses had been given included Copyright Productions Ltd, to do a thirteen part series of animated Noddy film that was transmitted by Thames Television; Phonogram, the record division of Phillips Industries, to record on audio cassette Noddy, Mary Mouse and other Enid Blyton characters and to David Wood, the British playwright, theatre producer and director to do a series of adaptations of Noddy for the stage.

Yet a third objective that was fulfilled many years later – in 1982 to be exact – was the bringing into being a trust to help children in need. It became known as The Enid Blyton Trust and was headed by Imogen Smallwood, Enid Blyton's younger daughter who, as we already know, was also one of the directors of Darrell Waters Ltd. Its main objective was to give financial assistance to the Great Ormond Street Hospital. (For more information on this Trust, see the article in Section Two: The Enid Blyton Trust.)

Finally, it is not known whether, or to what extent, the directors managed to fulfill the remaining twenty-two objectives that included things such as acquiring real and personal property and carrying on the business of an Investment & Holding company.

DARRELL WATERS CHANGES DIRECTION

As the years went by the company found itself dealing with changes that were to alter the structure and objectives of the company and steer it in another direction. These changes resulted from the passing of Kenneth Darrell Waters, Enid Blyton's second husband, who was also a director, on 15 September 1967, and of Enid Blyton, on November 28, 1968. She died peacefully in her sleep in a nursing home in

Hampstead. She is said to have left a personal fortune of £283,589 net (£330,946 gross). Most of her assets were said to have been tied of up in Stock Market quoted shares. [110]

Then in 1980 Eric Rogers, the Managing Director of the company, passed away. He is credited with using his financial and Stock Market expertise, especially in the early years of the formation of the company, to successfully manage Enid's financial affairs that, in the end, brought prosperity to her and her family, as pointed out in the following passage drawn from page 121 of Imogen Smallwood's book, *A Childhood at Green Hedges:*

> '...Behind all these ideas, negotiations and actions was the fertile brain of Eric Rogers and there is no doubt that the increasing wealth available to my parents was due to his management of their financial affairs.'

THE END OF DARRELL WATERS LTD

With the loss of these key persons at different intervals in the life of the company, the main objective of the company changed from managing Enid Blyton's business affairs to managing and conserving her vast literary estate, which included the copyrights to some 700 books she had written up to that time. At the helm were Enid Blyton's two daughters, Gillian Baverstock and Imogen Smallwood, who were still active directors in the company. While the staff carried out the day to day running of the company, it was they who had to make decisions when important company matters surfaced.

By this time both sisters were advancing in years – Gillian, who was born 15 July 1931 was approaching 65 years of age while Imogen, who was born 27 October 1935, was approaching 60, and were both leading busy lives. While Gillian was touring England lecturing on her mother's work at book festivals and exhibitions and giving interviews to the media, Imogen, along with her daughter, Sophie, was engaged in the running of The Enid Blyton Trust.

Therefore, to free themselves from carrying the weight of the company on their shoulders when the main objectives of the company had already been achieved, they decided that the time was ripe to sell the company; and what better time to do so than the approaching centenary of the birth of their mother on August 11, 1897.

Having decided that that was the best thing to do and after consultation with the company's lawyer and members of staff, they promptly called in Keith Tilson of Price Waterhouse Corporate Finance, who subsequently announced the intended sale in the media and monitored the results:

'*We are already getting quite a good response,*' said Keith Tilson, in an article written by Robert Winder for *The Independent*, in the issue of Saturday, November 18, 1995. '*Publishing companies, media companies and toy companies are all interested. Negotiations are expected to take several months.*' [111]

Surprisingly enough, Gillian herself had shown an interest in buying the company to conserve her mother's legacy:

'*I did try to raise the finance to buy the company,*' she said in an interview given to *The Independent*, reproduced in an article by Marianne Macdonald, in the issue of Wednesday 24 January 1996, '*but the money required was so great, and so many people were interested ... it was quite impossible.*' [112] In the end, Darrell Waters Limited was sold to Trocadero Plc for £14.7 m* and the company acquired it in February, 1996. [113]

Now while Gillian and her younger sister, Imogen, breathed a sigh of relief, others with whom they had been dealing in the years leading up to the sale, were also relieved, but for a different reason. According to an article in *The Guardian*, in the issue of May 7, 1996, the sale was met with general relief from those involved currently with Blyton projects. One such company was the BBC: '*Doing business with the family was becoming more and more difficult as there were lots of internal arguments. We're very pleased to have everything now on a clear business footing,*' said a source that was not disclosed to *The Guardian*.

Nevertheless, in judging the merits of the sale, we have to take into account that the company had fulfilled, many years earlier, the objective for which it had been set up, namely, to put Enid Blyton's financial affairs in order. In so doing, they had given her the peace of mind to carry on with her various writing projects and in the process made her and her family prosperous. It is this singular achievement, more than any other, that the company will always be remembered for.

*NOTE: There appears to be no agreement about the exact figure of the sale. I have seen quotes in newspaper articles ranging from £10m to £14m. However, the figure stated here, £14.7m, has been taken directly from a passage in Trocadero Plc. report to its shareholders on the acquisition of Darrell Waters Ltd, in its Preliminary Results for Year Ending December 31, 1996.

A SHORT HISTORY OF ENID BLYTON'S LITERARY ESTATE

AFTER IT HAD BEEN ACQUIRED BY TROCADERO PLC

As stated in the previous article, Trocadero Plc bought Darrell Waters Ltd in February 1996 from Gillian Baverstock and Imogen Smallwood, Enid Blyton's two daughters, who were running the company at that time, for £14.7 million. By so doing, it inherited Enid Blyton's literary estate comprising the copyrights of some 700 books as well as film, television, audio, translation and world rights in the bargain.

Trocadero plc came into being in November, 1995 when it demerged or split from Burford Holdings Plc, a property development group, and became a separate company. Its main activity was to manage the Trocadero building situated at the angle of Shaftesbury Avenue and Windmill Street in London (see illustration, Figure 34). At the same time it was managing the vast entertainment and leisure complex within the building itself.

One of the reasons for purchasing Darrell Waters Ltd was to find a home for Enid Blyton's favourite characters in a large interactive store in the entertainment complex. Here, visitors to the store could learn about Enid Blyton, buy her books, tapes and videos, and interact with some of her favourite characters in full body suits.[114]

FIGURE 34: A photo of the Trocadero building that was managed by Trocadero plc, the company that bought Darrell Waters Ltd from the Enid Blyton family. Enid Blyton's characters such as 'Noddy', 'Big Ears', 'The Famous Five' and 'The Secret Seven' were to find a home here in an interactive store. The project never got off the ground. Source: Evening Standard, in the edition of 16 August 2012 with the caption: Trocadero to be transformed into Tokyo-style 'pod' hotel. Photo credit: Tony Buckingham, photographer. Email: tonybuckingham@hotmail.com

The idea to do this must have come from the American entertainer, Walt Disney (1901 – 1966), who had similar stores throughout America in which visitors could interact with his creations, Mickey and Minnie Mouse, in full body suits, and buy the merchandise. However, for some unknown reason, this project never got off the ground and the company quickly turned its attention to fully exploiting Enid Blyton's copyrights.

To this end, it changed the name from Darrell Waters Ltd to Enid Blyton Ltd, set it up as a wholly owned subsidiary, and appointed David Lane, a former law lecturer and past director of Classic Licensing Ltd, as Managing Director to run the new branch of the company.

GETTING DOWN TO BUSINESS

The first task undertaken by David Lane and his team was to review the 7,000 existing publishing contracts, renegotiate their terms, increase the royalty rates and shorten perpetual rights to between two to ten years. In the end, the Enid Blyton Company managed to reduce the number of contracts to a much more manageable 500.[115]

Then they appeared at trade fairs around the world and, subsequently, established overseas representatives in twenty-one international markets to distribute licences for Enid Blyton productions.

Consequently, book sales were averaging eleven million copies a year worldwide and Enid Blyton's name, as well as the words Noddy and The Famous Five, became international brands in the same way Winnie the Pooh, Tintin, the Teletubbies and Thomas the Tank Engine became well known international brands.

Moreover, the Enid Blyton Company had done what its previous owners, Darrell Waters Ltd, could only dream of doing, namely, to break into the US Children's TV market. In the process, Noddy, who had by then become the company's star character, became a star in the States, breaking all TV viewing records. The production that propelled him into stardom, *Noddy in Toyland*, received high ratings and was subsequently sold to broadcasters worldwide. So popular had the show become that the company produced a sequel, *Make Way for Noddy* which also became a hit in the States and in countries worldwide.

Another thing they did was to establish in 1998 a new joint-venture company called Enid Blyton (Asia) Ltd to strengthen its presence in countries such as China, Japan, Korea, the Philippines and Singapore, as well as New Zealand and Australia. Here the company had the opportunity to sell translations of books and TV shows in a host of languages. This company, and another that was eventually formed in Singapore, became subsidiaries.[116]

Furthermore, on the home front, it had done successful deals with film and TV companies to take Enid Blyton's stories and characters off the pages of her popular storybooks, such as *The Famous Five* and the *Secret Seven*, and transported them unto TV and cinema screens in a number of adaptations that eventually resulted in increased books sales. In short, its success, both at home and abroad, had surpassed all expectations.

Meanwhile, changes were taking place at Trocadero Plc, the parent company, that eventually rebounded on the Enid Blyton Company which, as we already know, had been set up as a wholly owned subsidiary.

In the first place, it changed its name to Chorion Plc on 23 April, 1998 after acquiring the Agatha Christie, Georges Simenon and Robert Bolt's literary estates and branching out into the Bars and Nightclubs business. As these literary estates were already separate companies, Chorion established them as subsidiaries. Then it grouped the subsidiaries, including Enid Blyton Ltd, under the name Intellectual Property. In this way, it had two definite lines of business: The Bars and Nightclubs business and the Intellectual Property business.

In May 2002, after both lines of businesses had become successful, Chorion demerged or split into two, and the two lines of businesses become separate companies. The Bars and Nightclubs business became Urbium Plc and went its own way while the Intellectual Property business was established as New Chorion. Shortly after the demerger, New Chorion Plc changed its name back to Chorion Plc.

So how did The Enid Blyton Company fit into this new arrangement? Well, under the Intellectual Property umbrella it was classed as a portfolio, having by that time become one of many intellectual properties the company was managing at the same time. At one time Choron even tried to sell off Enid Blyton's literary estate for £30m. That was in November 2002 soon after the company demerged or split into two. The reason given was to maximise shareholders' value. However, poor response to the sale and the company's change of heart resulted in Enid Blyton's literary estate remaining in the fold.[117]

Meanwhile, the bright future the company had predicted from the excellent performances of its various portfolios soon turned into gloom when the worldwide financial crisis saw a heavy drop in book sales, project delays, bad debts and the cancellation or forestalling of orders for new TV programmes and films. To redress this situation, Chorion agreed to a £111m buyout in 2006 by the private equity firm 3i. It then changed its status from a public limited company to a private company.[118]

However, notwithstanding rapid growth in its business, the global economic crisis that eventually led to the company breaching its banking agreement plunged the company further into debt. Then, when the company failed to negotiate a new deal with its bank to alleviate its debt burden, both the company's chairman, Lord Alli and deputy chairman Lord Astor, resigned in August, 2011 and the company went into liquidation.

Consequently, the company began selling off its assets one by one. So it was that in March 2012, Enid Blyton's literary estate was sold to Hachette UK for an undisclosed sum, with the exception of Noddy, which by that time had become a separate portfolio. He was subsequently sold off to Classic Media, a US company.

Marlene Johnson, Managing Director of Hachette Children's Books was delighted with the acquisition:

I am absolutely delighted that we have acquired world rights to publish Enid Blyton. Hodder was her original publisher, so it is fitting that her whole portfolio has come home and will now be published and managed under one roof.

Mary Durkan, Managing Director Chorion was also delighted that a buyer had been found:

Chorion has actively managed a competitive and comprehensive sales process for this heritage estate over the last few months. The Enid Blyton estate has a wonderful literary heritage ...We are delighted that it is going to a publisher who understands and treasures this vast library of children's content. [119]

So Chorion that had done so much to advance the copyrights business and conserve Enid Blyton's literary estate was no more. It is now left for us to see what will happen to it now that it has found a new home at Hachette UK!

Further Reading

NEWSPAPER ARTICLES

Noddy Goes to the Trocadero, *The Independent*, January 24, 1996, article by Marianne Macdonald, Media Correspondent.

Gee Whiz, Noddy's a Sensation in the US: *The Times* p.1, 8 December, 1998, article by Helen Rumbelow.

Noddy Conquers America: the *Evening Standard,* 7 December, 1998, article by Hosking Patrick.

Noddy and Enid go West: *The Times* (London, England), Tuesday, April 21,1998, pg. 24.

Enid Blyton Ventures into Asia: *The Indian Express Globetrotter*, June 10, 1998.

Noddy's Asian Adventure: *The Sunday Times* (London, UK) June 7, 1998, article by Parsley, David.

Chorion hopes for £30 million windfall, Growth Company Investor, 07 November 2002, article by Leslie Copeland.

Make way for Noddy in China: *The Guardian*, Mon 22 March 2004, article by Stuart Jeffries.

Noddy heads for Japan, *The Guardian*, Mon 10 Jan 2005, article by Chris Tryhorn, City correspondent.

Chorion agrees £111m buyout, *Media Guardian*, Thursday 23 February 2006.

Chorion Set to be Broken Up, *The Mail on Sunday*, Sunday, August 28, 2011.

Noddy owner Chorion in sell–off: *The Daily Telegraph* (London, England) Friday, September 2, 2011.

THE ENID BLYTON TRUST

This Trust was started in 1982 by Darrell Waters Ltd, the company Enid formed to manage her business affairs. Its main objective was to give financial aid to the Great Ormond Street Hospital. As the years went by it extended its charitable giving to include grants to special schools for children, literacy schemes, arts activities and some holiday schemes. Grants were often made from £210 to a maximum of £2,500

Enid Blyton's younger daughter, Imogen Smallwood, was at the helm with a number of trustees, and her daughter, Sophie Smallwood, was also actively involved in its activities.

Then in June 2011 the trustees decided to wind up the Trust and donated its assets totaling £750,000 to Seven Stories, to set up a permanent fund at the Community Foundation Tyne & Wear and Northumberland.

This is how a spokesman for the Trust explained the decision to give its assets to Seven Stories, as carried in a post in the *Seven Stories' Enid Blyton Blog Site:*

Seven Stories is a truly inspiring place. We know that we have made the right decision and believe that Enid herself would feel very happy with everything Seven Stories is doing for her, her work and for the children.

Writing on behalf of Seven Stories in the same *Seven Stories' Enid Blyton Blog Site*, Hannah Green, the archivist, followed this explanation with the following statement:

This new Fund deepens Seven Stories' connection with Enid

Blyton and her outstanding contribution to children's literature in Britain. Grants from the Enid Blyton Fund for Seven Stories at Community Foundation will support our work to inspire more children from different walks of life to enjoy reading and the life opportunities that this brings. *

Hence the Trust that survived Enid's passing in 1968 for over forty years and disbursed some £500,000 to children in need has transferred its charitable work to an organisation with different activities and objectives. For just as Enid Blyton's storybooks have taught countless numbers of children to read, so the legacy to Seven Stories, a Centre for Children's Literature, will continue the trend but from a different perspective. Long may the new arrangement last!

*Hannah Green's full article, dated 22 June 2011, announcing the legacy can be read by visiting: *blytonsevenstories.wordpress.com*

A SHORT TREATMENT
OF
CLAIRVOYANCE

When we read about the wonderful demonstrations of clairvoyance by Enid Blyton, the blind Frances Browne, Robert Houghton and J.K. Rowling in the domain of fiction writing, as carried in Chapter VII, under *Enid: The Professional Storyteller*, we are both surprised and astonished.

Surprised because we never thought it was possible for fiction writers to see in their imaginations characters, scenes and settings from their stories as clearly as if everything were right before them and astonished because we never knew that blind people could also do the same thing.

We are even more amazed when we learn that clairvoyants can do things such as read the contents of a letter in an opaque envelope without opening it; see what lies on the other side of a solid brick wall; tell the picture, number or suit of a card turned down on a flat surface; find a missing person by holding in their hands some object, such as a wrist watch belonging to the person, and read a page in a closed book in a library without being anywhere near the book. All these wonderful things are done through a strange power that is called clairvoyance.

Clairvoyance may be described as the power to see with inner vision what we cannot see with the naked eyes. It is supposed to be dormant in all of us and is the heritage of all mankind, as can be seen from the following extract drawn from the opening lines in C. W. Leadbeater's book entitled *Clairvoyance: 'The capacity of clairvoyance ... lies latent in everyone, and those in whom it already manifests itself are simply in that particular a little in advance of the rest of us.'* [120]

If Mr Leadbeater's assertion is true, then we can all become clairvoyants. But what can we do to awaken this power that's supposed to be dormant in all of us? We can do so through training that is offered in England at a place called *The College of Psychic Studies* in South Kensington, London. [121]

Here our clairvoyant abilities will be assessed and if selected we could for a fee sit with others in comfortable surroundings for development or enfoldment of any branch of clairvoyance we may be good at. We'll also be invited to lectures and to consult the wealth of books on esoteric subjects in its library. Other means of development can be acquired through meditation classes under qualified teachers in yoga centres throughout the country. Then we'll no longer be surprised or astonished when we hear about people doing marvellous things as described in the preceding paragraphs and listed in Appendix 57. We'll be able to do them ourselves.

WIDER CONSIDERATIONS

Clairvoyance is as old as the hills. There's hardly a country in the world where it is not practiced in one way or another by peoples from all walks of life.

In the Bible, one of the world's oldest books to describe cultural practices among ancient peoples, we find references to it under names such as soothsaying, prophecy or fortune telling. However, because of its association with a branch of clairvoyance know as necromancy – convocation of or communication with spirits of the dead – Christians have been warned to stay away from it. Neither should they go to consult anyone working in that field.

However, this one-sided view has failed to impress upon the minds of Christians that clairvoyance, as portrayed in this article, is rife in the Bible, with Jesus being the greatest demonstrator of the art. To take an example drawn from the New Testament (the New International

Version), in the Gospel according to St John 4: 1 – 19, it is written there that Jesus met a Samaritan woman at a well while waiting for His disciples to return. During their conversation, Jesus told her of water He could give that no one would ever thirst (John 4:14).

The woman said to Him, 'Sir, give me this water so that I won't get thirsty and have to keep coming here to draw water.'

He told her, 'Go, call your husband and come back.'

'I have no husband,' she replied.

Jesus said to her, 'You are right when you say you have no husband. The fact is, you have had five husbands, and the man you now have is not your husband. What you have just said is quite true.'

'Sir,' the woman said, 'I can see that you are a prophet ...' [122]

Other example dealing with His exercising clairvoyance can be found in Mark 8: 31, where He predicted his death; Mark 14: 17 – 21, where He predicted that Judas would betray Him and in Mark 14: 27 – 31, where He predicted that Peter would disown Him. In the first example of the Samaritan woman, he was demonstrating Clairvoyance of the Past, and in others, Clairvoyance of the Future, two of the many branches listed in Appendix 57.

These examples rank among the good side of clairvoyance Christians are yet to discover. But the Church is so keen to protect Christians from the bad side of clairvoyance that it neglects to point out there's also a good side.

This state of affairs where the Church forbids the practice of clairvoyance in any of its forms was to continue with the Witchcraft Acts that were promulgated in England from time to time. [123] Among the practices the Acts forbid, under penalty of imprisonment or death, were convocation of or consorting with evil spirits, foretelling the future, casting spells and discovering the whereabouts of stolen goods. Consequently, England was gripped with fear that led to witch-hunts and denunciations of people suspected of witchcraft.

However, with the improvement in living standards and the rise of literacy among the so-called common people over the centuries, and the coming of the industrial revolution that provided work for idle hands and brains, witchcraft was no longer considered a threat to society.

Nevertheless, the Witchcraft Act of 1735 was to remain in force for over 200 years until 1951 when it was finally removed from the statute books, thanks to the Spiritualists National Union's successful campaign for its repeal, on the grounds that its members should be able to practice mediumship and demonstrate clairvoyance at church meetings, with no fear of prosecution. It was replaced with the Fraudulent Mediums Act that was promulgated 22 June 1951, a facsimile of which is presented in Appendix 74.

The new Act was subsequently repealed in 2008 when the Consumer Protection Regulations came into force May 26, 2008. Mediums, clairvoyants operating under the name of psychics, and others in the field of fortune telling are all regarded as providing a service to customers and had to comply with the new regulations.

However, even before these Regulations came into being, another organisation had been working tirelessly to help clairvoyants and others working in the field to gain respectability. This organisation is called the Society for Psychical Research. Set up in London in 1882 to investigate inexplicable phenomena, its various committees led by distinguished, open-minded people from all callings in life, soon accumulated a large body of evidence from participants to put clairvoyance in a favourable light. The cases they have investigated are carefully documented in the Proceedings and Journals of the Society.[124]

In this way clairvoyants need only to act in good faith at all times to uphold this respectability. It is also hoped that one day clairvoyance will be elevated to such a status that it will be fully accepted by the scientific community – a hurdle that is difficult to overcome because of fraud that is practiced by unscrupulous people and charlatans who are masquerading under the guise of clairvoyants.

Finally, for those of us who aspire to be good fiction writers, if the clairvoyant faculties were to awaken we would no longer have to struggle to invent plots. For once the idea to write a story comes to us, we could use our fully developed clairvoyant faculty to see in our imaginations the characters and settings in a story and listen to the dialogues with the additional faculty of clairaudience, which often accompanies clairvoyance. Then we could sit down like Enid Blyton and write it all out as it unfolds in our imaginations. In this way, we'll produce wonderful fiction books to fascinate and amuse children the world over – just as Enid Blyton and others have done. These would all be worthwhile goals to aspire to achieve if the wonderful faculty of clairvoyance, which is supposed to be dormant in all of us, is ever awakened!

NOTE: As this is just a short treatment of clairvoyance, those of us who would like to have a deeper understanding of the subject should try to get hold of a copy of C. W. Leadbeater's *Clairvoyance* which was mentioned earlier in this article and which has long since gone out of print. It is written in non-technical language, in layman's terms. It also provides a good grounding so that, were we to go for training in any way we choose to develop the faculty, we would be in a better position to understand what's happening.

Another copy is available to download from the Internet, free of charge, by typing the following link into the web browser: www.gutenberg. org/ebooks/29399. We can also explore the other books listed at the bottom of Appendix 57 for further reading.

PHYSIOGNOMY AND PHRENOLOGY

THE RISE AND FALL OF TWO GREAT 'SCIENCES'

In this essay we take a look at two great 'sciences' that came into the world like lightning, stood around for a century or two, and suddenly disappeared after influencing the thoughts and actions of countless numbers of people all over the world. How did they come into being? What circumstances hastened their demise? The answers may be found in this short essay, beginning with physiognomy.

PHYSIOGNOMY

In the summer of 1777, one of the most famous meetings ever arranged between two great men took place in the palace of the Holy Roman Emperor, in the city of Zurich, Switzerland. One of these men was Joseph II (1741 – 1790), the Holy Roman Emperor and the other, Johann Casper Lavater (1741 – 1801) the renowned author of *Essays On Physiognomy,* [125] a work in three volumes the Emperor himself had studied ever since Lavater presented him with a copy. (See frontispiece and title page illustration of one of the three volumes, Figure 30.)

'*Ah! You are a dangerous man!*' the Emperor said to Lavater as soon as he was brought before him. '*I don't know whether anyone ought to suffer himself to be seen by you. You look into the hearts of men. We must be very cautious when we come into your company.*' [126]

These are sentiments that almost anyone of the hundreds of thousands of people who had read his famous essays would have liked to express, if ever they had the opportunity to meet him face to face. For in that masterly work that was translated into many languages and ran through several editions, he laid bare the secrets of all the features of the human face for all to see. In exactly one hundred physiognomical rules, supported by some 800 of his own illustrations, he revealed the characteristics associated with every feature of the human face he had carefully studied – the forehead, eyebrows, eyes, nose, mouth and so on (see illustration of nine noses, Appendix 70).

As if overnight, avid readers of his essays had at their fingertips secrets of the human face that they could use to judge their neighbours. His books soon got the attention of employers who quickly profited by using his deductions to select the best workers, and those who employed servants had an invaluable tool for deciding whether their prospective employees would give the best service.

Even Charles Darwin (1809-1882), the English naturalist and author of *The Origin of Species*, could not escape his influence. In a passage in his autobiography, he stated how he had run a narrow risk of being rejected for the voyage of exploration because of the shape of his nose. The captain, Fitz-Roy, who had been an ardent disciple of Lavater, doubted whether, with such a nose, he had the energy and determination for the voyage. '*I think he was afterwards well satisfied that my nose had spoken falsely,*' Charles Darwin stated with satisfaction at the end of the passage. [127]

Thanks therefore to the publication of his three-volume set, he had brought physiognomy to the level of a science and, by so doing, freed it from the superstitions, astrological associations, fancies and occultism of former times. At one stroke, the treatments of the subject by authors such as Aristotle, Della Porta, Pliney the Elder and others were brushed aside. Here at last was a works to be taken seriously. Because of this, many people regard him as the father of physiognomy.

Since that time, many others have built on his legacy. A book worthy of mention is John Spon's *The Science of Physiognomy*, a passage from which is quoted in Chapter IX, *Enid: The Artist & Illustrator.*

Published in 1947 by Herbert Jenkins, it is still regarded as a standard reference book on the subject. Other books of equal importance are given in the *Bibliography* at the end of this book.

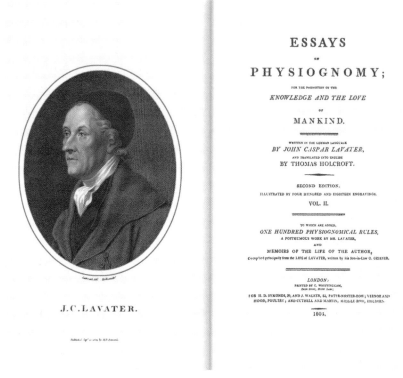

FIGURE 30: Left, frontispiece showing a photo of J.C. Lavater and right, title page of his book Essays on Physiognomy, *as they appeared in one of the English editions published by H.D. Symonds in 1804. Photo and page restoration credit: 2graphic Photo Restoration. Website: www.photo-restoration.co.uk. Reproduced with permission from Camden Libraries.*

Now in case we are wondering what Lavater's response was to the Emperor's less than laudable sentiments, given at the beginning of this essay, he was in no way lost for words:

'With permission of your excellence, I will say there is no honest and good man who needs to fear me, if I could really look as deep into the heart of some persons may imagine I can, which I am very far from being able to do… I am, besides, myself a sinful man who would not always wish that others should see into my heart…,' he said with an air of humility. [128]

A pastor by profession, he became interested in physiognomy while exercising his drawing skills. So striking were the similarities of features of faces he had drawn for recreation that he resolved to study the subject in its entirety. Years later he published his findings in his famous essays. He died in 1801 following a wound from a sniper's bullet.

Finally physiognomy might have survived had it not been displaced abruptly by a rival 'science' called phrenology that suddenly appeared on the scene with what appeared to be a better set of explanations for man's moral, animal and intellectual inclinations. Instead of the features of the face, the new 'science' was based on studies of protuberances or bumps on the head.

Let's now take a look at how it came into being, developed and now lives only in people's memories.

PHRENOLOGY

From hints given in the previous essay, we learned that physiognomy had been around long before Lavater came on the scene and overhauled the system. Phrenology, on the contrary, had no such history. It was a brand new doctrine that came entirely from the brains of Franz Joseph Gall (1758 - 1828) a French physician of Viennese origin.

Whereas Lavater's system was based on the features of the face, Gall based his system on elevations or protuberances on the head, commonly known as bumps. In time, he was able to show that these bumps are caused by overdevelopment of certain parts of the brain. He called each of these overdeveloped parts an organ. This is why his system was known from the beginning as 'organology'. At another time it was known as 'craniology'. Later on in this short history, we'll see how the name changed again, this time to 'phrenology' (see frontispiece and title page illustration of his book, Figure 31).

As time went by, he was able to show that each organ or overdeveloped part of the brain governs a particular faculty. A faculty is a natural or acquired ability to do something, such as to write poetry, compose music, do sums and so on. Consequently, people whose brains show, in several parts, signs of overdevelopment, are supposed to be endowed with extraordinary faculties. He went on to discover twenty-seven organs or bumps on the surface of the head, and linked each of them to a particular faculty. He even managed to find organs for offensive behaviour such as to steal, to commit murder and for sexual deviations of all kinds (see Appendix 71 for illustrations).

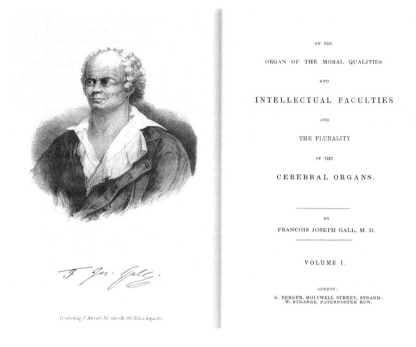

FIGURE 31: Left, photo of Franz Joseph Gall M.D. (1758 – 1828) who is the father of organology turned phrenology. Right, the title page of his book: On the Organ of the Moral Qualities and Intellectual Faculties and the Plurality of the Cerebral Organs, originally written in French under the title: Anatomie et physiologie du système nerveux en général et du cerveau en particulier, published by F. Schoell, Paris 1810. Source: British Library Board (SM: 7410.d.23, frontispiece and title page).

It was not long before he extended his system to animals with exceptional traits, such as dogs that easily lose their way, birds that steal from other birds, animals and birds that destroyed their offspring and those with excessive desires to copulate. To crown his research, he made plaster casts of heads of people with exceptional abilities or talents and, with much difficulty, managed to build up a collection of skulls.

Then he grouped these plaster casts and skulls according to the talents or special abilities of their owners and was surprised to find that they all possessed protuberances or bumps in exactly the same place on the surface of the plaster cast or skull. Later on, when he became a medical student, he went a step further and dissected or opened up skulls of dead men and animals and used his observations to elaborate his doctrine.

All this has led him to the firm conviction that talent, exceptional ability and acceptable or offensive behaviour in man and animal are innate, that is, that they exist at the time of birth. To many people this smacked of fatalism, the doctrine that all things are predetermined or unalterable. His doctrine left no place for free will or responsibility for one's actions. It was useless trying to reform people with tendencies such as to steal, murder, rape, destroy their offspring (infanticide) and so on. They are born that way. This teaching eventually brought his 'organology' into disrepute and hastened its demise.

For as much as he regarded them as truths about human behaviour, he should have paid attention to the axiom that not every truth is good to tell. People with exceptional gifts or talents would have gladly accepted his explanations for their endowments. But those without would have felt that since they did not possess them from birth, they could not be acquired. On the other hand, to have to live with the thought that kleptomaniacs or recalcitrant thieves, murderers, philanderers, rapists and nymphomaniacs are born that way and, consequently, are incapable of reform, would be too much for some people to bear.

In the light of this situation, the most sensible course of action opened to him would have been to form a society – or even a secret society – whose members could consider at length the implications of his discoveries.[129] Instead, he embarked on a series of lectures in his hometown in Austria and continued to publish a number of papers describing his discoveries. Eventually these lectures and papers got the attention of the authorities and he was banned by decree from spreading his doctrine in the country, whereupon he fled Austria and established himself in France.[130]

The problems he met with in France were no different from those he left behind in Austria. While he was able to impress ordinary people with the overwhelming amount of facts he collected to support his doctrine, he never manage to convince the scientific community. For them, the doctrine he advanced, that specific areas of the brain give rise to complex mental faculties such as composing music, writing poetry, doing sums, learning languages and so on could not be proved.

Even today, with the complex instruments and techniques that have since been devised to study the brain, the scientific community still regards his doctrine with scepticism. Notwithstanding this scepticism, many people who had studied Gall's doctrine still regard the bumps on the head as explanations for gifts and talents on the one hand, and excesses in human behaviour for good or bad, on the other. They continue to hold on to phrenology as they hold on to astrology, numerology and graphology – so called sciences that have stood the test of time. Come to think it, it is among these divinatory practices that it would have found its rightful place.

Having thus seen the basis of Gall's doctrine and how it came into being, let's now consider the following facts about phrenology.

- The person who is credited with popularising Gall's organology in England is Johann Gaspar Spurzheim (1776 – 1832). He was one of Gall's disciples and collaborated with him in the writing of his main work on the brain and its function. However, somewhere along the line, the two men fell out and Gall had to complete the work on his own. Spurzheim subsequently refined Gall's system and called it Phrenology – a name that stuck with it ever since (see Appendix 72 for illustration of the extent to which he modified the system. Then compare it with Gall's original system shown in Appendix 71). His book, *Phrenology or the Doctrine of the Mind*, published by Treuttel, Wurtz & Richter, London, 1833 became a textbook on phrenology. Gall subsequently accused him of plagiarism.[131] Spurzheim refuted the charge, claiming that he had the right to produce his own book on the subject.
- The first English translation of Gall's six volumes on the brain, written in French in 1810, was done in America in 1835. Entitled *On the Function of the Brain and each of its Parts* in six volumes,

it was edited by Nahum Capen and published in Boston by Marsh Capen & Lyon in the same year.

- Gall's theory that the excessive development of the cerebellum, and the corresponding elevation or bump at the back of the head, is the cause of sexual deviation set him at odds with physiologists who maintained the established theory that it's associated with motor functions in man. The theory explains things such as precocious sexual activity in children, philandering or lust, rape, and nymphomania or excessive sexual desires in women. It was so controversial that he had it published privately. George Combe, A leading Scottish phrenologist of intellectual standing, translated it from the French and it was published subsequently by Longman & Co. in 1838 under the title: *On the Functions of the Cerebellum*. Two distinguished physicians, Drs Vimont and Broussais collaborated in its production.

- The phrenologist who examined the surface of Enid Blyton's head – as described under *Enid: The Universal Teacher*, Chapter V – and predicted that she would turn to teaching as she developed, did so intuitively, for there is no protuberance or bump for teaching. It is believed he totalled a number of faculties, such as for language, form, comparison, order and firmness and deduced she would use them all for teaching.

Finally, it would appear that the real motive for Gall's research that eventually led to his elaboration of an entire doctrine was to understand the source of his own mental deficiencies and sexual excess. This is the conclusion I arrived at after studying accounts given in the short biography that appeared in the first part of the translation mentioned in a previous paragraph.

He had defects in both verbal memory and in the memory of persons and every kind of numerical calculation fatigued him. It is therefore no wonder that the first faculty he investigated, and the corresponding organ he discovered, dealt with the memory of words, facts, names and numbers. He was also a philanderer and this could be the reason for his discovery that the excessive development of the cerebellum was the cause of sexual deviations. Had it not been for these irregularities, it is unlikely he would have been motivated to delve into the mysteries of the brain and the whole doctrine of organology turned phrenology would not have been! He died August 22, 1828, aged 72, childless, following a paralytic attack.

NOTE: A list of books for further reading is given in the *Bibliography* at the end of this book.

EPILOGUE

ENID BLYTON'S MAIN HOMES

Elfin Cottage, situated at 83 Shortlands Road, Bromley (see illustration, Figure 26), one of the three main houses Enid Blyton lived in, is still standing, with new owners. The house is now a listed building and carries a plaque placed there by the Bromley Council in recognition of her having lived there between 1925 and 1929.

Old Thatch, the second, (see illustration Figure 4), is just as it was when Enid lived there from 1929 to 1938. Its present owners are landscape gardeners and have kept both their lovely garden and the house open to visitors just as Enid had done when she was at the height of her fame.

Green Hedges, the last house Enid lived in before she died November 28, 1968 and from which she achieved her gardening ambition to have a magnificent garden, as described under *Enid: The Passionate Gardener* in Chapter X, had changed owners before it was demolished in 1971. The place where it stood is now a small development of new dwellings known as Blyton Close.

LETTERS TO PROFESSOR PETER MCKELLAR (1921 – 2003)

The nine letters Enid Blyton wrote to Professor Peter McKellar in the 1950s describing how she wrote her stories were sold to an anonymous buyer at an auction held in Salisbury, Wiltshire November 9, 1994.[132] Peter McKellar had written to her for information about her writing method for his book *Imagination & Thinking* that was eventually published by Cohen & West, 1957. Barbara Story, her official biographer, carried extracts from these letters in Appendix 9, from page 205 of *Enid Blyton: A Biography*, first published by Hodder & Stoughton in 1974. Brief extracts are also carried in passages in this book, notably in Chapter VII, under *Enid: The Professional Storyteller*.

PHOTOGRAPHIC MEMORY

For those of us who are interested in the subject of precocious children and adults with photographic memories, as presented briefly under *Enid: The Professional Storyteller* in Chapter VII, Section One, we can read all about it in a paper Sir Francis Galton (1822 – 1911), the English scientist and cousin of Charles Darwin, wrote in *The Fortnightly Review* captioned Mental Imagery, published in Volume 28, pages 312 -324 [1880], and another in: *Mind* captioned Statistics of Mental Imagery, Volume 5, pages 301 – 318 [1880]. We can read these two papers online, or even downloaded them, by visiting the website: https://psychclassics.yorku.ca/Galton/imagery.htm.

CONTROVERSIES SURROUNDING HER STORYBOOKS

Those of us who want to know about the controversy surrounding Enid Blyton's storybooks for children should read Sheila Ray's *The Enid Blyton Phenomenon*, first published by Andre Deutsch in 1982. Here we'll learn about the banning of her storybooks from libraries and some schools and the rationale for such actions.

To learn about the controversy surrounding her Noddy books, we should read Bob Mullan's *The Enid Blyton Story*, published by Boxtree in 1987. Here we'll also find a psychological assessment of Enid Blyton's character.

TRIBUTE TO MARY POTTER ATTENBOROUGH

Enid's best friend from school days, Mary Attenborough, became a famous painter of landscapes, seascapes, still life, interiors and portraits in oils and watercolours. Among the places she exhibited her paintings are The New Art Centre, the Tate Gallery and the Fine Art Society in London. She received an OBE in 1979.

She was married to the writer and radio producer Stephen Potter from 1927 to 1955, and the couple had two children, Andrew (born 1928) and Julian (born 1931). Having outlived Enid by thirteen years, she died September 1981, and is remembered in a book written by her son, Julian Potter, entitled: *Mary Potter: A Life of Painting,* published by Aldershot in 2004.

TRIBUTE TO BARBARA STONEY (SEPT 18, 1924 – MARCH 6, 2009)

Barbara Stoney was Enid Blyton's official biographer. An accomplished journalist, she became interested in the life and work of Enid Blyton and was eventually commissioned by Gillian Baverstock, Enid's elder daughter, to write the biography. The resulting book, *Enid Blyton: A Biography* and the reprint, *Enid Blyton: The Biography,* is still regarded as the only authoritative biography of Enid Blyton.

First published by Hodder & Stoughton in 1974, it was well received and earned her warm praise and appreciation. The biography ran through several editions until 2006 when it was completely revised, showing a youthful Enid Blyton on the front cover. I'm indebted to her for the thorough research of the life of Enid Blyton, brief extracts from which are reproduced in various passages in this book.

TRIBUTE TO GILLIAN BAVERSTOCK (1931 – 2007)

Gillian Baverstock née Pollock, elder daughter of Enid Blyton, died of cancer June 24, 2007, aged 75. During her lifetime, she worked incessantly to protect her mother's name and reputation. '*My mother never wrote for grown ups*,' she has said time and again whenever critics reiterated the cliché that her mother's storybooks were of inferior quality and failed to stimulate a child's imagination.

Born July 15, 1931 at Bourne End, Buckinghamshire, just when her mother's writing career was taking off, she attended Benenden School before reading History at St. Andrew's University. Following in her mother's footstep, she took up teaching and held the post of primary school teacher at Moorefield School for Girls in Ilkley for twenty years before attaining the position of School Governor.

She married Donald Baverstock, a BBC television producer and executive, in 1957 and had four children, Sara, Owain, Sian and Glyn before the marriage was dissolved in 1994. Sian later died of a heart attack aged 48 and Glyn was involved in a car accident aged 22.

In 1999, she and the comic writer Tim Quinn founded Quill Publications Ltd, and launched *Blue Moon*, a monthly children's magazine that featured sequels to fairytales. The magazine was discontinued after twelve issues. She is also the author of *Enid Blyton*, published by Evans Brothers Ltd, 1997, in the *Tell Me About* series. Some three years later, she and Sheila Ray wrote: *Gillian Baverstock Remembers Enid Blyton,* published by Mammoth, 2000. Written in simple language with lovely pictures, they give children interesting sidelights into Enid Blyton's early life and work. She is survived by her younger sister, Imogen Smallwood, her two remaining children and six grandchildren.

EILEEN SOPER (1905 – 1990)

Eileen Soper, one of Enid Blyton's illustrators, who has illustrated the Famous Five series of books, is remembered in *Wildings – The Secret Garden of Eileen Soper* by Duff Hart-Davis, published by H.F.& G. Witherby in 1991.

NOTE: Her portrait, which can be seen in Figure 23 among five other talented women, is carried in the back page of the aforementioned book. It was done by Reginald Haines, 4 Southampton Row, W.C. The author, Duff Hart-Davis has carried no acknowledgement in the book.

ALEC ROWLEY (1892 – 1958)

Alec Rowley, the distinguished English pianist, composer and teacher who set the words of many of Enid Blyton songs to music, is remembered in: *Rowley Rediscovered – the Life and Music of Alec Rowley* by Beryl Kington, published by Thames Publishing, London, 1993.

EDMONIA LEWIS (1844 – 1907)

Edmonia Lewis was an African American sculptor who achieved international recognition for her artwork in marble during the second half of the nineteenth century (see her photo, Figure 23).

According to Biography.com on the web, she was orphaned at an early age and was raised by her mother's relatives. She had little training in sculpture. She attended Oberlin College in Ohio where she emerged as a talented artist. Her first commercial success was a bust of Colonel Robert Gould Shaw (1837 – 1863), an American officer in the Union Army during the American Civil War. The money she earned selling copies of the bust allowed her to sail to Rome, Italy, where she mastered working in marble. 'I was practically driven to Rome in order to obtain the opportunities for art culture, and to find a social atmosphere where I was not constantly reminded of my color. The land of liberty [America] had not room for a colored sculptor,' is one of her famous quotations. She achieved success as a sculptor and spent most of her working life there.

To see some of her astonishing artwork in marble, type the following into your web browser: *sculptures by edmonia lewis.* For a biographical sketch of this talented sculptor, type in your web browser: *biography.com and edmonia lewis.*

THE COSTA BOOK AWARD

Finally, who would have thought that some forty years after her passing, Enid Blyton would have been voted Britain's best-loved writer of fiction for children? This is exactly what happened when a poll carried out in 2008 for the Costa Book Award found her to be on top of the list, beating Roald Dahl, J.K. Rowling and Jane Austen who ended up second, third and fourth place respectively. How times have changed!

THE END

ENDNOTES

CHAPTER 1: ENID: THE NATURALIST

1   This book, although termed an autobiography, is really a book Enid wrote to give collective answers to questions posed by her fans. This is the explanation she gave in 'A Letter To You All', Chapter I of the book.

2   Barbara Stoney gave this information on page 36 of *Enid Blyton: A Biography* first published by Hodder & Stoughton, London, 1974.

3   Chapter VII, page 93 of the 1931 *Primary School Report*, revised version, from the government-appointed consultative committee headed by Sir W.H. Hadow. The full report can be read online at: http://www.educationengland.org.uk/documents/hadow1931.

4   The disparaging remarks referred to can be found in Chapter 1, 'A Country Home', pages 19 to 21of *Enid Blyton's Animal Lover's Book*, first published by Evans Brothers in 1952.

CHAPTER II: ENID: THE POET

5   *The Story of My Life*, p.70.

6   *The Story of My Life*, p. 74.

7   *The Story of My Life*, p. 74.

8   The page numbers in Barbara Stoney's *Enid Blyton: A Biography* where information about these poems are given are 36, 38 and 45 respectively.

9   We know today that 'H.A' are the initials of her first husband, H.A. Pollock who was the mysterious interviewer.

10   The long list of uncollected poems, as well as uncollected songs and plays, starts from pages 182 to 189 (Part 1), pages 208 to 210 (Part 2) and pages 202 to 206 (Part 3) of Tony Summerfield's

Enid Blyton: An Illustrated Bibliography which Milford Books published for the Enid Blyton Society. More information about these volumes is available from its website: www. enidblytonsociety.co.uk.

CHAPTER III: ENID: THE COLUMNIST & FEATURE WRITER

11   The Enid Byton Society republished these 'Letters from Bobs' and 'More Letters from Bobs' in two booklets, each containing 32 pages. They may be purchased from the society's online bookshop through its website: www.enidblytonsociety.co.uk.

12   For background information on this subject, see page 46 of Barbara Stoney's *Enid Blyton: A Biography,* published by Hodder And Stoughton, 1974.

13   In 2002, The Enid Blyton Society collected all her 'Friday Afternoon Stories' and published them in a booklet with the same name, a copy of which may be purchased from its online book shop by visiting the website: www.enidblytonsociety.co.uk.

14   'Notes for the Teacher', page 1076, *The Teachers World*'s edition of August 29, 1928.

15   A paladin is the French equivalent of an English knight. King Charlemagne and the Paladins is said to be the French counterpart of 'King Arthur and the Knights of the Round Table'. However, whereas King Arthur is said to have had 150 knights, King Charlemagne had only 12.

16   A joust is a fight between two knights in full body armour, mounted on horses and carrying lances that they direct against each other's shields.

17   These were people regarded at that time as irreligious, uncivilised, or unenlightened.

18   These *Chronicles*, written in French, deal principally with numerous battles during the so-called Hundred Years' War (1337 – 1453) between the English and the French.

19   Edmund Spenser (1552 – 1599), an English poet, presented in

the form of an epic poem the "Faerie Queene". It is supposed to be a celebration of virtues such as holiness, friendship, courtesy and so on.

20 A sample reading of one of her Country Letters can be found between pages 194 and 197 inclusive, in the appendices of Barbara Stoney's *Enid Blyton A Biography*, published by Hodder & Stoughton, 1974.

21 See Appendix 69 for more information about this club.

22 The extract is from a passage on page 32 of *The Enid Blyton Society Journal* No 36 (Summer 2008).

23 The account of her contributions to this newspaper and of the discovery of the Noddy stories can be read in full in Volume 20 (Spring 2003) and in Volume 21 (Summer 2003) of *The Enid Blyton Society Journal* respectively. Back issues can be purchased from The Enid Blyton Society's online bookshop by visiting their website: www.enidblytonsociety.co.uk.

24 Tony Summerfield gives a list of all the known periodicals with dates her article first appeared and an estimate of the number of contributions on page 124, Part I, page 172, Part II and page 162, Part III of *Enid Blyton – An Illustrated Bibliography* that Milford Books published for The Enid Blyton Society.

CHAPTER IV: ENID: THE EDITOR

25 Barbara Stoney gave a full account of her qualifications on page 36 of the first edition of *Enid Blyton: A Biography* (Hodder & Stoughton), 1974.

26 Source: The foreword to Volume I – History for Senior and Junior Schools (455 pages) published by H.M. Stationery Office, 1928.

27 The full text of this article can be found on page 1 of *The Times* (London), in the edition of December 21, 1995 captioned: Last stand of the printed word/feature.

28 The address of the British Library is 96 Euston Road, London NW1 2DB, England.

CHAPTER V: ENID: THE UNIVERSAL TEACHER

29   T*he Story of My Life,* page 78.

30   Barbara Stoney describes the events leading up to his leaving home from page 18 of *Enid Blyton: A Biography*, first published by Hodder & Stoughton, 1974.

31   *The History of St Christopher's The Hall School*, a 16 page booklet the school published to mark its centenary 1893 – 1993, a copy of which may be obtained from the headteacher.

32   See page 75 of *The Story of My Life* for a passing reference to this situation.

33   The full account she gave of the nerve-racking conversation with her father can be read on pages 76 and 77 of *The Story of My Life*, first published by Pitkin in 1952.

34   Source: *Enid Blyton: A Biography*, Chapter III, beginning from page 41.

35   See page 75 of *The Story of My Life*, and page 30 of Barbara Stoney's *Enid Blyton: A Biography,* for a passing reference to her Sunday school teaching at the Elm Road Baptist Church.

36   The British and Foreign Bible Society based in London published this book in 1954 and the Bibles Enid described therein are in the society's collection. From studying the wording of her preface, I get the impression she had been commissioned to write the book.

37   This is the official service book of the Church of England, the first issue of which appeared in 1549.

38   Royalties refer to a sum of money paid periodically to an author for every copy of a book sold.

39   Page 77, *The Story of My Life.*

CHAPTER VI: ENID: THE PROLIFIC SONGWRITER

40   Tony Summerfield of The Enid Blyton Society listed these songs between pages 182 and 190 in Volume I of his masterly works, *Enid Blyton: An Illustrated Bibliography* first published by Milford Books, May 2002.

41 According to Barbara Stoney, her biographer, in a passage on page 17 of *Enid Blyton: A Biography*, this 'school' was situated in a house at the corner of Clockhouse and Cedar Roads in Beckenham, Kent.

42 Aesop, who is said to have lived in the sixth Century BC, was a Greek compiler of fables such as 'The Lion and The Mouse', 'The Fox and The Crow,' 'The Hare and the Tortoise', 'The Goose That Laid the Golden Egg' and so on.

43 *The Story of My Life*, p. 49.

44 *The Story of My Life*, p. 52.

45 *The Story of My Life*, p. 52.

46 *The Story of My Life*, p. 52.

47 First delivered at The Royal College of Physicians in 1907, as part of the Fitzpatrick Lectures, and revised by his nephew who had it published posthumously in 1921 by Eric G. Millar, London England.

48 The papers in question are 'Mental Imagery', published in The Fortnightly Review in 1880, Volume 28, pages 312 -324 and 'Statistics Of Mental Imagery', in Mind in 1880, Volume 5, pages 301 – 318. These papers may be read online, or even downloaded, by visiting the website: https://psychclassics.yorku. ca/Galton/imagery.htm.

49 The *Iliad* is about the events connected with 'The Siege of Troy' and *The Odyssey*, about the wandering of Odysseus, king of Ithaca, during the ten years after the fall of Troy. They were written in the form of epic poems and are attributed to Homer, a Greek epic poet who lived in the ninth century BC.

50 The Story of My Life, p.106.

51 In Irish folklore, a leprechaun is a tiny elfin cobbler supposed to own hidden treasure, and a banshee, a woman fairy whose cries and wails are supposed to foretell death.

52   Published by D. Nult in 1893

53   Volume V, pages 678 – 689. The Encyclopaedia was edited by
      James Hastings M.A., D.D and published by T. & T. Clark,
      Edinburgh, in 1926.

54   Published by Methuen in 1925.

55   David Chambers while researching Enid Blyton's contributions
      to the Sunday Graphic brought this fact to light. The fascinating
      story of his find of the stories of Pip, before they were published
      in book form, can be read in *The Enid Blyton Society Journal*,
      Volume 20, Spring 2003, pages 32 – 37.

56   From a passage in Maggie Brown's article in *The Guardian*
      [Manchester UK], 07 May 1996, captioned: 'Noddy goes Moddy;'
      they're trying to bring Enid Blyton's 'outdated' creations into the
      multi-media...

57   Enid was to write nine letters to the professor over five years.
      Extracts from these letters are to be found from page 205 to 215
      in the first edition of Barbara Stony's *Enid Blyton: A Biography*.
      The letters were sold subsequently at an auction in Salisbury,
      Wiltshire in November 1994 to an anonymous buyer for £5400.
      The announcement to this effect was carried in *The Sunday Times*,
      p.2, Nov 10, 1994.

58   Page 15, Adventure With Inspiration, Morley & M Kennerley,
      1929.

59   Page 28, Adventure With Inspiration, Morley & M Kennerley,
      1929.

60   Page 15, Adventure With Inspiration, Morley & M Kennerley,
      1929.

61   From *The Case of Patience Worth* by Walter Franklin Prince,
      pp. 394 – 395, published in 1927 by The Boston Society For
      Psychic Research, Boston, USA.

62   In spiritualism, a 'Medium' is an intermediary between the world
      of the living and the world of the dead. He or she is specially
      trained to give evidence of survival of the human soul.

63   T P James, in his preface to the book, which followed that of the departed Charles Dickens, gave examples of the type of criticisms the book met with and stated how he dealt with them.

64   From *The Case of Patience Worth*, by Walter Franklin Prince, first published in 1927 by the Boston Society of Psychic Research, USA.

65   From a 'Short Biography of Patience Worth', carried in the website: www.patienceworth.org.

66   The Story of My Life, pp. 63 - 64.

67   The Story of My Life, p. 64.

68   The Story of My Life, pp. 64 - 65.

69   *Enid Blyton: A Biography*, page 210, Appendix 9, Correspondence with Peter McKellar (Hodder & Stoughton, 1974).

70   The Story of My Life, p. 70.

71   The Story of My Life, p. 72.

72   The Story of My Life, p.71.

73   Page 210, Barbara Storey's *Enid Blyton: A Biography* (Hodder & Stoughton, 1974).

74   The Story of My Life, p. 84.

75   From a transcript by Jimmi Thøgersen that's reproduced in the HP Survivor website: www. hpsurvivor.com that's no longer on the web. You can also listen to the broadcast directly by using the search string: J.K. Rowling on The Diane Rehm Show, (WAMU Radio Washington, D.C.,) October 20, 1999. (Re-broadcast December 24, 1999.)

76   Appendix 9, page 210 Correspondence with Peter McKellar, carried in Barbara Stoney's *Enid Blyon: A Biography* (Hodder & Stoughton, 1974).

77   *The Herald* (Glasgow), July 29, 2006, p.16. Reporter, Anne Johnstone. The 60th anniversary of 'Malory Towers' took place at the Edinburgh International Book Festival August 26, 2006 Reproduced with permission of *Herald & Times Group*.

78   Page 211, Appendix 9, Correspondence with Peter McKellar, carried in *Enid Blyton: A Biography* by Barbara Stoney (Hodder & Stoughton, 1974).

79   For a colourful history of the Saucepan Man in Enid Blyton's stories, see Anita Bensoussane's articles in *The Enid Blyton Society Journal*, issues No. 30, Summer, 2006, part 1 and No 31, Winter, 2006, Part 2.

80   Page 9, first paragraph of the abridged edition of *Little Women* by Louisa Alcott, first published in Boston, USA in 1868 by Roberts Brothers.

81   Page 13, *Five on a Treasure Island*, under the caption: *The Strange Cousin*, (1997 edition), first published in Great Britain in 1942 by Hodder & Stoughton.

82   The full account can be read on page 210, Appendix 9, Correspondence with Peter McKellar, in *Enid Blyton: A Biography* (Hodder & Stoughton, 1974).

83   For a full understanding of what the will is, see *The Will: Its Nature, Power and Development* by William Walker Atkinson, first published by L.N. Fowler & Co. Ludgate Circus, London in 1910.

CHAPTER VIII: ENID: THE PLAYWRIGHT

84   Barbara Stoney states on page 40 of *Enid Blyton : A Biography* that the family consisted of Horace, an architect and chartered surveyor, his wife Gertrude and their four children who were living in Southernhay at that time.

85   A full account of her teaching at the Thompson's family home is given in Chapter III, from page 41 in *Enid Blyton: A Biography*, published by Hodder & Stoughton, 1974.

86   Barbara Stoney carried this extract on page 161 of *Enid Blyton: A Biography* instead of carrying it in Appendix 9 where fuller extracts of her letters to Professor Peter McKellar and his replies are given.

87   Extract from a review carried in *Plays & Players* in the issue of February 1955, after the staging of its first performance, Dec. 23, 1954 at The Stoll Theatre, London.

88   Norman Wright published his findings in an article in *The Enid Blyton Society Journal*, issue No. 15, page 50, that came out in 2001.

89   Mr Greenfield has written this book as part of a Pocket Biographies series giving necessary information about famous writers.

90   A list of all the plays from books written by Enid Blyton can also be found in Tony Summerfield's *Enid Blyton – An Illustrated Bibliography*, Part 1, 1922 – 1942, pages 162 – 164, published in 2002 by Milford Books for The Enid Blyton Society.

CHAPTER IX: ENID: THE ARTIST & ILLUSTRATOR

91   A photo of Peter Wienk can be seen on page 63 in number 21 of *The Enid Blyton Society Journal,* [Summer 2003], edited by Tony Summerfield.

92   Source: Barbara Stoney's *Enid Blyton: A Biography*, pp.14 -15, first published by Hodder & Stoughton, London 1974.

CHAPTER X: ENID: THE PASSIONATE GARDENER

93   Barbara Stoney gives a full account of these events from page 18 in Chapter I of *Enid Blyton: A Biography*, first published by Hodder & Stoughton, London, 1974.

94   Details of the Suggestions in the *Primary School Report* that Enid Blyton used as a basis for elaborating the 'Round the Year with Enid Blyton 'Gardening Course' can be read online by clicking on this link in your browser:http://www.educationengland.org.uk/documents/hadow1931/ Search the site for: The Primary School/ Curriculum Suggestions – The Study of Nature, page 183 [Revised Version].

95   A full treatment of this situation can be found in the early chapters of Barbara Stoney's *Enid Blyton: A Biography*, first published by Hodder & Stoughton in 1974.

96   Full text of this long letter of February 15, 1953 is carried
     from page 205 to 208 inclusive, of Barbara Stoney's *Enid Blyton:
     A Biography*, first published by Hodder & Stoughton, London,
     1974.

97   Page 207, Appendix 8, Correspondence with Peter McKellar,
     Barbara *Stoney's Enid Blyton: A Biography* (Hodder & Stoughton,
     1974).

98   See an account George Greenfield gave of anomalies he found
     in a story submitted to him on page 53 of *Enid Blyton,* published
     by Sutton Publishing in 1998.

99   Sheila Ray gives an insight into this controversy in her well-
     researched book *The Enid Blyton Phenomenon*, published by
     Andre Deutsch, 1982.

100 To take the pressure off her shoulders Enid eventually formed a
     company, Darrell Waters Ltd, in 1950. A short history of this
     company is given in this section.

101   Lister, D. (1997) 'How the Famous Five became a burden
     for Enid Blyton', The Independent, 11th August, page 1. © The
     Independent.

102   Page 99, *The Story of My Life*, published by Pitkin,1952.

103   Source: *The Sunday Times,* p. 4, April 13, 1997. Article by Nicki
     Pope and Richard Woods with the title: 'Enid Blyton Wins Back
     Her Shelf Space'.

     THE SUNNY STORIES MAGAZINE: A PHENOMENAL
     SUCCESS

104   From retelling Joe Chandler's original Brer Rabbit tales in
     her own words, Enid went on to write completely new Brer
     Rabbit stories that conserved the Brer Rabbit character. The
     original tales can be read in *Uncle Remus his Songs and his
     Sayings* by Joe Chandler, republished in 1931 by D. Appleton &
     Co Ltd, Boston, USA.

105   Enid was inconsistent in the way she headed her letters.
     Sometimes they were headed: Dear Boys and Girls, went to

Dear Children then to Dear Girls and Boys.

106   The illustrated front covers of the 250 volumes of The *Sunny Stories for Little Folks* magazines and of the 553 *Enid Blyton's Sunny Stories* and, subsequently, the *Sunny Stories* magazines can be seen in the Enid Blyton Society's website in pages with the title: *Sunny Stories for Little Folk*s and *Enid Blyton's Sunny Stories.*

BRIEF HISTORY OF THE ENID BLYTON'S MAGAZINE

107   Source: *Enid Blyton: A Biography*, by Barbara Stoney, carried in a passage on page 145.

108   Source: Barbara Stoney's *Enid Blyton: A Biography*, last paragraph, page 145.

A SHORT HISTORY OF DARRELL WATERS LTD

109   Source: An article in *The Guardian*, in the edition of April 14, 1993 and from David Haslam's website: www.agraphic.co.uk/ nod.htm which is no longer accessible on the web.

110   Source: *The Daily Telegraph*, 12 August 1969. Title of article: Enid Blyton Leaves £283,000.

111   Winder, R. (1995) 'Noddy's Off to Treasure Island', The Independent, 18th November, page 19. © The Independent.

112   MacDonald, M. (1996) 'Noddy goes to the Trocadero', The Independent, 24th January, page 3. © The Independent.

113   Source: Trocadero Plc Preliminary Results for year ending December 31, 1996, distributed at that time by PR Newswire. co.uk on behalf of Trocadero.

A SHORT HISTORY OF ENID BLYTON'S LITERARY ESTATE

114   Source: Marianne Macdonald's report in *The Independent*, 24 January, 1996, in which she carried comments by Nick Leslau, the chief executive of Trocadero Plc about the intended interactive store in the entertainment complex.

115   Source: Trocadero Plc's first report to its shareholders for period ending 31 December 1996 that was distributed at that time by

PR Newswire on behalf of Trocadero.

116   Source:*The Indian Express Globetrotter*, Wed June 10th, 1998 from an article entitled: Enid Blyton Ventures into Asia.

117   Source: From Leslie Copeland's article entitled: 'Chorion hopes for £30 million windfall', published by Growth Company Investor 7 Nov 2002 and from a passage in the Company's Annual Report to its shareholders for year ending 31 Dec 2002.

118   Source: *Media Guardian,* Thursday 23 February 2006, in an article captioned: Chorion agrees £111m buyout.

119   Source: Hachette UK Press Release, dated 3 March, 2012, captioned: Hachette UK Acquires Worldwide Rights in Enid Blyton, published in their website: Hachette.co.uk.

A SHORT TREATMENT OF CLAIRVOYANCE

120   First published in 1899 by the Theosophical Publishing Society, 26 Charing Cross, S. W. London, England.

121   For information about this college visit their website: www. collegeofpsychicstudies.co.uk.

122   New International Version of the Bible.

123   The first Witchcraft Act in England was passed in 1542. Subsequent Acts were promulgated in 1563, 1604 and 1735.

124   The Proceedings of the Society for Psychical Research can be consulted at the Rare Books & Music Wing of The British Library, Euston, England under the shelf marks: x.529/799. Vol. II, published by Trübner & Co, Ludgate Hill, London, 1884. For information about the Society for Psychical Research visit their website: www.spr.ac.uk.

PHYSIOGNOMY & PHRENOLOGY

125   First published in German in 1775, it was translated into English by Thomas Holcroft and published by William Tegg in 1862. The full title of the works is: *Essays on Physiognomy for the Promotion of the Knowledge and the Love of Mankind.*

126   Source: 'Memoirs of the Life of J. C. Lavater', p. lxxxi, *Essays On Physiognomy*, London, William Tegg, 1862 English edition

127 Source: *Charles Darwin: His Life Told in an Autobiographical Chapter*, published by John Murray, Albemarle Street, London, 1902, Ch. II, page 26.

128 The conversation between these two great men can be read in full in 'Memoirs of The Life of J.C. Lavater', beginning from page lxxxi (81), contained *in Essays On Physiognomy*, published in 1862 by William Tegg, London [English Edition].

129 Phrenological Societies with different intentions were eventually established in different countries, not by him, but by enthusiasts of phrenology. Notable among these is the Edinburgh Phrenological Society that George Combe co-founded in Scotland in 1820.

130 John van Whye, Ph.D, gives a full account of this situation in a paper with the title: 'The Authority of Human Nature: The Schadellehre of Franz Joseph Gall', published in the *British Journal for the History of Science,* Vol. 35, No1, (March 2002), pp. 17 – 42. and republished on the Internet under the same title.

131 This situation is described by Dr Gall himself in volume III, pages IX – XIX of the original French edition with the title*: Anathaomie et Physiologie du Systeme Nerveux en General et du Cerveau en Particulier*, published by F. Schoell, Paris, 1810.
EPILOGUE

132 Source: *The Times*/Home News, p.2, London, England, in its edition of November 10, 1994.

APPENDICES

length equal to not less than half the number of years between the date on which they became certificated, and the date on which they become 65 years of age.

A new Clause, however, provides that the teacher can qualify for a pension by a minimum of ten years' recognised or contributory service, but the total service of such teacher must be not less than three-quarters of the number of years between the date on which he was first employed in contributory or recognised service and the date on which he attained or will attain the age of 65.

This provision extends to teachers other than those who contributed under the Act of 1893 the privilege of retiring with the certainty of a pension at age 60 before having served the usual 30 years. For instance, a teacher beginning to teach at the age of 37 must serve a minimum of $\frac{3}{4}$ (65—37) = 21 years. Under present conditions he could not qualify at all.

This new provision is of advantage only to teachers who enter pensionable service comparatively late in life.

It will be noted with considerable relief by our readers that the Government has not adopted the recommendation of the Emmott Committee to the effect that the teacher must serve five years after the age of 50 before becoming entitled to a pension at 60; but while making 10 years the minimum, has inserted the "¾" safeguard to prevent, in the words of the Emmott Report, "the expenditure of public money to the undue advantage of people with short teaching service."

Concession to Married Women Teachers.

The case of the woman teacher who leaves school on marriage is greatly simplified in the new Bill. In her case the 30 years' service necessary is reduced by the number of completed years (up to ten) "during which she was, while married, absent from recognised, contributory, or qualifying service."

Handwork for Seniors, Coarse Sewing and Design, A Number of Things.

In view of the unique topical interest of the middle page pictures in the issue, our readers will pardon the further postponement of Mr. Vinall's illustrations of Design.

NEW FEATURES FOR TEACHERS OF OLDER CHILDREN.

In a new feature, to begin shortly, Messrs. Birkett and Lewis will deal with the Geography of Europe in a series of comparative maps and pictorial diagrams on the lines of the Empire maps which achieved so remarkable a popularity when published in this journal, and which are now available in book form as the Pupils' Empire Atlas.

Another new series will present a novel and most effective method of teaching English grammar, while a third feature will be devoted to the teaching of arithmetic in the higher classes.

ENID BLYTON'S NATURE ARTICLES.

Miss Enid Blyton, the "T.W." children's poet and story-teller, is undertaking a series of Nature articles for juniors. Written in her delightfully entertaining style and illustrated by herself, these articles are assured of a warm welcome from every teacher of the younger children.

respect of him under this Part of this Act shall, be calculated, as respects service before the commencement of this Act, in whichever of the following ways is, in the opinion of the Board, most advantageous to him, that is to say:—

(a) he shall be treated as having served in recognised service only during his actual years of recognised service if any; or

(b) he shall be treated as having served in recognised service for all the purposes of this Part of this Act for one-half of the aggregate number of years for which he has served before the commencement of this Act either as a teacher in recognised service or in full-time service as an organiser:

Provided that—

(a) no contributions shall be required to be paid in respect of any period of service as an organiser in respect of which he is so treated as serving in recognised service; and

(b) in either case any full-time service as an organiser shall for the purposes of determining his qualification for a superannuation allowance or gratuity under this Part of this Act and of computing his average salary in accordance with the provisions of this Part of this Act, be treated as recognised service.

An important omission from the Bill is the provision of any machinery for enabling teachers to take part in administrating a fund to which they are called upon to contribute so heavily. There is not even any mention of the suggested advisory Superannuation Council which the Emmott Committee approved.

Finally, it may be noted that the Bill will, if it becomes law, come into operation on April 1, 1926.

***THE READER WHO HAS ANY SUPERANNUATION DIFFICULTY WHICH THE NEW BILL MAY SOLVE SHOULD SEND THE QUESTION TO THE T.W. BUREAU OF SPECIAL INQUIRIES (SEE COUPON ON PAGE 41), WHEN IT WILL BE IMMEDIATELY ANSWERED THROUGH THE POST.

Bottom half of a full page in *The Teachers World* edition of April 1, 1925, page 3, showing the announcement of the beginning of 'Enid Blyton's Nature Lessons' for juniors, termed 'Nature Articles' here (second column, bottom). Image restoration credit: 2graphic Photo Restoration. Website: www.photo-restoration.co.uk.

APPENDIX 2

THE TEACHERS WORLD, *April 15, 1925.*

ENID BLYTON'S NATURE LESSONS

In response to many requests to provide simple Nature lessons for younger children, we have arranged for Miss Enid Blyton to contribute this fortnightly series.

GORSE.

"Oh, come across the hillside, the April
month is here,
The lamb-time, the lark-time, the child-time
of the year."

(M. Woods.)

BUT it is the season for something else, too—something that clothes the hillside with blazing gold as far as the eye can see. Now is the time to see gorse in its full glory, a glory that brings artists rushing to the South Downs with brush and palette, trying in vain to catch the shining splendour spread before them.

A queer, unfriendly plant is the gorse. It won't let you come near it. "Keep off," it seems to say, "or I'll prick you with a hundred little spears, and woe betide any animal who tries to eat me!"

I shouldn't like to nibble a piece of gorse. I expect you've heard the story of the little hungry animal who tried to make a meal off a gorse-bush. The prickly spines he swallowed stuck out of his back, and he became the first hedgehog!

Spines.

It is a painful business to pick gorse because there is no place about it where it is possible to hold it without being pricked. Lower down the spikes are fewer and point towards the sandy soil. Can you guess why? It is to prevent any small animals such as mice from climbing up the plant to nibble at flowers or other parts of the stem.

Look at the spines. There are two kinds. One kind springs from the main stem, and is big and sharp like a stout needle. From this big spine you can see many little ones growing. The little ones are really the *leaves* of the gorse, which it has modified into sharp-pointed prickles. The big spines are *branches* of the gorse. You can easily tell which are which.

A Bleak Home.

Perhaps the gorse is unfriendly because it grows in a bleak, unfriendly place. Think where you have seen gorse growing—on open moors—on cold hillsides—on wind-swept commons—on bleak cliffs. If you were a plant living in places like these, think what you would do. "Ooh!" you would say, "how strong the wind is! I must make myself strong, too, and hug the earth or I'll be blown away." And you would grow a strong, tough stem like the gorse, or become wiry and springy like the heather.

I have seen gorse growing on a sloping cliff in Cornwall, where the wind swept in from the Atlantic and almost blew me off my legs. But the gorse stood firm and hardly shook in the great cold wind. Still I could see the effect that wind had had, blowing week after week for years—for the gorse cowered down on the cliff, and crouched so close to the ground that it was impossible to see under it. It was just a dense close mass of spines. It looked as if the gorse

were saying "I daren't look out—I daren't even stand up—or I'll be blown away to Europe. I'm going to hang on to this cliff like a limpet!"

You can quite well imagine that a bleak, wind-swept place will be dry, so that the gorse is unwilling to part with any moisture it can get. That is another reason why it has such queer narrow needle-like leaves. Plants not only breathe through their leaves, they give out moisture through them, too.

"And so," says the gorse, "I must have the narrowest leaves possible, then I'll be able to keep my moisture in as much as I can, for I do need it so badly!"

The Golden Flowers.

The glory of the gorse is its brilliant flowers of warm, rich yellow. There are two or three kinds of gorse, and here and there you will find a bush with paler yellow blossoms probably in July or August—but the gorse that is out in great, shining masses in April is the deep yellow kind. Sometimes I have found a bush of gorse so thickly covered with blossom that I could hardly see the dark spines.

They are beautiful little flowers. Soft and silky, and the loveliest contrast to the sombre green of the bush. If you look at them you can easily tell that the gorse is cousin to a garden flower you know very well—the sweet pea. It is the same "butterfly" sort of flower.

Look at the buds. They are carefully wrapped in a pair of strong, hairy brown sepals. The gorse takes great care of its babies. When the sepals open they don't fall off, but remain at the sides of the flower, almost as if they were "on guard."

Now take a flower carefully to pieces. First you will have one big petal—the *standard*—a very good name because it *stands* up at the back. Then you will have two side petals—*the wings*. and last of all a pair of joined petals called *the keel*, because they are boat-shaped.

Wouldn't the gorse be a good badge for our three military services—the army, the navy, and the air force? The standard for the army, the wings for the air force, and the keel for the navy! And the prickles around would say: "Keep off! We guard England."

What have you found inside the keel? The plant's most precious possessions—stamens and pistil. These are the means by which the gorse produces seeds, and everything is carefully planned for this purpose.

There are ten stamens hidden away, and each has at its tip a bag of pollen—fine golden dust fit for a fairy's baking-powder. All that pollen is going to be thrown at a bee. What a joke!

The Bee's Visit.

Have you ever watched bees working in a gorse-bush? I have.

Up comes a busy, energetic bee. He sees a nice yellow blossom.

"Good," he thinks, "there's honey there, I can smell it!"

He alights heavily on the boat-shaped keel and presses it down. With a tiny pop that I never can hear the keel bursts open and out spring the stamens with a shower of yellow pollen from their bags! Some of it goes on to the bee's velvet back, but he takes no notice at all. I always think if *I* were a bee I should either fall off the flower in fright, or else sneeze violently. But I suppose the bees get used to explosions and surprises as they go on their daily rounds.

What happens next?

The bee gets his honey and flies off again, still carrying the yellow dust on his back. The next gorse flower he visits greets him with another "pop"—but in brushing against the pistil among the stamens there he leaves a little of the first flower's pollen sticking to that pistil—and that's all the gorse wants. Directly *another* flower's pollen has been given to it, it can use it to make its seeds with. And it begins straight-away.

A curious thing is that once a bee has

visited a gorse flower and taken its pollen, the keel doesn't spring back to its original position—it stays where it is, drooping down as if to say to the next bee, "No need to come here. All the work's done." But I have noticed that some bees don't take any notice of that. They just blunder in all the same. Perhaps they are "dunce" bees.

Cocoanut Cakes.

It is not only the bright yellow blossoms that attract the bee, but the gloriously strong smell. There is something most delicious about the smell of gorse. To lie on a hillside in the shade of the gorse-bushes on a hot sunny day is to be perfectly happy. Have you ever tried it? You can see the golden gorse against the deep blue sky—you can hear the happy hum of the bees working in the blossoms—and you can smell the warm rich scent that is drawn out of the gorse flowers by the heat of the sun. It always, always reminds me of hot cocoanut cakes, and I expect it will remind you of them, too.

Fairy Pop-Guns.

In summer, if you walk among the gorse-bushes, you will hear "Pop! Pop-pop! Pop!" all around you. And you can almost imagine tiny elves sitting in the gorse-bushes firing little pop-guns at you. What is it making that noise?

The gorse-pods! You will find them all over the bush—little black pods with brown hairs. They are full of pea-like seeds. The lower part of the pistils we found among the stamens has grown and grown until it has become a pod, carefully protecting the baby seeds inside. And now that it is time for the seeds to seek their fortune in the world the pods are bursting in the heat of the sun, and sending out their babies.

Why do they pop? Why don't they just open and let the seeds fall out? You can easily guess.

If the seeds tumbled out and fell down they would simply fall through the mother gorse-bush to the ground beneath—and there is no room there for another bush to grow.

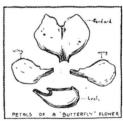

PETALS OF A 'BUTTERFLY' FLOWER.

But an explosion sends the seeds further off, away from the mother bush, and, in a clear space, the new baby plant will find room to grow and to breathe. It is all marvellously well planned.

The pods twist themselves up when they have shot out their little bullets, and after a time fall off the bush. Their good work is done.

An Old Saying.

"When the gorse is out of blossom, then kissing's out of fashion!"

You've surely heard that saying. And, as you very well know, we kiss all the year round, so that, therefore, the gorse must be out all the year, too!

And you'll find it is, even on the barest winter day. Here and there, actually in the snow, I have been able to spy a splash of yellow gold. Brave little blossoms, with no hope of bee or butterfly!

Some people call it "furze," some call it "whin." Most of us call it gorse. All three names are poetical, because all three suit the plant so well. Short and sharp, and yet pretty—just like the golden-blossomed bush.

SEE CAPTION OR EXPLANATION PAGE 319

APPENDIX 3

WEEKLY SUGGESTIONS FOR INFANTS' TEACHERS

Continued from page 813.

Let children find out by the picture card what letter is silent in these words—the letter *l*. What sound has *a* in these words? Remind children of the phonogram *ar*. "A" has the same sound before silent *l*. Let children spell the words and supply others if known, such as *balm, alms.* As these words are seldom in a child's vocabulary, they must have their meaning explained. Let children give sentences in which these words are used.

WRITING AND DRAWING.

Summertime,
Summertime,
Now at last has come.
Fragrant flowers,
Sunny hours,
Busy bees
low hum.

Children can decorate as they wish, and take home to parents.

Blackboard Work.
The *calf* is in the shed.
Would you like *half* of my apple?
Salmon are very large fish.
I have lines on the *palm* of my hand.

NUMBER-WORK.

Measuring in inches, and half-inches.
Let children have a ruler, marked with half-inch and quarter-inches, and a piece of plain paper. Revise the former lesson on measuring inches. Let them put a dot at the beginning and end of one inch, and draw the line one inch long. Let them make this into a square. Show the children how to put the ruler so that the angle is right, i.e., the line marking the inch should be in a straight

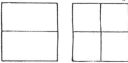

line with the top of the square. Let children divide the square into halves. What shape is each half? Are they squares? How long is the shortest side? How many inches is it round the square? How many round half the square? Let children divide the square into quarters. What shape are these? How long is each side? How long all the way round? Let children draw a half-square and a quarter-square by themselves. Then let them draw squares 1½ inches, 2½ inches, &c.

HANDWORK.

Drawing.—The Butterfly. (Food of the Bat.)
Modelling.—Miss Bat in the chimney. (From the story.)

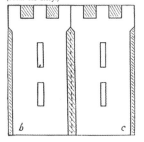

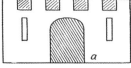

a

Cutting.—The tower where the bats sleep. One and a-half squares needed. Cut out shaded parts: drawing windows. Mount *a* in centre, with a tower *b* or *c* on each side.

SEVENS AND STANDARD I.
ENGLISH, NATURE TALKS AND LANGUAGE-TRAINING.

Let children talk of the summer flowers. Have some roses for them to see and pictures to illustrate talks. Let children examine the wild rose of the hedges first, both bud and flower. Right under the flower they will see the tiny, green cup which the rose-mother has made for the baby-seeds. At the top of this they will find five little green leaves which wrap up the bud, and which fall back when the five pretty pink petals open out. What can they see in the open rose? A great many stamens, full of pollen. Like the poppy the rose has no honey for the bees and insects, but very much pollen in-

stead. The pretty colour and the mass of pollen and the sweet scent all call to the insects to come and help the rose by carrying the pollen to the stigma of another rose, and so causing the seeds to grow. Let children look at a fallen rose and examine the little seed-box. It is shaped like an urn. If one is cut open they will see the seeds. As the seeds ripen, the seed-box swells and becomes soft, sweet, and juicy; then turns bright red; then we call them "hips." The birds come and eat them, but they drop the hard seeds down on the ground. Remind children that the rose is the emblem of England.

Story.
"The Rose and the Anemone." *The Greenwood Tree.* (Arnold.)

Composition (a) Oral.
Let children describe a summer day, speaking of the following points—the air, the sun, the flowers, birds, insects, trees, people. Put some descriptive phrases on blackboard to help, e.g., "full-blown flowers," "humming of insects," "leaves quivering in the breeze. Let child use these and supply others.

(b) Written.
Which do you like best—summer or winter? Why?

Spellings.

flowers,	leafy,	gardener.
fragrance,	leaves,	heat.
leaf,	garden,	holidays.

WRITING AND DRAWING.

Oh give to me
the roses red,
The queen
of fragrant flowers
Old Song

NUMBER-WORK.

Proving sums right.—Let children use very small numbers at first in order that they may understand the process. Let them put fifteen counters in a line on the desk and mark off 6.
Tell them to set this down as a subtraction sum.
Let them see that the number subtracted and the number left, if put together (added), make the number they had altogether, therefore, to prove their subtraction sum right, they must add the answer to the number subtracted, and if they get the number on the top line their sum is right. Let children practise 9 + 6 = 15 for some time with quite easy numbers, then let them apply what they have learned to larger numbers.

From 73   Add 54
Take 19   To 19

54 Left   73 Altogether.

Addition of two numbers can be proved in the same way, by subtracting one of the numbers from the answer, when the second number will result.

HANDWORK.

Drawing.—A wild rose. From Nature.
Free-cutting.—A spray of rose leaves.
Toy-making.—*A sunshade.*

A small stick, with a bit of silk thread for a tassel. Push top of stick through *a* (see diagram), and squeeze the folds downwards.

ENID BLYTON'S NATURE LESSONS.
SYLLABUS FOR SEPTEMBER, 1925, TO SEPTEMBER, 1926.

1925.
Sept. 2. Some Seeds and Fruits.
16. Migration.
30. Heather.
Oct. 14. Falling Leaves.
28. Getting Ready for Winter.
Nov. 11. The Squirrel.
25. The Cat.
Dec. 9. Holly and Mistletoe.
23. Footsteps in Snow.
1926.
Jan. 6. The Robin.
20. Buds of Trees.
Feb. 3. Flowers of Trees.
17. The Little Coltsfoot.
March 3. Frogs.
17. Moles.
31. The Cuckoo.
April 14. The Buttercup.
28. The May Tree.
May 12. Gnats.
26. The Hedgehog.
June 9. Foxgloves.
23. The Bat.
July 7. Wasps.
21. Flat Fishes.
Aug. 4. Jellyfish.
18. Crabs and Lobsters.

SEE CAPTION OR EXPLANATION PAGE 319

APPENDIX 4

THE TEACHERS WORLD, *September 1, 1920.*

ENID BLYTON'S NATURE LESSONS
ILLUSTRATED BY THE AUTHOR.

BIG CRABS AND LITTLE CRABS.

IN the last nature lesson I told you the life-story of the crab, and how it lived, grew, and changed its coat. This time I will tell you of some of the crabs you can look for and find at the seaside.

The Pea-crab.

This crab is so tiny that he is called the Pea-Crab. You may often have seen him, and taken him up in your hand to smile at his smallness. He is a dear little thing, and even when he is quite grown up he is hardly half an inch across, and so round that he really does look rather like a pea! Not a green pea, though, but a yellow one.

Now, where do you think the Pea-Crab lives? I don't think you would guess if you had a score of tries, for he lives inside the shell of a living mussel or cockle! Fancy being small enough to do that!

What he does there I really don't know. He certainly doesn't seem to harm his landlord or landlady. He probably skips inside the shell for safety, and is only too pleased when Mr. Mussel shuts up his front door, and hides him away from any enemy. Yet the curious thing is that if he finds a *dead* mussel he will gorge himself on the flesh and have a fine feast.

If you open a mussel shell that has a pea-crab hiding inside, you won't see him pop out in a hurry. Instead, he curls up all his tiny legs round his wee body, and lies so still that you almost begin to think he must be a stone or something which has got inside the shell. Take him out, and he will scuttle over your hand like a frightened spider.

In some places you will find a pea-crab in nearly every mussel shell you open, for this quaint family has found that it is far safer to take lodgings in a shell than to tramp the sandy pools and find holes for themselves.

The Shore-crab (illustrated last lesson).

This is a crab you are sure to have seen, for he is always to be found running about the shore when the tide is out, and loves to hide himself under stones or seaweed.

He is generally rather green in colour, but you will find almost as many brown or yellow, with black markings.

He does not grow very big, and it is a good thing for him that he doesn't, for his flesh is nice to eat—but there is so little of it that no one bothers about catching and cooking him.

You can watch this crab going hunting on the seashore. He loves sandhoppers for his dinner so he looks about for a few of these lively little fellows, and then creeps up to them carefully. Suddenly he gives a pounce, and one of the unfortunate sand-hoppers finds himself caught in a pair of strong pincers. Then the shore crab enjoys his meal.

This crab is really rather a jolly little fellow, and easily tamed. If you happen to live by the sea and keep a salt-water aquarium, you can easily keep one of these crabs and teach him to come to you for his food, and even (if mother allows it!) have a little run over the table to say how-do-you-do when visitors come.

Be careful, when you catch him, that he doesn't nip you, for his claws are very strong indeed, and will pinch you sharply if you are careless in holding him.

The Fiddler-crab.

This is a swimmer-crab. As I told you last time, most crabs only crawl, but the Fiddler can swim very well. Perhaps you have seen him swimming in a little rock-pool, and felt quite astonished to see a crab getting along quickly through the water.

How does he do it? Well, he has turned his hind legs into paddles, and uses them to row himself through the water. It's really a very good idea, isn't it?

If you can catch him, have a look at his hind legs. You will see that they are flattened out into oval plates, which have fringes of long hairs around them, instead of being thin and slender with little hooked claws at the tip.

You will wonder why he is called the Fiddler-Crab. He is given that name because when he moves his legs he makes rather the same movements that a fiddler does when playing his violin. You must watch him and see.

1. Thornback-crab.   2. Fiddler-crab.
3. Hermit-crab.   4. Pea-crab.

You can keep him, too, in an aquarium, and tame him. But don't put him with anything else alive, for he will fight it, and kill it if he possibly can. He is a most warlike little creature, and loves to eat his enemies.

The Fiddler is a pretty little crab. His shell looks rather like velvet, for it is covered with a soft down. He wears blue stripes on his legs, and has blue and scarlet claws, so you can see he is a gay and handsome fellow.

The Thornback-crab.

If you see this crab you will, perhaps, think he is an unpleasant-looking spider, for he has a small body and very long, thin legs. The family he belongs to is called the Spider-Crab. Long, sharp spikes grow on his shell, and you will probably find, to your surprise, that he has bits of seaweed or sponge growing on his back!

Can you guess why? It is because he does not want to be seen and eaten by his enemies. He is a very large crab, and it is difficult for him to hide himself completely, so he simply grows seaweed on his back, squats at the bottom of the sea, and pretends to be a nice patch of seaweed!

You will think the crab is very clever when I tell you that he *plants the seaweed himself* on his back! You can sometimes see him doing this if you go to the fine aquarium at the Zoo and look into the Spider Crab tank. First he scratches his back to make it nice and rough. Then he pulls up a neat little bit of seaweed, puts it on his back, and presses the roots nicely down. He has plenty of spines and tiny hooks on his shell to hold the seaweed for him. Then he plants a second piece and a third, and

so on until his back is covered. Then he is content, for he knows his enemies will think he is seaweed and not a crab at all.

Once a spiny spider-crab, whose back was covered with seaweed, was put in a tank with sponges at the bottom, instead of sea-weed. What must he do but tear off all the seaweed on his back and plant bits of sponges there instead!

The Edible-crab.

I must really tell you about this crab, because we eat him. He is not very likely to find him, for he lives in deep water. He is, as you know, a large crab, and sometimes weighs as much as twelve pounds. He has enormous claws, which can give a terrible pinch.

You can sometimes find him when young hiding in a rock-pool, but be careful of his pincers. If he pretends to be dead—which he probably will do—you can safely pick him up and look at him.

The shells of edible crabs are often covered with barnacles or sea-worm tubes, and sometimes carry so many that it is difficult to see any of their backs at all!

The Four-horned Spider-crab.

This is a common spider-crab, and you are quite sure to find him if you look. He has a long beak in front, and on it grow four horns, which give him his name.

His upper parts are covered with little short spikes and hairs, and he is usually so covered with funny little corallines seaweed that you can hardly see his shell at all.

The Hermit-crab.

This is perhaps the most interesting crab of all. He lives in a house of his own made of an old whelk-shell. You will easily find a hermit-crab if you hunt about the pools for a little while. Soon you will come across a whelk-shell whose entrance is guarded by a big claw. Then you may know a hermit-crab is inside.

But why does he live there? For a very good reason—his body is soft, and his tail is long like a lobster's. He is afraid of being eaten, so he looks for somewhere to hide his long tail. An empty whelk-shell fits him beautifully, so he walks in backwards, takes hold of the inside of the shell with a pair of curious pincers on the end of his tail, and guards the entrance with his armoured claws. You will usually find his legs hanging out, too.

Don't pull him out, or you will hurt him. If you really want to see what he is like out of his shell, take him and pop him on a big sea anemone. Then he will be afraid of being swallowed, and will hurry out of his shell at once. Put the shell down by him and watch him getting in again.

Sometimes a hermit-crab grows too big for his shell, and goes to find a bigger one. If he finds another hermit-crab in a shell he fancies, he will try to drag him out, and a terrible fight begins! You can see this at the Zoo Aquarium sometimes, and most thrilling it is.

Some hermit-crabs have small anemones growing on their whelk-shells. They like this, because the stinging rays of the anemone keep away hungry fish. The anemone likes it, too, because he gets a nice share of the hermit-crab's meals!

The Robber-crab.

Before I finish I must just tell you of one curious hermit-crab who lives on Christmas Island. This great crab lives in a snug burrow, which he lines with coconut fibre. When he wants food he climbs sixty feet or so up a coconut palm, shakes down a nut, and climbs back again.

Then he cleverly hammers in the "eye-holes" of the coconut, puts in his smaller pair of pincers, and takes out delicious bits of the nut.

I hope I have told you enough to make you want to look for crabs, and watch them. They are such interesting creatures, and we would like to know even more about them than we do, so see if you can find out something that nobody else knows!

SEE CAPTION OR EXPLANATION PAGE 319

THE TEACHER'S TREASURY

gregarious and " live with a pack," so to speak, they understand the mentality of a dog far more than that of a cat, which usually comes to them for what it can get, and not for what it can share or give. Naturally there are many exceptional individuals, but it is with cats as a whole that this lesson deals.

§ 7

The cat family is a large and successful one. Their many physical helps of claws, eyes, pads, teeth, and whiskers make them " winners in life's race," and they have cunning as well, an even greater **The Cat** asset to predatory animals. Lions, tigers, leopards, panthers, **Family** pumas, ocelots, caracals, and lynxes are some of the best-known members of this widespread family, of which the cat has, rather curiously, become our domesticated, if somewhat inscrutable, friend.

No. 26.—THE ROBIN

" The bird, who by some name or other,
All men who know thee call thee brother."
WORDSWORTH.

JUST as we love the dog for his willing comradeship and friend-liness, so do we love the robin for the same characteristics. No other bird has such a firm hold of our affections, and his place of honour on hundreds of Christmas cards shows the regard which we have for him.

§ 1

The robin is most astonishingly tame and friendly, and his con-fidence that we will return his engaging advances is most amusing. No one could repulse a robin. If he taps at the window, he **A Friendly** **Little Bird** knows it will be opened. If he builds his nest in our bedroom, he knows perfectly well it will not be disturbed. He is a living little example of perfect faith, and as a rule his faith is entirely justified.

§ 2

The robin is easily recognised by his tawny-orange waistcoat, which reaches right up to his face. His long, slender legs give him **A Fine** rather the air of a dandy, while his full black eyes are as **Dress** watchful and keen as can be. Young robins have no red breasts, but are speckled and dressed in various shades of brown, making it difficult to see them when they sit among brown twigs and branches. They gain their red waistcoats in the late summer.

244

SEE CAPTION OR EXPLANATION PAGE 319

THE 20 TEACHING FEATURES—HOW THEY WILL APPEAR

A PROVISIONAL TIME-TABLE SHOWING THE ALTERNATION OF FORTNIGHTLY SERIALS

IN BOTH EDITIONS — 9 REGULAR WEEKLY FEATURES

1. FRONT PAGE Leaders, Special Articles, Exclusive Photographs.
2. EDUCATIONIST'S DIARY (the most eagerly canvassed commentary in educational journalism).
3. Special articles by leading historians on CONTEMPORARY HISTORY, alternating with literary articles by Horace Shipp and others.
4, 5. NEWS AND VIEWS of the week ("T.W." is nearly always the "first out," with important educational news).
6. SCHOLARSHIP PAPERS (actually set by L.E.A.s).
7. LESSONS IN THE NEWS and Topical Celebrations, by Robert Henry, M.A.; alternating with the RURAL SCHOOL feature.
8. ENTERTAINMENT PAGE (Songs, sketches, plays).
9. Book Reviews and Notices.

JUNIOR EDITION ONLY

10 PAGES OF SERIAL TEACHING FEATURES

ONE WEEK

10. A YEAR'S LESSONS IN ENGLISH.—A carefully graded course in Composition, Grammar, Spelling.—By R.K. and M. I. R. Polkinghorne.—First instalment Page 758.
11. HISTORY THROUGH STORIES.—By Olive Enoch, whose Period Tales have proved so popular in "T.W."—Page 760.
12. HEDGEROW TALES.—A NOVEL NATURE STUDY COURSE. By Enid Blyton. See attractive Syllabus, Page 771.
13. HOW TO TEACH ON THE "NEW ART" LINES. For Infants and Juniors. By M. J. Welsch.—Pages 762-4.
14. THE DRAMATIC METHOD FOR ENGLISH.—By Rodney Bennett, the teacher-playwright.—Page 773.
15. P.T.—GRADED LESSONS FROM THE BOARD'S NEW P.T. SYLLABUS.—By A. T. Meakins—Page 775.
16. 17. LESSONS IN PICTURES.—Double-page "spreads" for display in classroom or hall.—Pages 766-7.
18. "OLD THATCH."—ENID BLYTON'S CHILDREN'S PAGE—Page 777.
19. "T.W." INQUIRIES BUREAU PAGE. For teachers of Juniors.—Page 779.

ALTERNATING WEEK

10. GEOGRAPHY FOR JUNIORS.—"At Home and Abroad": A novel syllabus, By Robert Finch.
11. HANDWORK IN THE JUNIOR SCHOOL.—By E. E. Kenwrick, the Froebel Examiner and Lecturer.
12. RHYTHMIC TRAINING.—An important series, By Ethel F. Gyford.
13. INFANTS' SCHOOL.—By Hilda Gall, the Liverpool Inspector.
14. CUT PAPER AND DESIGN.—A practical and colourful series, By Donald Milner, Principal, Bristol School of Art.
15. OUR READERS AS CONTRIBUTORS.—Novel lessons in all subjects.
16. 17. THE PICTORIAL FEATURES on the middle pages are, of course, a weekly feature.
18. So also is Enid Blyton's page, read by more than three quarters of a million children every week.

N.B.—The scheme of alternation here shown is provisional only; it may be modified.

> KEEP THIS SYLLABUS SAFE FOR REFERENCE

SENIOR EDITION ONLY

ONE WEEK

10. ENTICEMENT TO POETRY.—The Headmaster of Rugby, P. H. B. Lyon, M.A., shows how to overcome the Senior's distrust of poetry—Page 758.
11. GEOGRAPHY WITH "C" CLASSES. A detailed course of lessons, "Round B.S. Enquire, By B. G. Hardingham, Page 760.
12. BIOLOGY THROUGH THE SCHOOL GARDEN.—A sound and practical course, By Robert Beeks.—Page 762.
13. EXPERIMENTAL "SCRIPTURE." Our popular contributor, F. K. Chaplin, M.A., proves that Religious Instruction need not be dull or tedious.—Page 764.
14. MENTAL ARITHMETIC. "Something more than Mental Arithmetic." By W. W. Summerscales.—Page 771.
15. P.T. ROUND THE YEAR. A complete scheme based on the Board's new Syllabus.—Page 775.
16. 17. THE PICTORIAL FEATURES. For wall display. Pages 766-7.
18. MAKING HISTORY COME ALIVE —Stimulating and practical suggestions by E. H. Dance, M.A.—Page 775.
19. GENERAL KNOWLEDGE SEARCH CARDS. Covering a wide field. By A. Richardson-Wuhi. With answers.—Page 779.

10 PAGES OF SERIAL TEACHING FEATURES

ALTERNATING WEEK

10. ENJOYABLE ENGLISH.—A Course of Vocabulary Exercises. By Edwin Moore.
11. GEOGRAPHY BY THE "TOPIC" METHOD.—John G. S. Ward, M.A., describes exactly how his novel scheme works in a Senior School. A full year's course.
12. THE TEACHING OF CITIZENSHIP. —A Symposium by leading experts.
13. IDEAS FOR THE "C" CLASSES.—Practical help for all teachers who have backward pupils.
14. THE APPLICATIONS OF SCIENCE. —This popular course, of which only seven instalments have appeared, will be continued.
15. IDEAS FOR CRAFT LESSONS.—Suggestions for work in all the School Crafts.
16. 17. The pictorial displays in the middle pages are, of course, a weekly feature.
18. "T.W." INQUIRIES BUREAU PAGE For teachers of Seniors.

N.B.—The scheme of alternation here shown is provisional only; it may be modified.

Further new serial teaching features are already in hand. Each of the above will be followed by others equally strong and helpful, and many issues will contain even more material than is promised above. **Merit Stamps in colour, gummed and perforated, are announced on page 752.**

NO OTHER EDUCATIONAL JOURNAL HAS EVER COVERED THE TEACHER'S NEEDS SO COMPLETELY

SEE CAPTION OR EXPLANATION PAGE 319

THE TEACHERS WORLD, *August* 29, 1934. 771

HEDGEROW TALES—A Year's Course in Nature Study

By Enid Blyton

The many friends and correspondents of Enid Blyton—and they number, literally, thousands of teachers and children—will be glad to hear that she is to write the Nature Study lessons for the school year 1934-35. The scope of the series is described in characteristic terms by the author herself in column 3.

THE TIME TABLE OF THE SYLLABUS

September 5.	Rabbity Ways.	(Rabbits and Hares.)
September 19.	Prickly Friends.	(Hedgehog and Family.)
October 3.	New Tails for Old.	(Lizard and Newt.)
October 17.	The Adventurers.	(Swallows and Martins.)
October 31.	Dozymouse and Flittermouse.	(Doormouse and Bat.)
November 14.	Spinner in the Hedge.	(Spider, Flies.)
November 28.	The Grey Miner.	(Mole and Hedgehog.)
December 12.	Oak Tree Guests.	(Nuthatch, Woodpecker, Tree creeper.)
December 26.	One Warm Winter's Day.	(Field and Water Voles.)
January 9.	Keep Away!	(Robins and other birds.)
January 23.	Bushy Tails.	(Red and Grey Squirrels.)
February 6.	Never Say Die!	(Stoat and Weasel.)
February 20.	Hoo Hoo the Owl.	(Owl and Sparrowhawk.)
March 6.	Brer Frog and Brer Toad.	(Frogs and Toads.)
March 20.	The Wonderful Traveller.	(Eel.)
April 3.	One Dark Night.	(Badger and Fox.)
April 17.	Creepy Creatures.	(Viper and Grass-Snake.)
May 1.	The Whistler.	(Otter.)
May 15.	The Strange Egg.	(Cuckoo and Hedge Sparrow.)
May 29.	The Bumble Bee Hums.	(Bee and Wasp.)
June 12.	The Blue Visitor.	(Kingfisher and Moorhen.)
June 26.	Wicked Rat.	(Rats and Mice.)
July 10.	The Little Fawn.	(Deer.)
July 24.	A Friend and an Enemy	(Ladybird and Daddylonglegs.)

* A novel feature of this very attractive new Nature Serial is the large four-page picture of the hedge-row in Autumn which will appear with the first instalment of the series. It can be coloured by the children or the teacher, mounted on cardboard, and displayed on the class-room wall. For Winter, Spring, Summer, new pictures will be published. With each "Hedgerow Tale" will be published an outline drawing of the animal, bird or insect of the tale. This can be cut out and coloured and affixed in the appropriate place on the big picture.

FROM THE AUTHOR TO THE READER

EVERY bank, every hedgerow is a world of its own, with its own creatures, it casual visitors, its squabbles, friendships, big and little happenings. A rabbit is most truly a rabbit when sitting happily outside its burrow; a robin is wholly a robin when complete with its friends, enemies and natural background; that is why I have taken one particular hedgerow, with its over-shading tree, its sunny bank, its moist ditch below, and the little pond nearby, and have woven into this natural background the lives and personalities of the little creatures whose home it is. I want to present a truthful picture of this small country world, whose bounds are only a few dozen feet square. I myself have often sat on the bank below the hedgerow, shaded by an old tree, and have watched the little animal folk at their work and play. In these Hedgerow Tales I would like to take the children with me, so that they may watch and understand too—hoping, of course, that they will long for the real thing, and go out into the country to find and love all the little animal and bird characters in these Hedgerow Tales!

ENGLISH

Continued from page 758

(*b*) This year my birthday fell on Wednesday.

(*c*) I received many presents. One came from Canterbury in Kent, and another came from far-away Australia.

1. Write the names of the days of the week; of the months of the year. If you are not sure of the spelling ask about it.

2. Write three sentences like the three given above in (*a*) (*b*) and (*c*).

3. Write the names of five towns in five different countries; see sentence (*c*) above.

Notes for the Teacher

SOME of these lessons can be told or read to the children, the exercises are for written work. The simpler exercises are for the lowest forms. If they are used for children of seven they can be divided. For example, Exercise I. contains written work for three exercises for little ones, and so on. By arranging the exercises in this way it is hoped that material will be found for every form. The top form should be able to work *every* exercise completely.

When these exercises are corrected, it is useful to let the children keep their corrected papers in folders so that they build up a simple grammar book, though the exercises are as useful for spelling as grammar. The exercises can be written on the board or hectographed for the children. Exercise III. of Lesson II. is very interesting for older children from the point of view of general knowledge. It is always wise to associate the teaching of English with history and geography—as the one subject is hopeless without the other.

DRAMATICS

Continued from page 773

Simple Acting Points

RIGHT from the beginning, appreciation and criticism should be directed to the looks as well as the sound of the play. Thus the class will quickly appreciate what an improvement it is if the players move when occasion offers, thus producing new groupings. They will see that it is also a good thing if there is variety of level. (Thus the Ferryman may sit lower than the Girl, and presently rise.)

They will also observe that it is a fault for one player to hide the other from the audience. (This "masking" of one another is a favourite trick of children and needs constant attention.)

Next, we shall consider how from these simple beginnings we can develop something like a shapely little play.

HISTORY THROUGH STORY

Continued from page 760

THE ANCIENT BRITONS OR CELTS

The Celts lived in small settlements and hunted wild animals and grew crops. Their weapons were of bronze and iron.

DRUIDISM

Their belief was Druidism. They believed in immortality and offered human sacrifices to their gods.

Their priests, the Druids, were learned men who knew many secrets of science.

PERKUNOS

One of their gods was Perkunos, god of hills and battles. Before a battle sacrifices were offered to him in sacred oak groves.

THE TREASURE CAVES

Many valuable treasures of the Druids were hidden in underground caves known only to a few.

SUPERSTITIONS

Like all heathen beliefs, Druidism held many superstitions. Good and evil spirits were thought to haunt the dells and caverns. The Club Moss (grace-of-God) was supposed to protect its owner from danger if picked in the proper way.

SEE CAPTION OR EXPLANATION PAGE 320

THE TEACHERS WORLD, *September 5, 1934.*

HEDGEROW TALES

A YEAR'S LESSONS IN NATURE STUDY BY ENID BLYTON

1. Rabbity Ways

THE night had been very dark, for there was no moon. Now there was a grey light creeping into the eastern sky. Daybreak was near. Soon the owls would go home and the bats would fly back to the old barn to sleep.

The old oak tree that grew out of the hedgerow rustled its leaves in the chilly wind. It was a wise old tree, friendly to all creatures, and loved by a great many.

The hedgerow was old, too. In it grew hawthorn, whose leaves were out early in the springtime, green fingers held up to the sun. Bramble sprays flung long arms here and there, as prickly as the wild rose that forced its way up to the sun. Ivy covered one part of the hedge, and here, in blossom-time, feasted the last late flies and many beautiful red admirals.

***

BELOW was a sunny bank, for the hedge-row faced south. In summer-time the birds found sweet wild strawberries on this bank, and the primroses sometimes flowered there in the early days of January. In the ditch below there was moss growing, soft as velvet, and a few graceful ferns. It was always damp there and cool.

Near the old oak tree was a small pond, ringed round with rushes and meadow-sweet. Many creatures came to drink there—from the sly red fox down to the striped yellow wasp! All the creatures in the fields around knew the pond well, and often the swallows would come and skim above it, looking for flies.

The hedgerow was in a deserted corner of the field. Nobody came there, not even the children hunting for blackberries. The farmer had forgotten to cut the hedge for years, and it had grown tall and tangled. Sometimes the wind would bring the sound of the farmer's voice, talking in a distant field to his horses, but usually the hedgerow knew nothing but the sound of the wind, of bird calls and pattering paws.

Many, many things had happened in and around the hedgerow. The oak tree had rustled its leaves over thousands of insects, birds and animals. Its twigs knew the dif-ference between a squirrel's scampering paws and a bird's light hold, three toes in front and one behind. Its acorns had been stolen by all kinds of mice, and by the screeching jays and the hungry nuthatch.

Now it stood whispering in the cool wind of daybreak. Summer was passing over, and soon the oak leaves would lose their dark green hue and would turn brown.

***

THE grey light in the sky became brighter. Beneath the oak-tree, where the bank showed a sandy streak, a hole could just be seen. It was a rabbit's burrow. The burrow went down among the roots of the tree, exactly the size of a rabbit's body except now and again when it widened out to make passing-places for two meeting rabbits. The tunnel branched off into two or three different burrows, but the rabbits had learnt every foot of them, and always

knew which tunnel to take when they wanted to go to the gorse-bush, to the bank or to the other side of the pond.

Out of the hole in the bank a rabbit's head appeared. Her big eyes looked through the dim grey light, her nose twitched as she sniffed the air, and her big ears listened to every sound. She wanted to go out and feed on the grass, and she had with her a young family of five rabbits, who were just getting old enough to look after themselves.

"It is safe," she said to her young ones. "We can go out. There is no stoat about, and the owls have all gone home."

They trooped out of the hole. Other rabbits were in the field too, big ones and little ones, for there were many other burrows there.

***

"KEEP near the burrow," said the mother rabbit. "Then you will not have far to run if danger comes. I am going along the hedgerow. There is a young furze bush there and I shall feed on the juicy shoots. Keep an eye on the other rabbits, and if you see them turn so that their white bobtail shows plainly, dart into your burrow. Bobbing tails mean danger somewhere! And keep your ears pricked, too—for if one of the old rabbits scents danger he will drum on the ground with his hind-foot to warn us all. Then you must run as fast as you can."

The little rabbits began to nibble the grass. They felt quite sure they could look after themselves. Their mother ran silently along the hedgerow. Suddenly she stopped and stood so still that it seemed as if she had frozen stiff. She had seen another animal coming through the hedge.

It was a brown hare. As soon as the rabbit saw that it was a harmless creature she ran on again and came up to the hare. "You scared me, cousin hare," she said. "Is your burrow round here?"

"Burrow!" said the hare, looking in sur-prise at the rabbit, her soft eyes gleaming in the grey light. "I have no burrow. I live above ground."

"But how dangerous!" said the rabbit, in alarm. "Stoats and weasels could easily find you! Do you make a nest like the birds?"

***

"COME with me," said the hare. "I will show you where I live. My home is called a form, because it is simply a dent in the ground the size and form of my body. I make it the shape of my body by lying in it, you see. I like to live alone. I should not like to live with others, as you do."

"But it is safer," said the rabbit, going with the hare over the field. "I have left my young ones with the other rabbits, and they will warn them if danger is near. There is safety in numbers."

"My ears and my nose make me safe," said the hare. "I can smell faraway things and hear the slightest noise. Look at my

See page 790

ears, longer than yours, cousin. See the black tips, too. You have no black tips. Look at my hind legs. Yours are strong, but mine are much stronger. I can run like the wind!"

Suddenly the hare gave a great leap, and jumped about fifteen feet over the field. The rabbit was startled, but the hare called to her.

"Here is my form. I always jump like that before I go to it, so that I break my trail. Then if weasel or stoat come round they cannot follow my scent for it breaks where I jump! Come here, cousin. I have some young ones to show you, only a few days old."

***

THE rabbit went to the hare's form, which was simply a dent in the earth. Near it were other small holes, and in each lay a young hare, a leveret, its eyes wide open, its body warmly covered with fur.

"They have made forms of their own," said the hare, proudly. "Even when they are young they like to live alone."

"My young ones are not like this," said the rabbit in surprise, looking at the leverets. "My children were born blind and deaf and had no fur on them at all. I made a special burrow for them, and blocked up the entrance to it every time I went out. I should not think of leaving them out in the open like this. It is a good thing your children are born able to see and hear, for they would certainly be eaten by an enemy!"

"They are safe enough," said the hare. "Now take me to see your home, cousin rabbit. I should like to see your youngsters too."

***

THEY went back to the hedgerow. The hare gave another great leap when she left her form. It was a favourite trick of hers not only when leaving her home, but when she was hunted by dogs. Sometimes she would double on her tracks, too, to throw off her hunters. It nearly always deceived them.

The hare was astonished to see the burrow in which the rabbits lived. "But how do you manage about your ears?" she asked. "Do you bend them back when you run underground? That must be very uncom-fortable. It is a strange idea to tunnel in the earth. I am sure that our family were not meant to do so, or we would not have been given such long ears. It must be diffi-cult, too, to dig out all the earth."

"No, it is easy," said the rabbit. "I dig with my front paws and shovel out the earth with my hind paws. See, cousin, there are my children, feeding yonder."

The hare was looking at the young rabbits in the light of the dawn when a curious noise came to her long ears. It was a drumming sound, and it seemed to the hare as if the ground were quivering under her feet. The mother rabbit called to her young ones at once.

"Come here! There is danger about! That is the old rabbit drumming with his hind feet to warn us. Come, cousin, you must hide in our burrow, too."

Continued on page 807

NATURE NOTES

APRIL

" A cold April the barn will fill."

OF ALL THE MONTHS April is perhaps the most beautiful in her sudden changes from sun to rain, from blue sky to purple clouds. She gives us rainbows by the score, and piles up clouds like heaps of cotton-wool in the pure-blue sky. A most delicious month of young things growing, of brilliant greenery and dazzling flowers. It may be cold or warm, or both alternately. Note that a cold April is supposed to be good for crops. Let the children observe if this is so.

Trees in April

Most charming of all the trees this month is the golden " palm " in its glory of yellow blossom. The grey fur of the " pussy-willow " buds has, in the case of the male stamen flowers, burst forth into bright yellow heads of fluffy-looking " palm." It is a joy in any classroom. Tell the children only to cut (not break) what they need, for too many golden " palms " are spoilt in the spring through destructive pulling and tearing. Let the children find also the female catkins of the same species of tree— they are green and ragged looking, not a bit like the beautiful golden " palm."

Find the flowers of the ash, the oak, the beech, the yew, poplar and birch, as well as any others local to the district. Many people have no idea what kind of flowers the oak has, for instance, though they know the acorns well. Bring in some of the " rosy plumelets " that spring from the larch-tree, which is now beautiful in its bright green dress.

The almond-tree is lovely now, and the prunus, which may have been out in March, is most certainly blossoming now. Fruit-trees are also a lovely sight to see, particularly the early plums, which are as white as snow in the sunshine. Apple-blossom is lovely, too—let the children smell the unexpected sweetness of the pink blossoms. Pear-trees begin to blossom now, also.

Besides their flowers, the trees are putting forth their tender green

99

SEE CAPTION OR EXPLANATION PAGE 320

APPENDIX 10

SOME INTERESTING THINGS TO DO

	PAGE		PAGE		PAGE
JOHN'S "DRY GARDEN"	168	JOHN'S FLOWER AND BIRD CHARTS	171	JOHN'S LEAF-PRINTS	174
EGG-CUPS FOR THE TOYS	169	A LITTLE AQUARIUM	172	FIR-CONE BIRDS	176

DO YOU KNOW THESE FLOWERS?

	PAGE		PAGE		PAGE
ARUM, or LORDS AND LADIES	184	FOXGLOVE	189	PURPLE ORCHIS	188
BARREN STRAWBERRY	181	FUMITORY	194	RAGGED ROBIN	189
BELL HEATHER	191	GERMANDER SPEEDWELL	184	RAGWORT	193
BIRD'S FOOT TREFOIL	192	GORSE	183	RED CLOVER	186
BLACKTHORN	183	GRASS OF PARNASSUS	195	RED DEAD-NETTLE	180
BLUEBELL	186	GREATER STITCHWORT	184	RIBWORT PLANTAIN	187
BLUE BUGLE	188	GROUND IVY	183	ROSEBAY WILLOW-HERB, or FIREWEED	192
BRAMBLE, or BLACKBERRY	191	GROUNDSEL	180		
BROAD-LEAVED DOCK	196	HAREBELL	193	ST. JOHN'S WORT	194
BROOM	188	HAWKBIT	193	SCARLET PIMPERNEL	187
BUR MARIGOLD	197	HEART'S EASE, or WILD PANSY	187	SCENTLESS MAYWEED	190
BUTTERCUP	186	HEATHER, or LING	191	SHEPHERD'S PURSE	180
CAMPION	187	HEDGE PARSLEY	190	SILVERWEED	192
CHICKWEED	180	HEMP NETTLE	197	SNEEZEWORT YARROW	195
CHICORY	196	HENBIT	181	SORREL	189
CINQUEFOIL	192	HERB ROBERT	192	SPRING WHITLOW GRASS	181
COLTSFOOT	182	HONEYSUCKLE	191	STINGING NETTLE	193
COMFREY	197	IVY	197	TANSY	194
COW PARSNIP, or HOGWEED	190	JACK-BY-THE-HEDGE, or GARLIC MUSTARD	185	THISTLE	189
COWSLIP	186	KNAPWEED	193	TUFTED VETCH	187
DAISY	183	KNOTGRASS	198	VIOLET	182
DANDELION	186	LADY'S SMOCK, or MILKMAID	185	WALL PELLITORY	198
DEVIL'S BIT SCABIOUS	197	LESSER CELANDINE	181	WATER CROWFOOT	188
DOG DAISY, or OX-EYE-DAISY	189	MARSH CUDWEED	195	WHITE DEAD-NETTLE	184
DOG'S MERCURY	181	MARSH-MARIGOLD	184	WILD ROSE	189
DOVE'S FOOT CRANE'S-BILL	185	MEADOW SAFFRON, or AUTUMN CROCUS	196	WILD TEAZEL	195
DWARF FURZE	198			WINTER HELIOTROPE	198
ENCHANTER'S NIGHTSHADE, or BITTERSWEET	192	MEADOWSWEET	190	WOOD ANEMONE, or WINDFLOWER	182
EYEBRIGHT	196	MUGWORT, or WORMWOOD	195	WOOD SPURGE	188
		NIPPLEWORT	193	WOOD-SORREL	185
FIELD CONVOLVULUS, or BINDWEED	190	PERSICARIA	194	YARROW, or MILFOIL	187
FIELD GENTIAN	196	PETTY SPURGE	197	YELLOW BEDSTRAW	191
FIELD MADDER	196	POPPY	190	YELLOW IRIS	188
FIELD SCABIOUS	194	PRIMROSE	182	YELLOW TOADFLAX	193
		PURPLE LOOSESTRIFE	195		

6

SEE CAPTION OR EXPLANATION PAGE 320

"Well—we will see," said the little swallows. "We don't want to leave this farm-yard that we love, or the pond we skim over, or the barn we know so well. Maybe we will stay after all."

But one day in the autumn the young swallows felt very restless. A cold wind had begun to blow. There did not seem to be so many insects. They flew here and there on their wide, strong wings, and suddenly they did not want to stay near the farm-yard any more.

One swallow after another settled on the roof of the old barn. Dozens of them, scores of them, hundreds of them gathered together, twittering.

12

"It is time to go. Say good-bye! It is time to go! We will fly to-night, to-night!"

The young swallows said good-bye to the sparrows. "We must go after all. We cannot stay. The wind is blowing to help us. We shall never forget you."

"Come back again," begged the sparrows. "You were born here, in the old barn. You grew up in the sky above the fields and the farm.

13

SEE CAPTION OR EXPLANATION PAGE 320

THE ENID BLYTON NATURE READERS

1. The Brownie's Magic.
    The Friendly Robin.

2. The Squirrel Who Forgot.
    Jack Frost is About!

3. The Dog Who Wanted a Home.
    Where Shall We Nest?

4. The Little Hidden Spell.
    Betty and the Lambs' Tails.

5. The Cross Little Tadpole.
    Silky and the Snail.

6. The Clever Weather-Cock.
    The Very Queer Chicks.

7. The Fish that Built a Nest.
    The Lamb without a Mother.

8. The Dandelion Clocks.
    The Strange Bird.

9. Hats for Sale! Hats for Sale!
    Down Willow Way.

10. Mooo-ooo-ooo!
    Old Ugly, the Water-Grub.

11. Muddle's Mistake.
    The Birds go to School.

12. The Friendly Ladybird.
    The Spell that went Wrong.

13. Tick-Tock and the Buttercup.
    The Wonderful Carpet.

14. A Very Queer Home.
    Gloves for the Party.

15. The Unhappy Grass-Snake.
    Who-Who-Who-Who?

16. The Elf and the Poppy.
    The Tail that Broke Off.

17. Peggy Visits the Bees.
    The Two Little Friends.

18. The Queen who wanted a New Dress.
    The Family in the Corn-Field.

19. The Crab with a Long Tail.
    The Surprising Starfish.

20. Sea-Foam's Adventure.
    The Bad Bluebottle Fly.

21. The Three Bad Imps.
    Silly Sammy and the Corn.

22. The Swallows in the Barn.
    The Birthday Party.

23. The Water-Babies.
    The Rabbit's Party.

24. Ten-Toes the Tailor.
    The Brownie and the Ivy.

25. Diggy's Little Garden.
    Hoppetty-Skip and Crawl-About.

26. Freckles the Thrush.
    The Little Ploughman.

27. The Wonderful Conker.
    Nid-Nod's Mistake.

28. Good Old Miner the Mole.
    The Mistle-Thrush and the Mistletoe.

29. Susan and the Birds.
    The Very Lovely Pattern.

30. Woffly the Rabbit & Quick-Ears the Hare.
    The Little Fir-Tree.

31. The Lucky Bag.
    Down in the Pond.
    You Must Do as You're Told!

32. Umbrella Weather.
    The Brownie & the Yellow-hammer.
    Friendly Old Toad.

33. The Clever Fisherman.
    This is My Place!
    The Tale of a Goldfish.

34. Be Careful, Bubble!
    Oh, what an Unkind Plant!
    Master Prickly.

35. Looking for a Home.
    The Furry Caterpillar.
    Tap-Tap-Tap-Tap-Tap!

36. A Good Little Messenger.
    Hotels for the Birds.
    Sue had a Little Lamb.

SEE CAPTION OR EXPLANATION PAGE 320

THE TEACHERS WORLD, *March 2, 1923* 1143

MARCH

HERE comes March with a whirl and a rush,
    Setting the trees asway,
Swinging the daffodils round and about,
    In his headlong, blustering way.
Round goes the weathercock up on the church,
    And out stream the flags in the town,
For here comes March with a whirl and a rush,
    Racing all up the country and down!

Hedges are red with a myriad buds
    That soon will break out into green,
And sweet pussy-palm is awake in the woods,
    With its fairy-like silvery sheen.
Catkins of hazel are swung in the breeze,
    And shake out their powdery gold,
And everything's happy and young to-day,
    And nothing, oh nothing is old.

The blackbird is singing a wonderful song,
    The loveliest one that he knows,
The daffy-down-dillies keep time to the tune,
    And dance on the tip of their toes.
The almond tree feels that it's time to awake,
    And opens its buds just a chink,
Till the chaffinch calls out at the top of his voice,
    "Why it's pinkity, pinkity pink!"

Let's climb to the top of a very high hill,
    And hear the wind whistling by;
Let's call to the hustling, bustling clouds,
    That race down the slippery sky!
Oh! March, you are sweet with your green
                    and your gold.
    You are grand with your hurricane power,
And wouldn't I love to be you, just you,
    For a glorious, blustering hour!
                    ENID BLYTON.

SEE CAPTION OR EXPLANATION PAGE 321

APPENDIX 14

AN INDIAN DAY

THE coppersmith bird is awake, for I hear
His clinkity song,
He calls to the red, roundy sun in the East,
"Come along, come along!"

And slowly and drowsily down from the hills
Come oxen and carts,
Bringing the fruit of the country around,
To sell in the marts.

And sweet is the morning, and cool to the cheek,
While the red rising sun
Climbs to the top of the far-away hills,
The day is begun.

In bright-coloured robes come the folk of the town,
Wending their way,
To buy in the clamouring, crowded bazaars,
In the cool of the day.

But high climbs the glittering sun, and begins
To scorch and to burn,
Till it seems as if never and never again
Will coolness return.

And shimmering, quivering, almost alive,
The heat lies around,
Dancing a wavering, stifling dance,
From roof to the ground.

Drowsiness creeps over country and town,
The folks disappear,
To seek out a shelter, and sleep through the heat
Till ev'ning is near.

And now every minute the brain-fever bird
Sings all up the scale.
He sings it a million, million times,
An unending tale.

At last drops the sun in the westerly hills,
The land wakes from sleep,
The markets are crowded with chattering folk—
Long shadows creep.

The sun dips below the world's far-away rim,
Quickly comes night,
And out flash a myriad, glittering stars,
Crystally bright.

Mournful and slow sounds an Indian song,
Through the night air,
The moon swings her silvery lamp in the sky,
Silent and fair . . . .

ENID BLYTON.

PHYLLIS CHASE

SEE CAPTION OR EXPLANATION PAGE 321

257

THE TEACHERS WORLD. *July 3, 1925*

NEW ANIMAL POEMS

By ENID BLYTON.

VI.—SEA LIONS.

YOU really might think, when you hear my name,
That I and the lion are much the same,
But I haven't a mane, and I don't wear feet,
And I'm not such a frightening person to meet.

If you go to the Zoo, you will find us there,
We swim in a pond in the open air,
We're strong and swift, and we're graceful too
As we dive and swim all day at the Zoo.

It's not very often we're out on land,
For it's awkward for us to walk or stand,
Instead of feet we have flippers and so
When we travel by land we're clumsy and slow!

When the keeper feeds us at half-past four
(And I really do wish he would feed us more)
You'll see us catch all the fish he throws
Till his basket's empty and off he goes.

We're so good at catching, it's easy to tell
We'd all play at cricket remarkably well,
So if you should want a good fielder or two
Just borrow a sea-lion out of the Zoo!

SEE CAPTION OR EXPLANATION PAGE 321

POEMS OF THE OPEN AIR

BY ENID BLYTON

THE POPLAR TREE

A LITTLE goblin, bent and old,
One winter looked to see
Where he could hide his crock of gold,
In bush, or hedge, or tree.

A poplar tree he chose at last
In which his gold to hide,
'Twould keep his treasure firm and fast
'Mid branches spreading wide.

Said he, " Pray guard my money well,"
But, when the wind blew round,
The crock of riches almost fell
Upon the wintry ground.

The poplar held it close in fright,
And all its branches bare
In a twinkling grew upright
To guard the riches rare.

And since that day the poplar tree
Has held its branches high;
Tall and strong for all to see,
They point towards the sky !

SEE CAPTION OR EXPLANATION PAGE 321

THE QUIET SNOW

ALL night the quiet snow
Fell silently and slow,
And in the morning light
The countryside was white.
The trees, no longer bare,
Stood tall and white and fair.
And every rounded hill
Beneath the snow was still.
A white enchantment lay
Upon each bush and spray,
And when the sun so pale
Began its golden trail
Blue shadows, smooth and deep,
Lay on the snow asleep.

It fell so soft and slow—
How quiet is the snow!
ENID BLYTON.

THE LITTLE TREE-HOUSE

PRAY come for a walk in the woods to-day,
For I'm sure that a visit you'd like to pay
To the little Tree-House.
Josie, the Doll, will be longing to meet you,
And dear Bun, the Rabbit, will run out to greet you,
With Click, the wee mouse.
When we go up the stairs in the heart of the tree
A dear little room at the top we shall see,
Quite round and small;
Then up some more stairs to the bedroom we'll go,
Where three little wooden beds stand in a row,
Their heads to the wall—
And wouldn't we love in the Tree-House to stay—
With Bun, Click and Josie such games we would play
Till daytime was done,
And then into bed with them all we would creep,
And in the Tree-House we would fall fast asleep,
It would be such fun!

ENID BLYTON'S
Sunny Stories
Calendar
1942

GOOD LUCK!

HERE'S a Calendar for you
To keep you smiling all year through,
Your favourite story-folk are here,
There's old Brer Rabbit, sidling near,
And Galliano with his Show,
And Mister Twiddle down below;
There's dear Pink-Whistle, beaming bright,
The sheep-dog, Shadow, brown and white,
There's Mister Meddle, smart and vain,
And mischievous Amelia Jane;
And here are Josie, Click and Bun
To bring their love to everyone;
The Faraway Tree, the Wishing Chair,
Yes—all the things you love are there,
And now let Enid Blyton send
Good luck to every little friend!

SEE CAPTION OR EXPLANATION PAGE 321

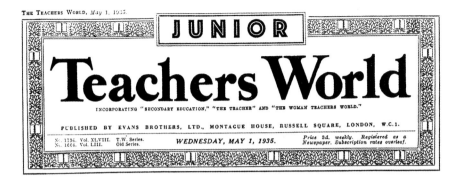

THE TEACHERS WORLD, May 1, 1935.

JUNIOR

Teachers World

INCORPORATING "SECONDARY EDUCATION," "THE TEACHER" AND "THE WOMAN TEACHERS WORLD."

PUBLISHED BY EVANS BROTHERS, LTD., MONTAGUE HOUSE, RUSSELL SQUARE, LONDON, W.C.1.

No. 1336. Vol. XLVIII. T.W. Series.
No. 1666. Vol. LIII. Old Series.

WEDNESDAY, MAY 1, 1935.

Price 3d. weekly. Registered as a Newspaper. Subscription rates overleaf.

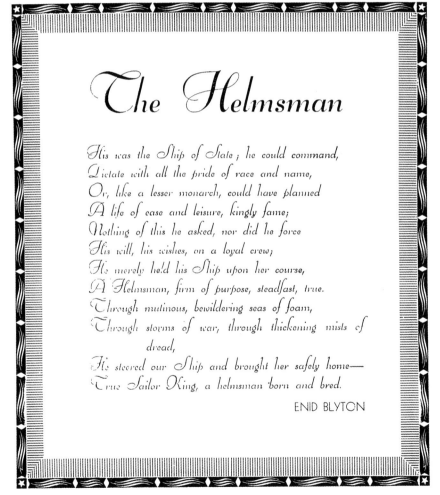

The Helmsman

His was the Ship of State; he could command,
Dictate with all the pride of race and name,
Or, like a lesser monarch, could have planned
A life of ease and leisure, kingly fame;
Nothing of this he asked, nor did he force
His will, his wishes, on a loyal crew;
He merely held his Ship upon her course,
A Helmsman, firm of purpose, steadfast, true.
Through mutinous, bewildering seas of foam,
Through storms of war, through thickening mists of
          dread,
He steered our Ship and brought her safely home—
True Sailor King, a helmsman born and bred.

ENID BLYTON

SEE CAPTION OR EXPLANATION PAGE 322

SUNDAY GRAPHIC, March 16, 1947

A Lion Once We Had

We have received the following poem from our famous contributor, ENID BLYTON.

A lion once we had that
roared for England,
That spoke with every
English heart and
voice,
Ranging behind him
every man and
woman,
At one with him and his
unfaltering choice.

★   ★

His was the voice of
England — when he
spoke
Our thoughts were
uttered, and his
burning phrase
Stung us to tears and
made us proud and
stubborn,
Unconquerable in
those tremendous
days.

★   ★

If ever a man was
England, this was he,
Old Lion-Heart, whose
heart was England's
own,
Leader of men, a
Marlborough grown
in stature,
He stood for us when
England stood alone.

★   ★

And now, when all our
glory's dimmed and
shadowed,
What would we give to
hear a dauntless
roar,
To range ourselves
behind a trusted
leader,
One for all and all for
one once more!

RECORD DROP IN HOME BUILDING

Chaos of form filling

Sunday Graphic Industrial Correspondent

NEW FACTS ABOUT A RECORD SLUMP IN BUILDING WILL BE REVEALED IN MR. BEVAN'S NEXT REPORT ON THE GOVERNMENT'S HOMES-FOR-ALL SCHEME.

Apart from the weather, controls, restrictions and form filling have reduced the building industry to a state of chaos.

With more than 4,000,000 names on waiting lists throughout the country, fewer than 5,000 permanent houses have been built in the last four weeks.

And, according to Sir Harry Selley, president of the Master Builders' Federation, the outlook is grim.

Facing Bankruptcy

Here are the facts about the building situation:

1. More than £1,000,000 worth of building material—in short supply here — is exported monthly.
2. At least 10,000 small builders —hit by bad weather and the fuel crisis—are on the verge of bankruptcy.
3. There are nearly as many civil servants and council officials (150,000) concerned in Government house-building as building operatives (188,700).

Houses Abandoned

4. It takes a month to build a house—eight months to fill up the 200 forms and await developments.
5. Work on more than 14,000 houses has had to be postponed indefinitely.
6. In 20 months more than 700 local authorities have not built one permanent house.
7. Several thousand building workers, held up by shortages and the crisis, have quit building for other jobs.

FOOTNOTE: Ministry of Health stated: Bad weather has made outside work and transport of materials impossible. And there may be worse to come.

BALKANS TANGLE

New U.S. move

AMERICA is intensifying her efforts to win over the nations in the Soviet sphere of influence from Communist control.

A fresh Note is being sent out to Budapest, Moscow and London this week, according to Washington sources.

This, it was stated, will again demand that the Russians should cease supporting the Communist-led minorities.

'May Declare War'!

Senator Taft asked bluntly in Washington last night for "an official estimate of whether Russia may declare war if we aid Greece and Turkey."

"I want to know what our top military people think ... just as we might be prompted to go to war if Russia tried to force a Communist government on Cuba," he added.

Mr. Lewis W. Douglas, new U.S. Ambassador to Britain, said before leaving New York: "This time we shall not withdraw from European and world affairs."

1,036 killed in India riots

JAMES MASON'S Own Story

THIS EXCLUSIVE series, written at James Mason's own request, with full access to letters and records, begins next Sunday.

DON'T MISS this story of struggle and success—personal, controversial, ACCURATE.

Sixteen Pages next week and every week.

Terrorists attack 2 NAAFIs

JEWISH terrorists launched simultaneous attacks on a N.A.A.F.I. club in Hadera

---

A section of a page in the *Sunday Graphic*, edition March 16, 1947, showing in the first column the poem, 'A Lion Once We Had' Enid Blyton dedicated to Sir Winston Churchill. The rest of the paper gives an insight into what was happening in the country and abroad at that time. © British Library Board (SM: MFM.MLD 36).

April Day

There is a copse I know on Purbeck Hills
That holds the April sun to its green breast;
Where daffodils
Are wild and small and shy,
And celandines in polished gold are drest.
Here windflowers dance a ballet full of grace,
And speedwell blue
Looks on with brilliant eye.
There, innocent of face,
The daisies grow,
And yellow primroses like children press
In little crowds together all day through.

Be silent, velvet bee,
And let me brood
At peace in this enchanted loneliness.
Chaffinch, take your merry song, and go
To some more distant tree.
'Tis not my mood
To have this silence stirred
By wing of bee
Or voice of bird.

Now, let me stand and gaze –
But ah, so lavishly is beauty spread
These April days,
There is no place to tread.
Then must I choose
To put away my shoes
And kneel instead.

SEE CAPTION OR EXPLANATION PAGE 322

THE TEACHERS WORLD, *February* 24, 1926.

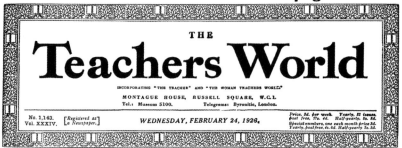

NEW PENSION RULES IN FULL—See pages 1083-4

THE

Teachers World

INCORPORATING "THE TEACHER" AND "THE WOMAN TEACHERS WORLD."

MONTAGUE HOUSE, RUSSELL SQUARE, W.C.1.

Tel.: Museum 5100.　　Telegrams: Byronitic, London.

No. 1,143. [*Registered as*] 　 WEDNESDAY, FEBRUARY 24, 1926. 　 *Price, 3d. per week. Yearly, 52 issues, post free, 17s. 4d. Half-yearly, 8s. 8d. Special numbers, one each month price 3d. Yearly, post free, 4s. 6d. Half-yearly 1s. 3d.*
Vol. XXXIV. [*a Newspaper.*]

MRS. MARGARET WINTRINGHAM, J.P.,
ON EDUCATIONAL REFORMS AND TEACHERS.
AN INTERVIEW BY R. L. MÉGROZ.

MRS. WINTRINGHAM.

PARTY politics are not dreamed of in my philosophy, but if they were I should be proud, if a Liberal, that Mrs. Wintringham, formerly independent Liberal Member for Louth, was one of the most important members of my party. She is so pleasant, so frank, and open-minded and gracious a personality, that it is not easy in her presence to realise her activity in political work, unless one has a very elastic conception of the party politician.

I met Mrs. Wintringham in London before the reassembly of Parliament this year. She had come to attend a conference of Liberal women, and I began by asking her a definitely political question :

"Have you noticed, during your own political career, any remarkable changes in the general attitude towards women in public life or merely as citizens? "

Legislation for Women.

"You can judge by one fact," she replied. " From 1900 to 1918 only five laws affecting women and children were passed. In 1918 women were given the vote and allowed to sit in Parliament. The effect of this revolution is indicated by legislation. In the six years following 1918 there were 15 important laws passed affecting women and children."

"You think, Mrs. Wintringham, that legislation will not only improve the position of women legally, but be altered for the better by the influence of women? "

"Yes. It is good that women should have responsibilities such as sitting on public bodies like county councils, and serving as magistrates; and their influence is bound to change legislation."

Franchise equality.

" Is there any reform which at the moment seems to be much wanted? "

" The franchise for women ought to be given on the same terms as for men. Sixty per cent. of the women of this country, between the ages of 20 and 30, work in industry. They ought to have the same say in the laws as men of the same ages."

" On these figures, the number of women up to 30 years of age working in industry must be nearly the same as that of men? "

" Yes."

" But are not most of such potential women voters ignorant of politics? "

" Yes, but the same is true of the men who are voters. I merely think that if a man ought to have a vote at 21 so ought a woman."

Temperance Reform.

I then asked Mrs. Wintringham what other reform engaged her attention.

" I am a keen temperance reformer," she said. " My design in legislation is for clubs to come under the same legislation as public houses. I believe also in the Sunday closing of public houses and a measure of local option."

" Would not this admit the danger of much local graft, of bribery in various forms? "

" In America prohibition came as a result of local option; that does not suggest much effective bribery on the part of 'the trade.' Local option simply gives the district the power to express its own opinion."

Education and the Government.

" I am very much concerned with the question of education at the present time," Mrs. Wintringham resumed. " I think there is a big gulf between the attitude of the present Government now and its pledge a year ago. I am very disappointed in its probable effect. My experience, sitting on the County Council Education Authority in Lincolnshire, showed me how nearly every progressive scheme formulated could be retarded. School buildings, for instance, which have never really been put right since before the war, with us have been continually made to wait a little longer. And now, when we were just going to do something, this Circular 1371 comes along. I think it will have an adverse effect also on the teachers' salaries, and on classes for adult education, and, worse still, on the position for children under five. The local authorities will be able to cut expenditure down. It is sometimes difficult to prove at once the need for expenditure in education. A very good beginning has been made in the establishment of nursery schools, for instance, and although you might not see or be able to measure the benefit in pounds, shillings, and pence, the effect on the after-life of the children concerned is bound to be immense. The Minister

Continued on page 1073.

SEE CAPTION OR EXPLANATION PAGE 323

The Teachers' World, *July 4, 1903.*

NATURE NOTES.
By RICHARD MORSE.
FORGET-ME-NOTS.

THE majority of our wild forget-me-nots are now at their best period for study, and form a little group of plants of quite remarkable beauty and interest.

Perhaps the general favourite is the true forget-me-not of marshes and river-sides, but other sorts abound in fields and way-sides, and any one of them may be chosen to illustrate the ingenious manner in which the flowers unfold, so as to secure the best advantage in the important process of cross-pollination by the insects.

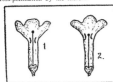

FLOWER OF FORGET-ME-NOT.
Semi-diagrammatic.
1. Young Flower, with short corolla-tube.
2. Old Flower, with lengthened corolla-tube.

The flowers themselves grow in that type of inflorescence which is known as a cyme, and in their young stage this cyme is coiled up tightly in a very characteristic manner. The end flowers are always the first to open, and as each one follows the other in attaining its maturity, so does the coil as a whole alter its position.

This change of position is one of the most beautiful contrivances in Nature, for it invariably happens that each new blossom that opens is placed in just that spot which is best calculated to give it greatest prominence; and, simultaneously with this, the flower which has already been fertilised is folded downwards, or otherwise turned out of the way.

These admirably contrived arrangements, however, are not confined to the forget-me-nots, but may be observed equally well in such closely related species as the viper's bugloss and the common comfrey.

How Fertilisation is Secured.

The little species known as the yellow-and-blue scorpion grass is really a forget-me-not, and has many points of interest in its structure and habits.

Thus, for example, if the tiny flowers are examined immediately after opening, it will be observed that the summit of the pistil shows quite plainly, jutting out prominently at the mouth of the corolla.

In a few days' time, however, the pistil is lost to sight, and you have to seek it low down amongst the stamens themselves.

These latter, it will be seen, are attached to the corolla, and if the length of the flower-tube be measured quite accurately, it will be found that it increases gradually in length after opening, and so the stamens and pistil are brought into actual contact with one another.

In its first stage, therefore, the plant obviously seeks insect-pollination, but if this should fail it, then it is practically certain to fertilise itself. (See illustration.)

Colour-Transformations.

Another interesting feature of this same little scorpion-grass is the varying colour of its flowers. When first they open they are always of a pale yellow. Later on they become pinkish, and finally bright blue, very much like those of its larger and better known cousins.

These and similar facts all go to show that the primitive colour of the forget-me-nots was not blue at all, but yellow. Even the commonest sort still has yellow " eyes " to its flowers, thus retaining in a similar way a very obvious ancestral feature.

The borage, the viper's bugloss, and a number of other plants in the same family, go through similar remarkable changes, and if a few specimens are kept in vases in the classroom, the various stages in these colour-transformations may be kept under constant observation.

A SYLLABUS OF NATURE STUDY.

The following series of Nature Study Lessons, which will cover a year's Course, will begin in September. The scheme is published this week for the benefit of teachers wishing to draw up their syllabus in advance.

GROUP I.—WOODLANDS AND HEDGE-ROWS.

1. The Hop Plant.	September.
5. The Fall of the Leaves.	October.
10. The Hedgehog.	November.
14. The Mistletoe.	December.
18. The Trees in Winter.	January.
22. The Hare and Rabbit.	January.
23. A Piece of Chalk.	February.
27. The Wild Arum.	March.
31. The Breathing of Plants.	April.
36. A Common Owl.	May.
40. The Honeysuckle.	June.
44. Co-operation in the Woodland.	July.
49. The Work of the Bees.	August.

GROUP II.—MEADOWS AND HEATHS

2. The Plants' Preparation for Winter.	
	September.
6. The Mole.	October.
11. The Chickweed.	November.
15. The Effect of Light on Plants.	December.
19. The Robin's Story.	January.
24. How Seeds Grow.	February.
28. The Celandine.	March.
32. The Grass Snake.	April.
33. A Grain of Sand.	April.
37. Buttercups.	May.
41. Wild Roses.	June.
45. The Grasshopper.	July.
50. Transpiration.	August.

GROUP III.—MARSHES AND WATER SIDES.

3. The Crayfish	September.
7. The Watercress.	October.
12. Common Wild Fruits.	November.
16. Hibernating Butterflies.	December.
20. How Mosses Grow.	January.
25. The Alder Tree.	February.
29. Frogs and Toads.	March.
34. Liverworts.	April.
38. The Water Buttercup.	May.
42. The Cuckoo.	June.
46. The Water Lily.	July.
47. The Story of a Pebble.	July.
51. Pondweeds.	August.

GROUP IV.—FIELDS AND GARDENS.

4. How the Plants' Food is Stored.	
	September.
8. The Study of Seeds.	October.
9. A Lump of Soil.	October.
13. House Flies	November.
17. The Shepherd's Purse.	December.
21. Bulbs.	January.
26. The Common Sparrow.	February.
30. Clover.	March.
35. The Dandelion.	April.
39. Snails and Slugs.	May.
43. The Pea.	June.
48. Nasturtiums.	July.
52. The Cabbage Butterfly.	August.

EDUCATIONAL NOTICES.

THE Festival of Folk Song and Dance at the King's Theatre, Hammersmith, this week is attracting much attention. The English Folk Dance Society and its director, Mr. Cecil J. Sharp, are to be congratulated on their enterprise. Performances will be given at 8 each evening until and including Saturday, the 7th, and there will be matinées to-morrow (Thursday) and Saturday at 2.30 p.m.

* * * *

An exhibition of geometrical designs in colour composed by children from five to seven years old in the Italian, Dutch, English, Spanish, and French Montessori schools is on show at the Montessori Society's office at 11, Tavistock Square, W.C. 1, until Friday, July 6.

FROM MY WINDOW.
ENID BLYTON'S WEEKLY TALK.

"WILL you write a weekly column for THE TEACHERS' WORLD?" was a question put to me recently.

" I would love to," I answered; " but what about? Salaries, conferences, lock-outs? Impossible, I couldn't."

" No, other things you're interested in, and that might interest other teachers—books and theatres, education, children, Nature. . . . ." Thus it was settled, and I visioned a new and delightful task before me every week.

Here am I embarked on the first column, and what shall it be about? Books? No. Nature? No. Children? Yes, because I have been with them all day, and my mind is full of them.

It has often struck me how like a child's mind is in its way of working to the mind of a genius. A compliment to children! some will say. I think it is a compliment to genius. A child's mind is wonderful in its simplicity, directness, and sensitiveness. The younger a child is, the more clearly these characteristics show. The older he gets, the more he learns to hide his mind from others, and in doing so, he loses in simplicity and naturalness.

I have been reading some lives of men and women of genius. Their characteristic attitude of mind was a questioning one. Why? How? When and where? they were continually asking. Just the words I have heard the children say to me all day. And then, too, like the genius, the child is always delightedly finding things which resemble each other. " Oh, isn't that piece of sorrel like a small red poplar tree! "

The genius works in the same way. The poet uses his lucid and beautiful similes, the scientist reasons by analogy, and a Linnæus minutely records the similar characteristics of a host of plants.

A young child is intensely original. He has not learnt to think as others think, nor does he know enough to realise he is ignorant. He thinks for himself, he imagines, he observes with a curiously thorough and penetrating eye, often with comical or embarrassing results. Genius also is tremendously original and independent, and observes with a child's own absorbed concentration.

And at last of all, as Froebel knew, a child is always seeking to express himself—to give out what he has taken in—and through the same need of expression, genius has given our greatest treasures.

The questioning, wondering mind, that analyses and puts together, that observes and records for itself, and that finally bursts out into an expression of the many impressions—there is a description equally applicable to mature genius, or to immature childhood. What is the explanation of the curious similarity? *Why does it in all but a few cases cease as the child grows?* Is it some fault of our education, that has not recognised the real trend of a child's mind, which is, surely, genius-ward in its simplicity and need for expression?

I do not think genius is a mysterious something with which one must be born. I think it is the natural result of using one's mind to the fullest extent, of loving beauty in any form and of directly expressing the powerful spiritual effects which clamour for release. If only we could train our children in the way that geniuses perforce have to train themselves, we should get a wonderful type of ordinary men and women.

I may be entirely wrong in my surmises, but the question is an intensely interesting one, and I, in common, I suspect, with many other teachers, would dearly love to hear the modern psychologist's reasoned solution of the problem.

SEE CAPTION OR EXPLANATION PAGE 323

THE WEEK IN THE INFANTS' SCHOOL

Continued from page 1077.

to allow him to drink unless he gave up his right eye. Odin grieved to lose his eye, but he paid the price and drank of the wonderful waters.

With his new gift of wisdom he went on to deal with three evil monsters who were troubling the earth. The first was a great serpent. This Odin seized and cast into the sea, where it grew and grew until its tail grew round the earth, and growing into its own mouth, could grow no more.

The second monster was half a queen and half a dead creature. Odin cast her down to rule over the dead.

The third was the terrible wolf Fenrir, and Odin took him back to Asgard, in the hope of taming him and training him to be gentle and good.

All the heroes rejoiced at Odin's return, and were glad to hear of all he had seen and done.

LANGUAGE-TRAINING (based on above story).

After telling the story two or three times, let the children retell it, talk about it, and discuss it.

Description of Odin.—Lead them to see the likeness between Odin and the sky. The blue or grey cloak is like the blue sky and grey clouds; the one piercing eye is like the sun. One day in the week is called after Odin. It was first called Odin's or Woden's day. Children will guess that the day is Wednesday and that this is how we have a " d " in it.

Work of Odin.—Talk about the early Northmen. They thought courage and bravery were the finest things in the world. Arms and weapons to help in fighting were great treasures to them. Fearlessness and daring and a love of fair play have come down to English children from these far-back forefathers.

Odin's Sacrifice.—Let the children express their own opinions about this. Impress that nothing good can be got without trouble; children need to work hard before they can be clever.

Composition (either oral or written). Description of the sky.

Spellings.—Odin. Woden. Wednesday. Sky—cloudy, bright, blue, grey, piercing light.

Bravery—fighter, courage, fearless, daring. Wisdom—work, trouble, treasure.

Each of the above words should be learned in its right context and their meaning made real by reference to the story.

EXPRESSION WORK.

Modelling.—The serpent.—(Fig. 9.) **Drawing.**—The battle-axe.—(Fig. 9.) **Tree-cutting.**—Odin's hat and cloak.—(Fig. 9.)

Writing and Drawing.—(Fig. 10.)

NUMBER WORK.

First lessons in place value.

Give the children a number of loose sticks; the inch-long sticks used in stick-laying are the best.

Pick out one. Teach the name "unit" as meaning one single thing. (Fig. 11.)

Let the children make a bundle of ten sticks, tying them together. They now have one bundle of ten sticks or one ten. Let ten children put their bundles of ten together. Tie them and let children tell how many. One hundred.

If we want to write how many units we have, we must write 1. If we want to write how many tens, we write 1. If we want to write how many in the hundred bundle, we write 1. Figure 1 may mean 1 unit or 1 ten or 1 hundred; therefore we must have some way of finding out which it means. We do this by giving each a special place. Figure 1, all by itself, means one unit, but if we put it one place to the left, it means ten. When we do this we put a nought in the unit's place to show that the 1 meaning ten is in the second place. If we write one hundred we put two noughts to show that

Continued at foot of column 3.

FROM MY WINDOW

Enid Blyton's Weekly Talk.

GREEN AND BLUE.

THERE are two of Nature's colours that never fail to make me marvel at them —the blue of the sky, and the green of the countryside. They are so satisfying. We can imagine no other colours in their place that would be so right. Marvellous as a red sunset sky is, or a translucent green or yellow, none of these is comparable to the soft purity of our blue sky. It always looks so fresh and clean. One might almost imagine that the big, white-piled clouds were mops of cotton wool, forever scouring the blue of the heavens and keeping it clean and bright.

And was ever there a colour so restful and so delicious as the green of fields and trees? Red would be unthinkable, blue too ethereal, pink too gaudy. Yellow, though exquisite, would be too dazzling altogether, and all the other colours would make our country too sombre for beauty. Green is right. Look out over a sunwashed field, and see how gloriously right the colour is! It is perfect.

I always think it is marvellous that green should be the result of the combination of two colours. I can understand orange being the result of yellow and red, and anyone could guess what made mauve and purple. But green! You might guess that yellow helped to make it, but not blue. It is so much a colour on its own, and its purity gives it the deep, elemental look that the primary colours have. And in no other combination of colours is there so great an element of surprise. It has always been astonishing to children to find that when they mix their blue and yellow paints together, and put the result on to paper, a bright green comes out. I shall never forget my own amazement when I first made that discovery at seven years old. It savoured of magic, it was something quite unbelievable, a fact that had to be repeated over and over again until it was bedtime. And I still think it is an amazing thing, and love to see the pure green coming on my palette when blue and yellow are mingled.

As I sit here and look out over the green lawn to the green fields beyond, and watch the oaks and elms waving in the strong breeze, I see a hundred different shades and tones of green. The brilliance of the lawn stands out against the duller green of the field, and the hawthorn hedge along the lane has a shadow as deep as night on the side that is away from the sun. The oaks are a mass of wonderful, changing lights and shades, all green. In the garden are a thousand different greens. Each plant has its own particular choice of green, from the soft grey-green of the lavender, to the vivid green of the little new London pride rosettes. Each green is an enchanting foil to the plant's own flowers, and the mingling of the whole foliage in the garden makes the most perfect background that is possible. There has never been an artist like Dame Nature.

One of the great charms of the green and blue symphony of the countryside and sky is the ever-moving quality of the one, and the unchangingness of the other. The wind shifts the greens to lights and darks, and the sun gilds and freckles them. They dance and shimmer, they run through all their shades in a twinkling—but behind and above them stretches the blue of the sky, still, unshadowed, unchanging.

And when, for the hundred-thousandth time, I look in delight at the two contrasting colours, I think of the two beginning lines in a thanksgiving poem written by a small boy in class—

" Blue of sky and green of trees, Now thank the Lord for both of these ! "

*** In place of this feature Miss Blyton will write—directly to the children—a Weekly Letter, commencing next week.

GEOGRAPHY OF WORLD DISCOVERY.

Continued from page 1058.

smoke. Then the Indians cast darts upon the Tartars, of whom many were wounded and slain."

* * * *

FRIAR WILLIAM DE RUBRUQUIS (William of Rubruck) was sent by Louis of France in 1253 to take letters to the Great Khan begging him to become Christian. He and his companions went to the Holy Land, whence they took ship by way of the Ægean Sea and the Black Sea to a port in the Crimea—Soldaia, he calls it— " where all the Turkey merchants which traffic into the northern countries do arrive . . . transporting thence ermines and gray furs with other rich and costly skins," and also " clothes made of cotton, or silk, and divers kinds of spices," as well as " dried fishes, sturgeons, and other fishes."

To please the governors of this city, Friar William took with him from Constantinople "pleasant fruits, muscatel wine, and delicate biscuit bread " as presents. But the governors were not at home, so Friar William put them back in one of his four covered carts and set out in June for the Volga lands. There were five persons in his little company—himself, Friar Bartholomew of Cremona, and three others.

Soon there came upon the Tartar hordes, who " came flocking about them on horseback after waiting for them sitting in the shadow under their black carts." The friars gave what they could spare of their wine and biscuit, receiving in turn "cow's milk after the butter was churned out of it, being very sour." When at last they departed it was, says Friar William, "as if we were escaped out of the hands of devils."

On they went for two long months. " We never lay in house or tent, but always under the starry canopy and in the open air or under our carts." Then they came to the lands of the western main body of the Tartars of the Volga—a multitude of great tents on wheels that looked like " a mighty moving city "; great droves of oxen and horses and flocks of sheep; and men armed, who inquired what presents the friars had for their lord.

After many sore trials and adventures the little company made its way across. the steppes towards the Altai and the city of Karakorum. The summer heat was intense. They passed the land of Batu, where they heard of the visit of Friar John de Plano Carpini, and travelled with Batu's Tartar hordes for five weeks.

The friars arrived at the court of the Great Khan just after Christmas, having suffered as severely from the terrible winter cold of the steppes as they had done from the summer heat. Barefooted, with frostbitten fingers and toes, the pious friars entered the golden tent of the Emperor, chanting the hymn of the Nativity. The Emperor was "a little man of moderate height, aged about forty-five, and dressed in a skin spotted and glossy like a seal."

The Great Khan asked many questions. Was France a rich country? Was it worth conquering? How many men had the King of France? And so forth. But he made no promise that he would become a Christian, nor did he once consider the question of ceasing his wars upon neighbouring peoples.

The friars left the country of the Great Khan in May, when they set out on their homeward journey. They retraced their steps to the Volga, whence they went South along the Western shores of the Caspian, and through the land of Armenia to the Holy Land.

the 1 meaning one hundred is in the third place to the left.

If we want to write eleven or 1 ten and 1 unit, we put 1 1. Let the children work out for themselves the notation from 10 to 20, using single sticks for units and bundle of tens for the tens column. This basic lesson will recur in other forms.

HOW THEY LIVED.

Continuation on page 1072.

APPENDIX 24

THE TEACHERS WORLD, *September 4, 1929*

Enid Blyton's — Children's Page

DEAR BOYS AND GIRLS,

Aren't you surprised to see that I have a whole page this week instead of just one column? Isn't it lovely! Now I shall be able to send you a poem and a story every week, as well as my letter. I am so pleased, and I hope you will be too.

Perhaps you will be able to write to me and tell me the kind of thing you would like to see on my page, because I want you to enjoy it. Bobs is most excited about it, for perhaps I can sometimes find room for him to send you a tiny letter. He is feeling rather sorry for himself just at present, because he has a bad eye.

He found a tiny kitten in the garden, and was so pleased with it that he took it to his basket, and told it to make its home there. He licked it clean, just like its mother would do, and then let it sleep between his paws. When it woke up and climbed out of his basket he followed it, and looked after it splendidly. The little creature loved him, and played with his front paws, patting them, and pretending to bite them.

Then the mother cat turned up to look for her lost baby. She ran to it, licked it all over, and then gave it her tail to play with. Bobs lay and looked on in astonishment, for he is not used to cats. He was very much upset that another animal should have taken his tiny playmate away from him. I wouldn't let him go too near, because I was afraid the mother cat might fly at him. At last she took her kitten away somewhere, and for a few days I didn't see it.

But dear old Bobs went to look for it. He found it, and brought it back with him. It ran by his side, as happy as anything, glad to be with him again. Then the mother cat appeared once more, and mewed for her kitten to go to her. The naughty little thing wouldn't obey, and snuggled down between Bobs' two front paws. Then without any warning the cat flew at poor old Bobs, and scratched one of his lovely brown eyes. He, wouldn't bite the cat, for he is too gentle, but he growled and then ran whining to me. He climbed up on my knee, and showed me his poor half-closed eye.

So of course I popped him into the car and took him to the dog-doctor at once. His eye is getting better now, and has to be bathed four times a day. He gets a chocolate afterwards if he is good, so he doesn't mind at all. In fact, yesterday he tried to make me bathe his eye five times, but I told him not to try tricks of that sort on me!

Do you see the picture of my cottage that the artist has drawn at the top of the page? It is taken from a photograph, so it is exactly like it. Is it like what you imagined Old Thatch to be? I hope you think it is pretty. Please come and see it if you are ever down my way.

Much love to you all from

Here is a photograph of some of my pets. You will see Bobs on my knee, looking very good indeed, but really wondering what mischief he can get into next. Just below is old Thomas the Tortoise, putting his head out to see if he shall walk out of the picture. I pulled him back just in time. On my wrist is Jackie Daw the Second, who died in the great frost we had in March, poor old thing. I tried to get Maggie Pie to come on my other wrist, but she wouldn't whilst Jackie was there, for she was jealous of him. I will try and put a picture of my five pigeons in for you later on.

AN INVITATION.

IF ever you come down my way
Please walk up to the door,
Then knock three times, and simply say
"Is Enid Blyton in to-day?"

Then soon, you may be sure,
I'll come to greet you, and you'll see
My home inside and out,
While Bobs will lick your hand in glee
And bark, "They've come to call on me,
Yes, ME, without a doubt!"

So don't forget, when down our way,
To come and see us some fine day!

A LETTER FROM BOBS.

Dear Children,

Would you like a letter from me sometimes? I would like to send you one, because I do love girls and boys. I have a bad eye this week. It is nice to have a bad eye, because I get four chocolates a day. A loving lick from

BOBS.

BRER RABBIT'S COW.

HAVE you heard this tale of wicked Brer Rabbit?

One day Brer Wolf was coming home from fishing, with a string of fish across his shoulder. Suddenly old Miss Partridge hopped out of the bushes, and fluttered along right under Brer Wolf's nose. "Ho, ho!" said Brer Wolf, "Her nest is somewhere near. I'll find it."

So he put down his fishes, and went to look. About that time Brer Rabbit happened along. There were the fishes and there was Brer Rabbit—but neither of them stayed there long, and when Brer Wolf came back, his string of fishes was nowhere to be seen.

He sat down and scratched his head, and after a bit it came into his mind that Brer Rabbit must have been along that way. So he set out for Brer Rabbit's house, and hailed him. But Brer Rabbit said he didn't know anything about strings of fishes. Brer Wolf vowed he did, and they argued it up and down till Brer Rabbit said, "Well, if I've got those fishes of yours, you can go and kill my best cow!"

He didn't reckon Brer Wolf would take him at his word, but that's just what he did. Off he went to the meadow to kill Brer Rabbit's best cow.

Well, Brer Rabbit felt mighty bad when he thought he was going to lose his cow, but he laid his plans, and told his children that he wouldn't lose his beef, they'd see! So he raced up to Brer Wolf, lippitty-clippitty and told him that the policeman was coming. "You run and hide," he said, "and I'll stay here and take care of the cow till you get back."

Brer Wolf shot into the bushes, for he was afraid of the policeman. As soon as he was gone, Brer Rabbit killed his cow, salted the hide down, cut up the meat and stowed it away in his smoke-house. Then he took the cow-tail and stuck the end of it in the ground.

"Run, run, Brer Wolf!" he shouted. "Run, run! Your cow's going into the ground!"

When old Brer Wolf got there, he saw Brer Rabbit holding on to the cow-tail, as if he was keeping the cow from going into the ground. Brer Wolf caught hold too, and after he had given a pull or two, out came the tail!

"There," said Brer Rabbit, "you've pulled the tail off, and your cow's gone!"

But Brer Wolf wasn't going to give up. He got a spade, a pick-axe and a shovel, and he dug for that cow till he could dig no more. Old Brer Rabbit sat up there in his front porch, smoking a cigar, and every time Brer Wolf struck his pick axe into the clay, Brer Rabbit giggled to his children·

"He diggy, diggy, diggy, but there's no meat there! He diggy, diggy, diggy, but there's no meat there!"

And all the time he knew that the cow was turned into beef in his smoke-house, and he and his children were eating fried beef and onions whenever they felt hungry.

Old Brer Wolf never found that cow—but I'm not surprised at that, are you?

SEE CAPTION OR EXPLANATION PAGE 323

GREEN HEDGES

Enid Blyton's Children's Corner

DEAR BOYS AND GIRLS,

We have a dear little grey squirrel that comes and plays on our lawn in the early morning. It is a graceful little creature, and bounds about all over the place. It has a little store of hazel nuts under a stone in the rockery. I found it by noticing two or three nut-shells lying around—so I hunted about, and there, neatly tucked under a big stone was the squirrel's larder! He loves to nibble a nut now and then, though he likes to eat tender shoots and buds as well now.

When the cats see him they are most surprised. They stand and look at him, sniffing hard, and I can almost hear them saying, "Is it a special kind of cat?" Or a sort of little grey dog?" Then they run towards the squirrel—and he is off in the trees as lightly as if he had wings! His bushy tail streaks out behind him as he goes.

I wish he would build a drey or nest in one of our trees, and have a family of baby squirrels there. Wouldn't we be lucky if he did! But I am afraid he won't. Have any of you seen a squirrel's drey? It is a big nest on a twiggy platform. Sometimes it is cup-shaped, sometimes domed, with a roof. It is lined with grass that the squirrels pull up or with hay from a hay-stack. It is a pretty sight to see a crowd of tiny squirrel faces looking out of the drey.

We found a most beautiful peacock butterfly yesterday—not a bit ragged, but quite perfect. When it suddenly opened its wings and we saw the four "eyes", in the corners of the wings we all cried out in delight. It is called the peacock butterfly because the eyes in its wings are rather like the eyes in the tail of the real peacock. Who has seen a real peacock open his tail? I have—and it was just like magic, it was so beautiful. Find a picture and then imagine

that the tail is as brilliant as a rainbow, and you will guess how lovely the real thing is.

Wild flowers are everywhere now. Who is making a collection of them month by month this year? As I have often said before, it is fun to have a good reference book that shows every flower in its right colours—then you have an exciting time hunting for your flower through the book. You do feel pleased when you have found it at last, and proudly printed its name.

Soon the may will be out, and then the golden buttercups will follow. The town children still in the country will have the joy, perhaps for the first time, of seeing and smelling the white may that lies like a drift of fragrant snow over the hedges. They will stand and look at the great carpet of butter-cups that spreads from their feet to the far-off hedge and beyond. How they will love it—and so shall we too. I could never get tired of a buttercup field, could you?

Would anyone like our little black kitten, Mewlie? It must go to a good home where it will be loved, and I would rather like it to go where there are rats and mice to hunt, for he will be a wonderful hunter. He is most amusing, very clever, and very healthy. He would make an excellent school cat, or farm cat. We shall miss him very much—but we cannot, alas, keep every kitten. He sends you mews. Gillian and Imogen

A Letter From Bobs

DEAR CHILDREN,

Have you heard of a stick that stretches to any size you want? It's called elas-stick. I didn't like the sound of it at all.

"Bones and biscuits!" I said to Sandy, "If the gardener gets hold of that stick, it won't be very nice for us! He'll just make it stretch to any length he wants and it will reach us, no matter how far away from him we are!"

"Well, let's find this elas-stick and bite it up," said Sandy. "I guess our teeth could crunch up any stick in the world!" So we hunted around but we couldn't find it.

I went to ask Gillian. "Elas-stick?" said Gillian. "What do you want elas-stick for? There's a big roll of it in Mummy's work-basket."

Well, fancy a stick being rolled up! Any-way Sandy and I soon found it. It wasn't a bit like a stick. It looked like a roll of wide tape. We "took it out of the basket and unrolled it. "It's funny stuff," I said. "Perhaps it gets stiff like a stick when some-body wants to use it. You take one end, Sandy, and I'll take the other, and we'll pull it to pieces." So we did—and we pulled and pulled and that elas-stick got longer and longer and longer. And then Sandy let go! Oh, boys and girls, what a smack on the nose I got from that elas-stick! I shot down to the bottom of the garden and nursed my nose all the morning.

A poor old nose from BOBS.

Love to you all from

Enid Blyton

send kisses.

THE TEACHERS WORLD, *February 15, 1922.*

FRIDAY AFTERNOON STORIES

PERONEL AND HIS POT OF GLUE.

ONCE upon a time, long, long ago, the King of Fairyland sat at dinner. He had a wonderful old dish in front of him, full of fairy cakes. He was very fond of that dish, for no one knew how old it was, and it was certainly a most convenient dish to have, for whatever you wanted to eat, you had only to tap the dish seven times and say what you wanted—

DOWN WENT THE PAGE.

when, lo! and behold, there it was on the dish in front of you!

The King found it very useful indeed for parties, for if the cook suddenly found he hadn't enough food for everyone, he simply borrowed the old dish and told it what he wanted.

When the King had eaten two fairy cakes at the end of his dinner, he rang the bell for the table to be cleared. The fairy pages bustled up, and started carrying off all the things. One of them, a new one, was very nervous.

"Be careful of that old dish," said the King to him.

"Yes, your Majesty," answered the page, But, alas! the King's cat suddenly ran

"IT'S THE STRONGEST GLUE IN FAIRYLAND!"

against his legs; down went the page, and *crash!* went the dish into three large pieces!

"Oh, dear! oh, dear!" said all the fairy attendants.

"Oh, dear! oh, dear!" said the King, sadly.

"Oh, dear! oh, dear!" wept the page-boy.

"Never mind," said the King at last, "we may be able to stick it together again."

All sorts of fairy paste and fairy glue were brought. The three pieces were carefully fitted together and glued.

"Now, we'll see if it's all right," said the King, cheerfully. He tapped the dish seven times, but just as he was saying what he wanted—crack! the dish was in pieces again.

The fairies tried again and again to mend it, but it was of no use. Directly the King tapped it, into three pieces it cracked!

At last the King offered a reward to any fairy who was clever enough to find a glue that would mend his dish properly.

Fairies came from far and near with all sorts of paste and glue, but none of them was any good.

At last there came to the King's Court a little dancing fairy, called Peronel, with naughty twinkles in his eyes and mischievous dimples in his cheeks. He swung a large pot of sweet-smelling stuff in his hand.

"Your Majesty!" he cried, as he knelt before the King, "I've found something to stick your dish together. It's the strongest glue in Fairyland!"

"What is it made of?" asked the King.

"Wild rose honey, and poppy-stalk milk, catkin dust, and honeysuckle juice!" sang Peronel, gaily. "And there's morning frost in it, too, and sticky spider's web! There are too many things to tell you, and I stirred it all up with my magic wand."

"Let's see if it will stick my dish together," said the King, greatly pleased.

The little fairy quickly glued the three pieces together, and put the dish in the sun to dry. Then the King tapped it seven times, and said: "I should like some apples."

Immediately the dish became full of rosy apples!

"Hurrah!" cried the King, "the dish is mended! You shall have the reward, and stay at my Palace for seven days!"

Peronel thanked the King, and went off with his pot of glue. But he was the most mischievous little fairy in all Fairyland. He was so proud of his glue, he couldn't stop glueing everything!

He glued the underneath of the plates so that no one could lift them off the table! He glued the seat of the Chamberlain's chair, and the poor Chamberlain had a terribly hard job to get up again!

Then he went into the kitchen and put glue on all the taps, so that the fairy cooks spent nearly all the morning trying to unstick their hands! He was a very mischievous little fairy, indeed. But somehow he was so merry and gay that no one had the heart to scold him very hard.

At last something happened that made the King say that all this mischief *must* be stopped.

The little fairy had spilt some of his glue in the great hall where the King received his visitors, so that when his visitors arrived and walked up the hall, they suddenly found themselves unable to stir, for something held their feet firmly to the floor!

The King was angry, and yet he could not help smiling at the mischievous little fairy, who was laughing by the door.

So when the visitors had gone at last, he called a meeting of the fairies, to decide what should be done with mischievous little Peronel and his pot of glue.

"Let him do something useful," said one of his councillors. "Then he will not need to waste his magic glue on playing tricks."

"Can anyone advise what work we shall give him?" asked the King.

"Yes, I can," answered a tree fairy. "Last year most of the chestnut buds died

PAINTING THE CHESTNUT BUDS WITH GLUE.

before they came into leaf, for it was so cold that the frost killed them. If only they were painted with that strong glue, the frost couldn't get through that, and they would be quite safe."

"That's a good idea!" said the King. "That shall be your work, little Peronel. You can start straight away now, as it's early spring, and perhaps that will keep you out of mischief."

So now the little glue fairy is very busy every spring painting the chestnut buds to keep the frost out. And if you touch one, you will feel how very, very sticky his magic glue is!

ENID BLYTON.

"PLEASANT EDUCATION."

To the Editor.

SIR,—In reply to R. J. (Aberystwyth), and also to H. P. D., whose view on the undesirability of "pleasant education" he supports, I should like to give my own experience.

For the average pupil I firmly hold that the methods of teaching to-day far exceed those of 15 years ago. If all children had equal brain power, retentive memories, and similar tastes and dispositions, perhaps it might be wiser to teach on the "hard work" principle, but this is not the case—there are thousands of young minds in our schools to-day which are "slow to take unto themselves knowledge," and there are also those children whose physical ability is below par, and thus they are naturally "lazy" (for so we teachers term it!), and need an added stimulus to their work. Now, is it not better that these varieties of pupils should receive their lessons in original and illustrative ways, and thus gain at least some education, than for them to be continually lagging behind their classes, and finally—I would emphasise this—leave school with practically no useful knowledge whatever? The "difficulties of life, &c.," would indeed be cruelly hard to these—far more so in proportion than is risked by "pleasant education."

A MIDDLESEX TEACHER.

SEE CAPTION OR EXPLANATION PAGE 324

HANDBOOK OF SUGGESTIONS

FOR THE CONSIDERATION OF TEACHERS
AND OTHERS CONCERNED IN THE WORK
OF PUBLIC ELEMENTARY SCHOOLS

BOARD OF EDUCATION

LONDON:
PRINTED AND PUBLISHED BY HIS MAJESTY'S STATIONERY OFFICE
be purchased directly from H.M. STATIONERY OFFICE at the following addresses
Adastral House, Kingsway, London, W.C.2; 120, George Street, Edinburgh;
York Street, Manchester; 1, St. Andrew's Crescent, Cardiff;
15, Donegall Square West, Belfast;
or through any Bookseller.

1927.

Price 2s. 0d. Net.

7177—O—27.

3

PREFATORY NOTE.

In its aims and content the present volume of Suggestions does not differ materially from previous editions. It does not pretend to be an exhaustive compendium of the subjects to be taught or of the methods to be adopted in teaching, but it is an attempt to bring together a body of opinion and practical experience of which it is hoped teachers will take advantage as their opportunities permit. The Suggestions remain "Suggestions for the consideration of teachers and others concerned in the work of Public Elementary Schools," and should be regarded as a challenge to independent thought on the subjects treated.

The Board desire to re-affirm the statement made in the following paragraph of the original Prefatory Memorandum :—

"Neither the present volume nor any developments or amendments of it are designed to impose any regulations supplementary to those contained in the Code. The only uniformity of practice that the Board of Education desire to see in the teaching of Public Elementary Schools is that each teacher shall think for himself, and work out for himself, such methods of teaching as may use his powers to the best advantage and be best suited to the particular needs and conditions of the school. Uniformity in details of practice (except in the mere routine of school management) is not desirable even if it were attainable. But freedom implies a corresponding responsibility in its use."

No detailed reference is now made in the Code to the subjects of the curriculum. As is pointed out in Circular 1375.

"Certain subjects of the curriculum are required by statute as, for instance, the provision of 'practical instruction' under Section 20 (1) of the Education Act, 1921. The list of additional subjects hitherto included in the Code probably represents a general concensus of opinion throughout the country as to the subjects suitable for children of elementary school age, but it is, and has long been, open to an Authority to vary the curriculum and there seems to be no sufficient reason for retaining in Grant Regulations a list which derives its authority from general agreement rather than from any exercise of the Board's statutory powers. The curriculum of a school will remain subject to the

(2505) Wt.21009/8914A/1441 25,000 5/27 Harrow G.31

A 2

SEE CAPTION OR EXPLANATION PAGE 324

APPENDIX 28

STORIES OF WORLD HISTORY

THE SIEGE OF TROY.—1. HOW THE TROJAN WAR BEGAN.

TOLD BY ENID BLYTON.

A DOUBLE PAGE ILLUSTRATION for this story—a map of ancient Greece and the theatre of the Trojan War—occupied the middle pages last week.

I HAVE an old, old story to tell you—the tale of the Siege of Troy, and all the brave deeds that were done there. But first hear how the war began.

Long, long ago the goddess Thetis consented to marry a mortal, King Peleus of Phthia. Zeus, father of the gods, went to the marriage, and brought all the gods and goddesses with him—all save one, Eris, the Goddess of Discord. She was not invited because she was bad-tempered and very ugly. But she heard of the wedding-feast, and she determined to go and spoil it if she could. So in the midst of all the laughter and merriment she appeared. The guests hushed their laughter and stared at the angry goddess, who stood by the laden table, too angry to speak. Then she raised her hand and threw something down among the dishes. It rolled along the table unheeded, for everyone was watching the goddess and hoping that she would not breathe her poisonous breath over the guests. She suddenly disappeared, and the gods looked to see what it was she had thrown amongst them.

"It is a golden apple!" said Zeus, picking it up "And see! It has words inscribed around it."

He read the words, and then threw the apple down again. The guests picked it up, and saw that the words clearly traced thereon were these: "To the fairest!"

"To the fairest!" cried Hera, Queen of Heaven. "Then the apple belongs to me!"

"Not so!" cried Athene, the goddess of Wisdom. "It is mine!"

GREEK WARFARE

But a third goddess picked up the golden apple. She was Aphrodite, the goddess of love and beauty.

"I think that none will take the apple from me!" she smiled. "Zeus, father of the gods, say that this apple is mine."

But Zeus shook his head. He knew that the apple could be given to only one of the three goddesses, and that the two passed over would be bitterly angry. The goddesses quarrelled more and more angrily, and had Eris, the uninvited goddess of Discord, been listening, she would have been delighted to see how the happy gathering had been spoilt. As none of the guests would judge which goddess was the fairest, they

From the Board's new Suggestions on History, p. 118.

"In the junior classes . . . . simple, attractive stories should form the substance of the instruction. These stories need not be confined to any one country or to any one age. They should be so arranged as to introduce the child to a gallery of striking pictures drawn from *the whole range of history.*"

Among the tellers of tales to children Enid Blyton stands in the front rank. No narrator more competent to help the teacher in carrying out the above suggestions could be desired. This series will prove a source of great pleasure to both the children and their teachers. It will appear fortnightly.

decided that they would ask Paris, the beautiful son of the King of Troy. "He shall judge between us," said the goddesses.

The Judgment of Paris.

They went to find Paris. He was standing on a lonely mountain top, looking out to the sea, a handsome, comely youth. Suddenly, from behind him, he heard a silvery voice. He turned, and there, near to him, he saw the goddess Athene, clad all in glittering armour. Then by her side appeared queenly Hera, very stately and tall. Paris looked in wonder as yet another goddess appeared, the lovely Aphrodite.

"We come to ask thy judgment, Paris," said Hera's silvery voice. "This golden apple is for the fairest of the three. Look well, and judge. Dost thou not think it should be mine? I will promise thee power without end, thou shalt be king over a hundred peoples, and many lands shall call thee lord—only give me the apple!" Then Athene of the glittering armour spoke. "The apple is mine," she said. "I am the fairest, and from me thou shalt have such wisdom as never mortal had before. Thou shalt be as wise as the great gods themselves!"

Paris listened in amazement and delight; but when the beautiful goddess Aphrodite spoke, he forgot the others. She was so very lovely—as lovely as the rosy dawn that flushed the mountain-tops of Greece. "Paris," she said. "Am I not the most beautiful goddess? Look thou into my eyes and tell the truth. Give me the golden apple, and I will promise to give thee the most beautiful woman in the world to be thy wife—even a woman as lovely as myself!"

Paris looked at the lovely Aphrodite and was lost. He gave her the apple and she took it, smiling in triumph at Hera and Athene.

The Promise of Aphrodite.

Then were Hera and Athene full of anger, and they went back to the gods to tell them that they had been slighted by Paris. "We will be revenged upon Paris and upon all his race," declared Hera. "Though he prosper in love through the goddess Aphrodite, he shall lose in war. We will make all the gods promise to help us in our revenge on Paris and Aphrodite!"

But Aphrodite laughed when she saw how angry they were. She cared nothing now that she had the golden apple. She told Paris that she would keep her promise to him, and when the time came she would give him the fairest woman in the world for his own. "Go to thy father's court," she said, "and beg for a fleet of ships. Say that it is thy wish to go and rescue thy father's sister, who was taken from Troy years ago. Then will I come to thy side and guide thee on thy way."

Paris did as Aphrodite bade him. "Father," he said to King Priam, the wise old ruler of Troy, "I pray thee give me ships that I may set out across the sea to Greece and bring back thy sister Hesione, who was taken from thee by Hercules."

King Priam looked at his comely son proudly. He was the fairest youth in the city of Troy, and in looks and manner was a prince to be proud of. "Son," said the King, "thou shalt have the ships thou desirest. May the gods prosper thy journey and bring thee back safely to Troy."

He gave Paris many well-manned galleys, and the youth set off across the sea to Greece. Aphrodite went with him, guiding the vessels in safety. They sailed for many days, passing little islands gleaming in the brilliant sea. Down the coast of Greece the wind took the high-prowed galleys, and at last they came near to the city of Sparta.

"Behind the walls of Sparta," said Aphrodite, "is the greatest treasure in the world, and all for thy taking. Go, Paris, and visit the court of King Menelaus of Sparta. There thou shalt see this wondrous treasure!"

Paris forgot his mission, and went to the court of King Menelaus of Sparta. There he was made welcome by the King, and by Helen, the Queen, his wife.

Continued on page 1106.

GREEK ART

SEE CAPTION OR EXPLANATION PAGE 324

1106

THE TEACHERS WORLD, *August* 31, 1927.

STORIES OF WORLD HISTORY

Continued from page 1090.

Helen of Sparta.

Now the first moment that Paris gazed on the face of Helen the Queen he knew that she was the treasure of which Aphrodite had spoken, for Helen was beautiful as no other woman had ever been before. She was—

" . . . fairer than the evening air,
Clad in the beauty of a thousand stars."

She smiled a welcome at Paris, and he fell in love with her, and knew that he could not live without her. This was the woman Aphrodite had promised him, the most beautiful in the world, even as lovely as the Goddess of Beauty herself. Paris thought no more of the errand on which he had set out. He forgot his father, his men and his honour. All he cared for was the lovely Queen Helen. King Menelaus saw nothing. He trusted his princely guest, and treated him well. He was glad that Helen should make him welcome and smile at him.

When a day came that Menelaus had to go on a long journey, and leave his Queen alone, he feared nothing. He went to her where she played with her little daughter Hermione, and bade her a loving farewell. "See that thou treatest the young Prince Paris well," he said. "Entertain him as befits the son of the King of Troy." Then he went down to his ships and departed.

Helen of Troy.

No sooner was he gone than Paris begged Aphrodite's help, and asked her to make Helen forget her husband and love him instead. So Aphrodite, remembering her promise, turned Helen's heart away from her husband and little daughter, and made her fall in love with handsome, blue-eyed Paris. She listened to the prince when he told her of his great love for her and was glad.

"Come with me over the sea to Troy!" begged Paris. "Fly from Sparta before Menelaus returns. Troy will welcome you and proclaim you to be the loveliest woman in the world!" Helen loved Paris, and was willing to go with him. She was willing to leave her child, and thought of nothing but this tall, princely youth who had come across the sea to woo her. When the time came she went down to the big red-prowed ship that Paris had prepared for her, and sailed away with him. And now was she no longer Helen of Sparta, but Helen of Troy, the cause of many battles, many sorrows and many tears. But for her fair face the brave history of the fall of Troy would never have been sung down the ages.

The Wrath of Menelaus.

When Menelaus returned from his journey, great was his wrath to find that his honoured guest had robbed him of his beautiful wife. "Now, by all the gods!" he swore, "I will get Helen back and punish the thief Paris by death! I will go to Troy and demand justice!" He sent messengers to all the kings and heroes of Greece, telling them of the great wrong done him by Paris of Troy, and begging them for help. He sent to his brother, the powerful Agamemnon, overlord of all the Greeks, and that strong warrior promised to send ships and men and come himself to help Menelaus avenge his wrong. Then from far and wide did the Greek host gather, until thousands of men and hundreds of ships were ready to go with Menelaus across the blue sea to Troy.

"We will send to the Oracle at Delphi to know whether our expedition will be successful!" said Menelaus, before the ships sailed. This was quite a usual thing to do before setting out on a journey, for the Oracle often gave good advice. So men were sent to ask the counsel of Delphi. The Oracle gave a curious answer :—"Troy will never be taken without the help of the warrior Achilles!" "That is good," said Agamemnon. "We have Achilles with us on our side, and by that we may know we shall be successful!"

Then did the brave ships set sail for the taking of Troy. A great sight they were, sailing grandly over the waters; but many were the tears of the women who watched them go, for they knew that few would come back again. There was Menelaus, King of Sparta, and his powerful and brave brother, King Agamemnon. There was the mighty Achilles, than whom was no greater hero, so mighty was his strength. When he was six years old he fought with lions and bears and killed them—now that he was a warrior none could stand against him in battle. There was Patroklus, his brave and kindly friend, and Ajax, a giant in size and of great courage. There was Diomedes, second only to Achilles in bravery, and Nestor, the wise warrior, whose advice was often sought. There was Odysseus, the wily King of Ithaca, and many, many others.

All these set sail for Troy, and of their brave deeds and wonderful adventures I will tell you.

(The next story will be of the Quarrel between Agamemnon and Achilles.)

NOTES FOR THE TEACHER.

First Story.

THE date of the Siege of Troy is usually placed about the twelfth century B.C., round about the time when Joshua was leading the Children of Israel. The story is mostly legend woven round a solid kernel of truth. Certainly adventurers from Greece did cross the Ægean Sea long ago, and after a ten-years' siege burnt the city of Troy. Archæologists have actually excavated the charred remains of the palace of King Priam of Troy—a fascinating thought, for the remains link us up with the happenings of three thousand years ago.

The reason for there being so many kings in the armies of the Greeks is that the Greek States were many and small, and all at this time owned kings. They were, in fact, city-states, all owning themselves Greek, and speaking the same language, but all independent and intensely patriotic. Any Greek would defend his own city with his life, and would also go to the aid of other cities—as we see in the story of the taking of Helen, when all the Greeks responded to the call of Menelaus.

It is worth while noting here that the name Greeks was not the name given by the Greeks to themselves, but was the name given to them by the Romans later on. The Greeks called themselves Hellenes, and their country they called Hellas, after their legendary founder, Hellen.

THE GODS.—The Greek gods were many, and mingled freely with the mortals on occasions, taking sides, and even inter-marrying, as in the case of Thetis and King Peleus. During the Trojan War they often fought with the armies.

MOUNT OLYMPUS.—This was a high mountain in central Greece, which the Greeks believed to be the dwelling-place of the gods. Away on the summit, beyond the clouds, where no mortal foot had ever trodden, lived these powerful beings.

THE DELPHIC ORACLE.—On the southern slopes of another mountain, Parnassus, was Delphi, the centre of the religious life of Greece, for here in a sacred cave on the mountain-side the priests of Apollo practised their arts. They gave counsel to those who sought it, and prophesied future happenings. Kings, rulers, and ordinary men came to ask the Oracle questions, and these were answered by the voice of the priests or priestesses, telling what Apollo the god replied to them. The Oracle at Delphi was famed throughout the whole of the ancient world. It was no wonder that Menelaus asked advice from Delphi before he set out on his journey to Troy. *See map in last week's issue.*

FIRST STAGE GEOGRAPHY.—CANTON.

Continued from opposite page.

filling the place with queer smelling fumes.

The rice market reminds us that in spite of the constant toil of the farmers in the river valley, a great deal of rice has to be brought in junks from other parts of China, and from distant Siam and Singapore, to feed the hungry people that swarm in the great city.

* * * *

NOW let us go to the country outside Canton to see the farmers at work. Every little bit of land that can be farmed, is used for growing things; and everything that can be used as manure is put upon the fields to make big crops grow—even the river mud and the city waste are brought to the fields in barges for this purpose.

In the delta lands are broad flat fields marked off by little embankments to keep in the water, and protected by tall dikes from the river floods. Here they grow rice—two crops in the year; and when the second crop of rice is reaped, the farmers will make the field into broad, flat fields on which to grow the winter crop of leeks and other vegetables. Even the dikes are planted thickly with bananas, and every little embankment has its heavy load of garden stuff for human food.

Sugar-cane is grown in some fields—tall stuff 8 or 10 feet high, from which the Chinese make the flat cakes of brown sugar that are sent by the ton in junks to ports in Northern China.

Look at these labourers, bare to the waist, turning with their feet the bamboo waterwheel that lifts the precious water in its little wooden buckets and pours it into a higher channel as it turns round and round, creaking dismally all the while. We cannot help thinking that China is a country where men do heavy work that is done by farm animals in other lands.

Here is a floating duck-farm—a great raft-like houseboat anchored to the riverbank; and round it is a huge flock of ducks feeding on the insects and frogs. At night they go to their floating home which can be moved to another place when the ducks have eaten most of the food to be found here. Farther up the river mulberry trees grow in long rows, and upon the low hillsides tea-shrubs are the chief things to be seen in the bigger fields. Other fields grow grain or beans and peas or huge crops of vegetables. We see people toiling in them, planting, hoeing, spreading black mud from baskets slung on bamboo poles or working at the waterwheels. In wet weather they still toil on, with enormous mushroom-like hats and straw coats to keep out the rain. So all through the year farmers work hard to feed the millions who live in the South of China.

NEWS BRIEFLY.

SEVERAL thousand people stood bareheaded in a rainstorm while Archbishop Keating laid the foundation-stone of the new St. Patrick's Educational Hall and Catholic Schools, Liverpool. Designed on original lines, these splendid buildings include a completely equipped stage, a lecture hall, and a cinematograph outfit.

* * * *

Several committees have been formed to carry out the arrangements for Sheffield's Education Week, October 9 to 15.

* * * *

Miss Ethel Strachan Henry has been appointed head mistress of Boston High School. Miss Henry resigned her position as head of Spalding New Girls' School in 1925 to make a world tour.

* * * *

Objection to a teacher not doffing his cap at the singing of the National Anthem at the Bideford and District Elementary School sports was taken at Bideford School Managers' meeting.

* * * *

Mr. Etienne Briouse, 39, a schoolmaster, of Birmingham, was drowned at Boscombe last Thursday while bathing.

* * * *

Fermanagh Regional Committee received a memorial from parents requesting them to appoint a male principal teacher for Mullaghmeen new school, and stating that their boys would not be satisfied with a female teacher. A male was appointed.

SEE CAPTION OR EXPLANATION PAGE 324

APPENDIX 30

A COURSE OF MENTAL ARITHMETIC.

By Dr. G. F. SMITH, B.A., LL.D.

FOR ALL STANDARDS.

Senior and Junior papers appear on alternate weeks. Tests for Standards I., II., and III. were given last week.

STANDARD IV.—THIRD TEST.

1. A train leaves Sheffield at 11.45 *a.m.* and reaches Manchester at 1.5 *p.m.* What is meant by *a.m.*? (Before 12 o'clock noon.)

2. Why is meant by *p.m.*? (After 12 o'clock noon.)

3. How many minutes did the train travel *a.m.*? (15.)

4. How many minutes did the train travel *p.m.*? (65.)

5. How many minutes altogether? (80.)

6. How many hours altogether? (1 hour 20 minutes or $1\frac{1}{3}$ hours.)

7. If the fare is 3s. 4d., what is the *distance* at a 1d. a mile? (40 miles.)

8. How long did it take to travel 1 mile? (2 minutes.)

9. How much did a person pay for 1 minute's travelling? ($\frac{1}{2}$d.)

10. How much did a person pay for 1 hour's travelling? (2s. 6d.)

11. What is the return fare. Same cost each way? (6s. 8d.)

12. What is the distance travelled? (80 miles.)

13. If the train started at 12.45 *p.m.* and arrived at 2.5 *p.m.* How long a.m. would it have been travelling? (No time *a.m.*)

14. How long *p.m.*? (1 hour 20 minutes or $1\frac{1}{3}$ hours.)

15. If a person arrived at the station at 1.10 p.m. to catch this train, how many minutes was he late? (25.)

STANDARD V.—THIRD TEST.

(Blackboard to be used very freely to connect the steps.)

1. One boy digs $\frac{1}{5}$ of a garden in a day. Another boy digs $\frac{1}{6}$. How much does one dig more than the other? ($\frac{1}{30}$.)

(Put on blackboard A $\frac{1}{5}$, B $\frac{1}{6}$.)

2. What do both dig in a day? ($\frac{11}{30}$.)

3. How much would then *remain* to be dug? ($\frac{19}{30}$.)

4. The *first* boy works at this for a day. How many $\frac{1}{30}$, would he dig? ($\frac{6}{30}$.)

5. What *remains* to be dug? ($\frac{13}{30}$.)

6. The *second* boy works at this for a day. How many $\frac{1}{30}$ would he dig? ($\frac{5}{30}$.)

7. What remains now to be dug? ($\frac{8}{30}$.)

8. The first boy works at this for $\frac{1}{2}$ a day. What will he dig? ($\frac{3}{30}$.)

9. How much does he leave for the second boy to finish? ($\frac{5}{30}$.)

10. How long will it take him to finish this? (1 day.)

11. If 30s. be paid for digging the garden, what would each earn in a day? (6s. and 5s.)

12. They each work 6 hours a day. What fraction of the garden does the *first* boy dig in an hour? ($\frac{1}{30}$.)

13. The second boy? ($\frac{1}{36}$.)

14. What does the *first* boy earn in an hour? (1s.)

15. What does the *second* boy earn in an hour? (10d.)

16. How many hours must both work to earn a total of 7s. 4d.? (7s. 4d. ÷ 1s. + 10d. Ans. 4 hours.)

STANDARDS VI. AND VII.—THIRD TEST.

1. I buy a book for 1s. 6d., my sister buys one for 4s. 6d. If we buy 6 books each, how much does my sister pay more than me? (4s. 6d. − 1s. 6d. × 6. Ans. 18s.)

2. If the difference between the money we spend is 54s., how many books do each buy? (54s. is 3 times 18s. Ans. 18.)

3. How much do I spend on these 18? (27s.)

4. How much does my sister spend on 18? (4s. 6d. is 3 times 1s. 6d. ∴ 27s. × 3 = answer 81s.)

5. If my sister spends 90s., what should I spend? (1s. 6d. is $\frac{1}{3}$ of 4s. 6d. Ans. 90 ÷ 3 = 30s.)

6. If my sister buys 60 books, how many could I buy for the same money? (60 × 3 = answer 180.)

Concluded in column 3.

JUNIOR ENGLISH & HISTORY

In answer to many requests we publish below outlines of two of the new series now appearing in "The Teachers World." Both will be found to be in complete harmony with the Board's new "Suggestions."

OUTLINE OF NEW JUNIOR ENGLISH COURSE.

By R. K. and M. I. R. POLKINGHORNE.

BOOKS TO BE USED.

Standard II.

(*a*) Bell's *Stages in Bookland*, Book II.—"Prince Charming in Bookland" (Bell, 1s. 10d.).

(*b*) *More Nature Myths*, by F. V. Farmer (Harrap, 1s. 3d.).

(*c*) *The Birthday Caravan*, by Douglas English (Bell, 1s. 3d.).

Standard III.

(*a*) *The Adventures of a Donkey* (Bell, 1s. 4d.).

(*b*) Bell's *Stages in Bookland*, Book III.—"Travels with Prince Charming" (Bell, 1s. 10d.).

(*c*) *Wonder Tales from Many Lands*, by K. Pyle (Harrap, 1s.).

(*d*) *Andersen's Danish Tales* (Selected) (Bell, 1s. 4d.).

Standard IV.

(*a*) *Stories from the Latin Poets* (Ovid and Vergil) (Horace Marshall, 1s. 9d.).

(*b*) Bell's *Stages in Bookland*, Book IV.—"In the Land of Books" (Bell, 2s.).

(*c*) *A Treasury of Flower Stories* (Harrap, 1s. 3d.).

(*d*) *Edgeworth's Tales*. A Selection (Bell, 1s. 4d.).

SCHEME OF WORK.

Standard II.

In Standard II. simple poems will be given each week connected with the seasons, or familiar happenings, or with the book being read. A very short story is also given with the poem to help to impress on the child's mind new words in the poem or new ideas, and for oral and, in some cases, written reproduction.

Spelling lists are built up in connection with this work. Many short written exercises interesting to the child are given each week, based on the week's work—these are designed to give practice in spelling, sentence construction, the right use of words, simple punctuation—simple rules or grammar such as singular and plural, nouns, &c., and to test the child's understanding of what is being read. The same words will be frequently introduced again and again, and revision of stories and poems is taken by introducing the children to new ones similar to the old—this suggests repeating the old and so comparison.

The oral work is based on the things the child observes and on the poems, since they are connected with daily life, on the little story and the book being read.

Standard III.

A very similar course is followed, but the little story is dispensed with as the children can read more for themselves. More continuous thought is expected, but plenty of short interesting written exercises are given—for spelling, punctuation and the right use of words, &c.—all based on the poem and story studied.

The parts of speech are introduced in connection with the extracts studied, so that the child learns them as he needs them. As far as possible the written exercises are self-teaching.

Standard IV.

Similar to above, but the grammar, uses of words, spelling, &c., are based on poems, prose descriptions, short anecdotes and legends of literary value. Both the poems and the prose extracts selected deal with subjects of interest to and familiar to the child.

Throughout the spelling and grammar is connected with the child's reading, and the reading with composition or written exercises.

Besides, of course, the prose extracts for

Continued at foot of column 3.

STORIES OF WORLD HISTORY.

TOLD BY ENID BLYTON.

SYLLABUS.

Based on the History Suggestions of the Board of Education.

TALES, from the Iliad and other sources, of the Siege and Fall of Troy.

Tales from the Odyssey. The Adventures of Odysseus.

Tales from Herodotus, the "Father of History," being stories of the Greeks and Persians. Alexander the Great.

A Persian story from "The Arabian Nights."

Stories from Roman history. Romulus and Remus, Horatius, Hannibal, &c. Julius Cæsar and his visit to Britain.

The Story of Jesus and His place in history. The Beginning of Christianity.

Roman Rule in Britain. Caractacus. Boadicea.

Christianity comes to Britain through the Romans. St. Augustine.

Tales of Christian Knights. King Arthur and the Round Table.

Stories from Froissart. Charlemagne, Roland and Oliver, fighting against the heathen.

The Coming of the Northmen. Story of St. Edmund.

Tales from the Eddas and Sagas of the Northmen.

This is a year's syllabus, and a lesson, in the form of a vividly written story, will appear once a week.

Continued from column 1.

7. How much money has my sister spent when I have spent £6 on books? (£18.)

8. How many books can I buy for £6? (240 ÷ 3. Ans. 80.)

9. How many books can my sister buy for £18? (80.)

10. What would 80 books at 1s. 6d. each, and 80 at 4s. 6d. each cost? (6s. × 80 or £4 × 6. Ans., £24.)

11. If I sold a score of books at 1s. 9d. each what profit should I make? (3d. × 20. Ans., 5s.)

12. If my sister sold a score at 4s. 9d. each what profit does she make? (3d. × 20. Ans., 5s.)

13. What is the total profit made by both in selling a score of books? (10s.)

Continued from column 2.

special study a book (see list) is also being read—for the most part silently in class. For oral work the chapters, &c., read are retold.

Care is taken that the extracts studied are from time to time connected with each other, so that revision is natural. This is a most important feature, as isolated extracts, like isolated or difficult words, are of little value. If not met with again they are completely forgotten.

More attention is now paid to paragraphing, to sentence construction, &c., &c., so that the child at the end of the course knows thoroughly the use of capitals, the use of the full stop, all the important occasions when the comma is used, use of the question mark and the exclamation mark, use of the apostrophe, use of quotation marks for titles, &c.

Letter-writing is taken in different ways in Standards II., III., and IV.

SEE CAPTION OR EXPLANATION PAGE 324

APPENDIX 31

THE TEACHERS WORLD, *August 29, 1928.*

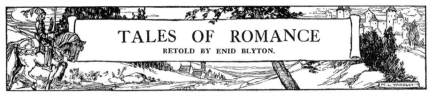

TALES OF ROMANCE
RETOLD BY ENID BLYTON.

KING ARTHUR AND THE KNIGHTS OF THE ROUND TABLE.

I. THE COMING OF ARTHUR

MANY years ago there lived in Britain a king called Uther Pendragon. He loved a fair maid called Igraine of Cornwall, but she would not look at the mighty prince who came to woo her. So sad at heart was he that he fell ill, and seemed about to die. As he lay grieving there, he saw a tall old man come to his bedside and stand there looking down upon him.

"I am Merlin, the magician," said the old man, and Uther Pendragon looked at him in awe. Merlin was so old that no man could guess his age, and so wise that he could see into the future as easily as into the past.

"I know why you grieve," said Merlin, "and I am come to help you. You want the lady Igraine for wife—you shall have her if you will promise that when your first son is born you will give him to me."

Eagerly Uther promised, and Merlin disappeared. The king leapt from his bed and went once more to woo Igraine, and this time, through Merlin's magic, she became his wife.

The Little Son.

Now when their little son was born the king rejoiced greatly. He named him Arthur, and looked with delight on the child's sleeping face. Then he remembered his promise to Merlin, and knew that he must part with his son and give him into the care of the magician. Deeply moved, he called a servant, and bade him wrap the child in a shawl and take him to the outer gate of the castle. "There you will find an old man, who will take the babe from you," he said. The servant, in great wonder, did as he was bid, and went to find the old man. Merlin, for of course it was he, took the child, and vanished into the night.

The Death of Uther Pendragon.

Not very long after this Uther fell ill, and knew himself about to die. He called his men around him, and bade every one of them swear to honour and obey his son Arthur as they had honoured and obeyed his father Uther. The men vowed to do so, but many did not believe that Uther had a son, and still more were angry to think that a child should rule them.

The king died. At once the nobles forgot their promises, and thought only of themselves. They cared nothing for any son of the dead king, and would not have let him rule them even if he had been put on the throne. But it seemed as if Arthur had completely disappeared. None knew of him, and none knew of Merlin's bargain with the king. The nobles began to quarrel among themselves, each wanting the throne, yet none strong enough to take it. Soon the country was in confusion, divided against itself, and open to any foe.

Sir Ector and His Wife.

Now when Merlin had taken the young child from his father he went with him to a nobleman called Sir Ector, a brave and good man with a young son of his own, Kay. "Here is a boy-child to bring up with your son Kay," said Merlin. "Give him to your wife, and bid her have as much care of him as if he were her own son. He shall be companion to Kay, and you will teach him all manner of knightly practices when he grows into boyhood."

Sir Ector took the child without question, and did not think even to ask who the boy was. His wife cared for him and loved him as her own son, and Kay thought that Arthur was his brother. As for Arthur, he was happy in his home, and loved Sir Ector and his wife, calling them father and mother, for he knew no different. He grew into a fine strong boy, truthful, courteous, and brave. Sir Ector trained both Kay and Arthur in all kinds of knightly ways, and was proud of both youths.

Merlin's Command.

Now when the right time was come Merlin went to the Archbishop of Canterbury, and

bade him call together all the great men of the kingdom. "Bid them come to the Cathedral in London," he commanded. "Every man must ride there at Christmastime, and there he shall see a marvel which shall show him who is the rightful king of this country."

The Archbishop sent out his messengers, and at Christmas-time there came riding to London all the barons and knights from east and west, north and south. None dared to disobey the bidding of the Archbishop, though many grumbled. Into the great cathedral they went to pray for peace.

The Sword in the Stone.

Now when they streamed out again from the doors of the cathedral they saw a strange sight, for in the open space before the church they found a great stone. On the stone there was an anvil, and thrust right through this was a mighty sword that glittered in the pale December sun. The barons and knights stared in the greatest wonder, for neither anvil nor sword had been there when they went into the church. Then two or three ran nearer, and saw that there was something written in gold letters on the marble stone:

"*Whoso pulleth out this sword from this stone and anvil is rightwise king born of all England.*"

Then all the amazed knights and barons knew that here was the marvel that Merlin had foretold, and they knew that the man who should pull out that sword would be king. One by one the men tried their strength eagerly, and sought to wrench out the sword from the anvil, but none could move it by so much as an inch. The Archbishop watched them step back ashamed, and then spoke loudly. "Set ten men to watch the stone and the sword night and

day," he said. "At Easter we will hold a great tournament, and brave men from everywhere shall try the sword to see if it is for them."

The Easter Jousts.

Now when Easter came Sir Ector took Kay and Arthur with him to see the tournaments and try their skill with spear and sword. On the morning of the jousts Arthur filled with excitement and delight. But before they had gone far Kay discovered that he had forgotten his sword! He clapped his hand to his side, and turned pale with dismay. Arthur saw him and knew what had happened.

"Take heart, brother," he said. "I will ride back to the house and fetch your sword for you. It will be easy for me to overtake you in time."

He turned his horse and galloped back the way he had come. But he found that the house was locked—everyone had gone to the tournament. Arthur stopped to think what he should do. He could not bear the thought that his brother Kay should lose the day's fun and glory for lack of his sword.

"Ha!" said the youth. "There is a sword in that anvil before the cathedral. I will take that for Kay!" He rode there, and found no one guarding the stone, for all the ten men were at the jousts. Quickly he pulled the sword from the anvil and rode off with it.

The King!

He gave it to Kay, who knew at once that it was the sword from the stone. He ran to Sir Ector, crying, "Father! I am the King of Britain! See, here is the marvellous sword!" "Where did you get it?" asked Sir Ector, startled. Arthur came up and confessed that he had taken it from the anvil before the church. To his great surprise, Sir Ector at once knelt before him and paid him homage, and made Kay do the same. Then the good knight told Arthur that he was no son of his, but had been entrusted to him by Merlin, and that no doubt he was the long-lost son of Uther Pendragon. Arthur had no thought for his kingship. All he could say was: "But are you not my father, and is not your wife my own dear mother? I would be her son, and none other."

Sir Ector comforted the weeping boy, and took him to the Archbishop. In amazement and delight the holy man called all the people before him, and told them what had happened. At once everyone followed Sir Ector, Kay and Arthur to where the great stone stood empty before the church. "Put back the sword and draw it forth again," commanded the Archbishop. Arthur obeyed, and the people held their breath to see him. But the barons began to shout loudly and angrily, for they had no wish for a youthful king. "What a boy can do a man can do better!" they cried.

Arthur is Crowned.

Then every man was told to take his turn at pulling the sword from the stone, but none could move it, try as he would. And when everyone had tried and failed, Arthur for the third time pulled the sword from the anvil as easily as from a scabbard. Then the people cheered, and shouted: "Arthur is king! He is king! We will have him for king and no other!"

The Archbishop stepped forward and took the crown from a waiting servant. At this

Continued on page 1076.

SEE CAPTION OR EXPLANATION PAGE 324

THE TEACHERS WORLD, January 16, 1929.

831

TALES OF ROMANCE
RETOLD BY ENID BLYTON.

KING CHARLEMAGNE AND THE PALADINS OF FRANCE.
6.—A ROLAND FOR AN OLIVER.

WHILE Ogier the Dane had been winning renown for himself, Roland had not been idle. He was younger than his friend Ogier, but very soon his strength was almost equal to the Dane's. He was much loved by everyone save the evil Charlot, and a traitorous knight called Ganelon. The youth had a ready smile, but when his face was stern it was fearful to see. A good friend was Roland, but a terrible enemy.

Charlemagne sent far and wide for armour to give his favourite nephew. Nothing but the best would do for one who, he was sure, would become a hero.

Roland's Armour.

The youth wore a coat of mail which had come from the distant north. It was made of the finest, best-tempered steel, and was so marvellously wrought that it would turn even the sharpest sword. Some said that the metal had been taken from the northern mountains by the dwarfs, and sent to the forges of the giants to be smelted.

Roland's helmet was a wondrous one. It was made of steel, and was inlaid with all manner of precious stones. It was wrought outside and inside with famous battle-scenes, and on the front was set a fierce golden eagle. A long ostrich plume waved above the helmet, and very splendid did Roland look when he donned the casque for the first time.

Roland's Horn.

Round his neck Roland wore a marvellous horn. It was made of sea-ivory, and hung from a thin golden chain. The ivory was set with brilliant stones that flashed in the sun, and seemed to set the horn afire.

But more wonderful than the stones that studded the horn was the sound that came from it. I have no words to tell of the enchanting music it made. When it was blown the noise went forth, and echoed from street to street, from hill to hill, from mountain to mountain until people in distant lands heard it, and looked round wonderingly, marvelling at the noise which seemed to come from nowhere.

None could blow the horn but Roland, for it needed a blast so powerful that ordinary men failed even to bring forth the smallest sound from it when they blew. The Emperor gave the horn to his nephew, and bade him never to sound it unless he was hard beset in battle. "For," he said, "it is a sound that will send men mad if they hear it often."

"I will only sound it when I crave help," promised Roland, slinging it round his neck.

Roland's Sword, Durindal.

Most wonderful of all Charlemagne's gifts to Roland was Durindal, the famous sword. So strong and so sharp was this that no sword could equal it. Not even King Arthur's wondrous sword Excalibur, nor Charlemagne's own beautiful weapon Joyeuse, were so glorious as Durindal. It was a famous sword, for it once belonged to brave Hector of Troy.

On one side of Durindal were written curious words that none could read save only Malagis, the enchanter, who was skilled in strange letterings. "These words mean 'Let honour be to him who most deserves it,'" said Malagis. "And on the other side is written, 'I am Durindal, that Trojan Hector wore.' Great good fortune is yours, Roland, to own the most famous sword in all history."

The Siege of Viana.

Now, some time after Roland had been given his famous arms the Emperor Charlemagne quarrelled with a certain Duke Gerard of Viana, who refused to do him homage. This Gerard sent word that he was no longer a man of Charlemagne's, and would never pay him a penny more in tribute money. The Emperor was angry, and vowed that he would not rest until the rebellious duke was brought to his knees.

Meanwhile the Duke Gerard had retired into his fortress and prepared for a long siege. So much food was brought into the castle that no more place could be found for it. Then Gerard sent for his four sons and two grandsons to help him, and they came riding swiftly to his aid with hundreds of men-at-arms.

Now, one of the two grandsons was no other than Oliver, who had been the boyhood friend of Roland. Neither had ever seen the other again, but both remembered the other and thought often of their long-ago friendship. Oliver had grown into a powerful young man, tall and strong, very skilful in combat. He was eager to help his grandfather, Duke Gerard, for he loved the old man and admired him.

Roland Sees Auda.

A long and bitter siege it was. It dragged through the winter and lasted into the spring, when the trees came into leaf and the birds sang sweetly. The castle had good stores of food, and would not surrender. If the Emperor's men attempted to storm it they were driven off by the cross-bow men, and often the Duke's soldiers would fling open the gates of the castle and ride forth themselves to attack the besiegers.

Still Charlemagne would not march away, for he had vowed to see the Duke kneeling in the dust before him.

There came a day when Roland rode out by himself into the sunshine, for the day was very beautiful. There was no fighting, and the young man rejoiced in the green meadows and the fluting of the birds. He rode towards Gerard's castle, and then, as he saw a figure standing on the ramparts, he galloped closer to see who it was, for it did not look like a knight.

It was Auda, sister of Oliver. She was a lovely maiden, as brave as she was beautiful. It was said that once she had even donned armour and ridden out to attack the Emperor's men herself. "Who are you?" asked Roland, reining in his horse, marvelling at Auda's golden hair that shone in the sun like purest silk.

"My name is Auda," answered the maiden, thinking that here was a splendid-looking knight, more glorious than even her brother Oliver. "Who are you?"

"I am Roland, nephew to Charlemagne," answered the knight. "I have something to say to you, fair Auda. Never have I seen a maiden so beautiful or so brave as you. I love you, and I will woo you and marry you, no matter what comes!" With that Roland rode away, and he carried with him the memory of the warrior-maiden smiling in the sunshine.

Single Combat.

Now, after seven months, news came to Charlemagne that Marsilius, the heathen king, was invading the southern parts of France, and the people there prayed him to come and save them from the Saracens. Charlemagne pondered over this, wondering how he could finish the siege of Viana.

At last he determined that the issue should be decided by single combat, and Duke Gerard agreed.

"We will draw lots," he said to his sons. "Write my name, and the names of my four sons and two grandsons, and put them into a helmet. The one which is first drawn forth shall be the knight chosen to fight the champion of the Emperor's."

This was done, and the name drawn forth was Oliver's, grandson of the Duke.

Meanwhile lots had been drawn by the Emperor also, and the choice fell upon Roland.

The Fight: A Roland for an Oliver.

The place chosen for the combat was a small island in the middle of the river Rhone. The men of each side stood upon the banks of the river to see the fight. Both Oliver and Roland were well mounted, and each felt certain of victory.

They rode full upon one another, and when their lances encountered each other's shields, they broke into pieces. Neither was unhorsed, but each jumped to the ground and drew his sword to fight on foot. They rushed upon one another, and the watchers on the banks held their breath to see the fury of the combat. Never were seen such strokes, such parries, such thrusts and cuts!

One hour went by, and another and yet another. Still neither knight had gained the victory. Each was marvellously matched to the other, so that no one could tell to which would fall the deciding blow. Roland marvelled at the endurance of his foe, and Oliver wondered at the strength of the tall knight opposed to him.

Then a strange thing happened. Roland struck so furiously at Oliver that Durindal, his sword, cleft through his foe's shield, and held there so that Roland could not remove it. At the same moment Oliver thrust so fiercely on Roland's breast-plate that his sword snapped off at the hilt. Thus both knights were left weaponless.

They rushed together striving to pull one another to the ground, but they could not. Then they tried to tear the helmets from each other's head, and both did so at the same moment. They stood there bareheaded, about to renew the fight, when they suddenly recognised one another. Oliver saw Roland, his dear boyhood companion, and Roland saw Oliver, his long-ago friend and comrade! For a moment they gazed in amazement, and then they rushed upon one another with joy. They embraced, and all the on-lookers gasped in surprise.

"I surrender!" cried Oliver.
"I yield me!" cried Roland.

The End of the Siege.

The knights on the banks of the river swiftly crossed to the island to see what had happened. When they saw the young men renewing their vows of brotherhood they all joined in the praise of the two knights' valiant combat, and shouted that each deserved the victory.

After a little while the quarrel between the Emperor and the Duke was ended, and Charlemagne went to the castle to feast in peace with his late enemies. With him went Roland, and great was the welcome that Oliver gave him.

Roland remembered the lovely Auda, sister of Oliver, and before he left the Duke's castle with his friend to follow Charlemagne back to France, he had won her promise to marry him.

NEXT WEEK: How Oliver Fought the Giant Fierifras.

SEE CAPTION OR EXPLANATION PAGE 325

THE TEACHERS WORLD, *April 24, 1929.*   215

TALES OF ROMANCE
RETOLD BY ENID BLYTON.

STORIES OF CHIVALRY IN THE FOURTEENTH CENTURY.
(Retold from Sir John Froissart's Chronicles)
I. THE SIEGE OF THE CASTLE OF AIGUILLON.

THERE was once a French King, Philip of Valois, who was full of wrath against the English, and vowed to vanquish them utterly.

"These English come to France and lay waste our fair lands," he said. "They have taken many of our noblest castles, and garrisoned them with their own men. It is time I gathered together a vast host, and destroyed every man of them."

The Victorious Army Besiege Angoulême.

Then the French King assembled a great army, and sent it forth to retake all the lost castles, and to do battle with the English wherever his men should find them. So vast was the army, and so brave were the leaders, that one after another the castles fell to them. At last they came to the castle of Angoulême, where an Englishman, John of Norwich, was captain.

The French army lay before the castle, and prepared for a siege. John of Norwich and his men watched from the walls, and wondered how long they could hold out before they had to surrender. The French overran all the district around and took many prisoners. John did not dare to sally forth and do battle, for his followers were few and the foe were many. Soon the food in the castle began to dwindle away, and the English feared starvation. John watched every day for the Earl of Derby to come to his rescue, but in vain.

The Trick that John of Norwich Played.

Then into John's mind there came a bold and daring thought. He would get all his men out of the fortress in safety, and would march to the strong castle of Aiguillon! But how was this to be done? John knew, but he told none.

On the eve of Candlemas he went to the walls of the city and looked down upon the great French host that lay below. Some of the Frenchmen saw him, and looked up at him in surprise. John took off his hat and waved it, signing that he would speak. Some of the Frenchmen ran up to the wall and asked him what he wanted. "I would speak to the Duke of Normandy," answered John.

Straightway the soldiers went to tell the Duke, and he with several knights came to the wall. "How is it with you, John?" asked the Duke. "Will you yield yourself, and give me the keys of the castle?"

"Not so," said John. "I came to beg for a truce of one day, my lord. To-morrow is Candlemas Day. Will you agree to a truce for the whole of that day, and promise that your men shall not harm or hinder mine? We, in our turn, will promise the same." "Be it so," answered the Duke, and they parted.

Away to Aiguillon.

Then John went to his men and bade them pack up what goods they wished to save, and tie them on their horses, and be ready by daybreak to depart with him for the fortress of Aiguillon. Then were his captains astonished, but he told them that a truce had been made for one day only, and that the Duke had promised not to harm any one of the Englishmen.

His men laughed when they saw through John's trick, but doubted much if the Frenchmen would allow them to ride off safely. At daybreak everything was ready. The castle gates were opened, and the Englishmen rode over the drawbridge.

The French host stirred, and challenged them in amazement when they saw the Englishmen riding by, with all their goods tied on to their saddles. But John bade them go to their Duke, saying that a truce had been promised, and therefore the French could not harm the English that day. When the matter came to the Duke's ears, he frowned and then laughed.

"This John is a cunning dog," he said. "He knows that I will never dishonour my word. We cannot harm them. Let them go as they will, in God's name, for I must keep what I have promised."

Thus John of Norwich and all his company came in safety to the castle of Aiguillon, and there amazed the knights with their tale.

The Siege of Aiguillon.

It was not long before the French Duke and his great army went to the fortress of Aiguillon. This was one of the most powerful castles. A broad river ran by the fortress, deep enough to bear ships, but there was no bridge.

The French set themselves all round about in the meadows, and began to lay seige to Aiguillon. There were a hundred thousand of them, both horsemen and foot-soldiers. Since they were so many they could assault the castle without ceasing. Morning, noon and night they assailed it, and gave the garrison no rest.

"We must approach nearer to the castle," said the French leader at last. "Until we have crossed the river we cannot hope for a victory."

"But there is no bridge," answered his captain.

"Then make one," commanded the Duke.

The Making of the Bridge.

Then three hundred carpenters came and set to work on the bridge. Day and night they worked, and those within the castle heard their hammering and wondered at it. "They are building a bridge!" cried one. "Let us enter our ships that lie on the river by the castle, and chase away the workmen!" cried another.

Then speedily the ships were got ready, and the knights entered into them. They sailed up to the bridge, and made such a fierce show that the carpenters fled away in terror. Then the knights broke down the bridge that had taken such a long time to make, and returned rejoicing to their castle.

Soon the French sent their workmen once more to build the bridge, and this time they set some of their own ships by them on the river so that they could resist the English if they came again. It was not long before the knights sailed up a second time and beat off the French. Then again they chased away the workmen and broke down the bridge. This went on day after day, but at last the French protected their carpenters so well that the bridge was finished and ready for use.

The Great Engines of War.

After that the French divided their army into four parts; the first to assault the castle from daybreak to nine o'clock, the second till noon, the third to evening-time, and the fourth till night. For six days they followed this plan, but those within the fortress defended themselves so valiantly that nothing was won from them.

Then the French took counsel together, and sent for great engines of war which could hurl stones right over the castle walls.

Twelve of these they used, and day and night they cast stones at the castle. But no harm was done except to the roof in some places, and not a man among the English was hurt. They too had great engines, and they put these in such a position that they cast back the stones so that they fell right on to the French engines of war and broke them to pieces.

A Hundred Crowns Reward.

Then the Duke of Normandy called all his host before him, and promised a reward of a hundred crowns to whatever man should win the drawbridge of the castle gate, and so get into the castle. So all the French went eagerly to the next assault, some over the new-made bridge, and some by ship. Then some of them took a little ship and went under the bridge. They threw great hooks of iron at the drawbridge, and when these caught and held they pulled with all their force. Soon the iron chains that held the drawbridge up broke in twain, and the bridge came crashing down.

At once the French leapt on it to pass into the castle, and pushed and jostled each other so that many fell headlong, for everyone wanted to win the hundred crowns.

But soon, hurtling down on their heads, came boiling water, pots of burning lime, baulks of timber and heavy bars of iron. The garrison in the castle meant to beat off the besiegers, and used everything that came to hand to force them away from the castle gate. As fast as the enemy swarmed on the drawbridge they were forced off, and numbers fell into the water below and were drowned. Still the bridge was held by the French, but try how they would they could not force the gate. When night came they had to retire to their tents, and then the English came forth from the castle and mended their drawbridge so that it was stronger than ever before.

The Four High Scaffolds.

Then the Duke of Normandy caused four tall scaffolds as high as the castle walls to be made on four ships, so that the French could shoot right into the castle itself. After some time these were finished, and the ships that held them sailed down the river to their appointed places, carrying within the scaffolds the knights that were to assail the castle.

But the English were ready for them. They cast such great stones on to the scaffolds that soon they were all broken, and one of them toppled over into the river and was lost, with all that were in it.

The End of the Siege.

So the siege went on, and the English grew tired of living in the castle. Then one day, to their great astonishment, they saw the French preparing to depart in haste.

At once the English dashed out from the castle gate, and went after the Frenchmen, harrying them at the rear and taking many prisoners. So joyful were they at the raising of the siege that not a man could withstand them.

"Why do you depart in such haste?" asked Sir Walter of Manny, the English leader.

"Have you not heard?" said the prisoners. "It is because your King, Edward of England, has heard of your plight, and has come to France to rescue you."

NEXT WEEK.—The King of England Does Battle in the Fair Land of France.

SEE CAPTION OR EXPLANATION PAGE 325

APPENDIX 34

The Teachers World, *July* 10, 1929.

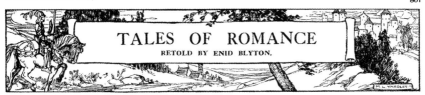

TALES OF ROMANCE
RETOLD BY ENID BLYTON.

TALES FROM SPENSER'S "FAERIE QUEENE."
1.—THE BEGINNING OF THE ADVENTURES OF THE RED CROSS KNIGHT.

A LONG time ago there lived a beautiful queen called Gloriana, who ruled over the realm of Faerie. Her long hair was golden and shone like the sun, and her skin was as white as winter snow. So lovely she was and so good that some of the bravest and best knights that ever lived came to her court to serve her.

There were many great deeds of chivalry done in her name, for she desired her kingdom to be freed from all evil men or monsters, and at that time there were very many of these.

Once every year Gloriana held a great feast which lasted for twelve days. People came from all over the world to see the dancers at this feast and to hear the wonderful music, and to admire the skill of the horsemen and the swordsmen. High above them all sat the Queen herself on a golden throne set with gleaming jewels.

This great feast was not simply for merriment and gaiety, but to help weak or oppressed folk; for on these feast-days anyone might come and beg for a knight's help. It might be that a wicked man, a giant or some other monster was causing distress to a town, and as soon as Gloriana heard of this, she would send a knight to the rescue. Never did she refuse a request of this sort.

The Coming of the Stranger.

On the first day of one of these feasts, when the musicians were playing a merry tune, and the knights and ladies were dancing gaily together, the great doors of the hall were flung open. The dancers paused to see who was coming—maybe a great knight, or some kinsman of the Queen.

To their astonishment a tall young man came in, dressed in rough clothes as if he had come straight from the fields. He made his way through the crowd of dancers, and went right up to the Queen's throne. All the merrymakers looked at him wonderingly, puzzled to see him, for he was not a knight.

He knelt down when he came to the Queen, and kissed her hand. Then she commanded the musicians to cease their playing whilst she heard what the youth had to say. "Welcome stranger," she said, "My gates are ever open so that all may enter and ask of me what they will. I refuse nothing that is good."

The young man lifted up his head and answered in a noble voice: "Oh Queen," he said, "I ask very little. Will you let me have the first adventure that happens at this feast?"

Gloriana looked at the strange youth in surprise. He spoke well, and he had a fine face—but his dress was very rough, and he did not look at all like a knight. But he seemed strong, and was very much in earnest.

"I never refuse to grant a wish at this feast," she said, "so I must grant you yours. But you have no armour, stranger, and I do not even know whether you are skilled enough to use spear and sword, nor can I tell whether you are versed in the rules of chivalry. But since I can see that you have a brave and sturdy heart and a wish to serve others, I grant you your request."

The stranger bowed with joy, and then, seeing that he made but a poor show in that richly dressed company, he sat himself apart, and waited patiently.

The Maiden on the Milk-white Ass.

The musicians struck up a merry tune again, and the knights and ladies danced and feasted merrily. Then once more the great doors swung open, and someone entered.

This time it was a lovely maiden riding on a milk-white ass. She wore a snowy wimple, and her cheeks were very pale, her looks sad and mournful. Slowly she rode through the doors on her little donkey, and by her side ran a tiny white lamb.

Behind her came her attendant, a crooked dwarf. He led a splendid war-horse by the bridle. Lying over the saddle was a suit of armour, rich and glittering. In his hand the dwarf carried the strong spear that went with the armour.

All the lords and ladies ceased their merriment as the maiden dismounted from her donkey and went to Gloriana's throne, where she stood with her eyes cast down in shyness.

"Welcome," said the Queen. "Whence do you come, maiden, and what is your wish?"

"I have come a long journey," said the maiden. "I am Una, daughter of a great king, who is ruler over a fair country. But, alas! a hideous dragon lays waste all his land, and my poor father is imprisoned in a tower of brass. I knew not what to do, so I have come to your court to beg for help against this dreadful monster."

"You shall have it," said Gloriana. Then she turned to her listening knights. "Who of you will undertake this adventure?" she asked.

But before anyone could answer the young stranger leapt to his feet. "Your Majesty!" he cried, in an eager voice. "Do you not remember your promise? You said I should have the first adventure that chanced?"

The Stranger Becomes a Knight.

The Queen turned to the youth, and looked on him for a moment. She did not know how this poorly clad stranger would fare when faced with a dragon. "Do you know how to fight?" she asked at last. "And what of your armour? Where is it, for you have none with you?"

Before the youth could make reply, the maiden Una spoke again, eagerly. "Madam," she said, "I have brought armour with me for the knight who will help me. This armour must be worn by anyone who would overcome the dragon."

"I know how to use arms," said the youth, "and I know the rules of chivalry, though I am no knight. This armour is very splendid. I should like to try it."

"Do so," commanded the Queen. Then the youth took the armour and donned it. It fitted him perfectly! It sat upon him as if it had been made for him and no other. Very splendid he looked in the glittering helmet and the breast plate with a bright red cross emblazoned on it. The shield shone brightly, and he held the long spear proudly. The watching lords and ladies murmured among themselves as they saw the noble youth. Una looked at him with pride and joy.

Queen Gloriana smiled with pleasure. "Without doubt he looks a noble knight," she said. "I will give him the order of knighthood, for I do not doubt but that he will prove himself to be brave and honourable. Give me your sword, stranger, and I will make you a knight before you set out on this adventure!"

The youth drew his sword from its sheath and handed it to the Queen. Then he knelt humbly before her, whilst she dubbed him a knight.

She touched him lightly on the shoulder and said: "Rise, Sir George, for that shall be your knightly name. Now go forth to your adventure, keep a knight's true vows, and win honour and glory for my court."

"This I swear," answered the knight. "I will keep all the rules of knighthood, help those in distress, and fight ever for truth and honour, God helping me."

Una and the Red Cross Knight Set Forth.

Then Sir George rose to his feet, kissed the Queen's white hand, and turned to Una. She smiled at him, and then once more mounting her milk-white ass, rode through the doors of the court. Sir George mounted the splendid war-horse, and followed her proudly, a strong and noble knight.

Out through the castle gates they rode together, to the sound of trumpets, whilst everyone cried God-speed after them, and wished them good fortune in their adventure.

For a long while the two travelled together, talking of many things. The dwarf lagged behind them, carrying the baggage with him. Suddenly the sun went in, and black clouds swept over the sky. The rain poured down, and Sir George looked about him for shelter.

"See," he said, "there is a wood nearby. Let us ride beneath the trees until the storm is past." So Una on her little white donkey, and the knight on his great war-horse, rode into the wood. There they took a winding path until the rain stopped, and the sun shone down between the trees.

But when they tried to ride out of the wood again, they could not find the way. The trees were very thick and every path they took seemed to lead them more deeply into the wood.

The Monster's Cave.

"Let us take this path," said the knight at last, pointing to a well-trodden one. "It should lead us somewhere from this place."

So they followed it through the trees. It twisted here and there, and at last brought them to a hollow cave in the very thickest part of the wood. The knight dismounted from his horse, and gave his spear to the dwarf to hold whilst he drew his sword.

"Be well aware," said Una. "This is a strange place, and dreadful peril may be near at hand. I have heard of this wood before. It is called the Wandering Wood, and in that dark and evil cave dwells a vile monster."

The dwarf began to tremble. "Fly, fly!" he besought the knight.

But Sir George took no heed of warnings. His sword in hand, he strode right up to the cave and looked inside. By the light of his gleaming armour he saw a horrid sight. Lying on the ground was a hideous monster, half human and half serpent. It had a long knotted tail with poisonous stings in it, and was ugly enough to put fear into the bravest heart.

But the knight would not turn back. He grasped his sword firmly, and waited to see what the monster would do. With a fierce bellow, the ugly creature leapt up and rushed out of the cave, seeking to slay him.

"Beware! Beware!" cried Una, in terror. "None may fight this monster and live!"

NEXT WEEK.—The Ugly Monster, the Wicked Magician, and the Saracen Knight.

778

TEACHERS WORLD AND SCHOOLMISTRESS, *September* 4, 1935

OUR PROGRAMME OF TEACHING FEATURES

IN the forefront of our programme are, of course, the two valuable presentation features.

1. A Presentation Series of **20** PORTRAITS of HISTORICAL CHARACTERS, resplendent in seven colours. No. I is presented this week, with the Junior School Edition. The complete list of 20 Pictures is as follows:

1. King Alfred's Mother	6. Thomas Becket	11. Wat Tyler	16. Cabot
2. King Canute	7. Robin Hood	12. Dick Whittington	17. Sir Thomas More
3. William the Conqueror	8. Prince Arthur	13. Joan of Arc	18. Mary Queen of Scots
4. King Henry I.	9. Robert Bruce	14. Caxton	19. Sir Francis Drake
5. The Empress Matilda	10. The Black Prince	15. The Princes in the Tower	20. Sir Philip Sidney

THE TWELVE NAMES ADDED TO THE LIST TO MAKE IT THIRTY-TWO CHARACTERS IN ALL

1. The Story of Guy Fawkes	5. The Duke of Marlborough	9. Captain Cook
2. James Graham Earl of Montrose	6. Sir Isaac Newton	10. George Washington
3. The Story of Oliver Cromwell	7. Bonnie Prince Charlie	11. Napoleon Bonaparte
4. Sir Christopher Wren	8. Lord Clive	12. Lord Nelson

SEE CAPTION OR EXPLANATION PAGE 325

APPENDIX 36

FOR THIS WEEK'S COLOUR PLATE

King Alfred's Mother

THE STORY OF A GREAT QUEEN—By Enid Blyton

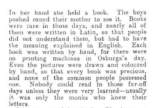

The beautiful seven-colour plates of great figures of history will dominate your class-room. Your class will want the story of each of these famous characters, and we have chosen Enid Blyton to be the narrator—for reasons which need no elaborating either for teacher or child.

MORE than a thousand years ago there lived a noble lady called Osburga. She was the daughter of the cup-bearer Oslac, who belonged to the old kingly family of the Jutes, and was as noble of heart as she was of birth.

Ethelwulf, a Saxon prince, fell in love with the beautiful Osburga, and they married. When Ethelwulf became King, Osburga sat by his side and shared with him all the joys and the troubles of his reign. Ethelwulf was King of the West Saxons, and in those days the great enemies of our land were the fierce Norsemen or Danes. The people were so terrified of these strong robbers that they prayed every day the same prayer—" From the fury of the Norsemen deliver us, O Lord !"

Osburga would dearly have loved a peaceful life. She wished to teach her sons all she knew, she liked to sew and to embroider, to hear and to tell all the old tales of heroes that she knew. But the Danes disturbed her peaceful life, for at any moment a messenger might come, breathless and terrified, crying, "The Norsemen are here !"

WAITING WITH HER BOYS

THEN Ethelwulf, her husband, hurriedly gathered together his men, bade good-bye to his anxious wife, and rode off to drive away the robbers from over the seas. Osburga waited fearfully until he returned, dreading that any messenger might bring news of the death of Ethelwulf, her kind and noble husband.

Osburga and Ethelwulf had five sons. The best of these, and their favourite, was Alfred, the youngest. The other boys were manly and of kingly bearing, but Alfred was even more princely, and his generous and noble nature made him everyone's favourite. He had a quick mind and was interested in everything, and he could not do a mean or unkindly act.

Osburga loved this small son of hers very much. As she sat sewing or embroidering she thought often of her many sons, and longed for them to become great men and noble kings. When Alfred grew into childhood and she saw his quick mind and kindly nature, she rejoiced—for she saw in him, young though he was, the makings of a great king, a leader and protector of his people.

Osburga had her sons around her as often as she could, and told them all the old tales and legends that she new. She bade .them be as brave as the heroes in her tales, and to behave always as noble princes, to be daring but not rash, to be merciful but not weak, to be strong in all things, so that when they became King in their turn they might have the friendship and loyalty of their people, without which no king could stand.

A GREAT TREASURE

THE five boys listened, but it was Alfred who stored away in his mind all the wisdom she offered to her small sons. It was he who hung upon her words, remembered them, and afterwards shaped his troubled life to follow his noble mother's teaching. He made her tell him again and again all the stories she knew, all the poems she had heard and learnt in her own childhood. He only had his mother for a few short years, but of all her sons Alfred loved and admired her most.

One day Osburga called her sons to her.

In her hand she held a book. The boys pushed round their mother to see it. Books were rare in those days, and nearly all of them were written in Latin, so that people did not understand them, but had to have the meaning explained in English. Each book was written by hand, for there were no printing machines in Osburga's day. Even the pictures were drawn and coloured by hand, so that every book was precious, and none of the common people possessed one. Nobody could read in those far-off days unless they were very learned—usually it was only the monks who knew their letters.

Osburga opened her book. The boys exclaimed in wonder at the coloured letters in it and the marvellously bright pictures of angels, the beautiful little designs of animals, birds and fishes here and there in the pages.

ALFRED'S FIRST VICTORY

THE children watched as their mother turned over the leaves. Alfred felt the thick pages, and his hands longed to hold the book. He wanted the lovely, hand-printed, hand-coloured book more than any toy he had ever seen.

"What is in this book ? " asked Alfred.

"There are many poems," answered his mother. Then, seeing the eager, admiring faces pressing round her, she smiled.

"The one among you that can first say these poems by heart shall have the book for his own," she promised.

It was Alfred who caught Osburga's hand in surprise and joy, and cried :

"Oh, mother, will you *really* give it to the boy who can first repeat the poems to you ? "

"I will," said Osburga, glad to see the delight in her youngest son's face and wondering what the small boy meant to do. Alfred begged her to give him the book to take to one of their teachers so that he might begin learning the poems at once. He

ran off with it, and surprised his teacher by insisting on hearing every poem at once.

Day after day the little boy listened to his teacher repeating the poems in the book, and said them after him. At last he knew them all, and he went to his mother, eager and proud.

"I can say the book by heart " he told her. In surprise, she listened to him repeating the poems, and when she found that he knew them all she gave him his reward—the beautiful hand-written book.

Alfred took the book joyfully. It was his own, the first he had ever had. He could not read it—few people in the kingdom could do that—but he knew all it contained, and he could turn over the pages and look at the pictures to his heart's content. He longed to read the words, he longed to be able to write down his thoughts, the stories he knew, the poems he could say. But it was not until he was twelve years old that at last he found someone who taught him to read and write. There were no schools then as there are now —it was considered a hard and a most learned task to master the art of reading.

His mother's teaching, when he was four or five years old, the book she gave him, which he treasured to the end of his life, and her love for the good and the noble were the beginnings of great things in the life of her little son, Alfred. He grew to be a fine and noble king, learned, wise, merciful and strong, the best and greatest king that England has ever had.

He had fierce enemies in the sea-faring Norsemen, but he learnt how to conquer them by building ships that were bigger and faster than theirs. He never lost his love for books, and he founded a school so that those who wished to read and to study might do so. He had many Latin books made into the English language so that the common people might understand them. Osburga, his mother, would have been proud and glad to see her favourite son fulfilling all her high hopes.

AN ANXIOUS PARTING

WHEN Alfred was still small, barely five years old, his father, Ethelwulf, decided that he would like to go on a pilgrimage to Rome. He wanted to pray at the shrines of the apostles S. Peter and S Paul—but his kingdom was in a troubled state then, so he resolved to wait for a little while before setting out himself, and to send instead some ambassadors or messengers to the Pope in Rome—and with them should go Alfred, his little, youngest son.

Ethelwulf was proud of Alfred—far prouder than of any of his older sons. He was so quick, so generous, so manly for his age. It would be a great honour and a great adventure for the small boy. Osburga was sad to hear that Alfred was going on such a long journey away from her—over the tossing sea, through thick forests, across great, towering mountains, in peril from robbers most of the way—who knew if he would ever come back in safety to her ? She was proud that her favourite had been chosen for such an honour, but sad at heart to lose him for so long—for in those days it took many weeks to travel to Rome, and the way was beset with grave dangers.

Continued on page 815

SEE CAPTION OR EXPLANATION PAGE 325

A LIST OF ALL THE STORIES IN THE SERIES
PUBLISHED IN *THE TEACHERS WORLD*

MONTH	STORY	EDITION
JANUARY	The Golden Promise	January 8, 1926
FEBRUARY	Lost - A Robin Called Sing-A-Song	February 5, 1926
MARCH	The Story of Dilly & Daffo	March 5, 1926
APRIL	The Giant's Easter Egg	April 2, 1926
MAY	Builders of the Empire	May 21, 1926
JUNE	The Sunset Fairies	June 4, 1926
JULY	The Red Imps	July 2, 1926
AUGUST	The Storm Fairies Get Into Mischief	July 16, 1926 (For August)
SEPTEMBER	Peeko's Prank	September 3, 1926
OCTOBER	The Flyaway Broom	October, 1926
NOVEMBER	Roundy and the Keys	November 5, 1926
DECEMBER	The Astonishing Christmas Tree	December 3, 1926

SEE CAPTION OR EXPLANATION PAGE 326

THE TEACHERS WORLD, *January* 11, 1929

777

A NEW FEATURE

JANUARY

BY ENID BLYTON.

JANUS, THE GOD OF JANUARY.

LONG ago, when the Romans were the greatest nation in the world, people worshipped strange gods. One of these was called **Janus**, and if you had seen him, you would not have known which way he was going, for he had two faces! One looked backwards and the other forwards. In his hand he carried a key, for he was the doorkeeper, or janitor, of Heaven. You will see part of his name in that word "janitor." The Romans called him the god of Beginnings and Ends, and when they wanted to be sure that a new venture of theirs would meet with success, they begged Janus to help them. They also prayed for his help when they wanted to bring something to a successful finish.

Janus had a temple of his own, whose doors were always open in time of war, and shut in time of peace. There were twelve doors, just as there are twelve months in the year.

Can you guess why the Romans chose Janus for the month of January? They chose him because of his two heads that look backwards and forwards—one head looks back over the year that is gone, and one looks towards the year that is come. We all look backward over the old year, on New Year's Day, and forward to the New Year, hoping it will bring us happiness, so I think it was a good idea to let Janus, the two-faced god, give his name to the first month of the year—don't you?

JANUARY WEATHER.

LONGER DAYS.—The days are becoming longer now. The sun is rising earlier, and setting later. By the end of the month we shall have 25 minutes more of daylight in the morning, and 46 in the evening. How much longer will the day be then?

WEATHER.—January is usually a cold, frosty month. The birds shiver at night, and try to find some sheltered place. Sometimes they die of thirst if all the pools are frozen. Many little animals are sleeping day and night— the hedgehog and the dormouse, the squirrel and the frog. Rabbits scrape away the snow to find the grass, and if it is too deep, they gnaw the bark of trees or of ivy, to keep away their hunger.

BIRDS AND FLOWERS.

EXCITED ROOKS.—If there are a few warm, sunshiny days in January the **rooks** begin to think of springtime, and visit their old nests in the high trees. They talk of what they will do, and pull a few twigs about, pretending that nesting-time has come. But when the cold night creeps on they forget their excitement, and fly swiftly back to their roosting-places. Other birds, too, are beginning to dream of the spring, and you will hear them trying to remember their song-notes. Watch the starling's beak, and see it turn bright yellow, and notice the cock-sparrows growing black bibs.

BRAVE FLOWERS.—You will not find many flowers in cold January. If there is thick snow, you won't find any except the lamb's tails on the hazel tree. Find some of these merry catkins if you can. They are the male flowers of the hazel. You will see the little spiky female flowers next month, looking just like red-fringed buds. Perhaps you will find some yellow gorse in bloom. You know the old saying that kissing's out of fashion when gorse is out of bloom, don't you? If you think that out for yourself, you'll see it means that gorse can always be found blossoming. Maybe you'll find chickweed too, and groundsel, and perhaps that funny little flower, shepherd's purse, with tiny green purses sitting all the way up the stem. Red deadnettle, dandelion, and speedwell are also somewhere about, waiting for sharp eyes to see them.

The Moon.—Look for the little **New Moon** on the 11th, and the round full moon on the 25th.

Snow Crystals.—Have you a little magnifying glass? If you have, use it to look at the snow crystals when snow falls. Catch a snow-flake on something black, and see what it is really like. You will find that it is made of tiny star-shaped crystals, all six-sided, and all different. They are very beautiful. I wonder how they grow, don't you? Snow is made of the moisture that hangs high up in the sky. It freezes, and falls as snow flakes, and the flakes are made up of millions of beautiful crystals. Nobody really knows why or how the crystals grow in such lovely patterns.

SPECIAL DAYS.

Twelfth Night.—Count twelve days from Christmas and you will find **Twelfth Night,** the 6th of January. It used to be the old Christmas Day, but nowadays most countries keep Christmas Day on December 25, as we do. Christmas holidays are supposed to be over by Twelfth Night, and men, women and children must go back to work, though, of course, most people are at work long before that date.

ANNIVERSARIES.

Robert Burns.—Have you ever heard of **Robert Burns,** the poet of Scotland? His birthday was this month, in the year 1759. He was a little plough-boy, and whilst he was ploughing he made up many of his lovely poems. Here is a bit of one, which he thought of when he was driving his plough, sad to see the bright daisies crushed into the ploughed earth :—

Wee modest crimson-tippéd flower,
Thou's met me in an evil hour;
For I maun crush among the stoure
Thy slender stem;
To spare thee now is past my power,
Thou bonny gem.

(*Maun* means *must,* and *stoure* means *dust.*)

James Watt.—I am sure you have heard the story of the boy who made his aunt cross, because he watched a boiling kettle for so long? His name was **James Watt,** and his birthday was in January, 1736, nearly two hundred years ago. The story may not be true, but he was certainly that kind of boy. He made many different engines to drive machines, but not the first steam railway engine. Steamers, railways, great machines of all kinds sprang from James Watt's discovery.

SEE CAPTION OR EXPLANATION PAGE 326

APPENDIX 39

ACTIVITIES IN THE INFANTS SCHOOL—12

I. Some Things to Find and Do

EACH child tries to count how many pet animals or birds he knows—his own, his friends or neighbours, etc. Lists of these pets and their names are written on the board. Some children may have a friend who has a canary or parrot. A parrot is a great find!

Choosing a pet. The children decide on the pet they would like to have in their class-room to watch them at work, and to be fed and looked after. It is to be a "make-believe pet," and when the pet is chosen a picture of it is found and pinned on the board. Next a name has to be chosen for the pet. Names are suggested and written on the board, and the name selected put under the picture of the pet. Perhaps the chosen pet is a dog called Spot (*Fig.* 1). Every morning he says, "Bow wow" to the children, "How are you? Are you ready to work?" Sometimes he tells them what he has seen yesterday, and so on. They "feed him" by pinning on the board near him slips of paper on which are printed the names of the things he likes to eat and drink, as bones, meat, water, etc. Drawings are also made. Stories are told about him, and the different things he can do are written on the board, as "Spot can beg." The keeping of a "picture pet" leads to the story of a particular animal, to "worth-while" writing, because children want "to feed" their pet with well-written words, to story-telling and oral work of different kinds.

II. Story Telling, Language and Creative Work

A riddle. Guess what the secret is.
"What do you think is in our backyard?
Perhaps you can guess if you really try hard.
It's not a puppy or little white mice,
But it's something every bit as nice!
It is not chickens, or kittens at all,
But something soft and round and small!
It's two little somethings as white as snow!
Two baby rabbits! There, now you know."

The children must be given time to guess before the last line is read. Children of six and over will be able to make up some riddles about pets. Other simple guessing games will be found in "The Land of Words," Book I (G. Bell & Sons).

The following story is useful for the younger children, and can be made into a reading book (see next section).

BOW-WOW AND MEW-MEW

Tom had a dog. The dog said "Bow, wow." Jane had a cat. The cat said "Mew, mew." So Tom called his dog Bow-Wow. Jane

called her cat Mew-Mew. Tom said, "Mother, my dog has no house." Mother said, "Make a little house for your dog, Tom." Jane took the hammer to Tom. Tom found wood, nails and the saw. Then with a tap, tap, tap, and a ZZZ-zzzzzz, he worked and he worked. He worked to make a little house for Bow-Wow.

One day the house was ready. "Here is your house, Bow-Wow," called Tom. "Look at your name on it."

"Bow, wow, wow," barked the little dog. "Thank you, thank you," and he ran into the little house. Then the cat came softly up. "Mew, mew," she cried. "May I come in?"

"Bow, wow, wow, do, do, do," said Bow-Wow.

The cat ran into the little house. "Purr-r-r, purr-r-r-r-r," purred the cat. "I like this little house." Bow-Wow and Mew-Mew stood in the doorway of their little house and looked out. Then they lay down on the soft straw and fell fast asleep.

Kindness to animals can be stressed in this story, and the children will have many experiences to add

III. Some Things to Make and Do

MAKING READING BOOKS

The children make a reading book about their class pet (*Figs.* 1 and 2). Perhaps a picture of Spot can be found for the cover. *Fig.* 2 shows the first page of a book made by children of six who were fairly good readers. The second page told about Spot's food. Two interesting pages told of Spot's doings at night when he was alone. Another booklet can be made for the story of Bow-Wow and Mew-Mew (*Fig.* 3). This booklet is shaped like a kennel. Inside the story is written in simple sentences.

NUMBER WORK AND DRAWING

A large bowl is drawn on the board so that every child can see it well. Inside the bowl goldfish are drawn, and some big stones as in *Fig.* 4. On the fish and stones little sums that the children can work are written. Each child draws a big bowl on a large piece of paper, and in the bowl the right number of fish and stones. Then they copy the sums and put in the answers, thus 3+2=5. When the sums have been worked correctly, the child takes

a yellow crayon and colours the fish, and with a green crayon draws in some water weed. The children have already had some experience in drawing fish (see Lesson 11). Quicker children can draw more fish and have little sums put on them. Colouring the fish yellow shows the sum is correct. Some little children must have practice in making the numbers 1—5 before they put them on the fish.

Take again the grouping of objects in the room and help the children to recognise 1—5, thus 2 chairs, 4 books, 5 pencils, etc. The children also draw groups of five objects arranged in different ways (see Lesson 9). They can draw goldfish and put the number drawn beside each group. For further stories of pets, see "Language and Speech Training Stories" (Univ. of London Press). Examples of reading books and other Self-Help Booklets will be sent to those who apply to the Authors, c/o TEACHERS WORLD, enclosing stamped addressed envelope.

FIG. 1   **FIG. 2**

> I
> Spot is our dog
> He is white
> He has black
> spots.
> He can run.
> He barks.
> Bow-wow

FIG. 3   **FIG. 4**

≋ GREEN HEDGES ≋

Enid Blyton's Children's Corner

DEAR BOYS AND GIRLS,

It is very difficult to write to you this week because Rufus the kitten will not get off my knee. Topsy is sitting beside me, and Rufus is afraid that as soon as he gets off my knee Topsy will take his place. He is a jealous little kitten, very loving indeed, and has the loudest purr I have ever heard in my life from a cat. The most enormous purr I ever heard came from a big tiger in a cage. It sounded like a large-size sewing machine going on and on!

Because of the unexpected warm weather all kinds of flowers are coming out in my garden here. Primroses, polyanthus, wallflowers are blooming side by side with late roses and chrysanthemums. I nip off the polyanthus and the wallflowers, because I am afraid that they will not bloom in the springtime if I let them flower now. I have had very many letters this last week from you telling me of all kinds of out-of-season flowers. If this warm weather goes on we shall have snowdrops popping up their heads, thinking that the early spring is near!

Imogen came home yesterday for the day, very thrilled to find her remaining birthday presents waiting for her. One of the presents she liked best was an enormous kite, which she is planning to fly on the next windy day. She says, "It's so big, Mummy, you'll have to hold on to me when the wind blows, in case I get carried away by the kite." When the time came for her to go back to her school she was torn in two—she wanted to stay with me, because she loves her home, and yet she badly wanted to go back to school because there was to be a firework party. I do hope you had some fireworks too. And I hope you will have many more things you have missed these last few years—crackers at Christmas time, really nice toys, and, when Easter comes, proper Easter eggs again.

Only six weeks till Christmas now! I have bought some of my Christmas cards already, and have been looking round to see if I can find anything exciting for presents. It is nice to give away things at Christmas, isn't it? I expect a good many of you are making your presents to give away, and that, of course, is a hundred times nicer than buying them. Do you do as Gillian and Imogen do—make a list of all the people you want to give presents to, and then mark them off as you get the presents? They love doing that, but, dear me, their lists get longer and longer every year.

And now, boys and girls, and teachers, too, I am going to say good-bye to you in TEACHERS WORLD. I think the time has now come for me to stop writing these long letters to you each week. We have had some lovely times together, and I have made thousands of boy and girl friends, and hundreds of teacher-friends too. We have hunted for flowers together, watched the birds, looked for twigs and berries, collected all kinds of things. You have learnt all about my many, many pets, and I have heard about yours. We have been very good friends, and we always shall be. Although I shall not be writing to you any more, you know that I shall be writing *for* you. I shall write you many books, you will have your "Sunny Stories," and some of you will read my tales in many papers. You can always write to me, if you want to. Go on doing all the things we have done together, won't you, work hard, be kind and just, be my friend as much as ever. I shall be here at Green Hedges just the same, with my children, my pets and my garden—writing books for you all as hard as ever I can!

Love to each one of you from

Enid Blyton

A Letter from Bobs

DEAR CHILDREN,

Bones and biscuits, what's this I hear? Mistress and I are not going to write our letters to you! Well, well, tails and whiskers, I feel as if the world is coming to an end. "What will the children say?" I said to Mistress. "Look, my ink bottle is almost full, Mistress, and I have a new nib in my pen. I know I'm a room-atticky old dog now, with front legs that limp a bit and paws that can't hold a pen very well—but perhaps I could dip my tail in the ink and write then."

I must say good-bye to you, dear boys and girls, and thank you for all the laughs you have given me when my letters have been read to you. And I say good-bye to you for Cosy and Rufus and Topsy and the doves and all the rest of us furred and feathered friends of yours.

Please be my friend still, and be kind to all animals because you have loved me. And I'll be kind to all children because I have loved you. That's fair, isn't it? I expect you will understand all dogs better because you have had so many weekly peeps into my doggy life. Now I shall sit back and be a lazy old dog who will soon forget how to spell even the word "dinner."

A very last letter from BOBS.

PENGUINS AND PUFFINS

FIRST the Puffins, beautifully illustrated in line and colour: "Our Horses," by Lionel Edwards; "Brer Rabbit"; "The Story of China," by Tsui Chi, illustrated by Carolin Jackson. Joseph Conrad's "Within the Tides," "Escape to Switzerland," by G. R. de Beer, F.R.S.; "A South Sea Diary," by S. W. Powell (the last two in "Travel and Adventure" series), and "Lady Hester Stanhope," by Joan Haslip (Biography), are the Penguins.

From Penguin Books also, in their Aircraft Recognition Series, comes the first annual edition of "Aircraft of the United States," corrected to November, 1944 (5s.). Copiously illustrated in line and from photographs, this is a book everyone must consult who is interested in aircraft.

SEE CAPTION OR EXPLANATION PAGE 326

ENID BLYTON PENNANT SERIES

1. Melia's Money-Box
   The Run-away Cows

2. Stones for a Donkey
   The Princess and the Cottage-Girl

3. The Boy who Found Sixpence
   The Wonderful Conjurer

4. The Little Girl who was Afraid
   We are Your Friends!

5. The Purple Pig
   He Couldn't be Trusted

6. Garry Give-up & Fanny-Find-a Way
   The Cat that was Forgotten

7. Mr. Trusty's Pennies
   He Wouldn't do Anything!

8. Buttercup Day
   Mike's Monkey

9. Eyes and No-Eyes
   The Very Old Teddy Bear

10. The Angry Pixies
    Sally the Screamer

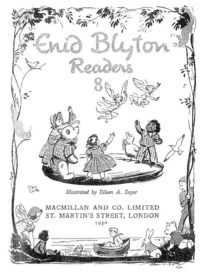

Illustrated by Eileen A. Soper

MACMILLAN AND CO. LIMITED
ST. MARTIN'S STREET, LONDON
1950

11. Which one are You?
    Little Mr. Kindly

12. House on Fire!
    The Fly-Away Money

13. The Wonderful Hooter
    Crack! Crack! Crack!

14. The Angry Toys
    Tell-Tale Tommy

15. The Bed that Took a Walk
    Binky the Borrower

16. It All Began with Jinky
    The Boy who Didn't Tell the Truth

17. Charlie the Cheat
    Three Wishes

18. It was only A Little Thing
    Dame Quickly's Wash-Tub

19. He'll Do for a Sweep
    Mr. Topple and the Egg

20. Sally Slapdash and Tabby Trust
    Jimmy Has a Funny Time

21. The Grand King-Doll
    The Dog that Remembered

22. The Ugly Little Girl
    The Frisky Little Goat

23. Lucy Lively and Dicky Dull
    The Magic Mirror

24. The Big-Boy
    The Forgotten Pets

25. The Rich Little Girl
    What a Silly Thing to Do!

26. The Two Rude Children
    Little Dolly Dawdle

27. Little Connie Careless
    Dame Topple's Buns

28. Teddy Makes a Mistake
    He Wouldn't Take the Trouble

29. The Little Boy in the Looking Glass
    The Little Dunce

30. Let's Pass it On!
    Little Mister Sly

SEE CAPTION OR EXPLANATION PAGE 327

THE
TEACHER'S
TREASURY

Edited by
ENID BLYTON N.F.U

With
an Introduction by
T. PERCY NUNN M.A.D.Sc.
Professor of Education in
The University of London

VOL. 1

THE
HOME LIBRARY BOOK COMPANY
(GEORGE NEWNES LTD)
67 & 68 CHANDOS STREET W.C. 2

E P

SEE CAPTION OR EXPLANATION PAGE 327

THE TEACHERS WORLD, *April* 14, 1926.

Dr. Percy Nunn says:—

"The right kind of help for the right kind of teacher"

No greater compliment to a book for teachers could be given than is made by that well-known educationist, Dr. Percy Nunn, about "The Teachers' Treasury."

THE
TEACHERS' TREASURY

Edited by

ENID BLYTON, N.F.U.

With an Introduction by

T. PERCY NUNN, M.A., D.Sc.,

Professor of Education in the University of London.

"The Teachers' Treasury" has been written by a teacher of the widest experience as a classroom aid for teachers of little children. Its help lies in all branches of Infant and Junior School work—in Story-telling—in Dances and Rhythmic Exercises—in Nature Study—in preparing Children's Plays—in Singing Games—etc., etc.—in fact, it covers practically the whole of the work of the Infant and Junior School. Miss Blyton's work is already well known to teachers, not only in this country, but all over the world. As Dr. Nunn points out in his introduction, "In the training of the young there will always be a place . . . for activities whose educative value lies in the very fact that they are social. The telling and hearing of story and fable, dancing, singing, and acting, are activities of this kind; our race in its childhood was largely humanised by them, and they form an essential part of the education of children to-day."

"The Teachers' Treasury" is compiled with this plan in view and therefore should be in the possession of every progressive teacher.

WHAT THE WORK CONTAINS:—

1. Stories to read to the children.
2. Rhythmic Exercises and Dances.
3. Nature Study. A year's course of lessons.
4. Children's Plays, with notes on Dress and Stage Properties needed.

5. Singing Games, with music by Percy Judd.
6. Twenty new Copyright Songs, with Staff and Tonic Sol-fa Setting.
7. Thirty Poems specially appealing to children.
8. Twenty-one Unfinished Stories. A unique feature.

The whole work is abundantly illustrated with Photographs and Black and White and Full Colour Illustrations by Horace Knowles, Lola Onslow, Kathleen Nixon, Ernest Aris, etc., etc.

FREE BROCHURE

All Teachers in Infant and Junior Schools are invited to send the attached coupon, or a copy of it on a postcard, for free Brochure, which fully describes this work and which contains specimen pages and illustrations.

"TEACHERS WORLD" COUPON (2).

To THE HOME LIBRARY BOOK CO.
(Geo. Newnes, Ltd.),
67/8, Chandos Street, London, W.C.2.

I shall be glad to receive Free Brochure of Miss Enid Blyton's "The Teachers' Treasury" and particulars as to how this work may be purchased by small monthly payments.

Name ....

Address ....

....

SEE CAPTION OR EXPLANATION PAGE 327

INTRODUCTION

MISS ENID BLYTON, by allowing me to read the proofs of her delightful book, has enabled me say a word in its praise. There is no difficulty in picturing to oneself the gaiety and happy interest that will spring up in every class-room to which this book finds its way.

During the last few years teachers of young children, stimulated by the preaching and practice of Dr. Maria Montessori, have given a great deal of their attention to developing methods of "individual work." In my opinion there can be no question of the value of this movement ; it has already been fertile in excellent results within the infants' schools, and is destined to have a vivifying influence over the whole field of education. But we may welcome the emphasis now laid upon a somewhat neglected aspect of educational work without thinking that other aspects are less important. In the training of the young there will always be a place, not only for tasks and enterprises which the little worker must face alone, under the watchful eye of the teacher, but also for activities whose educative value lies in the very fact that they are social. The telling and hearing of story and fable, dancing, singing, and acting, are activities of this kind ; our race in its childhood was largely humanised by them and they form an essential part of the education of children to-day.

Miss Blyton offers to the right kind of teacher just the right kind of help in using these fundamental means of civilisation : stories full of invention and instruction, fantasy and faery, stories happily addressed to the moralist in every natural child, stories left unfinished at a point of genuine interest and crying out for completion by eager young wits ; rhythmic exercises and merry dances ; nature studies free from sentimentality and likely to awaken true scientific interest ; singing games and songs set to tunes with melody and spirit in them ; a little anthology of poems in which Miss Blyton's own verses appear in not unworthy association with those of recognised laureates of childhood ; last, but far from least, little plays well within the dramatic capacity and power of stage-management of the average child. In all these sections of the work the skill of an experienced teacher of children is plainly visible, while artists and publishers have conspired to make it as attractive in form as a book should be. I wish it the good fortune it deserves.

T. P. NUNN.

SEE CAPTION OR EXPLANATION PAGE 327

THE TREES.

2.
Now the summer-time has come,
Everyone is hot,
But beneath our leaves you'll find
A cool and shady spot!
Chorus.

3.
Now it's Autumn, and our leaves
Flutter to the ground —
Red and yellow, brown and gold,
See them all around.
Chorus.

4.
Winter's come with frost and snow,
We are cold and bare;
Snow is lying still and white
Round us everywhere!
Chorus.

7

SEE CAPTION OR EXPLANATION PAGE 328

287

APPENDIX 45

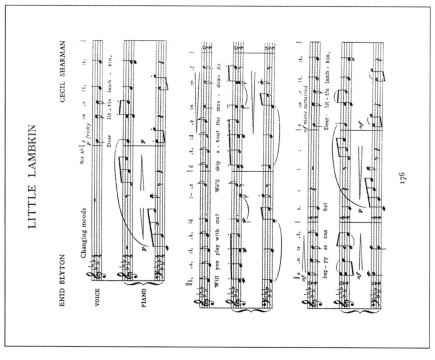

SEE CAPTION OR EXPLANATION PAGE 328

288

TABLE I

ENID BLYTON'S SONGBOOKS
WORDS BY ENID BLYTON

I – CONTAINING SONGS FOR UNISON SINGING

YEAR	TITLE	TYPE	COMPOSER	PUBLISHER	SONGS	REMARKS
1924	Songs of Gladness	Unison	Alec Rowley	J. Saville & Co	9	
1934	Songs of Summer	Unison	Cecil Sharman	Oxford University Press	3	
1935	Four Unison Songs	Unison	Cecil Sharman	York Bank & Sons	3	
1965	Mixed Bag	Unison	Carey Blyton	Boosey & Hawkes	6	(Plus 1 by B Hardy)
				SUB TOTAL	21	

II – CONTAINING SONGS BASED ON HER POEMS

YEAR	TITLE	TYPE	COMPOSER	PUBLISHER	SONGS	POETRY BOOKS
1924	Ten Songs from Child Whispers	Unison	Sydney Twinn	J. Saville & Co	10	Child Whispers
1926	Autumn Days	Unison	Cecil Sharman	Novello & Co	6	Child Education
1930	Round the Year Songs	Unison	Alec Rowley	Novello & Co	12	The Enid Blyton Poetry Book
1934	Snowy Days	Unison	Cecil Sharman	Novello & Co	6	(Untraced)
1949	Songs for Infants	Unison	F Fowler	E. J. Arnold	11	The Enid Blyton Poetry Book
1955	Enid Blyton's Happy Year Song book	Unison	R C N Johnson	J B Cramer	12	The Enid Blyton Poetry Book
				TOTAL	78	

SOURCE: The British Library Integrated Catalogue, Music Wing, Euston, London, England.

SEE CAPTION OR EXPLANATION PAGE 328

THE SINGER IN THE NIGHT

D ADDY called it a nightingale . . .
　　But it couldn't have been;
It sounded to me like a fairy-tale
　　Sung by the Queen—
The Queen of the Fairies, trilling high
A song to the moon and the list'ning sky,
And the dreamy clouds a-dawdling by,
　　A song of once-and-a-day.

And all the elves in Ring-a-ding Wood
　　Were list'ning too,
And the bunnies sat so quiet and good
　　The whole night through;
I saw them there for I went to see,
And nobody, nobody minded me;
But just as I came to the Fairy Queen's tree
　　She stopped—and fluttered away.

Daddy called it a nightingale . . .
　　But it couldn't have been.

TABLE II

MISCELLANEOUS SONGS AND SONGBOOKS

SONGS PUBLISHED IN THE ENID BLYTON'S BOOK OF THE YEAR

YEAR	WHERE PUBLISHED	TYPE	COMPOSER	PUBLISHER	SONGS	REMARKS
1941	Song Section	Unison	Alec Rowley	Evans Bros	12	

SONGS PUBLISHED IN THE TEACHERS' TREASURY

YEAR	WHERE PUBLISHED	TYPE	COMPOSER	PUBLISHER	SONGS	REMARKS
1926	Volume II, Section VI	Unison	E May & Others	Evans Bros	20 *	

* Eleven of these are drawn from *The Morning Post* and three, from *Teacher's Times*.

NODDY SONGBOOKS

YEAR	TITLE	TYPE	COMPOSER	PUBLISHERS	SONGS	PUBLISHED IN
1952	*Enid Blyton's Noddy Songbook*	Various	R. C. N. Johnson	G Ricordi	13	Songbook
1954	*Enid Blyton's Noddy in Toyland: Selection for Piano*	Various	Phil Green	G Ricordi	12	(Spin off from the play: 'Noddy inToyland'
1959	*Enid Blyton's New Noddy Songbook*	Various	R.C.N. Johnson	A H & Crew	8	Songbook
				TOTAL	65	

SOURCE: The British Library Integrated Catalogue, Music Wing, Euston, London, England.

SEE CAPTION OR EXPLANATION PAGE 328

TABLE III

SHEET MUSIC

SONGS BASED ON HER POEMS

YEAR	TITLE	TYPE	COMPOSER	PUBLISHER	DRAWN FROM
1925	The Singer in the Night	Unison	Cecil Sharman	Novello & Co	Punch*
1926	The Secret	Unison	Cecil Sharman	Novello & Co	The Enid Blyton Poetry Book
1927	The Fairies Lullaby	Unison	Cecil Sharman	Novello & Co	Untraced
1927	In The Doll's House	Unison	Cecil Sharman	Novello & Co	The Teachers' Treasury
1934	The Merry Breeze	Two-Part Song	Cecil Sharman	Oxford Univ Press	Child Whispers
1935	The Wild Rose	Two-Part Song	Cecil Sharman	Novello & Co	The Enid Blyton Poetry Book
1936	The March Wind	Unison	Cecil Sharman	Stainer & Bell	Enid Blyton Poetry Book
1937	When March Comes…	Four-Part Song	Cecil Sharman	York Bank & Sons	Untraced
1937	A Frosty Morning	Unison	Cecil Sharman	Auguner Ltd	The Enid Blyton Poetry Book
1953	The Adventurers	Unison	Cecil Sharman	J Williams Ltd	The Teachers' Treasury
1958	Miss Nan Nockabout	Unison	Cecil Sharman	York Bank & Sons	The Teachers' Treasury

*Later reproduced in The Enid Blyton Poetry Book

TABLE IV

SONGS WRITTEN SPECIALLY FOR HER MUSICAL PLAYS

MUSICAL PLAYS FOR SCHOOLS

YEAR	TITLE	TYPE	COMPOSER	PUBLISHERS	SONGS
1927	The Play's The Thing	Performance	Alec Rowley	George Newnes Ltd	66
1939	How The Flowers Grow	Performance	Cecil Sharman	A Wheaton & Co	40

MUSICAL PLAYS FOR THE THEATRE

1934	Noddy in Toyland	Stage	Phil Green	Live Performance	33
				TOTAL	139

SOURCE: The British Library Integrated Catalogue, Music Wing, Euston, London, England.

SEE CAPTION OR EXPLANATION PAGE 328

THE KING'S POCKET-KNIFE

ENID BLYTON   ALEC ROWLEY

GARDENERS' SONG
(The Final Song is also sung to this tune)

First part of the score for 'Gardeners' Song', one of the 69 songs in *The Play's The Thing*, Enid Blyton's first book of musical plays for schools. Image restoration credit: 2graphic Photo Restoration. Website: www. photo-restoration.co.uk

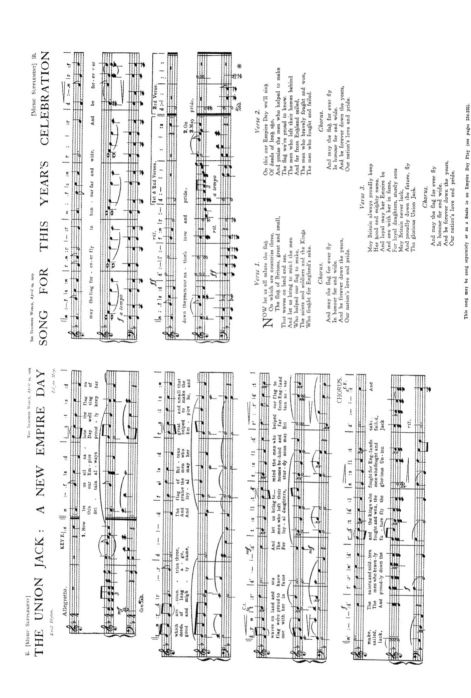

SEE CAPTION OR EXPLANATION PAGE 329

SHEPHERD SONG: A NEW CAROL

ENID BLYTON. ALEC ROWLEY.

SEE CAPTION OR EXPLANATION PAGE 329

TABLE V

CHRISTMAS CAROLS: WORDS BY ENID BLYTON

YEAR	TITLE	TYPE	COMPOSER	WHERE PUBLISHED
1924	Shepherd Song	Unison	Alec Rowley	The Teachers World Extra Number, edition Nov 7, 1924
1926	Christmas	Unison	Percy Judd	The Teachers' Treasury (Vol. II)
1938	His First Friends	Unison	Cecil Sharman	Two Years in the Infant School (Vol. II, page 626)
1938	Christmas Carol	Unison	Cecil Sharman	Two Years in the Infant School (Vol. IV, page 1267)
1941	In The Stable	Unison	Alec Rowley	The Enid Blyton's Book of the Year (page 355)
1955	Christmas Gifts	Unison	R. C. N. Johnson	Enid Blyton's Happy Year Songbook

TABLE VI

SINGING GAMES

YEAR	TITLE	TYPE	COMPOSER	PUBLISHERS	SONGS	PUBLISHED IN
1923	Responsive Singing Games	Unison	Not Known	J Saville & Co	8	Responsive Singing Games
1926	Singing Games	Unison	Percy Judd	George Newnes Ltd	10	The Teachers' Treasury

PATRIOTIC SONGS

YEAR	TITLE	TYPE	COMPOSER	PUBLISHERS	SONGS	PUBLISHED IN
1925	The Union Jack	Unison	Edgar May	The Teachers World	1	Edition April, 29, 1925
1926	The League of Nations	Unison	Alec Rowley	The Teachers World	1	Edition February 3, 1926

SONGS FOR INFANTS

YEAR	TITLE	TYPE	COMPOSER	PUBLISHERS	SONGS	PUBLISHED IN
1938	Song Section	Various	Cecil Sharman	George Newnes Ltd	45	Two Years in the Infant School

SOURCE: The British Library Integrated Catalogue, Music Wing, Euston, London, England.

SEE CAPTION OR EXPLANATION PAGE 329

APPENDIX 53

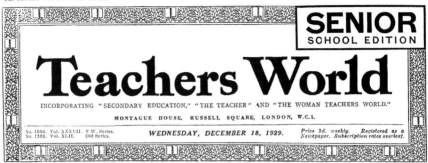

THE TEACHERS WORLD, December 18, 1929

SENIOR
SCHOOL EDITION

Teachers World

INCORPORATING "SECONDARY EDUCATION," "THE TEACHER" AND "THE WOMAN TEACHERS WORLD."

MONTAGUE HOUSE, RUSSELL SQUARE, LONDON, W.C.1.

No. 1056. Vol. XXXVII. T.W. Series.
No. 1386. Vol. XLII.   Old Series.

WEDNESDAY, DECEMBER 18, 1929.

Price 3d. weekly.   Registered as a
Newspaper. Subscription rates overleaf.

THE SHEPHERD KING.

A Carol.

WHILE Beth'ehem was wrapped in sleep,
  And drowsy shepherds watched their sheep,
    A little Child was born.
A King was He of heavenly birth,
Who yet for His first bed on earth
    A manger did not scorn.

No bells rang out to greet the Child,
None welcomed Him save Mary mild,
    Nor knew Him for their King,
Yet Heaven itself broke down its bars
And shone in glory 'mid the stars
    The holy news to bring.

The shepherds only were awake
And all of them with fear did quake
    To see the angels near,
And when the Heavenly host had passed
Then sped the wondering shepherds fast
    To see the Child so dear.

They worshipped Him as soft he lay
Half-sleeping on His bed of hay,
    Nor did they guess that He
Would name Himself a Shepherd too,
And seek His lambs the whole world through
    In sweet humility.

                    ENID BLYTON.

SEE CAPTION OR EXPLANATION PAGE 329

SEE CAPTION OR EXPLANATION PAGE 330

Brief Extracts

From

The Secret Commonwealth of Elves, Fauns and Fairies

By

Robert Kirk *

Fairies are said to be of a middle nature between man and angels…of light changeable bodies, somewhat of the nature of a condensed cloud and best seen in twilight…

They are distributed in Tribes and Orders and have children, nurses, marriage, deaths and burials … even as we do…

Their houses … are imperceptible to vulgar eyes…

Their apparel [dress] and speech are like those of the people and country under which they live…

They live much longer than we do yet die at last or, at least, vanish from that state … and are said to have aristocratically Rulers and Laws…

As birds and beast, whose bodies are much used to the change of the … open air, foresee storms, so these invisible people are more sagacious to understand by the books of nature things to come than we do…

These subterranean [living underground] have controversies, doubts, disputes, feuds and siding of parties … As to vice and sin, whatever their own laws be, sure, according to ours …they transgress and commit acts of injustice…

* * * * *

*First published in 1691 under the title: The Secret Commonwealth or a Treatise displaying the Chief Curiosities as they are used among diverse of the people of Scotland to this day.

Republished in 1893 under the title: The Secret Commonwealth of Elves, Fauns and Fairies By Robert Kirk, with extensions by Andrew Lang and published by D. Nult in 1893.

Notes:

The entire book, with its 17th century spelling, can either be read online or downloaded by visiting the website: www.sacred-texts.com. Then you can read all about Fairies to your heart's content for the book is in the public domain.

A fuller treatment of Fairies can be found in an article by J.A. Mac Culloch in The Encyclopaedia of Religion & Ethics, Volume Five, pages 678 – 689, edited by James Hastings M.A.,D.D., first published by T.& T. Clark, Edinburgh in 1926.

SEE CAPTION OR EXPLANATION PAGE 330

AUTHOR'S PREFACE.

DURING the progress of this work, as with all others on which I was engaged during my earth-life, I have felt a great desire to know the comments which would be bestowed upon it by its readers, and so have been glad when the last line was written, that I could obtain the different opinions which were to determine its success.

If I was apprehensive then, while on earth, it will be easily understood that I was still more so, when attempting to give the public a work, every word of which could only be placed on paper through the agency of earthly hands, used by me as the operator uses the instrument which transmits words thousands of miles by the power of electricity. The day is not far distant when this wonderful science will be better understood by millions who now believe it a delusion; and when that day comes, the world will be the better for it, and thousands who are in this happier world, and those who are yet to come, will be glad to know that the dear ones they have left behind regard their absence as a blessing certain, and so abandon the harrowing thought that it is possible a dear mother, father, sister, brother, wife, child or friend may be engulfed in a flaming sea which is to burn them for ever and ever. How little such people know of the wisdom and goodness of that dear Creator who made all things for a wise purpose; who has placed before the eyes of his earthly children so many evidences by which to convince them that nothing in nature is

---

PART SECOND

OF THE

Mystery of Edwin Drood.

BY THE SPIRIT-PEN OF

CHARLES DICKENS,

THROUGH A MEDIUM.

Embracing, also, that part of the Work which was published prior to the termination of the Author's Earth-Life.

"COGITO, ERGO SUM"

BRATTLEBORO, VT.:
PUBLISHED BY T. P. JAMES.
1873.

SEE CAPTION OR EXPLANATION PAGE 330

CLAIRVOYANCE

The branches of Clairvoyance may be summarised as follows:

SIMPLE (FULL OR PARTIAL)
The ability to see in the imagination people, objects, and scenes as clearly as in real life. The picture so seen may be static, as a picture on the wall, or in motion, as those seen on a cinema screen.
A SUBDIVISION OF SIMPLE
The ability to read, with the eyes closed, the contents of an envelope before it's opened; to see what lies on the other side of a brick wall; to tell the number and picture of cards turned down on a flat surface or to read a page of a closed book located in some other place, such as in a library.
HYGIENIC OR MEDICAL
The ability to diagnose disease without medical qualification. The bodies of people and animals appear transparent and the clairvoyant can watch the action of the various internal organs.
ASTRAL OR OUT OF BODY
Usually induced by going into a trance but can be done in full consciousness of one's surroundings. One seems to move out of the physical body and travel in spirit to some distant place and see people and things just as they would be seen in real life.
SPECTRAL
The seeing of spirits, ghosts or apparitions; the colour and forms of our thoughts; the aura surrounding people, animals and so on. This branch is further divided into clairaudience, the ability to hear spirit voices and clairsentience, to sense their presence.
PSYCHOMETRY OF CLAIRVOYANCE OF THE PAST
Seeing past scenes or finding missing persons by means of some object found in a strange place, such as rocks and stones, or belonging to a missing person, such as a piece of clothing.
SECOND SIGHT OR CLAIRVOYANCE OF THE FUTURE
The prediction of future events. In this category we find people known as psychics, mediums, seers and so on.
INTUITION
Regarded as the highest quality of the human mind. It's the effortless, instantaneous awareness of facts, events, principles and things and may be regarded as a branch of clairvoyance. When developed, it could lead to any of the other categories of clairvoyance described above.
SOURCES
Clairvoyance and Occult Powers by Swami Panchadasi, published by L.N. Fowler, USA, 1916.
Clairvoyance by C.W. Leadbeater, published by The Theosophical Publishing Company, London, 1899.
Seership: Guide to Soul Sight by Randolph, P.B, Confederation of Initiates, Quakertown, 1930.
Clairvoyance & Somnambulist Vision by Randolph, P.B, published by William White & Co, Boston, USA, 1869.
A *Course* of *Advanced Lessons in Clairvoyance and Occult Powers* by Swami Panchadasi, published by Advanced Thought Publishing Co, Chicago, USA, 1916

SEE CAPTION OR EXPLANATION PAGE 330

TABLE I

ENID BLYTON'S STRAIGHT PLAYS
AS CARRIED IN THIS BOOK
(In chronological Order)

YEAR	PUBLICATION	PUBLISHER

1927 *The Teachers' Treasury*, Volume II, Section IV   Goerges Newnes
1. The Land of Nursery Rhyme   4. The Union Jack
2. The Toys that Came Alive   5. The Christmas Fairies
3. Crying for the Moon   6. The Spick And-Span Stone

1927 *A Book of Little Plays**   Thomas Nelson
1. The Princess and the Swineherd (Specially written)
2. Sing a Song of sixpence (specially written)
3. Fairy Prisoners (recycled from *Merry Moments Annual*)
4. Robin Hood (recycled from *Teacher's Times*)
5. Peronel's Paint
*This book of plays was also used to give children reading practice
  and not for staging in schools

1935 *Six Enid Blyton Plays*   Methuen

Plays in One Act	Plays in Three Acts
Enchanted Cap	The Princess and the Enchanter
The Squirrel's Secret	Robin Hood and the Butcher
Play in Two Acts	The Whistling Brownies
A Visit to Nursery-Rhyme Land	

1939 *Cameo Plays*   Book III   E. J. Arnold
The Spick-And-Span Stone (recycled from *The Teachers' Treasury*)
Brer Rabbit Tricks Mister Lion (specially written)

1939 *Cameo Plays*   Book IV   E. J. Arnold
1. The Making of a Rainbow   5. Santa Clause Comes Down the Chimney
2. Poor Mr Twiddle   6. The Wind and the Sun
3. The Three Wishes   7. Brer Rabbit and Mr Dog
4. The Donkey's Tail   8. The Little Green Imp

1939 *The Wishing Bean and Other Plays*   Blackwell
1. The Hole in the Sack   4. The Queen's Garden
2. The Wishing-Bean   5. Sneezing Powder
3. Spreading the News   6. The Land of Nursery-Rhyme (recycled from
                                     The Teachers' Treasury

1941 *Enid Blyton's Book of the Year*   Evans Brothers
1. Mr. Stick-it-up   7. Who Will Hold The Giant?
2. The Lion and the Mouse   8. Mr. Sly-One and the Cats
3. The Runaway Rabbit   9. Good-bye, Swallows!
4. Brer Rabbit Raises a Dust   10. Finding the Tickets
5. The Mothers Meeting   11. Guy! Guy! A Penny for the Guy!
6. The Currant Bun   12. The Christmas Tree

SEE CAPTION OR EXPLANATION PAGE 331

"KING COLE CALLING!"

A HUMOROUS PLAY IN THREE ACTS.

By ENID BLYTON.

CHARACTERS.

Children.	KING COLE.
JACK.	CAPTAIN.
TOM.	SOLDIERS.
HUGH.	THREE FIDDLERS.
MARY.	MARY QUITE CONTRARY.
JILL.	JACK AND JILL.
*UNCLE REX.	TOM THE PIPER'S SON.
*UNCLE CARACTACUS.	THREE PAGES.
*AUNT PRISCILLA.	

COURTIERS, SERVANTS, &c.

Scene I.—Children's Playroom.
Scene II.—On borders of King Cole's Land.
Scene III.—King Cole's Court, and later, the Children's Playroom again.
Very few properties are arranged—mostly draperies of some sort—black, red, and purple.

DRESS.

KING COLE needs a tunic, long cloak and crown.

SOLDIERS red tunics with black belts, and tight-fitting caps with a feather. Swords.

PAGES, COURTIERS, FIDDLERS. Tunics of bright colours. Pages have short cloaks swinging from shoulder.

SERVANTS. Dressed in purple with a C for Cole stitched on front.

ACT I.

The children's playroom. There is a big chair at the back of the stage. Also a loud-speaker. The other furniture consists of ordinary chairs and stools, a table, etc. Four children, JACK, TOM, MARY, and JILL are in the room. JACK and MARY are doing a jigsaw puzzle on the table. TOM is reading, and JILL is sewing.

JACK:
We've nearly done the puzzle, Mary! Where's that little cornery bit that fits in here?

MARY:
Here it is! Hurrah! it's done. Come and look, you others.
(TOM and JILL go over to look.)

TOM:
Jolly good!

JILL:
And you've finished just in time, too, because it's almost half-past five, and the wireless will be on. Let's switch on the loud speaker, and listen in to the children's hour.

JACK:
Righto.
(Goes over and adjusts loud-speaker.)

UNCLE CARACTACUS *(supposed to be speaking on the wireless. The voice is arranged "off" in some convenient way. Probably curtains drooped over the back of the stage could be arranged to conceal someone)*:
Hullo, children! London Station calling! How are you, everybody? Hasn't it been a perfectly glorious day? Now, I've got lots of things to tell you this evening. First of all, thank you very much, Margery Brown, for your nice letter. I hope you'll have a very happy birthday to-morrow, and . . . .

* These names are introduced by permission of the B.B.C.

(The fifth child, HUGH, rushes into the room, carrying an old, dusty, ragged book. It is a big one, with "Book of Magic Lore" printed largely across it. He begins talking loudly, and interrupts the loud-speaker at "Margery Brown," drowning it in his excitement.)

HUGH:
I say! I say! What do you think I've found—what do you think I've found!
(Dances round in excitement, holding up the book.)

JACK:
Switch off the loud-speaker, Mary, quick.
(MARY does so.)

TOM:
What in the world have you got there, Hugh?

HUGH:
I found it under a pile of old rubbish at the far end of the cellar. Look! It's a Book of Magic Lore! I've been reading it!
(Puts it down on table. Children crowd round it.)

MARY:
Oh, Hugh! How glorious! What is it all about?

HUGH:
Oh, magic, and things like that! But there's one chapter that's perfectly marvellous. Here, let me find it.
(Turns pages rapidly.)

JILL:
Look! There's a chapter on " wireless " !

HUGH:
Yes, that's the one. It tells all about the coming of wireless, and it must have been written hundreds of years ago—fancy that !

TOM:
What does it say? Tell us.

HUGH:
It tells all about magic in connection with wireless. It gives directions about something called televi-travel !

JACK:
What on earth's that?

HUGH:
Televi-travel? Oh, it's a wonderful thing. Supposing Uncle Caractacus on the wireless to-night began talking about some place in Africa—well, we'd perform a few magic rites, and lo and behold ! we'd be transported to that very place and be able to explore it for ourselves !

MARY:
Goodness ! Do you suppose it's really true?

TOM:
Do you mean to say that if we switch on the wireless again, and hear about Paris, for instance, that we'd be able to go there this evening, if we use the magic written of in this book?

HUGH:
Yes, rather ! I say ! Do let's try, shall we?

EVERYBODY:
Yes, let's—do let's !

TOM:
I'll switch on the loud-speaker again ! I *do* hope Uncle Caractacus is talking about a foreign country !
(Switches on Loud-speaker.)

VOICE FROM LOUD-SPEAKER :
. . . . and they lived happily ever after. Now, that's a good story, isn't it? Here's another one for you. It's called " The Land of Old King Cole." Once upon a time, in the Land of Old King Cole, there lived a dwarf, who had three . . . .
(TOM switches it off again.)

JILL :
Oh, how disappointing ! It's no good trying to go to the Land of Old King Cole ! It's only make-believe, it isn't real.

JACK :
But we *can't* wait till to-morrow, we really *can't*.

HUGH :
No, we can't. We'll try the magic rites and see what happens, shall we?

EVERYBODY :
Yes, let's !

HUGH :
All right ! You must stand in a ring with me in the middle. I'm going to switch on the loud-speaker again, and while it's talking about the Land of Old King Cole, I'm going to do the magic part. I've got to say a rhyme of magic words. When I've finished it, you must shut your eyes, and take hold of each other's hands.

(The CHILDREN make a ring. HUGH switches on the loud-speaker, and then steps into the middle of the ring, holding the magic book open in his hands.)

LOUD SPEAKER :
" So, Old King Cole, as he felt very sad and unhappy, sent for his three fiddlers. But only two of them could be found. The third had disappeared, and no one knew where he had gone. Of course, the Red Dwarf could have told where he was, but he wasn't going to give away the secrets. So all up and down the palace scurried the King's guards, searching for the lost fiddler, and no one thought of looking in the . . .

(Whilst the voice from the loud-speaker is talking, not too loudly because HUGH's performance is the main theme, HUGH recites very loudly and monotonously the following, touching each child on the forehead as he does so:)

HUGH :
Rommany, rommany, fala garee,
Rommany, rommany rye,
Chikara, falaga, rommany ree,
Alus Talagrafal eye.
(As he ends rhyme, CHILDREN shut eyes and take hands. Suddenly all the lights go out and the loud-speaker stops. A loud bang is heard and a whistling sound. Complete silence.)

CURTAIN.

Continued on page 446.

SEE CAPTION OR EXPLANATION PAGE 331

APPENDIX 60

TEACHERS WORLD AND SCHOOLMISTRESS, *October* 23, 1935.

For Classroom and Study

PLAYS BY ENID BLYTON

Six Enid Blyton Plays. Methuen, 3s. 6d., 166 pp.

SHORT plays suitable either for school or private use. From the organiser's point of view, one of the best features of these plays is that they can be adapted for any number of characters. There are no fees, production is straightforward, scenery and "props" are easy to obtain, and the subjects are "right" for young children. "The Princess and the Enchanter," "Robin Hood and the Butcher," and "The Whistling Brownies" are in three acts apiece, "A Visit to Nursery-Rhyme Land" in two, and "The Enchanted Cap" and "The Squirrel's Secret" in one; but all are short and small. There are star parts for the more accomplished actors, but there are unlimited opportunities for "supers" and what the Admirable Crichton called "the odds-and-ends." Shy children after doing crowd-work and small parts will quickly overcome their reserve and clamour for the limelight. A very satisfying little book in every way.

Dramatic Verse. Edited by R. L. Mégroz. Pitman, 2s. 6d., 116 pp.
A selection of verse from Shakespeare, Marlowe, Beaumont, Fletcher, Kyd, Massinger, and one or two other Elizabethans. The anthology is specially intended to provide poetry-lovers with a good collection of dramatic verse suitable for verse-speaking. The editor has chosen with commendable judgment from a storehouse that he knows well.

Occupations for Little Folks. By Marjorie Pratt. Dryad Press, 2s. 6d., 36 pp.
Everything described in this book can be made with a minimum of trouble and with little mess. It will be specially useful to the kindergarten and infant school teacher. Among the "things to make" are paper clothes, baskets, calendars, jigsaws, bookrests, match-box cradles, necklaces, dolls' clothing (French knitting), bead serviette rings, raffia dish-mats, egg-cosies, slippers, and shopping bags. The book is well illustrated and instructions are clear.

The Animals' Broadcasting House. By Ernest Noble. Muller, 3s. 6d., 80 pp.
A collection of humorous animal caricatures which formerly appeared in a long series in *The Radio Times.* The drawings are accompanied by amusing comments. The book will probably be an acceptable Christmas present for young people. Uncles and aunts please make a note.

Old Peter's Russian Tales. By Arthur Ransome. Nelson, 1s. 6d., 309 pp.
The publishers are to be congratulated and warmly thanked for bringing out a cheap edition of this modern classic for young readers. It is a delightful collection of folk-tales by a man whom Hugh Walpole pronounced to be the best writer for boys and girls in England to-day. Teachers in search of good stories—and most teachers are—should get this wonderfully cheap little book.

An English Course for Adult Foreigners. By Walter Ripman. Dent, 2s., 136 pp.
A foreigner who studied this book thoroughly would know at any rate the principal features of the English language. There are 52 lessons with graded reading matter and exercises, a word-list with phonetic pronunciations, and the first 12 lessons are repeated at the end in phonetics. Mr. Ripman's book for foreign children, published years ago, had a big success, and the new volume is a sort of belated sequel for their elders. The illustrations strike the reviewer as being unnecessary.

The Golden Road, Second Series, Books I.-III. Compiled by W. Bertram White. University of London Press, 1s. 8d., 1s. 8d., and 1s. 10d. respectively. (These are in limp cloth. With cloth boards the price is 2d. more per volume.) Lengths: 160 pp., 160 pp., 192 pp. respectively.

THE poems in these anthologies, writes Dr. Ballard in the Foreword, "convey a message of cheer, of sympathy and of courage. Like Wordsworth's daffodils, they are indeed a 'jocund company' . . . It is in the conviction that these little books cannot fail to foster the finer graces of the spirit that I heartily commend them to their youthful readers."

Mr. Bertram White has gathered his poems from many sources, ancient and modern, and has deliberately excluded anything likely to depress the pupils. He has certainly found a great number of happy, inspiriting poems, and this is perhaps the keynote of the entire collection. No reviewer agrees with every single choice which an editor makes, but no teacher will complain that these books lack either quality or variety.

There are questions on each poem at the end of the volumes, and also some "Biographical Cameos" which will be useful to teacher and pupil alike.

Handbook of Botanical Diagrams. By Blodwen Lloyd, Ph.D., M.Sc. University of London Press, 8s. 6d., 108 pp.
A series of botanical sketches designed to illustrate a one-year lecture and laboratory course, and is suitable for pupils taking intermediate science, first year medical, etc. The diagrams are extremely well done, and to teachers of botany and to students working alone the book will be valuable.

Nelson's Bird Pictures for Individual Work, Sets I. and II. Nelson, 1s. per set of 12 pictures.
The pictures are beautifully reproduced in colour. Each species of bird is dealt with on a separate card, with a picture on the front and details about the bird's size, colour, food, habits, etc., on the back.

Regions of the World in Pictures, Set III., East Africa. Selected and with descriptive notes by G. J. Cons, M.A. University of London Press, 1s. 3d. per set of 16 pictures.
The "T.W." reviewer has already commended this series to the attention of teachers of geography. The pictures are reproduced from photographs, and the descriptive notes printed alongside give all the essential material without any waste of words. Mr. Cons's reputation as a lecturer on geography is already well-established.

Common Sense in the English Examination. By Sylvester Savigear, B.A. Pitman, 5s., 218 pp.
A modern manual of examination practice which incorporates the most up-to-date ideas on English teaching in Commercial, Technical and Secondary Schools, and intended particularly as a revision text-book for the Matriculation and School Certificate examinations. The author attempts a difficult problem, namely, the teaching of English for examination purposes without prejudicing the students against the subject for the rest of their lives. He deals with essay-writing, précis, direct and indirect speech, paraphrase, punctuation, grammar, prosody, etc., and, on the whole, succeeds in making the matter both instructive and palatable.

RECENT SCHOOL MUSIC
Reviewed by Mabel Chamberlain

"Rounds and Canons," collected and arranged for the pipes by Eric Bancroft (Novello, 1s. 6d.). Comprising a series of 13 rounds and seven canons, including some of the choicest of classical examples, the collection provides fascinating material for treble, alto, and tenor pipes.

＊   ＊   ＊

"The S.A.B. Book, a collection of well-known songs arranged by Cyril Winn for three-part singing with the melody part in the bass clef (Boosey, 1s.). Mr. Cyril Winn, in arranging this collection of 35 songs for the enjoyment of youths with changing voices, has made a valuable contribution to musical education. With a view to helping these singers who are only just finding their men's voices, he has given the melodies to this lowest part, and has set the soprano and alto singers the task of learning the accompanying harmony; an excellent idea. Most of the songs are taken from "Songs of Britain."

＊   ＊   ＊

"Further Steps in Sight-Singing," by J. W. Rossington (Novello, 8d.). Following Mr. Rossington's first steps for unison singing, there now appears this book comprising two-part exercises. The outstanding feature of the book is the fact that each test is provided with words, because the author believes, as stated in his previous book, that children should be introduced as soon as possible to the task of singing music straight away to words, which is one of the principal aims of learning to read and sing music. The 39 exercises are graded, beginning with the common chord, and should help in part-singing as well as in reading.

＊   ＊   ＊

"Ten Rhythmic Dances," by E. F. Gyford (Boosey, 1s 6d. net). The original feature of this set of dances is that they are arranged to be performed without a pianoforte, therefore are just the thing for the piano-less class or the class with a non-playing teacher. The rhythmic patterns, sol-fa of the melody, and one verse of words of these well-known songs are provided as well as the description of the dances. It is suggested that the class be divided into two sections, one to dance, the other to sing and tap the rhythm. This book should satisfy a need in the elementary schools.

＊   ＊   ＊

"Dances for the Seven-to-Eleven-Year-Olds," by Ruth Clark (Curwen, 2s. 6d. net). These dances have the great advantage of being designed for any number of children, all acting as soloists. The clear verbal directions and the excellent pictorial illustrations make the dances easy to follow. It seems a great musical pity, however, that with all the "picture" music available, it should be found necessary to read fairies, glow-worms, giants, elves in the rain, gnomes, and flower fairies into the classical works of Corelli and Beethoven.

SEE CAPTION OR EXPLANATION PAGE 331

SEE CAPTION OR EXPLANATION PAGE 331

SYNOPSIS
THE KING'S POCKET KNIFE
FROM
THE PLAY'S THE THING!
A MUSICAL PLAY IN ONE ACT BY ENID BLYTON

CHARACTERS: A king, six or more gnome gardeners, soldiers, an 'old-clothes fairy' 'brownie long-baird', 'tippytoes the pedlar', 'pixie bright eyes' and her servants.

The scene opens with a group of gardeners taking a break from work in the garden of the king's palace to sing the 'gardeners' song'. A rich conversation following the song is interrupted by the sudden arrival of the king. In due course they manage to pluck up enough courage to ask for a holiday, a request which the king turns down on the grounds their work is not up to standard. Whereupon he leaves the scene in haste.

Disgruntled, the gardeners are about to return to work when the king returns in full speed to announce he has lost his pocket-knife. Believing the gardeners are not telling the truth when he questions them, he orders his soldiers to search them. While pretending to carry out the search the soldiers sing the 'soldiers' song'. He then orders the soldiers to search in turn the 'old-clothes fairy' who often passes through the garden, and 'brownie long-baird', an old man who lives nearby, but to no avail.

Then all of a sudden 'tippytoes the pedlar' bursts on the scene singing the 'pedlar's song' while peddling his wears. When eventually he's questioned about the knife he suggests the king should ask 'pixie-bright eyes' to use her magical powers to help him find the knife.

When 'pixie-bright eyes' is finally brought before the king, with a train of pixie servants behind her, she offers to cast a spell to make the guilty person fall asleep. As she sets about casting the spell, her servants sing the 'spell song'. When the operation is complete, to everyone's surprise, the king falls asleep. Astonished, 'pixie bright eyes' searches him and finds the pocket-knife in his own pocket!

To make amends, the king who, apparently, suffers from amnesia, grants the gardeners their long sought holiday and the play ends with the singing of the 'final song' for the lazy gardeners get their holiday in a most spectacular way.

SEE CAPTION OR EXPLANATION PAGE 331

APPENDIX 63

```
┌─────────────────────────────────────────────────────────────────┐
│                                                                   │
│  TABLE II                                                         │
│                         ENID BLYTON'S MUSICAL PLAYS               │
│                           AS CARRIED IN THIS BOOK                 │
│                                                                   │
│                         ─────────────────────                    │
│                                                                   │
│     YEAR         PUBLICATION              PUBLISHERS              │
│                                                                   │
│     1927         The Play's The Thing     George Newnes Ltd      │
│                                                                   │
│   Plays in One Act                 Plays in Three Acts           │
│   The King's Pocket-Knife          Rumpelstiltskin               │
│   In The Toyshop                   The King's Jester             │
│   The Capture of the Robbers       The Magic Apple               │
│   The Cuckoo                                                      │
│   The Broken Statue                Play in Four Acts             │
│   The Wishing-Glove                Merry Robin Hood              │
│   Plays in Two Acts                                              │
│   The Rainbow Flowers                                            │
│   Rag, Tag and Bobtail                                           │
│                                                                   │
│   1939   The Blyton-Sharman Musical Plays for Juniors  A. Wheaton│
│   The Magic Ball                                                 │
│   How the Flowers Grow                                           │
│   The Fairy in the Box                                           │
│   The Toys at Night-Time                                         │
│   Who Stole the Crown?                                           │
│   Santa Claus Gets Busy                                          │
│                                                                   │
└─────────────────────────────────────────────────────────────────┘
```

A list of Enid Blyton's musical plays published in her own books for staging at school concerts and end of term parties. The plays listed under The Blyton-Sharman Musical Plays were published individually (see Figure 21 for cover pages illustrations).

ENID BLYTON'S NODDY IN TOYLAND

A Children's Play in Three Acts

SYNOPSIS OF SCENES

ACT ONE

Scene 1. Toyland Village, where Little Noddy lives.
Scene 2. The Enchanted Wood, with the Faraway Tree.

ACT TWO

Scene 1. Inside Moonface's little room at the top of the Faraway Tree.
Scene 2. A very lively Market in Goblin-Town.

ACT THREE

Toyland Village, as in Act One.

All enquiries regarding repertory and amateur acting rights in NODDY IN TOYLAND by Enid Blyton should be addressed to her agents, Messrs. John Farquharson, 8 Halsey House, Red Lion Square, London, W.C.1.

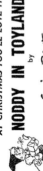

COME AND SEE NODDY IN HIS VERY OWN PANTOMIME AT CHRISTMAS YOU'LL LOVE IT!

NODDY IN TOYLAND
by *Enid Blyton*

BOOK YOUR SEATS NOW AND COME AND MEET NODDY, BIG EARS, MR. PLOD, TUBBY BEAR, MR. PINK-WHISTLE, SILKY AND ALL THE REST

WHAT FUN!

PRINCES THEATRE, SHAFTESBURY AVENUE, W.C.2

TEM BAR 6596

NODDY IN TOYLAND
Opening Thursday, December 22nd. 2.30 Daily, Wednesdays and Saturdays 2 Performances. 11 a.m. and 2.30 p.m.

THE FAMOUS FIVE
Opening performance Friday, Dec. 23rd. Nightly at 7.15 p.m. Apply : Box Office, Tem Bar 6596, Princes Theatre, Shaftesbury Avenue.

COME AND SEE A WONDERFUL PLAY

THE FAMOUS FIVE
by *Enid Blyton*

Book Your Seats Now and Come and Meet JULIAN, DICK, ANNE, GEORGE and TIMMY THE DOG

in one of their most exciting adventures ! You'll love it !

Enid Blyton's Magazine, December 7, 1955

732   THE TEACHERS WORLD, *August 24, 1932.*

Two more new teaching features—Courses in Nature Study and Drawing—will appear next week. The outlines of the schemes are set out below

ROUND THE YEAR WITH ENID BLYTON

A Weekly Course of Seasonal Nature Study

THIS course, which starts in next week's issue, has been worked out in accordance with the Primary School Report, which suggests that Nature Study should include :—

1. Weather observations, charts and calendars.

2. Common animals and insects found in gardens or round about. Pond animals in aquarium.

3. Common birds, their habits and appearance, and school feeding of birds in winter.

4. Common plants and trees. Bulbs, &c.

Miss Blyton writes :—Taking Nature under these four headings, I have allotted one of the above subjects to every month, making 48 lessons in all, so that, whilst each lesson is topical, the teacher will be able to follow out four different courses covering all the activities suggested in the Report. A glance at the time-table of articles below will show what I mean.

In addition to this syllabus there would be given, at the end of each lesson, THINGS TO DO, THINGS TO WRITE, QUESTIONS TO ANSWER, THINGS TO FIND or THINGS TO LEARN.

Also at the beginning of each month there will be included a short piece called " The Nature Table," listing what should find its place that month on the class " Nature Table," e.g., ashkeys, buttercups, celandines, toadstools, &c., at their respective times.

SYLLABUS—THE COURSE WEEK BY WEEK

	SEPTEMBER.	OCTOBER.	NOVEMBER.	DECEMBER.	JANUARY.	FEBRUARY.
WEATHER LESSONS.	Weather charts and how to make and keep them.	How things prepare for winter.	The rain and what it does.	How we get day and night, summer and winter.	Frost and snow. What they do.	The wind's work.
BIRD LESSONS.	The wonders of migration.	The making of a bird-table. The food, &c.	The house sparrow.	Robin and wren.	The friendly tits.	The skylark.
ANIMAL, INSECT AND AQUARIUM LESSONS.	The spider and its web.	Our tiny ploughman, the worm. How to make a wormery.	Snails and slugs.	Our cats and dogs.	Out in the snow. Snow-tracks we can read.	Making a school aquarium.
PLANT AND TREE LESSONS.	How to grow bulbs in the classroom. What to get and what to do—(bulbs to flower from Christmas onwards).	How seeds seek their fortune. A seed collection for next year.	All about Christmas decorations, (Ivy, mistletoe, evergreens).	Twigs and their story.	Germinating different seeds.	Our bulbs and how they are made.

	MARCH.	APRIL.	MAY.	JUNE.	JULY.	AUGUST.
WEATHER LESSONS.	Making a wind chart and wind vane.	The compass.	The sun and its work.	All about shadows.	The clouds we see.	Our school thermometer.
BIRD LESSONS.	Two singers—blackbird and thrush.	The strange cuckoo.	The swallow and the swift.	More summer visitors.	The seaside gulls.	All about owls.
ANIMAL, INSECT AND AQUARIUM LESSONS.	Stocking and keeping the aquarium.	The tale of the tadpole.	The keeping of caterpillars, moths and butterflies.	The silkworm's story.	Seaside creatures.	Bees.
PLANT AND TREE LESSONS.	Our school garden. (How to make it a success.)	Bees and flowers. How seeds are made.	Flowers for you to find.	Trees you should know.	Seaside flowers, seaweeds.	The corn field.

A YEAR'S COURSE IN DRAWING

DONALD E. MILNER, A.R.C.A. (Lond.), F.R.S.A., outlines his new series.

THE series of 15 articles on Drawing as a subject in Junior Schools will be based on a practical syllabus, and problems in teaching the subject will be discussed and demonstrated by means of large and clear illustrations.

Articles 1 and 2.

Short introduction dealing with aims and ideals. System and the most advantageous method of procedure. Mediums and their usage. A complete syllabus to cover a year of 42 weeks.

Article 3.

Nature drawing in pastel. Easy exercises with leaf shapes, twigs, &c. Training the pattern sense. Methods of using the medium. The finished drawing of the older child.

Article 4.

Nature drawing in pencil, ink and water colour. The suitability of different mediums for varying types of plant. Stages in a water colour drawing.

Article 5.

Object drawing without perspective. Types of objects and their expression in various mediums.

Article 6.

Object drawing. The approach to perspective. Interesting perspective demonstrations. Use of coloured paper. Introduction of shadows.

Article 7.

Natural objects. Treatment in various mediums. Group arrangement.

Article 8.

Memory drawing and illustration. Can illustration be taught? The pattern sense and conventions of very young pupils.

Article 9.

Colour. The distinctions between tone and colour. Use of coloured paper for demonstration. Simple exercises in pastel and water colour. Harmony and contrast. Sources of inspiration.

Article 10.

Pattern making. Patterns from simple units—the square, triangle, &c. Use of coloured paper units.

Article 11.

Pattern making. The use of nature in design. Exercises with leaves and flowers.

Articles 12 and 13.

The practical application of patterns by means of stick printing, potato cuts, paste cutting, &c.

Articles 14 and 15.

Elementary forms of block lettering. Simple written hands and their application. Suitable exercises. Methods of using decoration in lettering.

Attention will be given to making the more difficult problems as attractive as possible and distinction will be made between exercises suitable for younger and older Juniors.

The foregoing is provisional and liable to some small alteration.

SEE CAPTION OR EXPLANATION PAGE 333

ROUND THE YEAR WITH ENID BLYTON—20

Germinating Different Seeds

TO-DAY I am going to tell you a good many different ways of growing seeds, so that you may watch them developing all the time. I expect most of you have already grown seeds in one or other of the ways, so I will give you a wide choice, and you can choose some of the experiments you have not tried before, leaving out the ones you already know.

DIFFERENT SEEDS TO USE

THERE are many different seeds you may use for germinating experiments. You have probably tried the Bean, Maize, Pea, and Mustard and Cress. You can also grow Buckwheat, Sunflower, Marrow, Sweet-Pea, Sycamore, Onion, Grass, Lupin, and, of course, acorns and chestnuts in the glasses that are specially made for them. Do not stop at these seeds or fruits—gather seeds from the woods, and germinate those too. Gather them from the fields and grow little wild plants next spring! Save your date stones, and your apple and orange pips—grow those too. Why not?

THE BEAN IN THE CHIMNEY

You all know how a seed grows—first a root, and then a little green shoot—because you have planted seeds in your garden or in your window-box. It would be fun to see its root growing out and its shoot growing up, so you can try this experiment. It is quite an ordinary one, and if you already know it try another one.

You will want a glass lamp chimney, cylindrical in shape, a saucer and a piece of clean blotting paper. Cut the blotting-paper so that it exactly fits round the lamp glass inside. Slip it in. Stand the chimney in a saucer of water. Do you see how the blotting-paper is soaking up the water? When it gets halfway it may be very slow in getting further, so just turn the chimney upside down, and let the other half soak up quickly.

Now take some beans, which you have soaked for twenty-four hours, and slip them in between the blotting-paper and the glass. Pop a little saucer or slip of glass on top of the chimney to keep the moisture in, and your experiment has begun.

Now you may easily watch the bean put out its root and its shoot, and see it grow. Draw it as it develops. You will find it very interesting.

You may grow other big seeds, such as the pea, in this way.

SOAKING THE SEEDS

YOU will notice that I asked you to use soaked beans. Do you know why? It is because then they are in a fit state to grow. Look at a dry bean from the garden, or from the bean-bag. Isn't it hard and small, compared with a soaked one!

Did you see the beans as they were soaking? If you did you will have noticed that the skin wrinkled very much at first, and then gradually smoothed out as the bean itself took in water and swelled. Take up a soaked bean. Squeeze it. Did you see a tiny drop of water come out of a small hole at one side? Look at the little hole. It is through there that most of the water was taken up. Would you like to prove that? Very well, we will go on to another experiment.

HOW THE BEANS TAKE IN WATER

FOR this we shall want two large flat corks. Take about 10 beans and divide them into two equal heaps. Weigh each heap and write down their weight. Put

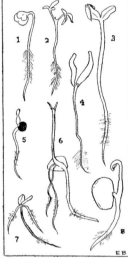

1.—Mustard seedling. Note root hairs.
2.—Cress seedling.
3.—Sunflower seedling. Note fruit: coat being cast off.
4.—Sycamore seedling.
5.—Pea seedling.
6.—Maize seedling.
7.—Wheat seedling.
8.—Bean seedling.

each lot of beans on their corks, and slip a rubber band across them to hold them in place. See that one lot of beans is placed with the little holes in the seed-coats uppermost, out of the water. In the others let them be downwards so that they touch the water when the corks are floated in saucers or jars with their burden of beans.

Leave your beans for 48 hours and then remove them from their corks. Wipe them carefully and re-weigh each separate lot of beans. The batch that had their little holes touching the water will weigh more than the others. Why?

A GERMINATION JAR

You can easily prepare a germination jar for almost any kind of seed. Get a glass jam-jar with a nice wide mouth. Cut a piece of clean blotting-paper to fit the inside of it neatly. Now get some sawdust and fill up the jar. It will press hard against the blotting paper and keep it close against the glass. Next get some water and pour in enough to wet the sawdust and keep the blotting paper moist. Then you may put your seeds between the paper and the glass, and watch them grow daily. The dampness from the blotting-paper gives them the moisture they need.

It is fun to put various different seeds into this germination jar, and watch how differently they grow. Would you like to do that? Draw them as they develop.

A FUNNY LITTLE EXPERIMENT

Here is a little experiment you may like to make with a few peas. Get some small corks—or cut a long cork into two or three pieces—and bore a neat hole in each one. Now put your peas one on each cork, just over the hole, and float them in a jar of water. Roots need water, and you will see your little peas putting their roots through the hole in the corks to reach the water down below! The shoot will grow upwards, of course.

THE KNITTING-NEEDLE EXPERIMENT

THIS experiment will show you the whole development of a germinating seed very clearly. For this you need a wide-mouthed glass jar again and a cork to fit it. Make a hole in the cork and pass through it a knitting-needle (or long darning-needle will do). Push a soaked bean on to the end of the needle. Now put the cork in the bottle so that the bean hangs in mid-air inside the bottle, over about an inch or so of water. The water keeps the air moist enough for the bean to germinate, and you will see it sending out root and shoot in a most interesting fashion.

WHICH PART OF A ROOT GROWS?

AS you watch a seedling developing and see the root growing longer and longer, perhaps you wonder which bit of the root is the growing part. Shall we find out? It is quite easy to do so.

For this we shall want a bean that has a root about an inch long. One that has grown on a knitting-needle in our glass jar will do very well. Take it out and wipe it very carefully. Now get a bit of cotton or silk and, holding it at each end, dip the middle of it into the ink-pot. Draw the inky part across the root at the tip, making a clear little mark. Now do it again a short distance above, then again and again until the whole root is marked evenly from bottom to top. Now place it carefully in your jar again.

Now you must make a careful drawing of the root, showing on it the exact number of lines, all evenly spaced. Make another drawing in about forty-eight hours—and you will have found out which part of the root grows! There will be a piece of root behind the tip which has no marks at all—and that is the piece that has grown, and so made the whole root longer! Isn't that interesting? You will be able to see this happening, if you look at the marked bean carefully about every three hours.

A GERMINATING BOX

Some schools like to make a germinating box for their seeds. This is how you do it. Get an ordinary wooden box without a lid. Take one side off, and get a sheet of glass to put in it slantways—i.e., the glass should slant in to the further corners, in-

Continued on page 537.

THE   SEE CAPTION OR EXPLANATION PAGE 333

GREEN HEDGES

DEAR BOYS AND GILRS,

A ship from Australia and New Zealand must have docked this week in England, because the pile of letters that suddenly came in from overseas was enormous! So far this week there have been over four hundred from the children who live on the other side of the world — and they make me feel glad and sad at the same time. Glad because I do love to hear their news, and sad because I haven't time to answer them — not time even to answer a quarter. I do try to send you each an autograph when I can't reply, but sometimes I haven't even time to do that so, children overseas, forgive me, please, and know that I love your letters even though I can't reply to all of them.

I've put a Brer Rabbit story in for you this time. You would be surprised how many mothers and fathers (and grandfathers) write to say they love Brer Rabbit, too. So do I —but I'm very, very glad he doesn't live with me!

Love to you all from

Enid Blyton

SEE CAPTION OR EXPLANATION PAGE 334

MY OFFICE,

DEAR BOYS AND GIRLS,

This week I have printed a lovely picture of Marion Crawford for you to see and on page 10 there are some more of her lovely stories about the Queen and Princess Margaret when they were children, for you to read. In this instalment she tells you all about some of the Princesses' favourite pets.

This week, too, you have a wonderful Royal Album, free, with your SUNNY STORIES. Isn't it exciting ? You can start right away sticking in those lovely pictures of the Queen when she was a little girl. And there will be another sheet of pictures with each of the next three issues of SUNNY STORIES. So don't miss them, will you ?

There is another exciting Cowboy Jim story this week. It's all about when Cowboy Jim went to a Rodeo—but you must read it yourself and find out what happened.

With lots of love from

YOUR EDITOR.

SEE CAPTION OR EXPLANATION PAGE 334

DIARY · 1957

To order this Diary give
number stamped on cover

A   **3/9** net
COLLINS   Incl. of P. Tax
DIARY

Published by
WM. COLLINS SONS & CO. LTD.
LONDON AND GLASGOW

THE THREE ENID BLYTON CLUBS

As most of you know, I have three Clubs or Societies for children, whose " meeting-place " is in my magazine (*Enid Blyton's Magazine*) each number.

Many of you suggested that it would be a good idea to put the Clubs into this diary, and tell you about them, so that those who did not know them might join if they wished—or so that those who *do* belong may always have the addresses and instructions handy. Each Club has its own badge, which I reproduce here. You have no doubt seen many children wearing them.

(1) **The Busy Bees.** This famous Club is for all children who are animal lovers (and most of you are!).

The Busy Bee Society is the youth section of the grand P.D.S.A. (People's Dispensary for Sick Animals) and I have well over three hundred thousand Busy Bees, most of them hard at work doing something to help animals or birds.

I am very proud to be Head of this fine Society, and to be known as their Queen

9

Bee. We have our own little paper, *The Busy Bees News*, and there I give news each month and tell you what the members are doing. Our badge is yellow with a bee flying on it.

The address of our Hive Headquarters is—Busy Bees, 44 Palace Road,
Bromley, Kent.
(*If you want to join send 6d. postal order for badge and instructions*).

(2) **The Sunbeam Society** is the youth section of the National Institute for the

Blind, and it helps to raise funds for little Blind Children, and to provide special " Sunshine Homes " for them, so that they may be taught to do everything for themselves and be happy. Sunbeams do all kinds of things to help and some of my very warmest-hearted readers are among them. Our badge is the head of a blind child turned towards the rays of the sun.

The address of the Sunbeam Society is
Sunbeam Society
224 Gt. Portland St., London, W.1.

10

(*To join, send 1s. postal order for badge and instructions*).

(3) **The Famous Five Club.** This is a club for all lovers of the Famous Five Books,

who like to meet together and make little clubs of their own, run small libraries, and so on. All profits go to the little Children's Home that I help to run in Beaconsfield, and it is to F.F. members that we owe such things as new beds, cots, prams, chairs, toys, birthday presents, a paddling pool and so on. Our headquarters is in my magazine, and in each number I give our latest news. We have members in every part of the world, and all members are expected to go up and speak to anyone wearing our badge. It is blue, and has the heads of the Five on it.

The address of the Famous Five Club is: F. F. Club, St. Paul's House,
Warwick Square, London, E.C.4.
(*To join, send 1s. postal order and stamped addressed envelope for badge and instructions.*)

11

THE ENID BLYTON'S MAGAZINE CLUB

This is a club I run for all boys and girls who read my magazine. At first members did not have to pay for their badge, but then parents (and children too, of course) wrote in and said, " Why can't *we* have a special cause to help, as all the other clubs do. We don't mind paying for our badges, and doing all kinds of things to raise a bit of money—so let us have something to work for and the profits on the badges can go to our new cause." I asked my readers to choose what cause we should have—and the great majority chose the little Spastic Children, who, because of an accident at birth, often cannot run about or play or use their hands or speak. So *this* club, the Magazine Club, helps the tiny children in the Centre for Spastic Children in Chelsea, London, for which (as some of you may remember), I broad-

12

cast one Sunday evening in the Week's Good Cause. We now have about 400,000 members and the good work they do in raising money to help these small afflicted children is beyond praise.

Our badge is red and gold. We hold many competitions for this club in my magazine, and every month one birthday child wins a beautiful Birthday Cake with his or her name and our badge on it in coloured sugar.

To join, all you have to do is to collect and cut out six of the coupons different numbers of my magazine, and send these in, with the enrolment form there, together with a 1/- postal order and 2½d. stamp to *Enid Blyton's Magazine Club*, Montague House, Russell Square, London, W.C.1. I do hope you will join.

SPECIAL NOTE: Do not write to me for the badges as I do not keep them at my home—write to the addresses given.

13

Title page and pages 9 to 13 from *Enid Blyton Diary* giving information in brief about her Fan Clubs whose meeting place was in The Enid Blyton Magazine itself. Published by W.M. Collins & Co. Ltd, London, 1957. © British Library Board (SM: p.p. 2466.k cover + 5 pages).

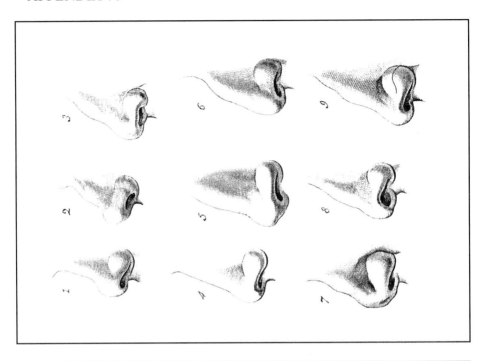

370

FRAGMENT FIFTH.

ADDITION D.

NINE NOSES, SHADED, IN PROFILE.

Neither does any one of thefe indicate, entirely, clear and found rea-
foning powers. You could except at moſt 4 and 5, and yet they too
afford matter of criticiſm. 4. Is good and honeſt, but to expreſs judgment properly ſo called, it is rather too much ſhortened, the wing is
too rounded, and not ſufficiently ſhaded—a fault with which I likewiſe
charge every noſe of this plate. The extremity of 5 is diſtinguiſhed
above the reſt by its character of force, which implies much penetra-
tion and wiſdom, a refolute mind and manly vigor.

1. Is deſtitute of every fpecies of delicate ſentiment, but I do not
think he wants malice.

2. The caricature of a noſe which fuppoſes good fenſe, and nothing more.

3. Naturally timid, he merits conſideration only for his love of order and propriety.

I will ſay as much of 6, in which I diſcern, at the fame time, a tint
of voluptuouſneſs.

7. Abandons himſelf to groſs brutality.

In 8 this expreſſion is ſomewhat modified by a fund of good-nature.

9. Deviates from truth: the contour of the upper part, and that of
the wing, are abſolutely defective. I queſ-
tion whether the Defigner copied after nature.

SEE CAPTION OR EXPLANATION PAGE 335

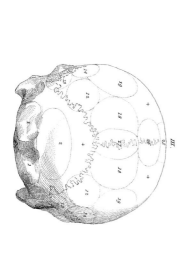

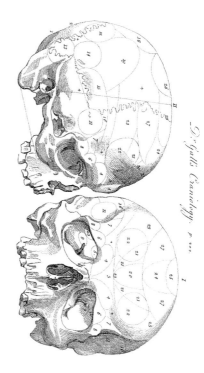

Dr Gall's Craniology. p. 201.

GUIDE TO UNDERSTANDING THE MATERIAL ON THESE PAGES

Fig. I - the number at the top of the skull - shows a front view.
Fig. II shows a side view.
Fig. III, a back view.

The numbers in the list below refer to the numbers in the different views. Example: No. 1, the organ of lust, is located at the bottom of the back view (Fig. III) and, at the back, near the bottom, of the side view (Fig. II) and so on.

Organs of Dr. Gall's System of Craniology*

Nos.

1. The organ of lust or of mutual instinct of both sexes. Fig. II. III.
2. The organ of a person's love for his children, or of an animal for his young ones. Fig. II. III.
3. The organ of being tractable in education, memoria realis. Fig. I. II.
4. The organ of finding, and remembering places. Fig. I. II.
5. The organ of recollecting persons (in the eye-hole.) Fig. I. II.
6. The organ of recollecting and comparing colours. Fig. I. II.
7. The organ of music. Fig. I. II.
8. The organ of arithmetic. Fig. I. II.
9. The organ of finding and remembering words (in the eye-hole.) Fig I
10. The organ of language (in the eye-hole) Fig. I.
11. The organ of mechanical arts. Fig. I. II.
12. The organ of friendship and attachment. Fig. II. III.
13. The organ of fighting. Fig. II. III.
14. The organ of murder. Fig. II. III.
15. The organ of cunning. Fig. II.
16. The organ of thieving. Fig. I. II.
17. The organ of highness. Fig. III.
18. The organ of thirst for glory, and that of vanity. Fig. III.
19. The organ of reflection. Fig. II. III.
20. The organ of comparing judgment. Fig. I. II.
21. The organ of philosophical judgment (includes No. 20) Fig. I. II.
22. The organ of wit. Fig. I. II.
23. The organ of the power of induction (includes the organs Nos. 20, 21 and 22.) Fig. I. II.
24. The organ of being good-natured. Fig. I. II.
25. The organ of theosophy. Fig. I. II. III.
26. The organ of constancy. Fig. II. III.
27. The organ of representation (includes No. 24) Fig. I. II. + are places not marked.

* Reconstructed from page 213 of the Medical and Physical Journal, Vol XV, Richard Phillips, 1806

SEE CAPTION OR EXPLANATION PAGE 335

POWERS AND ORGANS OF THE MIND.

AFFECTIVE.

I.—*Propensities.*

No.
1. Amativeness.
2. Philoprogenitiveness.
3. Inhabitiveness.
4. Adhesiveness.
5. Combativeness.
6. Destructiveness.
7. Secretiveness.
8. Acquisitiveness.
9. Constructiveness.

II.—*Sentiments.*

10. Self-esteem.
11. Love of approbation.
12. Cautiousness.
13. Benevolence.
14. Veneration.
15. Firmness.
16. Conscientiousness.
17. Hope.
18. Marvellousness.
19. Ideality.
20. Mirthfulness or gayness.
21. Imitation.

INTELLECTUAL.

I.—*Perceptive.*

No.
22. Individuality.
23. Configuration.
24. Size.
25. Weight and resistance.
26. Colouring.
27. Locality.
28. Calculation.
29. Order.
30. Eventuality.
31. Time.
32. Melody.
33. Language.

II.—*Reflective.*

34. Comparison.
35. Causality.

FRONTISPIECE

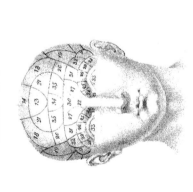

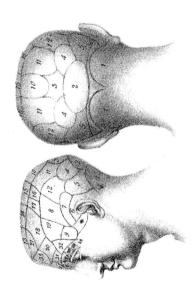

SEE CAPTION OR EXPLANATION PAGE 335

THE COMPANIES ACT, 1948

COMPANY LIMITED BY SHARES

MEMORANDUM OF ASSOCIATION

- of -

DARRELL WATERS LIMITED

1.   The name of the Company is "DARRELL WATERS LIMITED."

2.   The registered office of the Company will be situate in England.

*3.   The objects for which the company is established are:

(A)   (i)   To purchase or otherwise acquire and to hold, develop, turn to account, and dispose of and deal with real and personal property, assets and rights of all kinds and any interests therein and in particular, but without limiting the generality of the foregoing, rights of copyright in literary, dramatic, musical or pictorial works, scripts, film, motion picture, television and performing rights.

(ii)   To enter into engagements with authors, artists, printers, publishers, distributors and other persons, and to reimburse any such person by a salary or a royalty, or share of profits, or a salary varying with profits, or otherwise.

(iii)   To carry on the business of printers, publishers, distributors and proprietors of newspapers, magazines and periodicals.

(iv)   To carry on business of literary and dramatic agents.

(v)   To carry on the business of an investment and holding company and to invest and deal in property and in shares, stocks, debentures and securities of any kind issued or guaranteed by any body of whatever nature and wheresoever constituted or carrying on business.

---

*   The objects of the company were altered by Special Resolution on 7th April 1987

SEE CAPTION OR EXPLANATION PAGE 336

Fraudulent Mediums Act 1951

1951 CHAPTER 33 14 and 15 Geo 6

An Act to repeal the Witchcraft Act 1735, and to make, in substitution for certain provisions of section four of the Vagrancy Act 1824, express provision for the punishment of persons who fraudulently purport to act as spiritualistic mediums or to exercise powers of telepathy, clairvoyance or other similar powers.

[22nd June 1951]

1 Punishment of fraudulent mediums, &c.

(1) Subject to the provisions of this section, any person who—

(a) With intent to deceive purports to act as a spiritualistic medium or to exercise any powers of telepathy, clairvoyance or other similar powers, or

(b) In purporting to act as a spiritualistic medium or to exercise such powers as aforesaid, uses any fraudulent device, shall be guilty of an offence.

(2) A person shall not be convicted of an offence under the foregoing subsection unless it is proved that he acted for reward; and for the purposes of this section a person shall be deemed to act for reward if any money is paid, or other valuable thing given, in respect of what he does, whether to him or to any other person.

(3) A person guilty of an offence under this section shall be liable on summary conviction to a fine not exceeding fifty pounds or to imprisonment for a term not exceeding four months or to both such fine and such imprisonment, or on conviction on indictment to a fine not exceeding five hundred pounds or to imprisonment for a term not exceeding two years or to both such fine and such imprisonment.

(4) No proceedings for an offence under this section shall be brought in England or Wales except by or with the consent of the Director of Public Prosecutions.

(5) Nothing in subsection (1) of this section shall apply to anything done solely for the purpose of entertainment.

SEE CAPTION OR EXPLANATION PAGE 337

ENID: THE NATURALIST

CAPTIONS FOR APPENDICES 2 – 12

APPENDIX 2: A full page in *The Teachers World*, April 15, 1925 edition, showing the first in a series of fortnightly nature lessons for children. The illustrations are Enid Blyton's first demonstration of her drawing skills. Notice her initials E.B, bottom, left, in the frame of the illustration of 'Gorse'. Image restoration credit: 2graphic Photo Restoration. Website: www.photo-restoration.co.uk

APPENDIX 3: A full page in *The Teachers World*, July 15, 1925 edition, showing Enid Blyton's syllabus covering one year's nature lessons for children (third column, bottom). On this page can be seen the type of advice *The Teachers World* often gave teachers to help them to draw up their syllabuses or timetables. Image restoration credit: 2graphic Photo Restoration. Website: www.photo-restoration.co.uk

APPENDIX 4: This lesson, 'Big Crabs and Little Crabs' marks the resumption of the series of nature lessons, after the syllabus shown in Appendix 3 came to an end August 18, 1926 (September 1, 1926 edition). Image restoration credit: 2graphic Photo Restoration. Website: www.photo-restoration.co.uk

APPENDIX 5: A sample reading from Enid Blyton's 'Nature Notes' as it appeared in Volume I, Section III of her three-volume *The Teachers' Treasury* – a teaching book she wrote in 1926 for teachers. © The British Library Board (SM: X25/3694 vol. 1, Section III).
Image restoration credit: 2graphic Photo Restoration. Website: www. photo-restoration.co.uk

APPENDIX 6: 'The 20 Teaching Features', August 29, 1934 edition. Enid Blyton's forthcoming contribution, 'Hedgerow Tales: A Novel

Nature Study Course', is announced in Column 1, No. 12. Image restoration credit: 2graphic Photo Restoration. Website: www.photo-restoration.co.uk

APPENDIX 7: Enid Blyton's 'Time Table of the Syllabus' for 'Hedgerow Tales – A Year's Course in Nature Study', August 29, 1934 edition. Image restoration credit: 2graphic Photo Restoration. Website: www.photo-restoration.co.uk

APPENDIX 8: 'Rabbity Ways', the first lesson of 'Hedgerow Tales', the 'Novel Nature Study Course', published in *The Teachers World,* September 5, 1934 edition. Image restoration credit: 2graphic Photo Restoration. Website: www.photo-restoration.co.uk

APPENDIX 9: Sample reading from Enid Blyton's 'Nature Notes' for April, drawn from the Nature Section of *Enid Blyton's Book of the Year,* 1950 edition. © British Library Board (SM: 12831.dd.3, nature section). Image restoration credit: 2graphic Photo Restoration. Website: www.photo-restoration.co.uk

APPENDIX 10: This list of exactly one hundred flowers, compiled by Enid Blyton, is drawn from *Enid Blyton's Nature Lover's Book.* © British Library Board (SM: 7008.bb.3. page 6). Image restoration credit: 2graphic Photo Restoration. Website: www.photo-restoration.co.uk

APPENDIX 11: A sample reading from 'The Swallows in the Barn', the first story in book No. 22 in the series of Nature Readers. Among the basic facts of nature Enid Blyton wrapped up in this story is the migration of birds. © British Library Board (SM: 07001.a.2.). Image restoration credit: 2graphic Photo Restoration. Website: www.photo-restoration.co.uk

APPENDIX 12: A list of the 36 Nature Readers in the series. Inset, top right, the standard cover appearing on every book in the series. Source: The inside back cover of one of the Nature Readers published by Macmillan & Co. Ltd (1945 – 1946) and reconstructed for this list. Image restoration credit: 2graphic Photo Restoration Website: www.photo-restoration.co.uk

ENID: THE POET

CAPTIONS FOR APPENDICES 13 – 20

APPENDIX 13: This poem, illustrated by Phyllis Chase, is a facsimile reproduction of the first in a series of nature poems Enid wrote for *The Teachers World* (edition March 2, 1923, page 1143). Image restoration credit: 2graphic Photo Restoration. Website: www.photo-restoration. co.uk

APPENDIX 14: Enid Blyton wrote this poem for the Empire Day celebrations no longer observed in England. Here we can see Phyllis Chase's artistry, once again, in bringing to life scenes described in the poem (edition March 7, 1924, page 1191). Image restoration credit: 2graphic Photo Restoration. Website: www.photo-restoration.co.uk

APPENDIX 15: This poem is the sixth in a series of poems with animal themes Enid Blyton wrote for *The Teachers World*. Illustrations are by L.R. Brightwell (edition of July 3, 1925, page 731). Image restoration credit: 2graphic Photo Restoration. Website: www.photo-restoration. co.uk

APPENDIX 16: 'The Poplar Tree', one of twelve 'Poems of the Open Air', carried on page 162 of *Enid Blyton's Nature Lover's Book*. The illustration of the poplar tree is culled from another section of the book. © British Library Board (SM: 7008.bb.3, page 162).
Image restoration credit: 2graphic Photo Restoration. Website: www. photo-restoration.co.uk

APPENDIX 17: Left, The cover of the first edition of *Enid Blyton's Sunny Stories Calendar* for the year 1942 and Right, the first month. The calendar was published every year until 1951when it ceased publication. The total number of poems in the series is 98. © British

Library Board (SM: 12805.1.56, cover and first page). Image restoration credit: 2graphic Photo Restoration. Website: www.photo-restoration. co.uk

APPENDIX 18: 'The Helmsman', a poem Enid Blyton wrote to mark the Silver Jubilee celebrations of the then King George V. *The Teachers World* Junior edition carried it on the front cover, edition May 1, 1935, as can be seen in this illustration. Image restoration credit: 2graphic Photo Restoration. Website: www.photo-restoration.co.uk

APPENDIX 20: 'April Day', Enid Blyton's last known poem, published on page 185 in the Appendices of Barbara Stoney's *Enid Blyton: A Biography*. Courtesy Bob Stoney.

ENID: THE COLUMNIST & FEATURE WRITER

CAPTIONS FOR APPENDICES 21 – 39

APPENDIX 21: One of the front covers of *The Teachers World*, edition February 24, 1926, showing the type of material carried in the newspaper. Image restoration credit: 2graphic Photo Restoration. Website: www.photo-restoration.co.uk

APPENDIX 22: Enid Blyton's first article in her column, 'From My Window'*,* third column, published in the edition of July 4, 1923. She held this column for over four years. Image restoration credit: 2graphic Photo Restoration. Website: www.photo-restoration.co.uk

APPENDIX 23: 'Green And Blue', Enid Blyton's last article in her column 'From My Window' published in the edition of August 24, 1927. It was replaced with 'Enid Blyton's Letter to Children' the following week before its transformation into a 'Children's Page'. Image restoration credit: 2graphic Photo Restoration. Website: www. photo-restoration.co.uk

APPENDIX 24: A full page in *The Teachers World,* September 4, 1929 edition, showing Enid Blyton's first 'Children's Page'. Here she's seen sitting on the grass with some of her pets. Her 'Letter To Boys And Girls' that replaced her column, 'From My Window', became a prominent feature in the new 'Children's Page'. Image restoration credit: 2graphic Photo Restoration. Website: www.photo-restoration. co.uk

APPENDIX 25: Bottom half of a full page showing one of Enid Blyton's 'A Letter from Bobs', as it appeared in the edition of May 1, 1940. From reading this supposed letter we can see why they fascinated children since she began publishing them in her 'Children's

Page'. Image restoration credit: 2graphic Photo Restoration. Website: www.photo-restoration.co.uk

APPENDIX 26: A full page showing Enid Blyton's first Friday Afternoon Story, 'Peronel and His Pot of Glue' in the edition of February 15, 1922. This was her first story ever to be published in *The Teachers World*. The page was shared with other contributors before it was eventually phased out. Image restoration credit: 2graphic Photo Restoration. Website: www.photo-restoration.co.uk

APPENDIX 27: A reproduction of the Board of Education's *Handbook of Suggestions* that gave rise to two Modern Teaching books Enid Blyton edited and to her 'Stories of World History' that were serialised in *The Teachers World* (see *Enid: The Editor*, Chapter IV and *Enid: The Columnist & Feature Writer*, Chapter III, for details.). © British Library Board (SM: B.S.10/52. (5.), title page, prefatory note).

APPENDIX 28: A full page illustration of the first story in the series of 'Stories of World History' Enid Blyton ran in *The Teachers World* from August 31, 1927 to August 22, 1928. The name was changed to 'Tales of Romance' after the end of the first year, to renew the syllabus. The entire History course ended August 28, 1929. Image restoration credit: 2graphic Photo Restoration. Website: www.photo-restoration.co.uk

APPENDIX 29: Illustration of 'NOTES FOR THE TEACHER', third column, which Enid Blyton prepared at the end of some of the episodes of 'Stories of World History' to prepare teachers for questions children were likely to ask after listening to the stories in the classrooms. The rest of the page shows the continuation of the first episode, as shown in Appendix 28. Image restoration credit: 2graphic Photo Restoration. Website: www.photo-restoration.co.uk

APPENDIX 30: A full page showing Enid Blyton's syllabus, third column, for the entire History course she ran in *The Teachers World,* October 5, 1927 edition, from August 31, 1927 to August 28, 1929. The page also shows courses by other contributors in Arithmetic and English. Image restoration credit: 2graphic Photo Restoration. Website: www.photo-restoration.co.uk

APPENDIX 31: A full page showing the first episode of 'King Arthur & The Knights of the Round Table' in the edition of August

29, 1928. Enid Blyton narrated 15 episodes, each between 1,500 and 2,000 words, of this legend in her Weekly Page from August 29, 1928 to December 5, 1928. Image restoration credit: 2graphic Photo Restoration. Website: www.photo-restoration.co.uk

APPENDIX 32: A full page showing the sixth episode, 'A Roland for an Oliver', of 'King Charlemagne and the Paladins of France' in the edition of January 16, 1929. Enid Blyton narrated 18 episodes of this story in her Weekly Page from Dec 12, 1928 to April 10, 1929. Image restoration credit: 2graphic Photo Restoration. Website: www.photo-restoration.co.uk

APPENDIX 33: A full page showing the first episode, 'The Siege of the Castle of Aiguillon', Enid Blyton retold from Froissart's *Chronicles* in the series of 'Stories of Chivalry in the Fourteenth Century' carried in *The Teachers World* edition April 24, 1929. Fourteen more episodes followed until June 26, 1929 when the stories came to an end. Image restoration credit: 2graphic Photo Restoration. Website: www.photo-restoration.co.uk

APPENDIX 34: A full page showing the first episode of 'The Beginning of the Adventure of the Red Cross Knight' from book I of Spencer's 'Faerie Queene' carried in *The Teachers World* (edition July 10, 1929). Enid narrated seven episodes from this book, in her own words, from July 10, 1929 to August 28, 1929. Image restoration credit: 2graphic Photo Restoration. Website: www.photo-restoration.co.uk

APPENDIX 35: A part of a full page in the *The Teachers World And Schoolmistress,* edition of September 4, 1935, showing a programme of teaching features. Here we can see a list of the names of the historical characters for whom Enid Blyton was commissioned to write biographical sketches in the form of stories. I've added to this list the 12 other names to make it 32 historical characters in all. Image restoration credit: 2graphic Photo Restoration. Website: www.photo-restoration.co.uk

APPENDIX 36: A full page in *The Teachers World And Schoolmistress*, edition of September 4, 1935, showing the first story, 'King Alfred's Mother', in the series of 32 stories of Historical Characters which came to an end December 16, 1936. Image restoration credit: 2graphic

Photo Restoration: www.photo-restoration.co.uk

APPENDIX 37: Left, the second story, 'Lost – A Robin Called Sing-A-Song' in the new series of monthly stories for the year 1926, carried in *The Teachers World,* Feb 5, 1926 edition. Right, a list of all the stories in the series. Image restoration credit: 2graphic Photo Restoration. Website: www.photo-restoration.co.uk

APPENDIX 38: 'The Months', the first in a series of feature articles Enid Blyton wrote for *The Teachers World* (January 11, 1929 edition). Image restoration credit: 2graphic Photo Restoration. Website: www. photo-restoration.co.uk

APPENDIX 39: Enid Blyton's farewell letter to her fans, carried in the second section of the page in the second column, second paragraph, under Green Hedges. Notice how it is tucked in this second paragraph, as a passing remark, instead of being the focus of attention. Notice also that 'Bobs' her fox terrier, had also 'written' a farewell letter to his fans in the third column, top. (*Teachers World And the Schoolmistress* edition of November 14, 1945.)

Image restoration credit: 2graphic Photo Restoration. Website: www. photo-restoration.co.uk.

ENID: THE UNIVERSAL TEACHER

CAPTIONS FOR APPENDICES 40 - 43

APPENDIX 40: A list of the 30 readers in 'Enid Blyton Pennant Series'. Inset, top right, one of the book covers in another series, namely, Enid Blyton Readers (No 8). Source: the inside back cover of one of the readers published by Macmillan & Co Ltd in 1950.
Image restoration credit: 2graphic Photo Restoration. Website: www. photo-restoration.co.uk

APPENDIX 41: Title page of Enid Blyton's *The Teacher's Treasury*. The words 'Edited by Enid Blyton' are misleading. Apart from two sections dealing with poetry and handiwork which she did edit, she has written everything else in the book. The letters after her name, N.F.U. stand for National Froebel Union, the name of the organisation that awarded her the certificate to teach. © British Library Board (SM: 08310.i.31 title page).

APPENDIX 42: A full page advertisement carried in *The Teachers World* in the edition of April 14, 1926 for Enid Blyton's *The Teachers' Treasury*. The contents of the three volumes are summarised under the heading: WHAT THE WORK CONTAINS.
Image restoration credit: 2graphic Photo Restoration. Website: www. photo-restoration.co.uk

APPENDIX 43: Professor T.P. Nunn's introduction to Enid Blyton's *The Teachers' Treasury*. At that time, he was Professor of Education at the University of London. This introduction is proof that the volumes had been written, not edited, by Enid Blyton (see again title page illustration, Appendix 41). © British Library Board (SM: 08310.i.31 introduction).

ENID: THE PROLIFIC SONGWRITER

CAPTIONS FOR APPENDICES 44 - 53

APPENDIX 44: First part of the score for 'The Trees', one of a batch of eight songs in Enid's first songbook, *Responsive Singing Games*, published in 1923 by J Saville & Co Ltd. © British Library Board (SM: Music Collections VOC/1923/Blyton/ page 7).

APPENDIX 45: Left, part of the score for 'Little Lambkin', one of the 45 songs Enid Blyton wrote specially for *Two Years in the Infant School*, a teaching book whose preparation for publication she supervised. Right, 'Pop Goes the Weasel!', a traditional song that was also in the book. Cecil Sharman arranged the music for both songs. © British Library Board (SM (X24/1058, pages 176 and 219).

APPENDIX 46: This Table gives details of Enid Blyton's songbooks containing songs for 'unison singing' (I) and songs based on poems drawn from her poetry books and *Child Education* (II).

APPENDIX 47: Left, first part of the score for 'The Singer In The Night' that Novello & Co published in the *School Music Review* in the edition of November 15, 1925. Right, her poem from *Punch* on which the song is based. The poem was later reproduced in *The Enid Blyton Poetry Book*. Note: Novello & Co states that the company has no record of this poem in its repertoire.

APPENDIX 48: Table II showing Miscellaneous Songs and Songbooks as follows: songs published in *The Enid Blyton's Book of the Year*, *The Teachers' Treasury* and Noddy songbooks.

APPENDIX 48 A: Table III gives details of 'Sheet Music' whose words have been written by Enid Blyton. The songs are based on poems published in her poetry books, as shown.

Table IV gives details of songs Enid Blyton wrote specially for her musical plays for schools and the theatre.

APPENDIX 50: The complete score for 'The Union Jack', a patriotic song Enid Blyton wrote for the Empire Day celebrations that were observed in Public Elementary Schools in the early 1900s. From *The Teachers World Music Supplement*, edition April 29, 1925. Music by Edgar May. Image restoration credit: 2graphic Photo Restoration. Website: www.photo-restoration.co.uk

APPENDIX 51: One of two pages of the score for 'Shepherd Song: A New Carol' as it appeared in *The Teachers World,* edition of November 7, 1924. (See Table V for list of other Christmas carols and the publications that carried them.) Image restoration credit: 2graphic Photo Restoration. Website: www.photo-restoration.co.uk.

APPENDIX 52: Table V gives details of 'Christmas Carols' whose words have been written by Enid Blyton. Table VI gives details of 'Singing Games', 'Patriotic Songs' and 'Songs for Infants' written by Enid Blyton.

Appendix 53: 'The Shepherd King', one of Enid Blyton's Christmas Carols that made it on the front cover of *The Teachers World*, in the Senior School Edition of December 18, 1929. It is not known if it had been set to music. Image restoration credit: 2graphic Photo Restoration. Website: www.photo-restoration.co.uk

ENID: THE PROFESSIONAL STORYTELLER

CAPTIONS FOR APPENDICES 54 - 57

APPENDIX 54: Left, The inside cover of one of the 'Parts' of *The Children's Encyclopedia*. Right, the plan of the encyclopedia. When Enid Blyton was about twelve years old she read this encyclopedia from cover to cover and then read it all over again (see *Enid: The Professional Storyteller*, Chapter VII for development of this theme). © British Library Board (SM: W6/1224 cover, page 1).

APPENDIX 55: A brief extract from *The Secret Commonwealth of Elves, Fauns and Fairie*s by Robert Kirk, describing the nature and characteristics of fairies. © British Library Board (SM: L.P.12202. FF.1 extract).

APPENDIX 56: Left, title page of 'Part Second' of the *Mystery of Edwin Drood*. Right, first page of the 'Author's Preface', written by the spirit pen of Charles Dickens through the medium T.P. James. © The British Library Board (SM 012614.dd.40).

APPENDIX 57: Top, A description of some of the branches of clairvoyance, drawn from various sources.

ENID: THE PLAYWRIGHT

CAPTIONS FOR APPENDICES 58 – 64

APPENDIX 58: TABLE 1. A list of Enid Blyton's straight plays published in books between 1927 and 1941.

APPENDIX 59: A full page in *The Teachers World* edition of November 26, 1924, showing Enid Blyton's play: 'King Cole Calling!'. Image restoration credit: 2graphic Photo Restoration. Website: www.photo-restoration.co.uk

APPENDIX 60, A full page of *The Teachers World & Schoolmistress* edition of October 23, 1935 showing a review of 'Six Enid Blyton Plays' in the first column. The other two columns give an idea of the type of material the newspaper carried from time to time. Image restoration credit: 2graphic Photo Restoration. Website: www.photo-restoration.co.uk

APPENDIX 61: A full page advertisement carried in January's issue of *Child Education*, to promote *The Play's The Thing!* Enid Blyton's first book of musical plays. Image restoration credit: 2graphic Photo Restoration. Website: www.photo-restoration.co.uk

APPENDIX 62: Synopsis of 'The King's Pocket Knife', one of the twelve musical plays in 'The Play's The Thing!' published in 1927 by The Home Library Book Co. Ltd, a division of George Newnes Ltd. A sketch of the costumes in this play can be seen in Figure 20.

APPENDIX 64: A full page advertisement in *The Enid Blyton's Magazine,* issue of December 7, 1955, showing how Enid Blyton's two plays, 'Noddy in Toyland' and 'The Famous Five' were promoted. Right, a synopsis of scenes from 'Noddy in Toyland'. Inset, front cover of *Noddy in Toyland*, the book form of the play. Image restoration credit: 2graphic Photo Restoration. Website: www.photo-restoration. co.uk

ENID: THE PASSIONATE GARDENER

CAPTIONS FOR APPENDICES 65 AND 66

APPENDIX 65: Enid Blyton's syllabus for her 'Seasonal Nature Study & Gardening Course' in *The Teachers World*. The course ran for one year from September 1932 to August 1933. This is another example of her talent for teaching, through the medium of her pen. Image restoration credit: 2graphic Photo Restoration. Website: www. photo-restoration.co.uk

APPENDIX 66: A lesson on germination, one of the 48 lessons in 'Round the Year with Enid Blyton' published in *The Teachers World* between September 1932 and August 1933. Notice her initials [EB] in the corner of the main illustration (see *Enid: The Artist & Illustrator*, Chapter IX, for details). Image restoration credit: 2graphic Photo Restoration. Website: www.photo-restoration.co.uk

THE SUNNY STORIES MAGAZINE – A PHENOMINAL SUCCESS

CAPTIONS FOR APPENDICES 67 AND 68

APPENDIX 67: A Letter to Boys & Girls, from the new series of *Sunny Stories* published in the issue of June, 1952, showing the popularity of her Sunny Stories overseas. © British Library Board (SM: 12814.d). Image restoration credit: 2graphic Photo Restoration. Website: www. photo-restoration.co.uk

APPENDIX 68: A letter from the editor introducing a photo of Marion Crawford in the background, the woman who took over from Enid Blyton when she withdrew from the *Sunny Stories* magazine with no explanation to her devoted fans (Volume 558, March 24, 1953). (See *The Sunny Stories Magazine – A Phenomenal Success*, Section II for details.) © British Library Board (SM: 12814.d).
Image restoration credit: 2graphic Photo Restoration. Website: www. photo-restoration.co.uk

PHYSIOGNOMY & PHRENOLOGY

CAPTIONS FOR APPENDICES 70 - 72

APPENDIX 70: Two pages from Lavater's *Essays on Physiognomy* showing drawings of nine noses, right, with a description of the characteristics of their owners, left. According to Lavater, the straight outline of nose No. 4 could be that of an honest person.
(KEY to reading some of the words in the text: Replace the letter 'f' with 's'. Example: 'thefe' should be 'these'. This was a style of printing in the 18th century.) Reproduced with the kind permission of Camden Libraries.

APPENDIX 71: A map of the surface of the skull in three views showing the location of the 27 organs Dr Gall discovered. Right, description of the organs, each of which is linked to a protuberance or bump on the head. Source: The Medical & Physical Journal, Vol. XV, March, 1806, No. 85, Page 213. Courtesy Welcome Trust, 183 Euston Road, Euston, London, NW1 2BE.

APPENDIX 72: Left: The Frontispiece from Dr. Spurzheim's book on phrenology showing three views of the surface of the head where the organs or powers of the mind are located. An elevation or bump in any of the numbered parts indicates the possession of a faculty. Right: A list of faculties or powers of the mind. It was Dr Spurzheim who refined Dr Gall's organology, changed the names of the faculties, as shown above, right, and renamed it phrenology. His book *Phrenology or the Doctrine of the Mind*, published by Treuttel, Wurtz & Richter, London, 1833, was regarded as a textbook on the subject. Reproduced with permission from Camden Libraries.

BRIEF HISTORY OF DARRELL WATERS LTD

CAPTION FOR APPENDIX 73

APPENDIX 73: The first page of Darrell Waters's Memorandum of Association setting out the main objectives of the company. From this we can see that the objectives of the company went far beyond the mere management of Enid Blyton's business affairs. Source: Companies House. Licence to publish this docmment is granted by the National Archives on behalf of Companies House. Web Link: https://www.nationalarchives.gov.uk/doc/open-government-licence/version/3/

CLAIRVOYANCE

CAPTION FOR APPENDIX 74

APPENDIX 74: A copy of the Fraudulent Mediums Act of 1951 that gives clairvoyants the green light to practice clairvoyance provided it is done in good faith, for no reward and for entertainment purposes only. Source: National Archives. Link: www.nationalarchives/legislation. gov.uk/fraudulent mediums act 1951.

BIBLIOGRAPHY

FOREWORD

The books written by Enid Blyton, carried hereunder, are those referred to in this book, with extensions. It is not a complete list. Such a list can be found in Tony Summerfield's *Enid Blyton: An Illustrated Bibliography* in four parts, published by Milford Books, 2002.

NATURE BOOKS

ENID: THE NATURALIST

The Zoo Book, illustrated (62 pages)	George Newnes, 1924
The Bird Book, richly illustrated (124 pages)	George Newnes, 1926
The Animal Book, illustrated (124 pages)	George Newnes, 1927
Enid Blyton's Nature Lessons (187 pages)	Evans Brothers, 1929
Animals At Home, illustrated (62 pages)	W & K Johnson, 1935
Birds At Home, illustrated (62 pages)	W & K Johnson, 1935
Birds of Our Gardens, illustrated (160 pages)	George Newnes, 1940
Enid Blyton's Book Of The Year	Evans Brothers, 1941
Enid Blyton's Nature Lover's Book	Evans Brothers, 1944
Rambles with Uncle Nat	National Magazine Co, 1947

Enid Blyton's Animal Lover's Book, illustrated (224 pages)	Macmillan & Co, 1952
Hedgerow Tales, illustrated, (178 pages)	Methuen, 1935
My First, Second, Third etc, Nature Books (Republished as storybooks from *Enid Blyton Nature Readers).*	Macmillan & Co, 1952
L.J.F. Brimble, B.Sc. F.L.S.	Macmillan & Co, 1950
Stories & Notes to Enid Blyton Nature Plates:	
L.J.F. Brimble, B.Sc. F.L.S.	Macmillan & Co, 1949
A Reference Book to Enid Blyton Nature Readers:	

ENID: THE PASSIONATE GARDENER

The Children's Garden, illustrated (256 pages)	George Newnes, 1935
Let's Garden, illustrated (207 pages)	Latimer House, 1948
Round the Year with Enid Blyton (4 volumes)	Evans Brothers, 1934
Round the Year with Enid Blyton (New edition, combining the four volumes.)	Evans Brothers, 1950

POETRY BOOKS

ENID: THE POET

Child Whispers (28 poems)	J Saville & Co, 1922
Real Fairies (33 poems)	J Saville & Co, 1923
Silver & Gold (30 poems)	Thomas Nelson & Sons, 1925
The Enid Blyton Poetry Book (96 poems)	Methuen & Co, 1934
Noddy's Own Nursery Rhymes (25 verses)	Samson Low, 1958

BOOKS CONTAINING ENID BLYTON'S POEMS

Enid Blyton Book of Fairies (13 poems)   George Newnes, 1924
Fairy Tales (12 poems)   Birn Brothers, 1926
The Teachers' Treasury, Vol. II
(10 poems)   Evans Brothers, 1926
My First Reading Book (30 poems)   Birn Brothers, 1933
Read to Us (14 poems)   Birn Brothers, 1933
Enid Blyton's Book of the Year
(52 poems)   Evans Brothers, 1941
Enid Blyton's Nature Lover's Book
(12 poems)   Evans Brothers, 1944
Enid Blyton's Marigold St. Book
(8 poems)   John Gifford, 1954
Enid Blyton's Foxglove St. Book
(8 poems)   John Gifford, 1955
*The Enid Blyton's Treasury of
Verse*, a collection of Enid Blyton's
own poems (110 poems)   Purnell Books, 1979

SCHOOL STORY BOOKS

First Term at Malory Towers
(153 pages)   Methuen, 1946
Second Form at Malory Towers
(151 pages)   Methuen, 1947
Third Year at Malory Towers
(159 pages)   Methuen, 1948
Upper Fourth at Malory Towers
(147 pages)   Methuen, 1949
In The Fifth at Malory Towers
(146 pages)   Methuen, 1950
Last Term at Malory Towers
(50 pages)   Methuen, 1951

The Twins at St Clare's	
(217 pages)	Methuen, 1941
The O'Sullivan Twins	
(185 pages)	Methuen, 1942
Summer Term at St Clare's	
(153 pages)	Methuen, 1943
Second Form at St Clare's	
(157 pages)	Methuen, 1944
Claudine at St Clare's	
(153 pages)	Methuen, 1944
Fifth Formers at St Clare's	
(162 pages)	Methuen, 1945

OTHER SCHOOL STORY BOOKS

The Naughtiest Girl in the School	George Newnes, 1940
The Naughtiest Girl Again	George Newnes, 1942
The Naughtiest Girl is a Monitor	George Newnes, 1945
Here's The Naughtiest Girl	Hodder Children's Books, 1997

COMPILATION OF ENID BLYTON'S SCHOOL STORIES

A Treasury of Enid Blyton's School Stories (Compiled by Mary Cadogan & Norman Wright.)	Hodder Children's Books, 2002

SONGBOOKS

ENID: THE PROLIFIC SONGWRITER

Responsive Singing Games	(8 songs)	J. Saville & Co, 1923
Songs Of Gladness	(9 songs)	J. Saville & Co, 1924
Autumn Days	(6 songs)	Novello & Co, 1926

Round The Year Songs	(12 songs)	Novello & Co, 1930
Ten Songs from Child Whispers	(10 songs)	J. Saville & Co, 1930
Songs of Summer	(3 songs)	Oxford University Press, 1934
Snowy Days	(6 songs)	Novello & Co, 1934
Four Unison Songs (1 by B. Hardy)	(3 songs)	York Bank & Sons, 1935
Songs For Infants	(11 songs)	E. J. Arnold & Sons, 1949
Mixed Bag	(6 songs)	Bosey & Hawkes, 1965
Enid Blyton's Noddy Song Book	(12 songs)	G. Ricordi & Co, 1952
Happy Year Song Book	(12 songs)	J. B. Cramer, 1956
Enid Blyton's New Noddy Song Book	(8 songs)	A. H. & Crew, 1959

BOOKS CONTAINING ENID BLYTON'S SONGS

The Teachers' Treasury, Volume II   (20 songs, 10 singing games)
The Play's The Thing! Musical plays (69 songs)
How the Flower Grow (Sub-title for
The Blyton-Sharman Musical Plays) (40 songs)
Enid Blyton's Book of the Year   (12 songs)
Two Years in the Infant School   (43 songs)

BOOKS FOR TEACHERS

ENID: THE UNIVERSAL TEACHER

The Teachers' Treasury	Home Library Book Co, 1926
Enid Blyton's Book of the Year	Evans Brothers, 1941

BOOKS EDITED BY ENID BLYTON

ENID: THE EDITOR

Modern Teaching	George Newnes, 1928
Modern Teaching in the Infant School	George Newnes, 1932
Pictorial Knowledge	George Newnes, 1932
Birds of the Wayside and Woodland	Wayne Bros, 1936
Two Years in the Infant School	George Newnes, 1938
Daily Mail Annual	Daily Mail, 1944

BOOKS OF PLAYS

ENID: THE PLAYWRIGHT

The Play's The Thing! (12 plays)		The Home Library Book Co, 1927
(Reprinted as *Plays for Older Children* (6 plays) and *Plays for Younger Children* (6 plays)		George Newnes, 1940
Six Enid Blyton Plays		The Home Library Book Co, 1935
The Blyton-Sharman Musical Plays: (Published individually as follows:		
1. *How the Flowers Grow*		A. Wheaton, 1939
2. *The Fairy in the Box*		A. Wheaton, 1939
3. *The Magic Ball*		A. Wheaton, 1939
4. *The Toys at Night Time*		A. Wheaton, 1939
5. *Who Stole the Crown*		A. Wheaton, 1939
6. *Santa Clause Gets Busy*		A. Wheaton, 1939
Cameo Plays (Vol. 3)	(2 plays)	Arnold, 1939
The Wishing Bean & Other Plays	(6 plays)	Basil Blackwell, 1939
Six Plays for Schools		Basil Blackwell, 1939
*Finding the Ticket**	(1 play)	Evans Brothers, 1955
*Mr Sly One and the Cats**	(1 play)	Evans Brothers, 1955

| *The Mothers' Meeting** | (1 play) | Evans Brothers, 1955 |
| *Who Will Hold the Giant** | (1 play) | Evans Brothers, 1955 |

*These are reprints, in book form, of plays Evan Brothers published 1941 in *Enid Blyton's Book of the Year.*

MUSICAL STAGE PLAYS

| *Noddy in Toyland* | Premier at the Stoll Theatre, Dec, 1954 |
| *The Famous Five* | Premiers at the Prince Theatre, Dec, 1955 |

PLAYS FOR ADULTS

The Summer Storm   This play was never staged

BOOKS CONTAINING ENID BLYTON'S PLAYS

The Teacher's Treasury, 3 volumes (6 plays)	Evans Brothers, 1926
Enid Blyton's Book of the Year (12 plays)	Evans Brothers, 1941
Enid Blyton's Book of Her Famous Play Noddy in Toyland	Samson Low, 1956

RETOLD STORY BOOKS

ENID: THE PROFESSIONAL STORYTELLER

Old English Stories Retold (64 Pages)	Thomas Nelson & Sons, 1925
Aesop Fables Retold (64 pages)	Thomas Nelson & Sons, 1925
Tales of Robin Hood (128 pages)	George Newnes, 1930

The Knights of the Round Table	
(126 pages)	George Newnes, 1930
Heyo, Brer Rabbit! (128 pages)	George Newnes, 1938
The Baber Story Book (226 pages)	Methuen, 1941
The Land of the Far-Beyond (63 pages),	
from *The Pilgrim's Progress*	
by John Bunyan	Methuen, 1942
Tales from the Arabian Nights (94 pages)	Latimer House, 1951
Favourite Book of Fables, 4 stories	
(28 pages), from *La Fontaine's Fables*	William Collins, 1955
Tales of Brave Adventure	
(184 pages)	Dean & Son, 1963

RELIGIOUS BOOKS

The Children's Life of Christ,	
59 stories (191 pages)	Methuen, 1943
Tales from the Bible,	
31 stories (158 pages)	Methuen, 1944
Before I Go To Sleep	
35 stories & prayers (128 pages)	Latimer House, 1947
The Little Girl at Capernaum,	
1 story (64 pages)	Lutterworth, 1948
The Boy with the Loaves & Fishes,	
1 story (64 pages)	Lutterworth, 1948
The Enid Blyton Bible Stories	
Old Testament, 14 books	Macmillan, 1949
Reference Book to Old Testament	
Bible Plates (77 pages)	Macmillan, 1949
The Children's Book of Prayer	Muller, 1953
The Greatest Book in the World	Bible Society, 1954
The Enid Blyton Bible Stories New	
Testament, 14 books	Macmillan, 1954
New Testament Stories	Johnston & Bacon, 1955
Old Testament Stories	Johnston & Bacon, 1955

Enid Blyton Bible Stories
(94 pages) — Frederick Muller, 1955
Tales from the Bible (94 pages) — Frederick Muller, 1955
A Story Book of Jesus, 39 stories
(158 pages) — Macmillan, 1956

FAIRYTALE BOOKS

Adventures of the Wishing Chair	George Newnes 1937
The Enchanted Wood	George Newnes, 1939
The Adventures of Pip	Sampson Low, 1948
More Adventures of Pip	Sampson Low 1948
Enid Blyton Book of Fairies, 16 stories (128 pages)	George Newnes, 1924
Prinkity's Pranks & Other Nature Fairy Tales	Thomas Nelson &Sons, 1925
Enid Blyton Book of Brownies, 1 story (124 pages)	George Newnes, 1926
Fairy Tales, 12 poems (12 pages)	Birn Brothers, 1929
The Red Pixie Book, 17 stories (128 pages)	George Newnes, 1934
The Yellow Fairy Book, 1 story (123 pages)	George Newnes, 1936
Pippy & The Gnome, 7 stories 80 pages)	Pitkin, 1951
Pixie Tales	William Collins, 1966
Pixieland Story Book	William Collins, 1966
Brownie Tales	William Collins, 1968
Enid Blyton's Fairy Folk Story Book	Collins, 1966
Jinky & the Birds	E.J. Arnold, 1948
Jinky & the Animals	E.J. Arnold, 1948
Jinky & the Flowers	E.J. Arnold, 1948
Jinky & the Insects	E.J. Arnold, 1948

READING BOOKS

FROM ENID BLYTON'STORIES OF WORLD HISTORY

ENID: THE COLUMNIST

Tales of the Romans, Kingsway Supplementary Readers	Evans Brothers, 1934
Tales of the Ancient Greeks and Persians	Evans Brothers, 1934
The Story of the Siege of Troy	Evans Brothers, 1934
The Adventures of Odysseus	Evans Brothers, 1934

OTHER READING BOOKS

My First Reading Book (Simple verses for juniors.)	Birn Brothers, 1933
Let's Read, 5 stories	Birn Brothers, 1933
Read to Us (Simple verses for juniors.)	Birn Brothers, 1933
Treasure Trove Readers Book 1 (112 pages)	A Wheaton, 1934
Treasure Trove Readers Book 2 (136 pages)	A Wheaton, 1934
Treasure Trove Readers, Book 3 (144 pages)	A Wheaton, 1934
Treasure Trove Readers, Book 4 (160 pages)	A Wheaton, 1934
Treasure Trove Readers, Book 5 (208 pages)	A Wheaton, 1934
Enid Blyton Readers (Books 1 — 3)	Macmillan, 1942
Enid Blyton Readers (Books 4 — 12)	Macmillan, 1944 —1950

*Enid Blyton Pennant Series**

(30 books)   Macmillan, 1950

*Enid Blyton Nature Readers***

(36 books)   Macmillan, 1945 — 1946

Easy Readers (Books 1 - 4)   Collins Publications, 1965

*See Appendix 40 for list of titles

**See Appendix 12 for list of titles

BOOKS ABOUT ENID BLYTON

Baverstock, Gillian:

Enid Blyton

(Published in the

'Tell Me About' series.)   Evans Bros, 1997

Baverstock, Gillian, and Sheila Ray:

Gillian Baverstock

Remembers Enid Blyton   Mammoth, 2000

Endecott, Vivienne:

The Dorset Days of Enid Blyton   Ginger Pop, 2003

Greenfield, George: *Enid Blyton*   Sutton Publishing, 1998

Livingstone, Tess:

Enid Blyton at Old Thatch   Connor Court
                                     Publishing Australia, 2008

Mullan, Bob:

The Enid Blyton Story   Boxtree, 1987

Ray, Sheila:

The Blyton Phenomenon   Andre Deutsch, 1982

Smallwood, Imogen:

A Childhood at Green Hedges   Methuen, 1989

Stoney, Barbara:

Enid Blyton: A Biography   Hodder & Stoughton, 1974

(Reprinted 1992, 1997)

Summerfield, Tony and

Brian Stewart:

The Enid Blyton Dossier	Hawk Books, 1999
Reed, Nicholas:	
Enid Blyton in Beckenham	
and Bromley	Lilburne Press, 1997
Rice, Eva:	
Who's Who in Enid Blyton	Orion, 2003
Rudd, David:	
Enid Blyton and the	
Mystery of Children's Literature	Macmillan Press, 2000
Rudd, David*: The Famous Five:*	
A Character Guide	Norman Wright, 1995
Wright, Norman: *The Famous Five:*	
Everything You Ever	
Wanted To Know!	Hodder Children's Books, Dec, 2000

CLAIRVOYANCE

Bhakta Vishita, Swami*:*	
The Development of Seership:	
The science of knowing the future,	
Hindoo and Oriental methods	Advanced Thought Publishing Co, Chicago, 1915
Butler, W. E:	
How to Develop Clairvoyance	Aquarian Press 1977
Clayton, Arthur:	
Clairvoyance:	
Its Nature, Development	
and Purpose	Arthur Clayton, Nottingham, 1928
Count de St Leon:	
(Pseudonym of P.B. Randolph, M.D.)	
Clairvoyance and Somnambulist Vision	
(Contained in Part II of	William White & Co,
Love & Its Hidden History)	Boston, USA, 1869

Fodor, Nandor:
Encyclopaedia of Psychic Science   Arthus Press, 1934
Grumbine, J C Fremont:
Clairvoyance   L.N. Fowler & Co, 1915
Leadbeater, C.W:
Clairvoyance   The Theosophical
Publishing Society,1899

Panchadasi, Swami:
*A Course of Advanced Lessons in
Clairvoyance and Occult Powers*   Advanced Thought
Publishing Co, Chicago, 1916

Panchadasi, Swami:
Clairvoyance & Occult Powers   L.N. Fowler & Co, 1916
Randolph, Paschal Beverly:
Seership: Guide to Soul Sight   Quakertown,
Confederation of Initiates, 1930

Society for Psychical Research:
*Proceedings of the Society
for Psychical Research*   The Society for Psychical
Research, 1884

(Can be consulted at the Rare Books & Music Wing of The British
Library, Euston, London, England, under the shelf mark: X.529/799)

Samuel Sagan M.D.:
Awakening the Third Eye   http://www.clairvision.org

THE SUBCONSCIOUS

Atkinson, William Walker:
*The Subconscious and
SuperconsciousPlanes
of Mind*   The Progress Company,
Chicago, 1909
(British Library shelf
mark 87/01139 DSC.)

Atkinson, William Walker:
The Inner Consciousness:
A course of Lessons
on the Inner Planes of the Mind   Advanced Thought
Publishing Co, Chicago, 1908

Jung, Carl Gustav and others:
The Collected works of C.G. Jung:
The symbolic life, Vol. 18   Routledge, & Kegan Paul, 1953
Williams, John K:
Wisdom of Your
Subconscious Mind   Englewood Cliffs, Prentice Hall,
1964

Davies, Jim:
Imagination:
The Science of Your Mind's
Greatest Power   Pegasus Books, 2019

FAIRIES

Campbell, John Gregorson:
Superstitions of the Highlands
and Islands of Scotland   J. MacLehose &Sons,
Glasgow, 1900

Croker, Thomas Crofton:
Fairy Legends and Traditions of
the South of Ireland   Thomas Tegg & Son, 1838
Doyle, Sir Arthur Conan:
The Coming of the Fairies   Hodder & Stoughton, 1922
Douglas, Sir George B Scott:
Scottish Fairies & Folk Tales   W. Scott, 1893
Hastings, James, (editor):
Encyclopaedia of
Religion and Ethics   T. & T. Clark, Edinburgh,
1908

Hartland, Sidney Edwin:
The Science of Fairy Tales   Methuen & Co, 1925
Kirk, Robert:
The Secret Commonwealth of
Elves, Fauns & Fairies   D. Nult, 1893

PHYSIOGNOMY

Brophy, John:
The Human Face Reconsidered   George G Harrap & Co, 1962
Kurth, Hanns:
Se Connaître et Connaître les Aurtes
(Know thyself and others)   Editions Ramon F Keller,
                                   Geneva, Switzerland, 1974

Lavater, Johann Casper:
Essays on Physiognomy   William Tegg, 1862
                                 (Translated from the German
                                 by Thomas Holcroft.)

Penry, Jacques:
Character from the face   Hutchinson & Co, 1938
Looking at Faces and
Remembering Them:
A guide to facial identification   Elek Books, 1971

Spon, John:
The Science of Physiognomy   Herbert Jenkins, 1947
Spon, John:
Faces: What they mean and
how to read them   E. & F. N. Spon, 1934
Wells, Samuel R: *New*
Physiognomy or Signs of Character   Samuel R. Wells, Publisher,
                                      N.Y. 1867
Zebrowitz, Leslie:
Reading faces: Window to the Soul? Westview Press, 1997

PHRENOLOGY

Gall, Franz Joseph
and Spurzheim, George:
Anatomie et Physiologie
du Systeme Nerveux   F. Schoell, Paris, 1810
Gall, Franz Joseph:
On the Functions of the Brain
and Each of its Parts
in 6 volumes (English
translation from the
French.)   Marsh Capen & Lyon,
                                    Boston 1835

Gall, Franz:
On The Functions of the Cerebellum
(Translated from the French
by George Combe)   Maclachlan & Stewart,
                                    Edinburgh, Longman & Co,
                                    1838

Hedderly, Frances:
Phrenology: A Study of Mind   L N Fowler & Co, 1970
Hollander, Bernard:
Scientific Phrenology:
An illustrated text-book   Grant Richards, 1902
Hollander, Bernard:
The Unknown Life & Works of
Dr. Francis Joseph Gall   Gall Society, 1909
Spurzheim, George:
Phrenology or the Doctrine
of the Mind   Treuttel, Wurtz & Richter,
                                    1833

Wells, R.B.D:
A New illustrated Handbook

of Phrenology   H. Vickers, 1885

SPIRITUALISM

Doyle, Sir Arthur Conan:
The History of Spiritualism
(Sir Arthur Conan Doyle
is also the author of the
Sherlock Holmes stories)   Cassell, 1926
Grant, T:
A Scientific View
of Modern Spiritualism   J. Burns, 1872
Roberts, Eileen:
A Chronological History of
Outstanding Events in
Modern Spiritualism, 1848-1998   Institute of Spiritualist
                                   Mediums, 1998

Bennett, Edward T:
The Direct Phenomena of Spiritualism
— speaking, writing, drawing, music,
& painting — a Study   W. Rider & Son, (1908)

BOOKS DESCRIBING LIFE AFTER DEATH

Atkinson, William Walker:
(Pseudo) Yogi, Ramacharaka:
The Life beyond Death   Yogi Publishing Soc, 1937,
                                   (British Library
                                   shelf mark: 091166209X.)

Randolph, Paschal Beverly:
The "Ghostly Land"
the "Medium's Secret",
being the mystery of the human soul:
its dwelling, nature, and power
of materialization, pp. 33   Kate Corson, Toledo, Ohio,

1874, British Library shelf
mark 8631.dd.33. (1)

Thompson, Elizabeth Mary:
Life in the Hereafter:
Automatic writings and dictation
From Sir Arthur Conan Doyle,
Sir Walter Raleigh,
Mary, Queen of Scots,
Lady Jane Seymour and
Catherine of Aragon   Regency Press, 1969

SELECTED BOOKS WRITTEN BY SPIRIT PENS THROUH MEDIUMS

Hawley, Elizabeth &
Rossi, Columbia:
Bertie:
Life after Death of H.G. Wells   New English Library,1973
Douce, P. M:
Incredible Alliance,
Transmissions from
T. S. Eliot, through the
mediumship of P. M. Doucé   Dorrance, 1975
Leichtman, Robert:
Mark Twain Returns
(From Heaven to Earth)   Ariel Press, 1982
Leichtman, Robert:
Nikola Tesla Returns
(From Heaven to Earth)   Ariel Press, 1998
Toomey, Christine:
In Her Own Words:
The After-death Journal
of Princess Diana   English Rose Press,
                                         November, 1999

BOOKS WRITTEN BY PATIENCE WORTH

Worth, Patience:
The Sorry Tale   Henry Holt and Company,
                                       New York, 1917

Worth, Patience:
Hope Trueblood   Henry Holt and Company,
                                       New York, 1918

Worth, Patience:
The Pot Upon the Wheel   The Dorset Press, St. Louis, Mo,
                                       1921

Worth, Patience:
Telka, an Idyll of
Medieval England   Patience Worth Publishing Co,
                                       1928

BOOKS WRITEN ABOUT PATIENCE WORTH
& PEARL CURRAN

Prince, Walter Franklin:
The Case of Patience Worth   Boston Society for Psychical
                                       Research, Boston, 1926

Litvag, Irving:
Singer in the Shadows:
The Strange Story
of Patience Worth   The Macmillan Company,
                                       New York, New York, 1972

Yost, Casper S:
Patience Worth:
A psychic mystery   Good Press, Dec, 2019
Behr, Herman:
Light from Beyond   Patience Worth Publishing

Co, New York, New York, 1923

CHARLES DICKENS IN SPIRIT

Dickens, Charles:
The Mystery of Edwin Drood,
Part II
(Written through the medium
T. P. James who was also
the publisher.)

T.P. James, Brattleboro, Vt,
1873

MISCELLANEOUS

Duff, Hart-Davis:
Wildings, The Secret Garden
of Eileen Soper
Guthrie, Leonard:
Contributions to the Study of
Precocity in Children
Kington, Beryl:
Rowley Rediscovered:
The Life and Music
of Alec Rowley
McKellar, Peter:
Imagination & Thinking
Potter, Julian:
Mary Potter: A Life of Painting
Smallwood Sophie:
Noddy and the Farmyard Muddle

(Sophie Smallwood is

H.F. & G. Witherby, 1991

Eric G Millar 1921

Thames Publishing, 1993

Cohen & West, 1957

Aldershot 2004

Harper Collins Children's
Books, Oct, 2009

Enid Blyton's granddaughter.)
Swaffer, Hannen:
Adventures with Inspiration   Morley & M Kennerley, 1929

Atkinson, William Walker:
The Will:
Its Nature, Power and Development L.N. Fowler & Co, Ludgate
                                     Circus, 1910

AUTOBIOGRAPHICAL

Blyton, Enid:
The Story of My Life   Pitkin, 1952

ILLUSTRATED BIBLIOGRAPHY

Summerfield, Tony:
Enid Blyton:
An illustrated Bibliography
in 4 volumes   Milford Books, 2000 — 2004

INDEX

(The main subject index is in **bold**)

'A Lion Once We Had' (poem), 37

— Illustration of, in *Sunday Graphic*, Appendix 19/262

Adventures of Pip, The 104

— Publication of, first, 105

Adventures of the Wishing Chair, **124**

— Illustration from, Figure 35/124

Adventures with Inspiration, **110**, 358

Allen, H. E., 45

Alzheimer's disease, 176

Animal Book, The, 11, 339

— Title page illustration of, Figure 3/9

April Day, Enid's last known poem, **37**

— Illustration of, Appendix 20/263

Arnold, E. J., 131

Ascherberg, Hopwood & Crew, 93

Atkinson, William Walker, 127

— Endnote reference to, 83/236

Attenborough, Mabel, 129

— Mary, 224

Austen, Jane, 227

Automatic Writing, 95, 111-**112**, 113-114, 122

Bach, Sebastian, 145

— Photo of, among composers, Figure 22/147

— Family of musicians, 153

Baverstock, Donald, 225

Baverstock, Gillian, 37, 121, 174, 176, 201, 225-226

— At the helm of Darrell Waters Ltd, 198

— Defender of her mother's reputation, 176

Beach, Amy, (American composer), 146

— Photo of, among female composers, Figure 23/148

Before I Go to Sleep, 81

— Title page, illustration of, Figure 15/102

Bestall, Alfred, 134-135

Bickley Park School for Boys, 24, 39, 79, 129

Bird Book, The, 11, 155, 158-159

— Graphic illustration of birds from, Figure 1/4

— Illustration of Title Page, Figure 3/9

Birds of Our Garden, 16, 166

Birds of the British Isles, 74

Birds of the Wayside & Woodland, **74**

— Title page illustration of, Figure 11/67

Blackwell, Basil, 131, 344

Blyton, Carey (Enid's brother), 22, 98, 156

Blyton, Carey (Enid's nephew), 85, 89, 153

Blyton Close, 223

Blyton, Enid:

— Announcement to her father, to give up music, 78

— Date and place of birth, 1

— Death, place, and cause of, 176

— Discovered *The Children's Encyclopedia*, 96

— Fan Base, origin of, 174

— Main Homes, 223

— Nursery Governess, 79, 129

— 'Night Stories' or 'Night Thoughts', 116

— Presented with Magazine's Club badge, 188

— Rehabilitation, 175-176

— St Christopher's School, student at, 77-78

— Stories, criticism of, **169**

— Stories, moral lessons in, 81-82

— Sunday school teacher, Elm Road Baptist Church, 81

— Teaching, classroom, 5, 83, 95, 129, 149, 166-167

— Teaching through the medium of her pen, 84, 58, 129, 167

— Teacher Training Course, 83, 123, 160

— Teaching, qualifications for, 5

— Took up teaching, reason for, 83

— Withdrawal from *The Teacher's World*, **62**

— Writing Method, 95, 107—108, 111, 114, 118, 122, 223

  — Adapted, to write stage plays, **136-137**

  — Analysis of, **108**

Blyton Hanly (Enid's brother), 22, 98, 156

Blyton, Mary Ann (Enid's grandmother), 96, 103

Blyton Phenomenon, The, 224, 238

Blyton, Theresa (Enid's mother), 77, 156

Blyton Thomas (Enid's father), 4

Blyton-Sharman Musical Plays, 91, **134**, 139, 307

  — *How The Flowers Grow*, play, 91, 134, 136

  — Front cover illustration of, Figure 21/139

Board of Education, 46, 58, 67, 177

(See also Handbook of Suggestions)

Book of Common Prayer, The, 81

Book of Little Plays, A, 131, 133

  — Title page, illustration of, Figure 19/130

Book of One Thousand Poems, A, 36

Books written by spirit pens, 356

Botany, 3, 17, 21, 160, 166

  — First class pass in, 5

Brimble, L. J. F., BSc. 17, 18

BBC, incorporation of, 11

Bowne, Frances, 97, 119, 124, 209

  — Photo of, 109

Browning, L. J, 178

Burford Holdings Plc, 201

Busy Bees Club, 187

Byron, G (Lord Byron), photo of, Figure 22/147

Cameo Plays, 131

Carroll, Lewis, 125

Case of Patience Worth, The, 109

Cassell & Co, 50

Centre for Research into Children's Literature, 176

Chamberlain, Neville, 11

Chambers, David, 64, 234

Chapman & Hall, 113

Chase, Phyllis, 24, 46, 150, 321

Child Education, 63, 134

Child Whispers, 1, **25**, 28, 29, 90, 150

    — Front cover illustration of, Figure 7/26

    — *Ten Songs from Child Whispers* (songbook), 86, 90, 341

Childhood at Green Hedges, 37, 152, 164, 165, 191, 195, 198, 349

Children's Book of Prayer, The, 81

    — Title page illustration of, 102

Children's Encyclopedia, The 69, 70, 96, 97, 98, 100, 103, 107, 116, 124, 125

    — About the Book, Appendix 54/298

    — Inside Cover, illustration of, 54/ 298 (See also Mee, Arthur),

Children's Garden, The, 155, 340

    — Display advertisement for, in The Teachers World, 162

Children's Life of Christ, The, 81, 346

    — Title page illustration of, Figure 15/102

Children's Poet, The, 29

Chorion Plc, origin of, 204

    — Demerged, 204

    — Sold Enid Blyton's Literary Estate to Hachette UK, 205

    — Went into Liquidation, 205

Christmas Carols, 73, 85, 87, 88, **92-93**, 129

    — List of, Table V, Appendix 52/296

    —'Shepherd Song: A New Carol', 92

    — Illustration of score for, Appendix 51/295

Churchill, Winston, 37, 262

Clairvoyance, 96, 109, 112, **118-122**, 126, 138
    — A Short Treatment of, **209-213**
    — Books on, listed in Bibliography, 350-351
    — Branches, description of, Appendix 57/301
    — Enid's demonstration of, in story of 'Faraway Tree', 118-119
    — Mention of, in Fraudulent Mediums Act, Appendix 74/318
    — Rife in the Bible, 210
Cohen & West, 108, 224, 358
Coleridge-Taylor, photo of, among composers, Figure 22/147
Collins Educational, 36
Collins Sons & Co. Ltd, 188, 189, 313
College of Psychic Studies, The 210
Combe, George, 221, 241, 354
Commonwealth Day, 92
Complete List of Books, A, 84, 108, 193
Contributions to the Study of Precocity in Children, 98-99, 358
Costa Book Award, 227
'Country Letter from Enid Blyton, A', 63
Coward T.A, 74
Crawford, H. M, 24
Crawford, Marion, 184, 334
    — Photo of, Appendix 68/312
Croker, Crofton Thomas, 97, 103, 352
Curran, Pearl, 111, 114, 357
    — Photo of, Figure 18/109
Curriculum, 6, 66, 67, 73, 179, 237

Dahl, Roald, 227
Daily Mail Annual, The, 74, **75**, 344
    — Title page illustration of, Figure 11/67
Daily Mail, The, xi, xx
Daily Telegraph, The 140, 146, 206, 335
Darrell Waters, Kenneth, 164, 191
    — Passing of, 197

Darrell Waters Ltd, 36, 141, 201-203, 207, 238
   — Memorandum and Articles of Association, 191
   — Directors of, 191
   — End of, 198
   — Inaugural meeting, 191
   — Incorporated, 191
   — Objectives of, Appendix 73/317
   — Short History of, **190-200**
   — The end of, 198
   — Sold to Trocadero Plc, 199
Darwin, Charles, **215**, 127
'Days of the Week Poems', 61
Diane Rehm Show, xi, 120
Dickens, Charles, 97, **113-114**, 115, 235, 358
Dicksee, Margaret Isabel (British painter), 146
   — Photo of, among female composers, Figure 23/148
Dimple in the chin, types of, 145
   — Cause by, 145
   — Explanations of, 152-153, 154
   — In the chins of male musicians, Figure 22/147
   — In the chins of female musicians, Figure 23/148
   — In Enid Blyton's chin, 145
Duff Hart-Davis, 148, 150, 226, 358

Edinburgh Phrenological Society, The, Endnote 129/241
Edison, Thomas, 99
Elfin College, 43, 103, 160, 164, 166, **223**
   — Photo of, Figure 26/158
Eliot, T. S, 114, 356
Ellis, Walter 67-70
Empire Day Celebrations, 28
Enid Blyton – An Illustrated Bibliography, 37, 74, 231, 237, 359
Enid Blyton, (pocket biography), 172
(See also Greenfield, George)

Enid Blyton Bible Stories, The, 81, 346, 347
— Title page illustration of, Figure 15, 102
Enid Blyton Book of Fairies, 32, 46, 181, 341, 347
— Title page illustration of, Figure 17/106
Enid Blyton Diary, 188, 313
— Fan clubs, information in, Appendix 69/313
Enid Blyton's Literary Estate, short history of, **201-205**
— Sold to Hachette UK, 205
Enid Blyton Nature Readers, 19, 150
— Eileen Soper's illustration for, Figure 5/18
— List of the 36 book in the series, Appendix 12/255
— Reference book to, 18
— Sample reading from, Appendix 11/254
— Standard front cover of, Appendix 12/255
— Story books from, Figure 6/19
Enid Blyton Pennant Series, 80, 349
— Ilustration of books in the series, Appendix 40/283
Enid Blyton Phenomenon, The, 224, 238
Enid Blyton Poetry Book, The, 31, 32, 328, 340
— Title page illustration of, Figure 7/26
Enid Blyton Society, The, 74, 141, **176**, 230, 231, 234
— Journal, 64, 119, 176, 231, 234, 236, 237
— Website, 176
— Forum, 119
Enid Blyton Story, The, 224, 349
Enid Blyton's Animal Lover's Book, 20, 229, 340
— Title page illustration of, Figure 3/ 9
'Enid Blyton's Children's Page', 12, 39, 58, 62, 70, 163, 174, 178
Enid Blyton's Magazine, 2, 64, 138, 140, 168, 174
— Brief history of, **186-189**
— First issue of, 186
— Meeting Place of Fans in, 187
— Termination of, 188
— Illustration, two book covers of, Figure 32/187

Enid Blyton's Magazine Club, 140, 187
— Celebration party, at Montague House, 188
Enid Blyton's Book of Her Famous Play Noddy in Toyland, 140, 345
— Book cover, illustration of, Appendix 64/308
Enid Blyton's Book of the Year, **16**, 32, 89, 129, 142, 320, 328
Enid Blyton's Nature Lessons, 6-7, 16, 21, 61, 80, 104, 151, 230, 339
— Beginning of, in *The Teachers World*, Appendix 1/244
— Illustrations from, Figure 25/151
— Syllabus for, Appendix 3/246
— Title page illustration of, Figure 2/8
Enid Blyton's Nature Lover's Book, 16, 32, 166, 320, 321
— Title page illustration of, Figure 3, 9
Enid Blyton's Noddy in Toyland: Selection for Piano (songbook), 93
Enid Blyton's Noddy Songbook, 93
— Cover page illustration of, Figure 13/86
Enid Blyon's New Noddy Songbook, 93
— Cover page illustration of, Figure 13/86
Enid Blyton's Sunny Stories Calendar, 33
— Illustration of, Appendix 17/260
Enid Blyton's Treasury of Verse, 36, 341
'Enid Silver Screen Technique', 119
Epigraph, 115,127
Essays On Physiognomy, 214, 240-241, 335, 353
— Title page illustration of, Figure 30/216
— Illustration of nine noses from, Appendix 70/ 314
Evans Brothers, 7, 49, 50, 129, 162, 166, 186, 188, 226
Evans, Edward, 177
— Robert, 177
— Creator of *The Teachers World*, 179
— Knighthood, 177
Evening Standard, 64, 145, 148, 202, 206

Fairytale books, 104, 106-107, 169
— Title pages illustration of, Figure 17, 106
— List of, in *Bibliography*, 347

Famous Five Club, 140, 187, 189

Famous Five Series of Books, 141, 148, 226

Famous Five Stage Play, **140**

    — Advertisement for, in *Enid Blyton's Magazine*, Appendix 64/308

Fine, Ann, 176

Five on a Treasure Island, 123, 125, 236

Fortnightly Review, The, 99, 224, 233

Fraudulent Mediums Act, 212, 337

    — Copy of, Appendix 74/318

Friday Afternoon Stories, 46, 61, 230

    — Example of, Appendix 26/269

Froebel Teacher Training, 85

Froissart's *Chronicles*, 55, 57, 81, 100, 325

'From My Window', (Enid Blyton's column), 39, 43-45, 122, 155, 166-168, 178, 323

    — Book Reviewed in, 42

    — Categories of articles in, 40-41

    — First article in, Appendix 22/265

    — Last article in (Green and Blue), Appendix 23/266

    — Termination of, 43-45

Gall, F. J, (Father of Phrenology), 217, 335, 354

    — Banned by Decree from spreading doctrine, 219

    — Basis of his belief, 217

    — Death, cause of, 222

    — Fled Austria for France, 219

    — His work, first English translation of, 220

    — Photo of, Figure 31/218

Galton, Francis (cousin of Charles Darwin), 99,

    — Papers written in *Fortnightly Review and in Mind*, 224

'Gardeners' Song', 91

    — Illustration of the score for, Appendix 49/293

     (See also T*he Play's The Thing*),

Gifford, John, 32

Gillian Baverstock *Remembers Enid Blyton*, 226, 349

Golders Green Crematorium, 176

'Gorse', first nature lesson in *The Teachers World*, 6, 104, 149, 319
— Illustration of, Appendix 2/245

Granny's Wonderful Chair, 119
— Book cover, illustration of, Figure 35/124

Greatest Book in the World, The, 81
— Title page illustration of, Figure 15/102

Green Hedges (Enid's last home), 62, 152, 164-165, 172, 188, 326
— Demolition of, 223
— Moved to, 164

Green, Ronald, 150

Green, Philip, 85, 138, 140

Greenfield, George (Enid's Literary Agent), 142, 171-172, 349

Guildhall School of Music, The 77, 78

Guthrie, Leonard, M.A, 98, 358

Hachette UK, 205, 240

Hadow, W. H. Sir, 229

Handbook of Suggestions, 46-47, 67, 324
— Title page illustration of, Appendix 27/270
    (See also Board of Education)

Hartland, Sidney, 105, 353

Haslam, David, 195
— Pencil drawing of Noddy, Figure 33/196

Hatch, Susan (Child Actress, 'Noddy in Toyland'), 140

'Hedgerow Tales', 12, 15-16, 21, 61, 80
— Book form, title page illustration of, Figure 2/8
— First lesson in, illustration of, Appendix 8/251
— Time Table of the Syllabus, Appendix 7/250

Holy Grail, The 52

Homer's Iliad, 57, 80, 97, 100

Houghton, Robert, 119, 209
— Demonstration of Clairvoyance, 119-120

Hundred Years' War, The, 55, 80, 230
(See also 'Tales of Romance')

Humphreys, A. J. H, 69

'I'm Off To Sea' (poem), 35
Imagination & Thinking, 108, 223, 358
Ipswich High School, 5, 146, 160
    — Froebel Teacher Training Wing of, 24, 79
    — Trainee teacher at, Figure 12/78

James, T. P, (publisher and medium), 113, 235, 330, 358
Jenkins, Herbert, 145, 216, 353
Johnston & Bacon, 346
Johnson, R. C, 85, 93
Jones, Henry Arthur, 110
Joseph II, Holy Roman Emperor, 214
Judd, Percy, 85, 88

'King Arthur & The Knights of the Round Table', **51-53**, 230, 324, 346
(See also *Knights of the Round Table, The*)
'King Charlemagne and the Paladins of France', 51, **53-54**
 (See also *Tales of Romance*)
'King Cole Calling!' (play), 129, 331
    — Illustration of, in *The Teachers World*, Appendix 59/303
King George V, 37, 322
    — Death of, 11
'King Alfred's Mother', (Historical Character), 60, 325
    — Illustration of story, Appendix 36/279
    — Drawing of, Figure 10/59
'King's Pocket Knife, The' (musical play), 133, 134
    — Illustration of costume for, Figure 20/135
    — Synopsis of, Appendix 62/306
Kirk, Douglas, 146
Kirk, Robert, 105
Knights of the Round Table, The 53, 100

Lake, Richard, 140

'Land of Hope & Glory' (patriotic song), 92

Lane, David, 202-203

Latimer House, 53, 162, 163, 340, 346

Lavater, Johann Casper, 214-217

— Pastor by profession, 217

— Photo of, and title page of his book, Figure 30/216

Leadbeater, C. W, 210, 213, 351

League of Nations, 92

'League of Nations' (play), 129

Let's Garden, 162, 163, 340

'Letters from Bobs', (Enid Blyton's fox terrier), 44

— Illustration of, Appendix 25/268

— Farewell letter from, Appendix 39/282

Lewis, Edmonia, 146

— Photo of, among female composers, Figure 23/148

— Tribute to, 226

London Royal Academy of Music, (LRAM), 77

Low, Sampson, 140, 347

Mac Culloch, J.A, 105

Macaulay, Thomas, 99

'Magic in the Snow' (poem), 30

Magic Faraway Tree, The 106, 124, 125

Make Way for Noddy (American TV show), 203

Make Way for Noddy in China, 206

Malory Towers, 81, 121, 235, 341

Malory, Thomas, Sir, 57, 100

Man and the Attainment of Immortality, 42

Marshall, A. C, 69

May, Bunny, 140

May, Edgar, 329

McLaren, William (illustrator), 163

McKellar, Peter, Professor, 108, 117-118, 120, 122-123, 137, 170

— Letters, sold to an anonymous buyer, 223

Mee, Arthur, 23, 69-70, 96, 103, 116
 (See also *The Children's Encyclopedia*)
Mediumship, 212, 356
Menzies, John, 84, 108, 193
Modern Teaching – Practical Suggestions, **65-68**
    — Title page illustration of, Figure 11/67
Modern Teaching In The Infant School, **70-72**
    — Title page illustration of, Figure 11/ 67
Morning Post, 29, 89
Morse, Richard, 6, 14
Mozart, Wolfgang, 152
Mullan, Bob, 224
Mystery of Edwin Drood, 113
    — Title page illustration of, Appendix 56/300
    — Author's Preface, Appendix 56/300

Nash's Magazine, 24, 29
National Froebel Union Higher Certificate, 5, 24, 65
Nature books, 3, 16, 21, 122, 166
    — Title pages illustration of, Figure 3/9
    — List of, in Bibliography, 339-340
Nature Lover: The Magazine of the Countryside, 63
'Nature Notes', 8, 24, 33
    — Sample reading, from *The Teachers' Treasury*, Appendix 5/248
    — Sample reading, from *Enid Blyton's Book of the Year*, Appendix 9/252
Nature Readers, 16-19, 21, 80, 95, 122, 142, 166, 168
 (See also *Enid Blyton Nature Reader*s)
Necromancy, 210
Nelson, Horatio, (Lord Nelson), 60
    — Drawing of, Figure 10/59
Nelson, Thomas (publishers), 29, 340, 345, 347
Newnes' Pictorial Knowledge, **68-70**, 73
    — Title page illustration of, Figure 11/67
'Night Stories' (See under Blyton, Enid)

Noddy, 34-35, 176, 188, 191, 196-197, 205
Noddy in Toyland (musical stage play), 91, 93, 137, **138**, 140-142
188, 193, 203
    — Synopsis of scenes from, Appendix 64/308
Noddy vs The Real World, 195
 (See also Haslam, David)
Noddy books, 93, 146, 169, 188, 193, 196, 224
Noddy Songbooks, list of, Table II, Appendix 48/291
    — Book covers, illustration of, Figure 13/86
Noddy trademark infringement, 195, 196
Noddy and the Farmyard Muddle, in *Bibliography*, 358
Noddy's Own Nursery Rhymes, 34, 340
Norman, Diana, xi
    — Quotation from, xx
Notes for the Teacher, 47, 50, 52, 310
    — Example of, Appendix 29/272
Novello & Co, 90, 328, 343
Nunn, Percy, 82
NUT (National Union of Teachers), 178

Old Thatch, 159, 163-164, **223**, 349
    — Illustration of, on front cover of *The Teachers World*, Figure 4/10
On the Function of the Brain and each of its Parts, 220
On the functions of the Cerebellum, 221
Organology, (Previous name for Phrenology), 217-220, 222
Outline, The 64

Pitkin, 5, 108, 347, 359
The case of Patience Worth, 109, 114, 234
'The League of Nations' (patriotic song), **92**
'The Union Jack' (patriotic song), **92**
    — Score for 'The Union Jack', Appendix 50/294
'Peronel and His Pot of Glue', **46**
    — Illustration of, in 'Friday Afternoon Stories', Appendix 26/269
Photographic Memory, 57, 66, 69, **98-100**, 107, 111, 123, 125,

171, 180, 190, 224

Phrenologist's report, 77, 83

— Enid's father's disappointment with, 77

— Enid's refusal to believe, 83

Phrenology, 2, 76, 83, 144, 214, **217-222**, 241

— A map showing the location of the organs, Appendix 71/315

— List of books in *Bibliography* on, 354

Physiognomy, 2, 76, 144-145, 152-153, 167, **214-217**

— List of book in *Bibliography* on, 353

Picasso, Pablo, 153

'Picking The Apples' (poem), 33

Plays & Players, 140, 237

'Poems of the Open Air', 32

— Illustration of a poem there from, Appendix 16/259

Poetry Review, 24

Pollock, H. A., 11, 66, 68, 156-157, 229

Portraits of Historical Characters, **58-59**

— Announcement in *The Teachers World*, 59

— List of Historical Characters, Appendix 35/278

Potter, Beatrix, 146,

— Photo of, as a child, Figure 23/148

Potter, Harry, 120

Potter, Julian, 225

Potter, Mary née Attenborough, 224

— A Life of Painting (biography), 376

'Primary School Report, The', 15, 160, 229

Prince, Walter Franklin, Dr, 109, 111, 235, 357

'Princess and the Enchanter, The' (play), 129

Public Elementary Schools, 5, 58-59, 61,

Punch, 23, 29, 63

— 'Singer in the Night', poem published in, 90

Purnell Books, 36, 341

'Rabbity Ways', **13-14**

(See also Hedgerow Tales)

Ray, Sheila, 224

Ready-made stories, 95, 108, 110-112, 118, 126, 170-171, 174

'Real Fairies' (poem), 26

Real Fairies, (book, 29, 340
   — Title page illustration of, Figure 7/26
   — Review of, 27

Reference Book to Enid Blyton Nature Readers, 18, 340

(See also Brimble, L. J. F.)

Religious books, 81-82
   — Title pages illustration of, Figure 15/102
   — Listed in *Bibliography*, 346-347

Responsive Singing Games (songbook), 87-88, 150, 328, 342
   — Front cover illustration of, Figure 13/86

Retold Story Books, listed in Bibliography, 345-346
   — Title pages illustration of, Figure 14/101

Ricordi, G, 93

Rogers, Eric, 191, 198

Roland and Oliver, **53-54**

'Roland for an Oliver, A', Appendix 32/275

(See also Tales of Romance)

Roncesvalles, battle of, 54

(See also Tales of Romance)

'Round the Year with Enid Blyton', 12, 58, 72, 80, 150, 155, 160, 340
   — Syllabus for, Appendix 65/309
   — Front cover illustration of, Figure 27/162
   — Illustrations from, Figure 25/151
   — Gardening lesson from, Appendix 66/310

Rowley, Alex, 85, 89, 91-92, **226**

Rowley Rediscovered, 358

Rowling, J.K, 173, 209, 227
   — On Diane Rehm Show, 120
   — How Harry Potter first appeared to her, 120

'Rule Britannia' (patriotic song), 92

Saucepan Man 125

Schoolmistress, The 131

— Supplement to, 25

— Incorporation of, by *The Teachers World*, 177

School Music Review, The 90, 328

School story books, listed in *Bibliography*, 341-342

Science of Fairy Tales, 105, 349

Science of Physiognomy, The, 145, 216, 353

Seaman, Owen, 23

Second World War, 16, 37, 75, 92, 136, 142, 166, 183

Secret Commonwealth of Elves, Fauns & Fairies, The, 105, 107, 353

— Brief extract from, Appendix 55/299

Secret Seven, 173, 175-176, 191

— Transported to TV screens, 203

Seven Stories, **207-208**

Sharman, Cecil (composer), 73, 85, 88, 90-91

Snowflower, 119, 124

Shaw, George Bernard, 110

Sheet Music (based on her poems), 87, **90**

— Table of, Table III, Appendix 48A/292

'Shepherd, The' (poem), 31

'Shepherd King', (Christmas carol), 93

— On front cover of *The Teachers World*, Appendix 53/297

'Shepherd Song: A New Carol', 92

— Score for, Appendix 51/ 295

'Silver & Gold' (poem), 29

— Review of, in *The Teachers World*, 30

— Title page illustration of, Figure 7/26

Singer in the Night', (poem), 32, 90

Singer in the Night, (song), score for, Appendix 47/290

Singing Games, **87-88**

— Listed in Table VI, Appendix 52/296

Six Enid Blyton's Plays, 131

— Review of, in *The Teachers World*, Appendix 60/304

— Title page illustration of, Figure 19/130

Smallwood, Imogen, 37, 152, 164-165, 191, 194, 198, 201, 207, 226
— Head of Enid Blyton Trust, 197
(See also *Childhood At Green Hedges, A*)
Smallwood, Sophie, 207
Society for Psychical Research, The 212, 351
Songbooks, Illustration of title pages/front covers, Figure 13/86
— Listed in Bibliography, 342-343
Songs, categories, 87
Songs based on her Poems, 90
— Listed in Table I, Appendix 46/289
Songs for Unison Singing, 89
— Listed in Table I, Appendix 46/289
Songs for her Musical Plays, 90-91
— Listed in Table III, Appendix 48A/292
Songs, patriotic, 91-92
— Listed in Table V, Appendix 52/296
Songs, miscellaneous, 93-94
— Table II, Appendix 48/291
Songs Written for Infant Schools, 88
Songs of Gladness (songbook), 89
— Cover illustration of, Figure 13/86
Soper, Eileen, 17, 21, 146, 150,153, 226
— Photo of, among composers and artists, Figure 23/148
— Nature Plate, Figure 5/18
Spectator, The, 99
Spencer's *Faerie Queene*, 100
Spiritualism, 112, 121
— Books on, in the *Bibliography*, 355
Spon, John, 145, 215
Spurzheim, Johann Gaspar (phrenologist), 220
— His book, *Phrenology or the Doctrine of the Mind*, 220
— Faculties he modified, illustration of, Appendix 72/316
St. Christopher's School for Girls, **77**
Statistics of Mental Imagery, **224**
— Reference to, endnote 48/233

Stoll Theatre, The, 91, 138

Stephenson, Robert Louis, 36, 123

Stoney, Barbara, 24, 37, 45, 63, 91, 129, 140, 146, 149, 184, 189
  — Tribute to, 225

Stories and Notes to Enid Blyton Nature Plates, 17

Stories of Chivalry in the 14th Century, **55**

 (See also Tales of Romance.)

'Stories of World History', **46-50**, 66, 80, 100, 129
  — Change of name, to 'Tales of Romance', 50
  — Commission to write, 47
  — First story, 'The Siege of Troy', illustration of, Appendix 28/ 271
  — Notes for the Teacher in, Appendix 29, column 3/272
  — Reading books resulting from, Figure 9/49
  — Syllabus for, Appendix 30/273
  — Syllabus, Winners and losers in, 57-58

Story of My Life, The 5, 22, 77, 79, 83, 94, 96-98, 104, 108, 123, 137-138
  — Reason for writing, Endnote 1/ 229

Subconscious Mind, 95, 111, **115-118**, 122-1123, 125-127, 138
  — Books on, listed in the *Bibliography*, 351-352

Sunday Dispatch, The 64

Sunday Mail, 64

Sunday Times, The 64, 206, 234

Sunny Stories for Little Folks, 70, 75, 99, 168, **180-183**
  — Change of title to *Enid Blyton's Sunny Stories*, 182
  — Front cover illustration of, Figure 29/182

Sunny Stories, 62-64, 70, 174, **182-184**
  — Front cover illustration of, Figure 29/182

Summer Storm, The (play for adults), **141-142**

Summerfield, Tony, 37, 74, 339

 (See also *Enid Blyton: An Illustrated Bibliography*)

Sunbeam Society, 140, 187

(See also *Enid Blyton's Magazine, The*)

Sunday Graphic, 37, 64, 105, 234, 262

Supernatural Agents, 112

Swaffer, Hannen, 109, 358

Tables of songbooks/ songs, Appendix 46/289, 48/291, 48A/292, 52/296

'Tales of Romance', **51-57**, 70, 80, 100

Tatler & Bystander, The 140

'The Helmsman' (poem), 37

— On cover of *The Junior Teachers World*, Appendix 18/261

The Play's The Thing (musical play), 91, 133-134

— Full page advertisement for, Appendix 61/305

— Title page, and illustration of costumes for, Figure 20/135

— Plays for Older and Younger Children, 134

The Teachers World:

— Brief History of, **177-179**

— Cover Page, illustration of, Appendix 21/264

— Music Supplement, 92

— Extra Number, 28, 35, 178-179

— Divided into two editions, 44

— Enid's Withdrawal from, **62**

Times, The, 69, 206

Teachers' Treasury, The, 8, 11, 36, 66, 71, 82, 88-89, 129, 131, 142

— Advertisement for, Appendix 42/285

— Professor T.P. Nunn's introduction to, Appendix 43/286

— Sample reading of Nature Notes from, Appendix 5/248

— Title Page, illustration of, Appendix 41/284

Tesla, Nikola, 114

— *Nikola Tesla Returns* (book), 356

'To Hang or Not To Hang' (poem), 37

'Too Hot', (poem), 35-36

Treasure Island, 123

Tresco (nursery school), 96, 149

Trocadero Plc, 199-200, **201-204**

— Acquired Darrell Waters Ltd, 201

— Changed the name of Darrell Waters Ltd to Enid Blyton Ltd, 202

— Changed its own name to Chorion Plc, 204
Trocadero Building, Figure 34/202
Two Years in the Infant School, 65, **72**
 — Songs specially written for, 88
 — Title page illustration of, Figure 11/67
Twinn, Sydney, (composer), 85, 90
Teacher's Times, 89
Thompson Family, 129
Tucker, Nicolas, 176
Traditional Stories, 82, 99, 180-181, 184-185

'Union Jack, The' (patriotic song), **92**
 — Score for, Appendix 50/294

Wallace, Edgar, 110
Walter de la Mare, (poet), 36
WAMU Radio, Washington DC, 120
 — Reference to, in endnote 75/235
Warne, Frederick, (publisher), 74
Wheaton, A, (publisher), 134
Wildings: The Secret Garden of Eileen Soper, 148, 150
 (See also Soper, Eileen),
Wishing Bean & Other Plays, The, 131
Witchcraft Act, 211
 — Acts passed in England, reference to, in Endnote 123/240
Witherby, H.F. & G (publisher), 150
Wood, Michael, (psychologist), 176
Worth, Patience, 109, 111, 114, 115
 — Books written by, through Pearl Curran, 357
 — Books about, 357
Wright, Norman, 141
Yeats, William (poet), 146
 — Photo of, among composers and artists, Figure 22/147

Zoo Book, The, **11**, 339
   — Title page, illustration of, Figure 3/9
Zoology, 3, 5, 21, 160, 166